EMILIO CORSETTI III

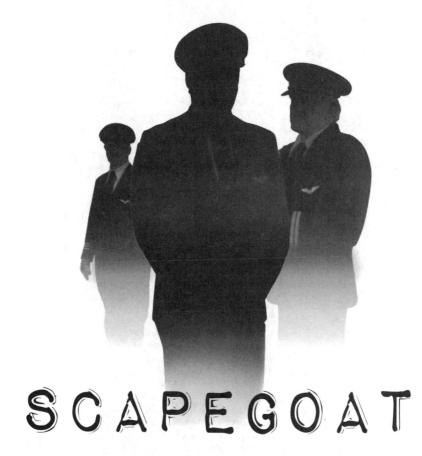

SCAPEGOAT

A Flight Crew's Journey
from Heroes to Villains
to Redemption

For information about this title or to order other books and/or electronic media, contact the publisher:

Odyssey Publishing, LLC.

www.ipgbook.com

ISBNs:

Hard Cover: 978-0-9972421-0-2
Paperback: 978-0-9972421-1-9
ePub: 978-0-9972421-2-6
Mobi: 978-0-9972421-3-3
Downloadable Audio: 978-0-9972421-4-0
PDF: 978-0-9972421-5-7

Printed in the United States of America
Cover and Interior design: 1106 Design
Front cover photos by Roger Peterson.
Back cover illustration by Mike James Media.

Corsetti, Emilio, author.
Scapegoat: a flight crew's journey from heroes to villains to redemption / by Emilio Corsetti III.
pages cm
Includes bibliographical references and index.
LCCN 2016904959
ISBN 978-0-9972421-0-2
ISBN 978-0-9972421-1-9
ISBN 978-0-9972421-2-6
ISBN 978-0-9972421-3-3
ISBN 978-0-9972421-4-0
ISBN 978-0-9972421-5-7

1. Aircraft accidents--Investigation--Case studies.
I. Title.

TL553.5.C663 2016   363.12'465
                          QBI16-600054

For Allison

Contents

Author's Note

When TWA 841 departed JFK on April 4, 1979, no one onboard had any idea of the drama that would soon unfold. One passenger, travelling with her husband, wrote in a journal about the smooth takeoff. She had been keeping a personal journal of her travels to share with her children on her return. She documented everything down to the most inconsequential detail such as her ears popping as the aircraft climbed. Days, weeks, and years later, after TWA 841 had become the subject of one of the longest NTSB investigations in the agency's history, investigators would scrutinize every minute of the flight in a similarly detailed manner. Much like a criminal investigation, the movements, actions, and whereabouts of each crew member were documented. Routine tasks such as when and where the meal trays were exchanged between the cockpit and cabin crew would take on added significance. Unraveling the mystery of TWA 841 was a monumental puzzle that needed to be solved. But unlike any accident investigation before or since, the same evidence investigators would use against the crew would be used by others to challenge the theories put forth by Boeing and the NTSB. Readers can draw their own conclusions as to which version is correct.

Illustrations

N840TW Seating Diagram

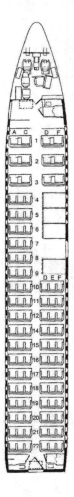

TWA 841 FDR Readout

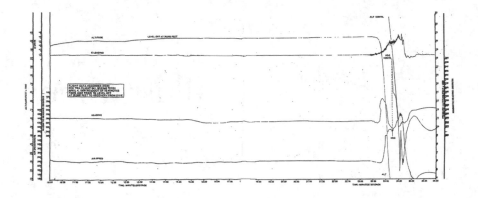

TWA 841 FDR Readout Close

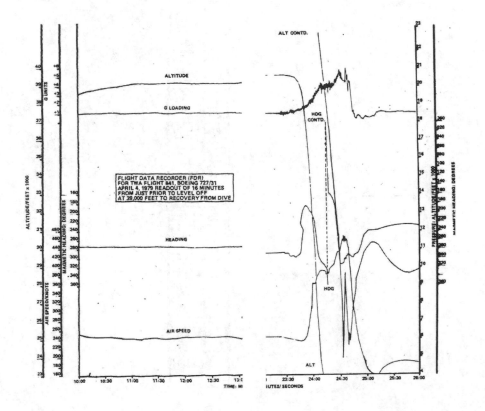

Boeing 727-100 Flight Controls

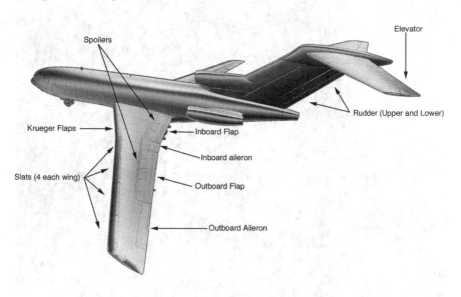

Boeing 727-100 Flight Controls Deployed

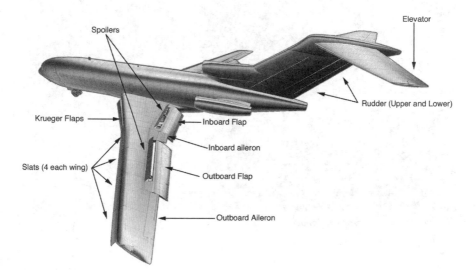

Figure 1 Captain Harvey "Hoot" Gibson

Chapter One

Headwinds

S*ome pilots can work their entire career* and never face anything more challenging than a blown landing light. Most pilots, however, will at some point encounter a problem that tests their skills and knowledge: a precautionary engine shutdown, a system failure, an electrical problem. Most of the time the malfunction is dealt with, and the flight lands without incident. Occasionally, a pilot will experience an emergency that is life threatening. A useful metaphor in demonstrating the random nature of emergencies involves a basket filled with marbles. Imagine that before every flight a pilot must reach into a basket and pull out a single marble. There are thousands of white marbles; there are a handful of red marbles; there is one black marble. On April 4, 1979, Captain Harvey "Hoot" Gibson reached into the basket and pulled out a black marble.

Hoot's day began in Columbus, Ohio. It was day two of a three-day trip. After a routine flight from Columbus to Philadelphia, Hoot, along with his two fellow crew members, First Officer Scott Kennedy and Flight Engineer Gary Banks, departed for New York's John F. Kennedy International Airport (JFK). The weather was overcast with light winds out of the northeast and temperatures in the upper forties. A light rain fell as the wheels touched down at JFK.

Figure 2 Aircraft N840TW

After a few hours on the ground, Hoot, Scott, and Gary, along with four flight attendants, boarded aircraft N840TW. The "TW" in the plane's N number designated the plane as a Trans World Airlines (TWA) aircraft. The Boeing 727-100 was a few months shy of fourteen years old. It was one of the first 727s purchased by TWA. The new car smell, however, had long since been replaced by a malodorous mixture of sweat-soaked seatbacks, spilled drinks, vomit, cleaning chemicals, and cigarette smoke. The worn-out interior was matched on the outside with an assortment of nicks, scrapes, dents, oil stains, and two faded red stripes that ran the length of the short fuselage. Of course, nowhere did the aircraft show its age more than in the cockpit, where countless crews had left signs of their presence from the worn seats, to the fingerprints on the instruments and flight controls, to the dust and food crumbs wedged into every crevice.

Some pilots refuse to fly in such an unhealthy environment and will spend an inordinate amount of time "sanitizing" the cockpit before a flight. That wasn't the case with the previous crew on this day. The three crew members entered to find a filthy aircraft. Newspapers and empty water bottles littered the floor. Gary Banks, a detail-oriented former fighter pilot, was especially irked at the mess. He gathered up the papers and bottles while Hoot and Scott took their seats and began their preflight checks.

In the cabin, lead flight attendant Mark Moscicki prepared the aircraft for boarding. There were eighty-two passengers, two of whom were lap children, meaning age two or younger and without a ticket or assigned seat.[1] Many of the passengers were connecting from international flights. They had already spent ten-plus hours flying to the U.S. from Portugal, Spain, Italy, Israel, and other international departure points. For these travelers, TWA 841 to Minneapolis, Minnesota, would be the last leg of a very long journey.

Of the twelve first-class seats, only six were occupied, unless one was to count the guitar case that one coach passenger secured against seat 1F. The owner of the guitar, a young, male passenger, had taken the instrument with him to his seat but soon realized that there was no space for it in coach. Since there were open seats in first class, Mark let the gentleman secure the case to a first-class seat with a seatbelt.

The flight was scheduled to depart for Minneapolis at 6:55 p.m. That time came and went as the flight was held for connecting passengers and a minor maintenance write-up. TWA 841 didn't push back from the gate until 7:49 p.m. The delay put the flight right in the middle of the evening push. Hoot taxied his Boeing 727 into position behind a long line of aircraft. Traffic congestion at JFK at this time in the evening was as common as the traffic jams on the New York freeways during rush hour. All Hoot could do was inch his plane forward and wait his turn for takeoff.

Despite the delays, it was a relaxed cockpit. Hoot made sure of that on day one. His first briefing to his fellow crew members included his disclosure that this was his first trip back as a 727 captain. He had just returned from a three-month medical leave after suffering from a broken ankle. Prior to that he had spent fourteen months on the Boeing 747 as a first officer. Hoot had flown as a 727 captain before, but he wanted his crew to treat him like a new captain. He told them to watch over him to ensure he didn't make any mistakes. The statement did two things: It let the other crew members know important facts about his currency on the aircraft, but it also put the first officer and flight engineer at ease. Hoot wasn't going to be a hard-nosed captain, the kind with whom no one likes to fly. Finally, at 8:25 PM, TWA 841 departed JFK for Minneapolis, Minnesota.

The climb to the planned cruising altitude of 35,000 feet, or flight level (FL) 350, was smooth and uneventful. After leveling off and engaging the autopilot, Hoot reached up to the overhead panel and turned off the seatbelt and no-smoking signs. He made a brief announcement over the PA and then removed his tie and unbuttoned the top button of his uniform shirt. When in the public eye, Hoot was the model of professionalism: a crisp white shirt, dark blue tie, neatly pressed pants, and polished black shoes. That professional crispness extended to his physical appearance. Hoot's dark hair and mustache were always neatly trimmed. Medical issues sometimes led to weight gain, but Hoot had a way of hiding his fluctuating weight behind a buttoned suit jacket. He would don his jacket and captain's cap anytime he left the cockpit. Behind the closed cockpit door, however, was a different matter. The cockpit was his office, and Hoot liked to be comfortable in his office.

With the aircraft trimmed and the power set, the next task was to perform a ground speed check. Pilots back in 1979 didn't have the benefit of the technology available to today's pilots. A pilot today can simply look at his primary flight display and read the ground speed right from the instrument. Wind direction and speed are also displayed. The fourteen-year-old 727, delivered in 1965, had no such capability. Determining ground speed was accomplished by performing a time and distance check. If the aircraft traveled seven nautical miles in 60 seconds, or seven nautical miles a minute, the ground speed (the speed over the ground) was 420 nautical miles per hour (7 * 60). The difference between the ground speed and the true airspeed (the speed through the air) provided the wind speed. When Scott performed the ground speed check, he determined that they had a headwind of more than 100 kts.

Hoot's first inclination after learning of the strong headwinds was to descend. But he remembered reading a company memo about fuel conservation. He also had the recent memory of being chastised by the last check airman he flew with for not climbing to a higher altitude to conserve fuel. The company wanted pilots to fly at the highest altitude the aircraft was capable of flying, considering weight and temperature. Jet aircraft burn less fuel the higher they fly. Fuel is the highest operating cost for an airline, and anything pilots can do to help lower the fuel burn directly impacts the bottom line. So Hoot asked Gary to check the numbers for flight level 390. Gary did as requested and said it looked like they were light enough to climb. About this time there was a double knock on the cockpit door. A double knock was the signal that a flight attendant wanted access to the cockpit. This was long before the strict protocols now in place for flight attendants communicating with the cockpit. Standing just outside the cockpit door was lead flight attendant Mark Moscicki. Mark wanted to know if the crew was ready for their crew meals. Hoot said yes and told Scott and Gary that they would delay the climb to flight level 390 until after they ate. That way they would burn off a little more fuel and further lighten the aircraft.

Mark handed Gary three meal trays. Hoot took his but Scott passed. Scott had grabbed a bite to eat in New York and wasn't hungry. Gary placed Scott's meal tray on the floor. The crew meals weren't restaurant-quality cuisine, but they weren't bad, either. Hoot finished his meal and handed his tray back to Gary. He then asked Scott to contact Toronto Center to request flight level 390.

Hoot slid his seat forward and disengaged the autopilot. He planned on hand-flying the plane to the higher altitude. Just before beginning the climb, something caught his attention. He glanced behind him and saw that Gary Banks had just sat down at the flight engineer panel. Hoot assumed that Gary must have just handed the meal trays back to the flight attendant and was now returning to his seat. Hoot advanced the power and started the climb.

———◦◦———

In the back of the plane, flight attendant Mark Moscicki stepped back to coach to assist the other three flight attendants with their meal service. In 1979, every passenger received a meal. With only six first-class passengers, Mark had finished the first-class meal service early. The three flight attendants working coach, stewardesses Francine Schaulleur and Carol Reams, and Steward Carlos Machado-Olverdo, indicated that they were almost finished with their service. So Mark went back to the galley to prepare the flight-attendant crew meals. While the meals were heating, he walked through the cabin and picked up trash. The cabin lights were on.

Mark, Carol, and Francine were New York-based flight attendants. Flight attendant Carlos Machado-Olverdo, a gregarious individual originally from Ecuador, was a Los Angeles-based steward working as an extra on the flight. Flight 841 was the beginning of their trip pairing. None of the four flight attendants had flown with the three Los Angeles-based cockpit crew members, and prior to TWA 841, none of the four had flown together. For Mark Moscicki, this was also his first flight after returning from his vacation.[2]

With the passengers content for the time being, the flight attendants grabbed their own meals. Carol Reams found an open seat in first class in which to eat her meal. She sat near the window on the right side of the aircraft in seat 2F. Mark Moscicki and Carlos Machado-Olverdo ate their meals sitting in the aft-facing jump seats. Carlos sat in the seat nearest the cockpit door. The two men balanced their meal trays on their laps while they ate.

Flight attendant Francine Schaulleur wasn't eating. She was back in the galley warming up a bottle of milk for an infant cared for by passenger Holly Wicker. Earlier she had taken the apple pie off her meal tray and entered the cockpit so she could enjoy her dessert away from the scrutiny of the passengers. The flight deck at night is one of the only places where a flight attendant can find a little peace and quiet. Seeing the crew looked busy, she finished her apple pie and stepped back out as quietly as she had entered.[3]

— • —

As TWA 841 continued the climb they reached the end of Toronto Center's area of radio coverage and entered Cleveland Center's airspace. The radio crackled with the frequency-change request from the Toronto Center controller.

Toronto Center:	TW841 change to Cleveland Center 133.25
TWA 841:	133.25
Toronto Center:	Roger.
TWA 841:	Cleveland, TWA's eight-forty-one is out of three-seven-zero climbing to three-nine-zero.
CE:	TWA 841, ident, squawk code two-seven-zero-two.
TWA 841:	Twenty-seven-zero-two, TWA's 841.

Hoot made the climb from flight level 350 to FL 390 at 400 feet per minute (fpm), a relatively slow rate of climb, perhaps to keep the ride smooth and the deck angle low. He leveled off at FL 390 at 9:38 pm central time. The 4000-foot climb had taken fourteen minutes.

Once Hoot was level at flight level 390, he reengaged the autopilot. Gary Banks set the power based on a power setting he read off the performance chart. By climbing to a higher altitude Hoot was hoping to get a smoother ride and less headwinds, but by doing so he was also pushing the aircraft to its maximum capabilities based on weight and altitude. The service ceiling on the Boeing 727-100 was 42,000 feet. That was the highest altitude in which the aircraft was certified to fly. On this night, however, with a gross weight of 130,000 pounds, the maximum altitude the aircraft could fly was 39,000 feet.

Flying any aircraft near the service ceiling is a delicate balance. Fly too slow and the aircraft can experience low-speed buffet. Fly too fast and there is the possibility of high-speed mach buffet. Both conditions occur when the air flowing over the wings begins to separate either because of excess speed or a high angle of attack. Increasing the g-loads on the aircraft has the same effect as increasing the angle of attack. Turbulence or a steep turn then can be enough to make the plane become unstable and even uncontrollable. Some pilots describe it as feeling as if the plane is balanced on the head of a needle. There's even an aerodynamic term for this flight regime: It's called the coffin corner.

This is not to say that climbing to the higher altitude was unsafe. The aircraft was well within safety limits. The performance margins, according to later analysis, showed that the aircraft was 70 knots above the low-speed stall buffet and 36 knots below high-speed mach buffet. In smooth air, the aircraft could have sustained level flight at 43 degrees of bank without entering a stall.[4]

While the ride at FL 350 had been relatively smooth, with only an occasional bump, the ride at FL 390 was even better. One passenger would later comment that the ride was as smooth as if he were sitting in his living room. It was also clear. It was so clear that Hoot could see the distant glow of lights from Chicago. A half-moon provided just a hint of light on the cloud deck below. The stars were unusually bright that night. Hoot would later say that it was as bright a night as he'd ever seen.

Despite the smooth ride and favorable weather conditions, Hoot wasn't entirely comfortable. The Boeing 727 wasn't the most stable aircraft at high altitudes due to a number of factors, including the short, highly swept-back wings and a large rudder. One thing was certain, though, at FL 390 Hoot and the other two crew members were more apt to notice any unusual vibrations or other aerodynamic abnormalities than what they might notice at a lower altitude. Hoot slid his seat back and closed his eyes briefly. The time was 9:42 p.m.

At the Cleveland Air Route Traffic Control Center (ARTCC) in Oberlin, Ohio, controller Leon Cleaver, who was working the high-altitude Peck sector, had TWA 841 on his screen. Sitting next to Leon and plugged into Leon's console listening in, was a pilot who was taking part in a two-day program called "Rain Check." The Rain Check program was a chance for civilian pilots to learn about the operations of the Air Route Traffic Control Center. A half-dozen other pilots were scattered throughout the room sitting next to other controllers. The only other aircraft on Leon's screen was a Northwest Airlines flight. Leon pointed out the radar blip that represented TWA 841 and explained to the pilot the significance of the information in the accompanying data block that showed the aircraft's transponder code of 2702 and FL 390 altitude readout. The pilot moved in for a closer look.[5]

The center controllers didn't get visitors very often, and there wasn't much traffic, so Leon spent a little extra time answering questions about his job. The loquacious pilot was commenting about some experience he'd had recently when Leon saw something strange on his radar screen. The altitude readout for TWA 841 went from 390 to 227 and then to XXX.

Leon held up his hand to stop the pilot from speaking while he stared at his screen and tried to make sense of what he was seeing. He watched the blip representing TWA 841 suddenly change course from a westerly heading to a southwest heading. Leon keyed his mike.

> CE: Trans World eight-forty-one, Cleveland.
> CE: Trans World eight-forty-one, Cleveland.

There was no reply.

Chapter Two

We've had a
Slight Problem

fter leveling at FL 390, Scott Kennedy prepared to make another ground-speed check. Hoot used the time to put away his New York charts and pull out the approach charts for Minneapolis. Hoot's flight bag was on the floor next to him on his left. As he leaned over to retrieve his chart book, he sensed a light, high-frequency vibration in the balls of his feet. Hoot glanced at Scott to see if he had felt anything. Scott was staring intently at the clock and didn't seem to notice the vibration.

Hoot sat upright and moved his seat forward. He put his feet on the rudder pedals. Something didn't feel right, but he couldn't place it. Hoot glanced around the cockpit for clues as to the source of the vibration. He looked outside and noticed the nose of the airplane yawing right and then pausing, and then yawing right again. Inside he saw that the control yoke was turned to the left, but the instruments and a quick glance outside confirmed that the plane was in a right bank. The plane was on autopilot. Something was causing the plane to bank and turn to the right while the autopilot tried to maintain heading by turning the yoke to the left.

Wanting to get a feel for what the plane was doing, Hoot grabbed the yoke and used the quick disconnect on the yoke to disconnect the autopilot. Almost immediately the right bank increased. Hoot applied left aileron and left rudder. The vibration increased to a slight buffet. The bank to the right slowed briefly; then the plane yawed severely to the right, and the bank increased.

"Hold on!" Hoot yelled out. "I think she's going over."

The roll continued until the plane became inverted. Hoot's first thought was that the ride had been so smooth that he was sure passengers were out of their seats. So he pulled back on the control wheel to create some positive Gs to keep people seated or from hitting the ceiling of the plane. The plane did a complete roll followed by another 360-degree roll, but this time the nose had dropped, and the plane entered a spiraling vertical dive.

Hoot had his hands full trying to arrest the roll. With his left hand, he began pointing towards the flight spoiler handle and yelling for Scott to "Get 'em up! Get 'em up!" Scott had been so focused on the clock that he wasn't even aware that the plane had rolled. But now he felt a force driving him against the cockpit window. He had no idea what Hoot wanted him to do.

Hoot reached over with his left hand and ran the spoiler handle full aft. It had no effect. The plane was now in a steep vertical dive, rotating at about 90 to 120 degrees a second. Hoot looked at his attitude indicator and saw something he had never seen before—solid black. The altimeter was unwinding at a rate so fast it was impossible to read. Hoot glanced at his airspeed indicator and saw that it was pegged at 475 knots. The plane dove through a cloud deck in a matter of seconds. Below that, much closer to the ground, was another broken layer of clouds. Hoot could see the lights from the cities of Flint and Saginaw, Michigan, rotating in and out of view. Since the plane wasn't responding to the left aileron and rudder input, Hoot tried reversing the control wheel to the right.

He also pushed and pulled on the yoke. Neither action had any effect. He briefly considered deploying a thrust reverser on one engine to stop the rotation but decided against it.

Scott was pressed up against the cockpit window on the right side. Gary, who was sitting facing forward, eventually passed out as the g-forces became too great for him to withstand. He fell forward, with his head landing on the center console. Scott was still trying to process what was going on. His instinct was to grab the control wheel. He placed his hands near the control wheel and glanced back at Hoot. Hoot gave him a look that indicated that he did not want Scott's assistance. Scott thought that maybe Hoot had been yelling at him to lower the landing gear. He put his hand over the gear selector and again glanced back at Hoot. Running out of options, Hoot signaled to Scott to lower the gear. Scott put his hand on the gear selector and yanked it downward.[1]

As the gear extended into the rushing air, there was a tremendous bang that sounded like an explosion. This was followed by the deafening sound of rushing air and metal tearing off from the aircraft. The noise level increased and made the experience even more frightening. Seconds later Hoot began to feel some feedback in the control wheel. The rotation stopped, but the plane continued to oscillate left and right. Hoot pulled back on the yoke and felt the elevator responding to his input. He continued to pull back on the yoke, but he was also concerned that if he pulled too hard the wings might come off. He could feel the g-forces intensifying. As the g-forces reached near 6 G's, a terrible thought raced through his mind. They weren't going to make it. He could see the ground rapidly approaching. They were entering a cloud deck or fog layer, and he could see hazy lights from the ground rushing up at tremendous speed. The plane was now in control, but they were too late. They were going to hit the ground.

Just how close the plane came to actually hitting the ground would be a subject for later debate. Hoot did, however, manage to pull the plane out of the dive. As the plane shot skyward, Hoot looked outside and saw the half-moon above him. He locked onto the moon and didn't let it out of his sight, knowing that as long as he had the moon in view he couldn't be headed for the ground.

It took only seconds to shoot up from nearly hitting the surface to climbing through eight thousand feet. About this time Gary Banks started to come out of his blackout. Sitting away from the instrument panel gave Gary a unique perspective. He could see the nose of the airplane and the horizon. It was obvious to him that they were climbing too steeply. He looked over at the airspeed indicator and saw the speed bleeding off rapidly.

"Watch your attitude and your speed," Gary said over Hoot's shoulder. "You're in a forty-five degree bank to the left. Airspeed's decreasing."

Gary's feedback broke Hoot's fixation on the moon. He started to ease the nose over, but he over-compensated and created negative G's. Now they were floating out of their seats. The plane was flying, but it wasn't stable. It was vibrating and shaking and oscillating from side to side.

"Watch your speed!" Gary yelled out again.

Hoot was trying to get a feel for what he could and couldn't do with the plane. He let the nose drop through the horizon and they quickly went from 9,500 feet back down to below 3,000 feet.

Hoot climbed back up to ten thousand feet and brought the plane into a somewhat level attitude. The plane was still shaking, and the noise level was so high that they had to shout in order to be heard. Adding to the slipstream noise and vibrations was the constant wailing of the "gear unsafe" horn. The gear had extended, but the nose gear and both main landing gear were indicating that they were not down and locked. The warning horn became so annoying that Gary Banks pulled the circuit breaker to silence it.[2] Gary scanned the flight-engineer panel looking for problems and reported that the system A hydraulics was indicating zero for both pressure and fluid level. He didn't see anything else on the FE panel, but when he made a scan of the instrument panel, he noticed a failure flag in the lower yaw damper. He pointed that out to Hoot and Scott along with the three unsafe gear indications. About this time, they heard the call from Cleveland Center.

CE: Trans World eight-forty-one Cleveland.

TW841:   TWA's 841; go ahead.

CE: Yes, sir, looks like you're on a southbound heading, sir, ah, verify your intentions.

TW841:   Okay, listen. We've had a problem. We've lost about twenty thousand feet and we got it level at ten thousand now under control. We got a severe vibration and, ah, probably ought to have a vector to a suitable airport close by, probably Detroit Wayne.

CE: Okay, sir. I have Saginaw airport directly below you and Flint is about, oh, eleven o'clock and thirty miles and Lansing is about one o'clock and forty miles.

TW841:   Okay, we have a vibration and I think we probably, ah, would like to—what's the weather at Metro?

CE: Okay, sir. Stand by.

When they were at cruise altitude, Hoot remembered seeing the lights from Chicago. He knew the weather at Chicago had to be clear. He suggested to Scott and Gary that they head for Chicago. Hoot's thinking was that if the plane had held together this long, it should be

15

able to get to Chicago without falling apart. O'Hare Airport was also a TWA base. There would be better maintenance available there, and it would also be easier for the passengers to find other flights. Scott and Gary, however, were adamantly against that idea. They wanted to get the plane on the ground as soon as possible. The debate about where to go for an emergency landing was interrupted by the controller.

> CE: Okay, Trans World eight-forty-one. The current Detroit weather is special eight-hundred scattered, measured twenty-thousand broken, and the visibility seven with light snow. The wind is three-twenty at eight knots—and I got an altimeter of two-nine-seven-four.

Pilots needing to make an emergency landing are required to land at the nearest suitable airport. The term "nearest suitable airport," however, doesn't always equate to the closest airport. There could be an airport a few miles away but it may not be suitable for a number of reasons such as weather, runway length, or approach capability. There were several airports in close proximity to TWA 841; Saginaw and Flint airports were both just minutes away. But Hoot didn't want to have to make an instrument approach in poor weather with an aircraft he was still having difficulty controlling. He picked up his mike and called Cleveland Center.

> TW841: We have a complete hydraulic system "A" failure. The airplane is shaking. We would like to be vectored someplace that has some pretty decent weather.
>
> CE: Okay, sir. Stand by one.

CE: Eight-forty-one Saginaw is about fifteen to twenty miles to your six o'clock position right now.

TW841:   Okay, what kind of weather do they have?

CE: Trans World 841, looks like they got a ceiling of four hundred, sky obscured, visibility is two and a half miles with the RVR at six thousand, winds three-six-zero at one-one.

TW841:   Okay, I'm not even sure we have a plate for Saginaw. If you want us to hold we can hold right here.

CE: No, sir. Detroit weather looks a little better than Saginaw. Detroit is at your eleven o'clock and sixty miles.

TW841:   Okay, we'll take vectors to Detroit.

With the aircraft somewhat stable, Hoot knew he had to say something to the passengers. He picked up the handset to make an announcement but hesitated before speaking. He wanted to update the passengers, but he also didn't want to alarm them. "Ladies and Gentleman, I think it is apparent that we've had a slight problem," Hoot began. "We're going to be pretty busy up here for the next few minutes. We'll get back to you as soon as we can."

Hoot turned to Gary and told him to brief the lead flight attendant and have him prepare the cabin for an emergency landing. Gary opened the cockpit door and found Mark Moscicki standing there waiting for instructions.

"Do you remember your training at the Breech Academy?"[3] Gary asked.

When Mark indicated that he did, Gary told him rather directly, "Well, you'd better go back there and do it." Gary then closed the door and pulled out his emergency checklist.

Cleveland center controller Leon Cleaver stayed with TWA 841 even though the plane was no longer in his airspace. He could tell by the stress in the pilot's voice that whatever was going on with the plane was serious. He didn't want to add to the pilots' workload by having them change frequencies. But he also knew that he couldn't let an aircraft enter another controller's airspace without notifying him. Once the situation seemed to be under control, Leon gave TWA 841 the frequency change to the low-altitude controller. He also reached up and pressed the button that connected him directly to controller Tony Mealy, who was sitting at a radar screen about fifteen feet to Leon's left. Leon told Tony there was an emergency aircraft in his sector at 10,000 feet south of Saginaw. As Leon was passing on the information about TWA 841, Tony also got the call from the aircraft.

Anthony Mealy didn't know anything about TWA 841. At that time of night, the center facility was working with a reduced staff, and he was working multiple sectors. Anthony frantically scoured his scope looking for the emergency aircraft. He had other planes he was controlling and needed to know exactly where TWA 841 was. He looked south of the Saginaw airport and didn't see anything. The realization that an aircraft had suddenly dropped into his airspace and he had no idea where it was caused him to do something he had never done before or since—he stood up from his seat. Finally he caught a glimpse of the transponder readout from TWA 841 southwest of Saginaw as it was climbing through 4,200 feet. At some point during the hand-off, Hoot had descended below Anthony's radar coverage, which in that area was around 5,000 feet.[4]

Anthony's first thought was to vector the aircraft to the closest airport, which at that time was Lansing, Michigan. He didn't know of the crew's prior decision to divert to Detroit. He gave Hoot a heading and the distance to Lansing. He contacted the Lansing tower controller and told him to roll the emergency equipment for an emergency aircraft headed their way. TWA 841 was lined up for a straight-in approach to Lansing, but Anthony wasn't so sure that Lansing was the best option for making an emergency landing. It was a smaller airport with a short runway. He contacted the aircraft and suggested that Detroit might be a better option. After a brief pause, TWA 841 came back on the radio and asked for vectors to Detroit.

Anthony Mealy called his supervisor and asked him to coordinate the emergency landing with the Detroit tower controllers. He sat back in his seat and watched TWA 841 track across his screen. He had no idea how serious the situation was inside the plane. He wished the pilots good luck as he handed them off to the Detroit approach controller.

——◆◆——

Despite surviving a dive that approached six G's, nearly twice the amount of g-forces experienced by Space Shuttle astronauts during liftoff, TWA 841 was not yet out of danger. The plane was severely damaged, and there were multiple emergencies that had to be dealt with before any landing could be made.

After some discussion, it was decided that the first problem to address was the three unsafe-gear indications. If they were going to land anywhere, they were going to need three green down and locked indications. Gary Banks was given the task of performing the emergency gear extension procedure, which involved manually turning a hand crank for each individual landing gear. Gary grabbed the hand crank from the aft bulkhead and removed the access panel on the cockpit floor. He rotated the crank clockwise to unlock the nose gear. He next rotated the crank counterclockwise to lock the nose gear into place. Almost immediately the noise level in the cockpit subsided as the red unsafe gear indication for the nose gear turned green. Gary went through the same procedure for the two main landing gears, but both gear lights remained red.

The two red unsafe lights meant that Hoot had no idea in what condition the landing gear was. He knew that they had exceeded the speed limitation for extending the gear. For all he knew, there might not even be any landing gear still on the plane. He had heard the loud explosion when the gear had extended. It was possible that the gear had been torn from the plane or at least been severely damaged. He didn't want to land not knowing the condition of his landing gear. His only option was to do a flyby to have the gear inspected by someone on the ground. He passed on his request to the Detroit approach controller.

Scott and Gary were running the alternate flap extension procedure when the plane suddenly banked hard to the left as the slats and flaps started to come out.

"Stop what you're doing!" Hoot shouted. "I'm having control problems."

Hoot was busy flying the plane and communicating with ATC and didn't know which emergency checklist they were running. But he knew that something had changed that caused the airplane to want to yaw and bank hard left. Hoot saw the flap handle in the five-degree detente.

"Bring the flaps back up," Hoot told Scott. "Something is causing the plane to want to roll to the left."

Scott reversed his steps to bring the flaps up again. Everything had happened so quickly that the flaps hadn't yet extended. The slats, however, had extended fully. Unfortunately, because they were using the alternate flap extension procedure, they were unable to retract the slats. They were out permanently. For some unexplained reason, the plane continued to yaw and bank left. Hoot had to use almost full opposite right aileron just to keep the plane upright. Hoot had no idea how much damage the plane had suffered. It certainly wasn't flying normally. He would comment later that he believed the aircraft had been damaged to the point where the wings were just hanging on.

Hoot wanted to know which systems he had lost with the loss of system A hydraulics. Gary read off the list of affected items: lower rudder, lower yaw damper, outboard flight spoilers, ground spoilers, and nose-wheel steering. The one word Hoot didn't hear was braking. Not having flaps for landing meant that they were going to have to make a faster-than-normal approach. The runway was likely to be slick due to the weather, and he would not have the use of aerodynamic braking from the ground spoilers, but he would have normal braking. Hoot was sure that he could stop the plane once they were on the ground, assuming the gear held up.

As they were vectored for the flyby, Hoot decided to see how much control he had. He tried slowing the aircraft and discovered that when the plane slowed below 200 kts, he was unable to stop the plane from rolling to the left. At 220 kts the aircraft was fairly stable. So that was the speed he decided he would use for the approach. A normal approach speed would have been around 130 kts.

When they broke out of the clouds around 700 feet above the airport, Hoot saw the flashing lights from the emergency vehicles lining the runway. He told the tower operator that he was going to do the flyby at around three hundred feet. Ground personnel were ready with spotlights to shine on the undercarriage. Gary and Scott were still running emergency checklists, but Gary took a moment to check on the cabin. When he opened the door he noticed that the passengers were all in the brace position. Gary called Mark over and told him that they weren't landing just yet and that he would let him know when the passengers needed to assume the brace position.

Keeping the speed at 220 kts, Hoot flew as low as 100 feet above the runway. The report from the tower operator, who was in contact with the emergency and fire and rescue vehicles, was not good. The nose gear and left main landing gear looked normal, but the right main landing gear appeared to be dangling in an unusual position.

Hoot climbed back up and asked for vectors for the approach. There was nothing he could do about the landing gear now. As Hoot made the turn to the downwind leg, the plane was in and out of the clouds. Hoot tried to keep the runway in sight to see if it was contaminated with snow or slush. At one point Hoot was so focused on examining the runway that the airplane went into a steep left bank. Scott took the control wheel and righted the plane.

After a long vector to final, Hoot was ready. He was running on adrenalin. He made a perfect approach and flew over the runway threshold at 217 kts. He kept the speed up as long as he could and touched down on the left main landing gear at about 187 kts. It held. The nose gear held as well. As the speed bled off, Hoot couldn't hold the right gear off any longer. He let the plane settle and hoped for the best. The right gear touched the runway. It held. Now Hoot was barreling down the runway with fire trucks and emergency vehicles in close pursuit.

The runway was wet and slick, but Hoot had normal braking and was able to bring the plane to a stop on the runway. Once he was certain that everything had held up, he used differential power and braking to taxi off the runway and onto a high-speed turnoff where the majority of the emergency vehicles were waiting. As soon as he was clear of the runway, he set the brakes. Without nose-wheel steering, he wasn't going any farther.

Hoot told Gary to start the auxiliary power unit (APU) so they would have power after shutting down the engines. While this was happening, emergency vehicles surrounded the aircraft and sprayed foam around the main landing gear area. Hoot received a call from the tower advising him that they had seen sparks as the aircraft rolled down the runway. Not long after hearing that news, Hoot heard a voice come over the intercom saying, "Hello, cockpit."

Standing by the nose of the aircraft, connected to the maintenance intercom, was TWA mechanic Mel Brown. Mel had learned of the emergency and was told by the Wayne County airport supervisor that he needed to tow the 727 off the taxiway. So Mel headed out to the plane with a tow tractor and tow bar. When he arrived on scene, the first thing he did was try to insert safety pins into the main gear. He saw the condition of the right gear and feared the gear was about to collapse. But when he shined his flashlight on the damaged gear, he could see that he wasn't going to be able to insert the safety pins because the holes didn't line up. He was examining the right landing gear when a fireman indicated that fuel was leaking from the left side of the plane and that they needed to get the people off the aircraft as soon as possible. Mel rushed back to the front of the aircraft to advise the captain.[5]

When Hoot learned of the fuel leak, he became alarmed. He was certain that the sparks seen by the tower operator were the result of the gear doors dragging on the runway; he had heard the metal scraping against the pavement. But the news of the fuel leak was reason to be concerned. He contemplated having the passengers use the emergency exits but quickly decided against it. Having passengers slide down emergency slides was just asking for trouble. He decided that everyone could be safely deplaned by the aft stairs. He notified the flight attendants, who then made an announcement over the PA.

By the time mechanic Mel Brown unplugged from the intercom and walked back to the rear of the plane to lower the stairs, he found that the flight attendants had beat him to it. The stairs were already down, and passengers were streaming from the aircraft.

Mel came back on the intercom and asked the captain to contact operations to arrange for transportation for the passengers back to the terminal. Hoot radioed operations and requested the transportation. He started to perform a cockpit-secure checklist, but as he started his flow, he realized that there were a number of switches that were not in the normal position. He decided to leave everything just the way it was. He felt it would help maintenance later when they tried to determine what had happened. He told Gary and Scott to grab their bags. They were getting off the plane.

As Gary Banks gathered his flight bag and coat and opened the cockpit door, a passenger saw him and came forward. "It's interesting that it isn't anyone's time on this plane to die," the passenger said, before turning and heading for the rear of the plane.[6]

Figure 3 Missing number seven slat

Before exiting the aircraft, Hoot glanced around the cabin as he worked his way rearward. He saw broken dishes and glasses in the aisle. He noticed a couple of barf bags sitting on the floor in the galley. A few oxygen masks dangled from the ceiling. He spotted a portable oxygen bottle lying on a passenger seat, indicating that one or more passengers may have needed oxygen. Several overhead lights had come loose and were hanging by their electrical wires. Hoot thought it looked like a scene from a disaster movie.

Figure 4 From left to right: Captain Hoot Gibson, First Officer Scott Kennedy, Flight Engineer Gary Banks. This image was taken during the making of the documentary "The Plane That Fell From The Sky."

Once outside the aircraft, Hoot, Scott, and Gary did a quick walk-around to survey the damage. The first problem they saw was the right gear that jutted out at a weird angle. By this time most of the emergency vehicles had departed the scene. Passengers huddled together on the wet taxiway.

An ambulance attended to several passengers. As the three men examined the damaged aircraft, several passengers came up and congratulated them on getting the plane back on the ground safely.

Hoot shook the hands of a few passengers and then continued his examination of the plane. He looked at the damaged right gear and saw something that looked out of place. When he moved in for a closer look, he saw a tree branch wedged into the gear. He yanked on it and tossed it aside. About this time, he heard Scott yelling to "come look at this." Scott was standing in front of the right wing, where an entire slat panel was missing. There was a gaping hole where the number seven slat should have been. One half of the slat track hung from the bottom of the wing, twisted and broken. It was obvious that very strong forces had been involved in the breaking away of the slat. Hoot was amazed that the plane had held together at all.

It wasn't long before everyone was gone and the three men were left alone by the side of the plane. Gary, overjoyed at having survived the dive and no longer under the scrutiny of passengers, ran towards Hoot to give him a bear hug. Gary was a good seven inches taller than Hoot. Hoot tried to maintain his balance but re-injured his ankle trying not to fall backwards.

Knowing that the mechanic was there to secure the plane, and realizing that no one was coming out to get them, Hoot, Scott, and Gary headed for the terminal building on foot. Moments later they were picked up by someone in a truck and dropped off at TWA operations.

Chapter Three

Roller Coaster

S*hortly after finishing his meal,* passenger Arthur Gaultier, age seventy, got up from his seat and walked to the back of the plane to have a smoke. Smoking was allowed in 1979 in designated smoking sections, usually the back of the plane. Passenger Barbara Merrill, a tall, attractive brunette, stood up and headed for the aft lavatory to freshen her makeup. Barbara's fourteen-year-old daughter, Susan, flipped through a magazine while she waited for her mother to return. The two were returning from a trip to Cairo, Egypt.

Robert and Jeannine Rakowsky were among only six passengers sitting in first class. They were returning from a week-long visit to Portugal along with two other first-class passengers, Floyd and Patricia Carlson. Floyd's company, *The Comfort Center,* had one of the best sales records in the country for residential furnaces. The supplier of the furnaces had rewarded Floyd with four round-trip tickets to Portugal. Robert Rakowsky managed Floyd's Duluth branch, so Floyd invited Bob and his wife on the all-expenses-paid trip.

The Rakowskys were sitting in the last row of seats in first class, which was up against a bulkhead. Directly behind that was an aisle-facing galley. The Carlsons sat in seats 1A and 1C on the left side of the aircraft. The Rakowsys and Carlsons were exhausted, having flown from

Portugal to New York and then on to TWA 841, going to Minneapolis. They were enjoying the first-class service and having cocktails. They had just finished dinner. Jeannine Rakowsky pulled out a pillow and leaned against the cabin window in an effort to get some much-needed rest. She hadn't been in that position very long when she felt a slight vibration. She looked at her husband, who also felt the slight vibration. The vibration was followed by a noticeable shudder. As the plane started to roll over to the right, Jeannine leaned left against her husband as if she were trying to will the plane upright. Suddenly they heard the sound of dishes and glassware breaking. Bob turned to his left to see what had happened and saw Flight Attendant Francine Schaulleur thrown to the floor; shards of broken plates and glasses lay scattered all around her. Bob reached out and held Francine by the arm.

Flight attendant Carol Reams knew something was wrong. She placed her meal tray down on the seat next to her and was headed back to her emergency position near the emergency exit across from the galley. She didn't make it. She saw Francine on the floor. She felt the pressure on her body and flung herself into seat 3C, where she strapped herself in.[1]

For the passengers in the front of the aircraft, there was no doubt that the plane was descending. Passengers sitting near the aft, however, had the sensation that the plane was climbing. Passenger Douglas Page, a design engineer for IBM, was sitting near the aisle in the very last row of seats on the right side of the aircraft. He felt a slight shudder that he later compared to light turbulence. But he also heard a strange thumping sound. Doug had just ordered a drink from Flight Attendant Francine Schaulleur.

Passenger Roger Peterson, sitting in seat 21A, was a new flyer. He could count on one hand the number of commercial airline flights he had flown on. He was returning from a trip to Israel, where he had met up with his mother, father, and younger brother and sister. His dad, who was a minister, was studying in Jerusalem.

Roger, at age twenty-five, was one of the younger passengers onboard. He was a musician. He worked days at Sears and Roebuck and played in a rock-and-roll band at nights and on weekends. He also played piano at his local church.

After eating his meal and handing his tray back to the flight attendant, Roger relaxed in his seat. He noticed a tall, slender woman walk by him on her way to the bathroom. Roger didn't feel any shuddering or hear any strange sounds. His first sensation was the g-forces acting upon him. He remembered hearing the woman in the bathroom call out for help. But Roger was pinned to his seat, unable to even raise his arms off the armrest. It felt to Roger as if he were in a rapidly climbing elevator. He remembered looking up at the seatbelt sign and noticing that it wasn't illuminated. This was an indication to him that whatever was going on with the plane could not have been that serious; otherwise, he reasoned, the captain would have turned on the seatbelt sign.

Roger Peterson's lack of concern was not shared by most of the other passengers. The increasing g-forces and the screaming sound of the jet engines left little doubt that something was terribly wrong. From inside the cabin, with the cabin lights on, the passengers had no way of determining the attitude of the aircraft. There was no sensation of the rapid rotation. The main sensation was of being forced into their seats, unable to raise their arms. As the g-forces increased, the skin on passengers' faces began to pull back, like that of a pilot undergoing high G training in a human centrifuge. It was a natural reaction to the forces, but it was frightening to see.

The aircraft jolted as the landing gear extended. Several oxygen masks fell from the ceiling, but the passengers sitting beneath the masks were unable to reach up and grab them. The sound level inside the aircraft intensified. One passenger would later describe it as sounding like a dive bomber from an old WWII movie.

One by one the passengers' thoughts turned to the possibility that they were not going to live through the experience. Chell Roberts, a twenty-two-year-old junior at the University of Utah, thought of his pregnant wife, Louise, sitting next to him and the possibility that he might never get to see his baby.[2]

Douglas Page's traveling companion, Lou Dougherty, turned to him and asked him if he thought they were going to be okay. Doug said he didn't think so. At that moment, several thoughts raced through Doug's mind. He did a quick mental calculation and realized that the flight number TWA 841 added up to thirteen. He wasn't superstitious but the number thirteen now crossed his mind. That was followed by thoughts of whether or not he had adequate and up-to-date life insurance. He was married with two children and hoped that he wasn't about to put them in a financial hole. After giving it some thought, he decided that he had sufficient insurance.[3]

Passenger Peter Fehr was sitting in seat 12D. He was returning from New York after attending the annual convention of the American College of OBGYN. Earlier, he had handed his meal tray to the flight attendant and then contemplated pulling out a medical paper he was working on. The paper, which he hoped to publish, was in a briefcase under his seat. Prior to the meal service the captain had made an announcement that they were going to be late getting into Minneapolis due to strong headwinds, but it had already been a long day, and the thought of just closing his eyes for a short nap seemed like a more appealing option. So he put off retrieving his paper and let his mind wander to the next day. He was scheduled for surgery in the morning. That's about the time he noticed the plane shudder.

Peter would later describe the shudder as more of a vibration within the plane itself rather than turbulence. The vibration was strong enough to catch his attention but not enough to cause alarm. His next recollection was of the heavy g-forces acting upon him. The g-forces were so great that he was unable to reach up and adjust his glasses, which had slid down to the tip of his nose. As the plane continued descending, he heard the passenger in front of him speaking out loud.

"You can do it," the man said in a pleading tone. "You can do it. You can pull it out!"

Peter thought the man's attempt to will the plane out of the dive was fruitless. He was certain that they were going in. It was then that his thoughts turned to his wife and family. The next thing he remembered was hearing what he believes was a sonic boom as the plane broke the sound barrier. This was followed by the loud sound of rushing air. Peter compared it to how he imagined a tornado might sound.

The sound from the aircraft was loud enough to catch the attention of a number of people on the ground. Several witnesses reported what they thought was a sonic boom. A woman and her two children heard the loud boom as they exited a movie theater in downtown Saginaw, Michigan. A group of sorority girls ran outside their dorm rooms at the Delta College in Saginaw when they heard the loud boom. Whether or not what witnesses heard was a sonic boom or perhaps the sound made when the gear extended has not been determined. It has been estimated, however, that the plane did exceed the speed of sound.[4]

One person on the ground who heard TWA 841 that night was Randall Deshano. Randall didn't hear a sonic boom. He was home watching TV when he heard what sounded like an airliner that was about to crash into his backyard. He ran to his kitchen window and looked outside expecting to see a ball of flames. Instead he saw nothing but darkness and then silence as the plane swooped overhead. Weeks later, parts from TWA 841 would be discovered in a farm field less than a mile from Randall's house.[5]

—•◦•—

No one inside the aircraft had any idea just how close to the ground they had come. They knew that the plane had experienced a malfunction. They also knew that they weren't out of trouble. The plane vibrated and shook and swayed from side to side. Adding to their fears was the deafening wind noise and the sound of metal under stress.

A few passengers reached up to try to pry open the panels containing the oxygen masks. They saw masks dangling above other passengers and were concerned when their masks did not drop.

Floyd Carlson, who was sitting in first class with his wife Pat, looked down at his armrest and noticed that the cocktail he had ordered was still sitting there. It hadn't spilled a drop through the entire ordeal. He downed the contents in one long gulp.

The passengers looked to the flight attendants for guidance as to what to expect next. Hoot's brief announcement did little to allay their fears. He hadn't said anything about what had happened. He hadn't said anything about where they might be diverting to or how long it might be before they landed. He hadn't said anything about the condition of the plane or given any reassurances that they would land safely. In Hoot's defense, he didn't know what the condition of the plane was other than that it was difficult to control. As for Scott and Gary, they were occupied with running emergency checklists. Still, the lack of communication from the crew about what was happening would be cited later by passengers filing lawsuits as a contributing factor to their anxiety and emotional distress.

After the brief exchange between lead flight attendant Mark Moscicki and Gary Banks, Mark gathered the other three flight attendants in the forward galley to brief them. Not wanting to alarm the passengers, he closed the curtain to the galley. He spoke softly as he told his fellow crew members that they had less than ten minutes to prepare the cabin for an emergency landing. Some passengers who were trying to get a glimpse of what was going on behind the curtain believed that the four flight attendants had huddled together to say a prayer. The four split up as Mark retrieved his emergency manual and, using the PA system, instructed the passengers to remove their shoes, ties, and any sharp objects from their pockets and to place those items in the seat pockets in front of them. He explained the brace position and mentioned that additional information could be found in the briefing cards located in the seatback pockets. For flight attendant Carol Reams, preparing the cabin for an emergency landing was a surreal experience. She had completed her yearly recurrent emergency training only the day before. Carol remained in the galley and began securing it.

Flight attendant Francine Schaulleur took off her shoes and walked on the armrests of passenger seats going from overhead bin to overhead bin pulling out towels and pillows to hand to passengers. Mark and Carlos went through the plane making sure that the seatbacks were up, the tray tables were secured, and the exit rows were free of obstructions. The four flight attendants did what they were trained to do in an emergency, but the stress of the situation was evident in their hectic preparations.[6]

Sitting in the exit row on the left side of the aircraft facing forward was passenger Holly Wicker. She was holding a two-month-old infant, Asha, on her lap secured by a Gerry-pack child carrier. Sitting next to her were two more children: Jasmine, age eight; and Tepi, age six. Holly and a coworker, Sheryl Fisher, both worked for an adoption agency. They had flown to New York the previous day in order to escort the children to Minneapolis, where the children were to be handed over to their new parents. Sheryl Fisher was sitting in the exit row opposite Holly with twenty-two-month-old Debi sitting beside her. Holly expressed some concern to Mark Moscicki that she might have trouble opening the emergency exit with the baby strapped to her. A passenger sitting behind Holly offered to help with the emergency exit door if it came to that. Other passengers agreed to help with the children if necessary.

Had a similar emergency occurred today, the children would not have been seated in the emergency exit row. Today, passengers must verbally acknowledge that they are willing and able to open the emergency exit if called upon. That's why the emergency exit rows are the last rows of seats filled. Airlines want to give their boarding agents an opportunity to pick individuals who are capable of working the emergency exit doors in an emergency.

The two older children traveling with Holly and Sheryl spoke no English. They had been given new clothes and shoes for the trip. As soon as Holly removed their shoes to prepare for the emergency landing, they would put them back on. Finally, one of the flight attendants took the shoes away from the children and placed them under the seats, where the toddlers couldn't reach them. One of the little girls had been given a toy by a boy at the New York Airport. She wasn't about to give that up. All attempts to remove the toy were met with screaming, so the toy remained in her possession.[7]

At some point the crew gave the instruction for the passengers to assume the brace position. They were in that uncomfortable position for quite a while until finally there came an announcement that they were going to be doing a flyby to have the landing gear checked. That's when passengers first learned about a problem with the landing gear. That's also when they learned that they would be landing in Detroit.

———◆•◆•◆———

It wasn't until after the recovery, as the flight attendants began preparing for the landing in Detroit, that passenger Roger Peterson became aware of the gravity of the emergency. One particular phrase uttered by a flight attendant caught his attention, "upon impact." From that moment on he knew that they were in a life-or-death situation.

As they did the flyby, Roger caught a glimpse of the numerous vehicles lining the runway. Those images combined with the sullen faces of the flight attendants convinced him that this was not going to end well. The news that the crew did not have a safe gear-down indication convinced him that they were going to end up in a ball of flames as the plane careened down the runway. It was then that he tried to make peace with his fate and silently say his goodbyes.

———◆•◆•◆———

Peter Fehr was relieved when he realized that the pilots had, in fact, pulled the plane out of the dive. That relief was short lived, however, as his concerns turned to the emergency landing he knew was coming. He determined from the actions of the flight attendants and the announcements over the PA that they were still in danger. So he listened intently as the flight attendants gave their instructions regarding preparations for an emergency landing.

There was little conversation as the plane continued on to Detroit and during the subsequent flyby over the runway. A small group of passengers, led by a catholic priest, recited the Lord's Prayer. Passenger Patricia Carlson, sitting in first class, recited the twenty-third psalm. Other than that, the passengers remained silent. Everyone was intent on not missing any important instructions.

As the plane made its final approach into Detroit, Peter Fehr assumed a brace position with his head down and his arms resting on the seat-back in front of him. He couldn't help but think of everything that could go wrong. Since he was a physician, his thoughts turned to the possible injuries that might result from a plane crash-landing on a runway.

Figure 5 Passengers and crew deplaned through the aft stairs

Peter's main recollection of the actual landing was the sound of metal scraping against the pavement. What he was hearing were the gear doors, which hadn't retracted, scraping the runway. The touchdown, however, was smooth. A few passengers would later comment that it was the smoothest landing they had ever experienced. When the plane came to a stop, a brief moment of silence was followed by a quick round of applause. Several minutes went by before an announcement informed them that they would be deplaning through the aft stairs.

As the passengers began standing up, retrieving items from the overhead bins and walking towards the back of the plane, Peter noticed one of the flight attendants administering oxygen to an older woman a few rows ahead of him. The flight attendant asked if there was a physician onboard. Peter waited for the aisle to clear and then stepped forward to offer aid to the woman.

Peter's first thought was that the woman was having a heart attack. He checked her pulse and breathing. Both were normal. After speaking with the woman, he decided that she was well enough to deplane with assistance. He helped her off the plane and into a waiting ambulance. Peter noticed other passengers huddled together in small groups. It was a strange sight to see them standing around in the cold with their bags beside them on the wet pavement.

Passenger Holly Wicker moved down the aisle to the rear of the plane with the infant in the Gerry-pack and the two smaller children leading the way. They were met by a fireman who ran up the rear stairs and into the aircraft. "Get off!" the fireman yelled, indicating that they weren't hurrying along as quickly as they should. The man picked up the two girls in one arm and Holly and the baby in the other arm. He carried them down the stairs through the narrow passageway.[8]

Outside the aircraft, a light snow fell. The two children from India, Jasmine and Tepi, wandered off to examine the snow that had accumulated on the grassy area next to the taxiway. It was cold out, and they were wearing light-weight cotton dresses, but the experience of seeing snow for the first time took precedent over any discomfort the two might have been feeling. Other passengers passed the time by strolling around the aircraft to survey the damage. One passenger, Douglas Page, an amateur photographer, unpacked his camera and took a couple of photos of the plane. Unfortunately, poor lighting and his trembling hands resulted in unusable images.

Eventually a beat-up station wagon pulled up alongside the plane. A TWA representative stepped out of the car and said he had room for four or five people. Passenger Chell Roberts, who was pregnant, took a seat. She was followed by passenger Holly Wicker and the baby, Asha.

"Anybody else?" the station manager shouted to the group of passengers standing nearby. "I have room for a few more."

Patricia Carlson looked around and didn't see anyone else heading for the car, so she slid into the seat, leaving her husband Floyd with the Rakowskys and the other passengers. She was cold and shaking and just wanted to get inside to calm down.

It would be another twenty or thirty minutes before a shuttle bus arrived. The shuttle bus, which was really a repurposed school bus, wasn't large enough to accommodate all of the passengers, so a number of people had to wait for a return trip.

Roger Peterson didn't make it onto the first shuttle bus. He had been walking around the aircraft to survey the damage. He stood by one of the crew members as he studied the damaged right wing. Roger didn't know anything about aircraft design, but it was obvious that a large section on the leading edge of the right wing was missing. Roger didn't speak to the crew member standing next to him. He saw the shuttle bus returning. The temperature was dropping, and he didn't have a jacket, so he joined his fellow passengers for the ride back to the terminal.

Peter Fehr was about to climb onto the same shuttle bus but remembered that he had left his briefcase on the plane. He reentered the aircraft via the aft stairs. When he exited the plane, he saw the shuttle bus driving off. He could see the terminal building and a sign saying Eastern Airlines, so he decided to walk to the terminal without waiting to see if the bus would return. But before he did, he stopped and vomited in the grass.

When the passengers were dropped off near the terminal, no one was present there to greet them or to direct them into the terminal building. They tried several doors until finally finding one that opened to a staircase leading up to the main terminal. It was late, and only a few places of business were open. The manager of a restaurant/bar opened up a closed section of the restaurant to give the passengers a place to sit down. The restaurant was closed, but the bar was still open. By this time a TWA representative, a tall, attractive African American woman, had handed out food and drink vouchers to the passengers. For most of those passengers on TWA 841, the $7.50 voucher would be the only compensation they would ever receive from TWA. A few passengers tried to use the food vouchers at the bar, but the bartender refused to accept them because he had no agreement with the airline.

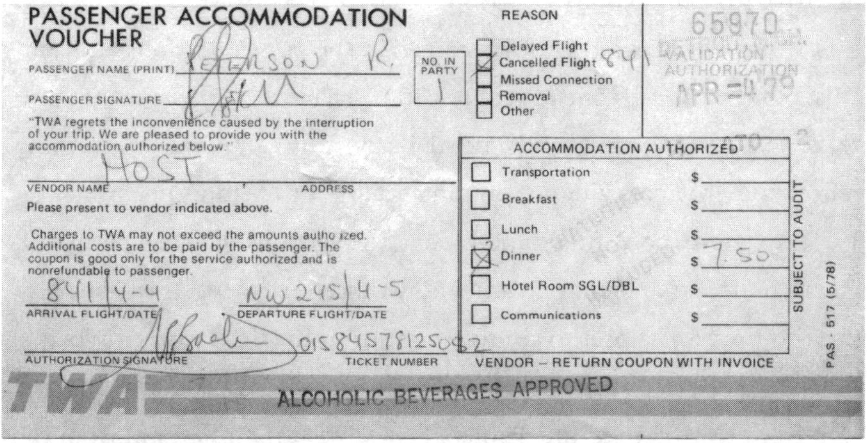

PASSENGER ACCOMMODATION VOUCHER

PASSENGER NAME (PRINT) Peterson R.
PASSENGER SIGNATURE

NO. IN PARTY 1

REASON
Delayed Flight
[X] Cancelled Flight 841
Missed Connection
Removal
Other

65970
VALIDATION AUTHORIZATION
APR 4 79

"TWA regrets the inconvenience caused by the interruption of your trip. We are pleased to provide you with the accommodation authorized below."

HOST
VENDOR NAME ADDRESS
Please present to vendor indicated above.

Charges to TWA may not exceed the amounts authorized. Additional costs are to be paid by the passenger. The coupon is good only for the service authorized and is nonrefundable to passenger.

841 4-4
ARRIVAL FLIGHT/DATE

NW 245 4-5
DEPARTURE FLIGHT/DATE

AUTHORIZATION SIGNATURE

015 8457812504 2
TICKET NUMBER

ACCOMMODATION AUTHORIZED
Transportation $
Breakfast $
Lunch $
[X] Dinner $ 7.50
Hotel Room SGL/DBL $
Communications $

SUBJECT TO AUDIT

PAS - 517 (5/78)

VENDOR – RETURN COUPON WITH INVOICE

TWA

ALCOHOLIC BEVERAGES APPROVED

Figure 6 Passenger Roger Peterson's unused food voucher from TWA 841.

One passenger was worried sick about a dog that was being transported in the cargo compartment. The woman had carried one poodle with her on the flight. The second dog was still in the belly of the plane. She pleaded her case with a ticket agent, insisting that someone go back to the plane to retrieve her dog. The agent placed a call, and the woman and dog were soon reunited.

The passengers had been shepherded to the terminal in groups and by different drivers and vehicles. They didn't all end up in the same place. Some found their way upstairs to the main terminal, where many wandered off in search of phone booths and bathrooms. Others were told to wait downstairs in a large, windowless room with only a few folding chairs to sit on.

Over the course of several hours, the general mood of the passengers had gone from relief and gratitude for having survived the ordeal to anger and frustration over their current predicament. They wanted answers. How were they going to get to Minneapolis? What about their bags? When was the next flight? One passenger announced that he wasn't about to get on another airplane. He was going to rent a car and drive to Minneapolis.

The passengers waiting downstairs had the same questions and concerns, but they had no one to vent to except each other. Every thirty minutes or so a TWA agent would enter the room with an update, informing them that they were trying to coordinate a flight to Minneapolis and that they would have more information soon. The agent would then disappear, and the murmurs and angry comments would start anew. The passengers were too tired and upset to see the situation from the TWA employees' point of view. Detroit was not a TWA base. There was no direct TWA flight from Detroit to Minneapolis. It was late at night, and most of the staff had already gone home by the time the incident occurred. Besides dealing with upset passengers, these same TWA employees were fielding calls from TWA management in New York and Chicago.

They were also dealing with passengers who needed medical attention. Of the eighty-two passengers on board, five reported injuries. Two passengers were taken by ambulance to a local hospital, where they were treated and released. Three passengers reported pain in their chests, necks, and backs but refused medical treatment. The injuries consisted primarily of strains and bruises. Barbara Merrill, who had entered the aft lavatory just before the incident, had bruised her arm, hip, leg, and tailbone after being thrown against the toilet and bathroom fixtures.

Holly Wicker, the adoption organizer, was asked to give a written statement to a TWA representative. Holly wrote that moments before the incident she had seen someone whom she believed to be one of the flight crew members hand the meal trays to a flight attendant. She said that the two chatted a little before the flight crew member returned to the cockpit.[9] Holly's written statement would later play a crucial role in the investigation.

After spending nearly three hours on the ground at Detroit, the passengers from TWA 841 heard an announcement that they would be continuing on to Minneapolis on a Northwest Airlines flight. The eighty-one passengers (with one electing to drive to Minneapolis) walked to the Northwest Airlines gate and boarded a Northwest Airlines Boeing 747 that had diverted to Detroit to pick them up. As the TWA 841 passengers boarded the large plane, they got more than a few quizzical stares from those already aboard the Northwest flight. The TWA passengers took the empty seats and filled in the Northwest passengers on their "roller coaster" ride earlier that evening.

The Northwest flight finally landed in Minneapolis at 3:07 a.m. Those passengers needing to rent a car found that none of the rental car agencies were open. Those hoping to meet friends or family coming to drive them home found that their rides had left the airport hours earlier. Many swore that they would never fly TWA again.

Mechanic Mel Brown was worried about the landing gear. He returned to operations and retrieved two jacks, which he put under the wings of N840TW while he worked inside the plane. His instructions were to secure the aircraft, remove the cockpit voice recorder and flight data recorder, and tow the aircraft to a nearby United maintenance hangar.

With the aircraft secured and the APU shut down, Mel hooked up the tow bar and slowly began moving the plane forward. He had just got the plane rolling before he had to stop. It looked to him like the right main gear was about to collapse. He jumped off the tug and placed the jacks back under both wings. When he jacked up the plane, the main landing gear retracted into the gear wells on its own accord.

Later that night, Mel handed the cockpit voice recorder and flight data recorder to TWA station manager Frank Cook, who placed the recorders in the trunk of his car. When two FAA inspectors arrived on scene later that evening, they asked for the recorders. Frank advised them that the recorders were in his possession and that he had instructions to send the recorders to Kansas City. If they wanted the recorders, they could find them there.

Chapter Four

Hero for a Day

Not long after being dropped off at TWA operations, Hoot received a call from the Chicago-base Chief Pilot, Harry Jacobson. Jacobson wanted to know what had happened. Hoot told him that they had a control problem and that they had to divert to Detroit. He said he didn't think there had been any injuries. Hoot did not convey the seriousness of what had just happened. Jacobson asked Hoot if there was another airplane available to fly the passengers to Minneapolis. When Hoot indicated that he thought there might be, Jacobson suggested that he continue on to Minneapolis with the passengers. Hoot wasn't about to get back on an aircraft that night. He told Jacobson that he thought it would be best if they not fly. Jacobson quickly dropped the idea. He told Hoot to go to a hotel and get some rest. He mentioned that he was planning to catch a flight to Detroit first thing in the morning and that he would see Hoot when he arrived.

Hoot asked the station manager for the phone number for the crew hotel. When he called to reserve three rooms, Hoot learned that the van driver had left for the night, and the hotel had no way of picking up the crew. With no other option, the three exhausted crew members trudged their way through the snow and slush to the Detroit Airport Hilton.

As soon as Hoot entered his room, he began rummaging through his belongings looking for a phone number. He was searching for the emergency phone number of the ALPA union rep who handled accidents. Hoot remembered receiving a reference card from the union that contained a to-do list if he were ever involved in an accident. Hoot had saved the card just in case he would need it someday. Hoot now felt a sense of urgency to locate the card. He spread out the contents of his flight bag across the bed. He found the worn and tattered card, but when he dialed the number, he found it was a wrong number. The card was out of date. Hoot looked over the list of do's and don'ts. The first item on the list was, "Don't talk to anyone before speaking with your union rep."

Hoot put the card down and then collapsed on the bed. He had just closed his eyes when the phone rang. He glanced at the clock and saw that it was after midnight. On the other end of the line was an FAA inspector by the name of Ronald Montgomery. Montgomery asked Hoot if it would be okay if he and another FAA inspector asked him a few questions. Hoot was dead tired. He hadn't slept a wink. He told the FAA inspector that he didn't feel like talking.

"I only need a few minutes of your time to get a statement," Montgomery insisted.

Hoot glanced at the union card sitting on the dresser with the admonition not to talk to anyone before speaking to a union rep.

"We just need a brief statement about what happened," added Montgomery.

Hoot knew the FAA inspector was only trying to do his job. "Okay," Hoot told him. "Come on up."

At a little after 1:00 a.m. the two FAA inspectors knocked at his door. Hoot hastily put on a shirt from his overnight bag but no pants.

"You know, we have always been told not to talk to you [FAA] when something happens like this," Hoot told them as they stepped inside the room. "But I don't have anything to hide. I really don't know what happened."[1]

Ron Montgomery, the senior of the two inspectors, thanked Hoot for agreeing to meet with them. He told Hoot that he was not wired for sound and that their conversation was not being recorded. He opened up his briefcase for Hoot's inspection.

Montgomery later said that Hoot appeared frazzled and nervous. He asked Hoot if he needed a drink to calm down. Hoot mentioned that he was thinking about going downstairs before the lounge closed, but that he was okay for the time being. Ron asked Hoot to tell them what had happened. Hoot began with the climb from 35,000 to 39,000 feet. He told them that they had just finished their meals and had the food trays removed from the cockpit. He said that not long after leveling off at 39,000 feet, he reached down beside his seat to get his Minneapolis approach charts. That was when he felt a slight vibration or buzzing sensation. He described how the plane was banking to the right, but the autopilot was trying to compensate by turning the wheel to the left. He then went through the entire event from the upset to the landing at Detroit. He paced back and forth as he recounted the ordeal of a few hours earlier. He spoke rapidly and with few pauses. He didn't cover every detail. It was more a summary of events.[2]

"Was everyone in their seats when it happened?" Montgomery asked.

Hoot said he didn't think anybody was out of their seats. He thought about it a few seconds longer and then commented that he remembered the flight engineer sitting down sometime before the event. Hoot repeated his comment that they had just finished their crew meals.

Neither of the two FAA inspectors took notes. They stayed less than half an hour. As they left, they thanked Hoot for his time and handed him their business cards. As Hoot thought back on his conversation with the two FAA inspectors, he realized that he had gotten some details wrong. He remembered saying that they had finished their crew meals, but he failed to indicate that they had finished the crew meals before the climb to 39,000 feet. It was a minor detail, and he was too tired to worry about it. Hoot didn't know it then, but his statement to the two FAA inspectors was the beginning of an investigation that was soon about to spiral out of control.

Sometime around four or five in the morning, Hoot was awakened by the ringing phone. TWA Vice President of Operations, Ed Frankum, was on the line. When Frankum asked Hoot what he thought had happened, Hoot said he didn't know and then made the comment, "The stupid airplane shouldn't be allowed to fly that high." Frankum agreed. At the end of their conversation, Frankum told Hoot to stay clear of the media. Hoot tried to go back to sleep but the images, sounds, and sensations from a few hours earlier occupied his mind, playing in a continuous loop starting with the vibration he felt just before losing control, to the discovery of the missing slat.

Around 8:00 or 9:00 in the morning, after a mostly sleepless night, the jarring ringing of the phone caused Hoot to bolt upright. Jerry Lawler, the ALPA captain representative and chairman of the Chicago base, was downstairs wanting to meet with Hoot. Jerry, along with the Chicago-base Chief Pilot, Harry Jacobson, had flown to Detroit to speak with the crew. Jerry had the task of interviewing the crew while Jacobson went off to talk to the station and maintenance personnel.

When Jerry received the call telling him that he had to fly to Detroit to meet with a cockpit crew about an incident, he had no idea what the incident was about or who the crew was until he got to the hotel. He was surprised to learn that Hoot was the captain on the flight. Jerry and Hoot were good friends. Hoot was six months ahead of Jerry on the seniority list.

"Hoot, what the hell happened?" Jerry asked, as Hoot let him into the room. Hoot was again hastily dressed in a shirt and no trousers, looking disheveled.

Hoot spent the next fifteen minutes describing in detail the near-disaster of the night before. Jerry couldn't believe what he was hearing. He had no idea of the seriousness of what had transpired. He sat spellbound as Hoot described the 727 rolling and then going into a vertical dive. Jerry didn't detect any stress or anxiety in Hoot's voice. It was one of those "and there I was" stories, except this was unlike any flying story Jerry had ever heard before, and he had heard a lot of them. Jerry thought that Hoot wasn't grasping the seriousness of the situation. He told Hoot that there was going to be a meeting later that afternoon with the FAA and the NTSB. He and Harry Jacobson, along with other TWA ALPA representatives, would be in attendance. The one word of advice he told Hoot before leaving was, "Just make sure you tell 'em the truth."

Jerry Lawler's next visit was with Scott Kennedy, the first officer. Scott, who was a deeply religious man, didn't react at all like Hoot. He was much more reserved and quiet. He would later say that he spent the day after the incident thinking about family and God. Scott was married, with three children, and his wife was pregnant with his fourth child. He was convinced that the actions they took helped prevent a tragedy, but he was also sure that divine intervention had played a role in their successful recovery. Those are the thoughts that were running through Scott's mind when Jerry Lawler came to visit.

Scott described the events very much the same way as had Hoot. He told Jerry that he had been focused on the clock because he was doing a groundspeed check and wasn't aware of any problems until Hoot started pointing with his hand and yelling something that he couldn't understand. Scott tried to process what was happening when he thought that maybe Hoot had been pointing at the landing gear. It was too noisy to communicate, so he put his hand over the gear selector. That's when Hoot motioned for him to put the landing gear down. The rest of what Scott had to say was in agreement with Hoot's recollection. Jerry told Scott about the meeting later in the afternoon and added the same comment he had made to Hoot about telling the truth.

The next person on Jerry's list was Gary Banks. Gary's reaction to the events the night before was completely different from Hoot's and Scott's. Gary told Jerry Lawler that he felt both helpless and angry. He felt helpless because as a flight engineer he could do nothing to help save the plane from crashing. All he could do was sit and watch as the plane was about to corkscrew into the ground. He was angry because he had experience flying fighter jets, and he thought he could have helped more had he been in a pilot seat rather than sitting at the flight engineer's panel. He described holding on to the flight engineer's panel with one hand and grasping Hoot's seatback with his other hand as he held on for dear life. He said it was a frightening experience. He described how he was finally able to offer some assistance after the recovery when he noticed the speed bleeding off as Hoot went into a steep climb.

After leaving Gary's room, Jerry walked downstairs, where he ran into Tom Kennedy, a JFK based ALPA council member. Media were milling about in the lobby, so the two men stepped outside. A few reporters eyed them suspiciously through a window but didn't approach them. Jerry was relaying what he had learned from the crew when they spotted

Jim McIntyre approaching. Jim McIntyre was the TWA ALPA representative in charge of accident investigations. Jim had a stern appearance with a pronounced jaw. He resembled Charlton Heston but lacked the actor's height. They spoke briefly about the day's events up to that point and about the meeting scheduled for that afternoon. Jim thanked Jerry for speaking with the crew and told him that he would be handling the investigation going forward.

Figure 7 TWA ALPA Accident Investigator Jim McIntyre

Hoot made his way downstairs after showering and getting dressed. He saw the media in the lobby and tried to avoid making eye contact, but a reporter spotted him and stuck a microphone in his face. The reporter happened to be an attractive female. "Were you the captain on TWA 841?" the reporter asked Hoot.

Hoot acknowledged that he was.

"Tell us what happened."

Hoot told the reporter that he couldn't comment on the incident but then started to do so anyway. He mentioned how he had experience flying aerobatics and how that had helped in his ability to recover the plane. He was enjoying the spotlight and flirting a little. He suggested to the reporter that she might want to come fly with him sometime. An ALPA union rep listening in stepped forward to break up the interview.

After getting a bite to eat, Hoot was ushered into a small conference room that had been converted into a makeshift hearing room. The setup was in the typical U-shape, with a table facing three chairs for the crew members and two tables on either side. About a dozen people were in attendance. Hoot recognized a few faces. Jerry Lawler was there as well as Harry Jacobson. He recognized the two FAA inspectors he had met the night before. There were four representatives from the NTSB. The rest of the participants in the room were accident investigators with ALPA and TWA. Shortly after taking his seat, Hoot was joined by Scott and Gary.

For most in the room, it was their first time hearing just how close the plane had come to crashing. Jerry Lawler remembered watching the astonished faces of Harry Jacobson and a few others as Hoot recounted the upset and recovery. The panel didn't spend a lot of time questioning Scott and Gary. Hoot was the captain. He was the one they wanted to hear.

Jerry Lawler listened carefully for any inconsistencies in Hoot's story. Jerry was the first person to speak directly to the crew after the incident. He was first to speak with each crew member individually. He didn't find any discrepancies in the three stories he'd heard earlier or at any time during the mini-hearing. As far as Jerry was concerned, the crew was being truthful.[3]

The unofficial hearing lasted a little more than an hour. The hearing wasn't recorded, and no one took notes. It was mostly a retelling of the events by the crew to bring the investigators up to speed on what had happened from the crew's perspective. Hoot left the meeting and went directly to the airport to catch a flight to St. Louis. Scott Kennedy was also on the flight, but they boarded separately and didn't sit together. The same was true for the flight from St. Louis to Los Angeles. They were both exhausted. The three-and-a-half-hour flight offered the possibility of some uninterrupted rest.

When Hoot returned to his house in Las Vegas early the next day, he had just set his bags down when the phone rang. A reporter for the *Detroit News* wanted to ask him some questions. Hoot told the reporter that he couldn't comment and suggested that the reporter contact TWA. Next came a call from a friend who had heard about the incident and wanted to learn what had happened. All Hoot wanted to do was get some rest, but the phone kept ringing. He spent most of that day taking calls. At some point the phone quieted down, and Hoot tried to get some rest. He got one or two hours of solid sleep before the phone started ringing again. By this time, reporters from every newspaper, magazine, and television news show were clamoring for a chance to get hold of hero pilot Hoot Gibson. He even had a call from someone from Hollywood wanting to purchase rights for a movie. The numerous distractions and phone calls made it impossible for Hoot to get adequate rest. Completely exhausted, he finally unplugged the phone. He went to his room and collapsed in bed.

A few hours later Hoot was awakened by the sound of his doorbell. This was followed by knocks on the door. Hoot rolled over and tried to go back to sleep. A few minutes had passed when Hoot thought he heard sounds outside his door. He dragged himself out of bed and cracked open the door to find a wide-eyed reporter staring back at him. Hoot couldn't believe it. Hoot put on some clothes and went into his living room where he found four or five reporters milling about and one guy with a television camera. Hoot politely asked them to leave and escorted them out the front door.

Over the next several days TWA Flight 841 became a national news story. "Jet Pilot Averts Disaster," read one headline. "Pilot's Skills Avert Crash," read another. The *Los Angeles Times* ran a story on the front page titled, "Pilot Saves Nose-Diving Jetliner." The *New York Times* ran a story with the title, "Pilot Was Trained to Keep Cool."

After turning down all requests for interviews, Hoot agreed to speak to a reporter when the Los Angeles-base General Manager of Flying,

John Rhodes, suggested that Hoot talk to Associated Press Reporter Norm Clarke. Rhodes told Hoot that the reporter had gone through the proper channels and that TWA had given Clarke the green light for an interview.

When Norm Clarke showed up the next day along with a photographer, the interview was brief, mostly because of the numerous interruptions from phone calls and Hoot's instructions not to discuss details concerning the upset. Hoot talked about his aviation background and where he had grown up. He talked about riding his pony to the airport as a kid. He hardly said a word about the incident. Later, after the reporter had left, Hoot spotted Clarke across the street talking with the neighbor kids. Hoot had taught some of those same kids how to fly.

Vegas pilot relives miracle flight

By Norm Clarke
Associated Press Writer

Training to "keep cool" and 31 years of flying experience helped pilot H.G. "Hoot" Gibson, who saved 87 lives by pulling a tailspinning TWA airliner out of a death dive.

Fatigued from only three hours sleep in 48 hours, Gibson said: "I feel like I'm 400 years old.

"Sure, everybody thinks about it," he told the Associated Press Friday night in an interview at his Las Vegas home.

"Things like that happen. But the people I work with have their act together. From the start, we (pilots) have been taught to keep cool...hold up under the worst."

His harrowing rescue came Wednesday night over Michigan when the Boeing 727 — on a New York-to-Minneapolis flight — went into a barrel roll at 39,000 feet. Breaking the sound barrier during a five-mile plunge, the airliner pulled out "maybe two seconds before crashing," according to a source who asked not to be identified.

"It seemed like it lasted 20 seconds," said Gibson, a veteran of 16 years with TWA.

"People say pilots are overpaid. The reason we get good money is for those critical few seconds every 4-5 years. You can't put a price on that,"

said Gibson, 44, who keeps in shape by jogging up to seven miles a day.

Gibson declined to cite specifics of the ordeal Wednesday night until TWA completes an investigation.

His thoughts varied as the plane thundered groundward.

"I didn't have time to talk to The

Man, but we could have held a group prayer session at the end," he said.

Keeping with company policy, he would not discuss why he resorted to putting down the landing gear — a move that brought the plane out of the dive.

"It comes down to doing the right

thing at the right time," he said.

Since the near-disaster, he said the phone has rung off his wall.

"I've had calls from all over the country — and I've got an unlisted phone number. Somebody from Hollywood called and wants the rights for a movie."

H.G. GIBSON ...TWA pilot at Vegas home

Figure 8 Norm Clarke's Article on Hoot

When the article came out the next day, Hoot laughed when he saw the photo that accompanied the article. Hoot was standing with his arm raised above his head. The photo, which took up half the space of the short article, was under the headline, "Vegas Pilot Relives Miracle

Flight." The image gave the impression that Hoot was demonstrating how the aircraft had rolled over. Hoot remembered that he had been telling the reporter how he used to tie his pony to the airport perimeter fence and then have to climb over the fence to get to the planes.

Few pilots have experienced the amount of praise and attention that Hoot enjoyed in the immediate days following the incident. Hoot received the same level of media attention that Captain Chesley "Sully" Sullenberger of "Miracle on the Hudson" fame would receive some thirty years later. There were a number of similarities between the two pilots. Both had long aviation careers, both had colorful nicknames, and the word "miracle" had been used to describe the outcome of each event.

"I can't think of any other incident," said Langhorne Bond, head of the FAA, "in which a commercial, passenger-carrying plane has done a complete 360-degree rollover and survived. The miracle is that it held together under such extraordinary speed and circumstances."[4]

But even before the crew had a chance to absorb the praise coming their way, rumors started flying about possible causes of the upset. Many of the rumors were started by armchair pilots eager to punch holes in the heroic story touted by the press. One early story was that the plane was too heavy to climb to flight level 390 and had simply stalled. Some claimed that the incident was caused by clear air turbulence. One outrageous theory was that Hoot, having had aerobatic experience, wanted to prove that he could roll the plane without the passengers even knowing it. Then there were the bizarre theories involving UFOs and meteors. The rumors spread quickly through the aviation community. Pilot training centers became breeding grounds for many wild hypotheses.

In some ways Hoot expected the criticism. It's human nature for people to want to find fault with someone receiving positive recognition, maybe even more so among egotistical pilots. What Hoot didn't expect, though, was that the very people investigating the incident would end up becoming the source of some of the most damaging and unsubstantiated rumors.

The first hint that the story of hero pilot Hoot Gibson was about to take a turn in a different direction came just three days after the upset. A *New York Times* article on April 7, 1979 reported the following: ". . . the cockpit voice recorder, which ordinarily contains the last half hours' worth of transmissions in the cockpit, had nothing on it when it was examined by federal officials."[5]

Hoot was at home when he first learned about the CVR erasure. John Rhodes called to tell him that the tape had been bulk erased and wanted to know if Hoot had erased it. Hoot said that he wasn't sure but that if he did erase it, it was unintentional. In truth, the tape had been bulk erased, but it wasn't completely blank as had been reported in the press and would continue to be reported. Nine minutes of useful audio remained on the thirty-minute tape. Hoot never said that he had erased the CVR, only that he could have but didn't remember doing so. These early, inaccurate accounts tainted the investigation and set in motion all that was to transpire in the days, weeks, months, and years ahead.

Chapter Five

An Inquisition

In the days immediately following the incident, Hoot, Scott, and Gary were taken off the line while the investigation continued. It was a stressful period for the three crew members. All three had trouble sleeping. Hoot, who was hounded by reporters, stopped answering his phone. One reporter from a Detroit newspaper, unable to reach Hoot by phone, decided to retaliate by writing an unflattering and factually inaccurate article accusing Hoot of deliberately erasing the CVR.

The *Detroit News* article by writer Edwin G. Pipp was titled, "Tape of jet's dive erased by crewman." In the article, writer Pipp, citing a knowledgeable source, claimed that a crew member had admitted to erasing the tape.[1]

The article painted the crew in a negative light, first by reporting inaccurate information related to the CVR and then subtly insinuating that Hoot was trying to hide something. "Gibson now is reported to be at his home in Las Vegas, but not answering his telephone," Pipp wrote.

Later in the same article Pipp had this to say about previous 727 accidents. "The Boeing 727 is the most common airliner in use today and is considered one of the safest. Investigation of all recent 727 accidents shows that they were at least partly—if not entirely—caused by pilot error."[2]

Hoot wasn't the only one hounded by the news media. The NTSB in Washington was inundated with media requests. Since those involved had no serious injuries and the plane had landed safely, the investigation into TWA 841 was handled as an incident. There was no need to send a "go team" since there was no crash.[3] The plane was sitting in Detroit. The investigation into TWA 841 became the responsibility of the Chicago field office. NTSB investigator Fred Rathke was assigned as the Investigator-in-Charge (IIC). Fred was in Detroit the day after the incident. He had taken part in the mini-hearing held that day. When TWA asked if they could begin repairs on the aircraft, Fred told them that they were free to begin repairs as soon as investigators documented the damage and took some photographs. The investigation was handled like any other incident where physical damage had occurred. Instead of treating the incident with the seriousness it deserved, investigators treated it the same way they might an aircraft that had scraped a wingtip or taxied off the taxiway into the mud.

The media, however, had locked onto a compelling story. They had a real mystery on their hands. What caused an airliner to suddenly fall out of the sky? Was there a problem with the plane? Did the pilots do something to cause the incident? They wanted answers. It wasn't until the NTSB got news that the CVR had been bulk erased that they began to take a closer look.

The most obvious clue of what might have happened to TWA 841 was the missing number seven slat. The crew reported that the plane had rolled to the right at the initiation of the maneuver. Having a single slat extended in isolation certainly could account for this right-rolling tendency. The question was what had caused the number seven slat to extend. Early reports from Boeing were that it was impossible for a slat to extend on its own. Then there were the reports that Gary Banks had

Figure 9 Most experts looking at the TWA 841 upset believed that the uncontrolled rollover and dive was the result of the number seven slat extended in isolation.

been out of the cockpit just prior to the incident. Investigators had two corroborating reports of this. One supposedly came from Captain Gibson himself during his interview with the two FAA inspectors, and the second came from the written statement provided by passenger Holly Wicker. Holly's written statement had since been lost, but enough people had read it to know that she claimed to have seen a flight crew member hand meal trays to the flight attendant and that the incident happened shortly after that crew member returned to the cockpit. In the investigators' minds, a clear connection existed between these events. The flight engineer leaves the cockpit, the captain and first officer decide to do something while the flight engineer is out of the cockpit, the flight engineer returns, and something happens to cause the plane to roll over and dive some 39,000 feet. Add to this an erased CVR, and you have the makings of a cover-up.

When the chairman of the NTSB, James King, learned of the early findings regarding the erased CVR and the intense media interest, he decided to re-assign the investigation to Leslie Dean Kampschror and make him the new Investigator-in-Charge (IIC). Kampschror was a lawyer who had worked on a handful of investigations prior to the TWA 841 case. King gave Kampschror instructions to depose the crew. He also told Kampschror to make sure that media was present. If the press wants to know what happened, King told Kampschror, let them hear it directly from the crew.

Hoot had never been involved in an NTSB investigation. So when he was told that he was going to have to testify at a hearing just eight days after the upset, he had no reason to question it. "If that's what they want me to do," he told Jim McIntyre, "then I'll answer their questions the best I can." He didn't know that a televised hearing so soon after an incident wasn't only unusual—it was unprecedented. Public hearings are normally held many months following an accident or incident, after the facts and probable cause have already been determined. The purpose of a public hearing is to allow the public to hear the facts of a case before the final report. Additionally, a public hearing involves all parties involved in an investigation and is not limited to the flight crew.

Leslie Dean Kampschror, the acting Board chairman, told anyone who cared to question the timing of the hearing that it wasn't a hearing at all. It was a fact-finding proceeding, he explained, and didn't need to follow the usual guidelines of a public hearing. He said that the depositions had been requested by the Chairman of the National Transportation Safety Board. He never explained to anyone's satisfaction why it was necessary that the crew's depositions be attended

Figure 10 NTSB Investigator Leslie Dean Kampschror (wearing glasses)

by members of the media. If his goal was simply to get the sworn testimony of the crew, he didn't need to make it a media event.

By the time of the televised depositions, all three crew members were physically and emotionally exhausted. None of them had been able to sleep more than three or four hours a night since the incident. They had been hounded by the media, they were dealing with the stress and anxiety that normally occur after a traumatic event, and each had been haunted by nightmares.

Adding to the crew's anxiety was the grilling they received just prior to the depositions by the Manager of Flying, John Rhodes. Rhodes requested that all three crew members report to his office one hour prior to the depositions. When they arrived at TWA operations, the secretary indicated that Captain Rhodes wanted to speak to each of them individually. Hoot went first.

A half dozen or so people dressed in suits were in the room. Hoot spotted Jim McIntyre and Harold Marthinsen, whom Hoot had met

Figure 11 Harold Marthinsen in the foreground. Hoot is talking to a reporter in the background.

earlier that day, standing off to the side. Harold Marthinsen was the Director of ALPA's accident investigation department. Harold's background was in aeronautical engineering, though he also held a private pilot's license. Harold Marthinsen and Jim McIntyre would soon become the crew's biggest advocates. Also in attendance were a couple of flight managers, as well as TWA attorney Jim Mollenkamp. Hoot, who was usually calm under pressure, felt intimidated by so many sullen faces.

Hoot didn't know Rhodes all that well, which was a good thing. The less time spent in the Chief Pilot's office, the better. After asking Hoot how he was doing, Rhodes asked him if it were possible that Scott had accidentally caught his shirt sleeve or his boot on the flap handle.

"That didn't happen," Hoot responded. "He was busy doing a ground speed check. I would have noticed something like that."

Rhodes switched gears and told Hoot that this was the time to come clean. "If you know something you haven't told us, I suggest you tell it to us now," Rhodes said, staring intently at Hoot. "The truth will come out eventually."

Hoot glanced around the room. No one was making eye contact. "I intend to answer whatever questions they have for me truthfully," Hoot responded.

Realizing that Hoot wasn't going to be giving a last-minute confession, Rhodes offered his support and the support of the company. Hoot shook a few hands as he left the room. He smiled and tried to maintain his composure, but his stomach was in knots. He would later confide in friends that he had left the meeting with Rhodes terrified at the prospect of having to testify.

When Hoot arrived at the Inglewood City Hall an hour later, Jim McIntyre pulled him aside and told him to be careful with his answers. He wanted Hoot to tell the truth, but he warned him that the investigation had taken some unexpected turns. "You don't know where this thing is headed," Jim cautioned. "Be truthful and concise, but don't volunteer any information."

Hoot entered the hearing room with ALPA attorney Ken Cooper accompanying him. Ken Cooper was a young attorney who stood out with a wild afro-styled hairdo that made him look like a DJ in a disco club. The two men took seats in the middle of the room with the deposition panel sitting at tables in front and on either side. Captain Marshall Hydorn and Jim McIntyre, the two ALPA representatives, sat on the panel as interested parties. Opposite Hoot were eleven men representing five different parties to the investigation: the NTSB, the FAA, ALPA, TWA, and Boeing.[4]

Hoot surveyed the room as he took his seat. He was more than a little surprised to see so many people in attendance. He was uncomfortable at the presence of the many television cameras and microphones. He was sworn in and then Kampschror gave a brief introduction.

The proceedings had the look and feel of a public hearing. The setup, the microphones, the panel of interested parties, the television cameras. Not one person from ALPA or TWA questioned the formality of what was supposed to be a simple deposition. Dean Kampschror, who by this time had been assigned the job of Investigator-in-Charge, oversaw the proceedings. Kampschror took on the role of a fair and impartial judge as he peered over glasses he wore on the tip of his nose. In an effort to underscore that this was not a public hearing, Kampschror began with the following statement: "The ground rules are pretty much the same as they would be at a public hearing; but, of course, this is not a public hearing. It is a public depositional proceeding."[5]

One of the men on the panel, representing the Federal Aviation Administration (FAA), was Deputy Assistant Chief Counsel James

Dillman. This was a man whose main role at the FAA was in enforcement actions. He spent most of his time in proceedings such as this with the sole intent of leveling fines, civil penalties, and certificate actions against pilots and aircraft operators. Wearing a light-gray suit and seventies-style oversized glasses, he made his presence known at the start. "Mr. Kampschror," Dillman began, "this may seem picky, [but] is Mr. Cooper here as Captain Gibson's personal counsel or merely as an out counsel?"

Hoot stated that Ken Cooper was staff counsel and represented the entire crew. When Kampschror asked a follow-up question as to whether Ken Cooper was Hoot's personal counsel, Hoot said that he was. What was lost in this brief exchange was that Hoot had not gone out and hired his own attorney. ALPA had provided the attorney and was paying his fees. But to anyone not listening closely, it sounded as though Hoot had felt the need for legal protection.[6]

After answering a few questions related to his background, his training, and time at TWA, Hoot was asked about the events leading up to the April 4 upset. Hoot gave a detailed description from the initial buzz he felt just prior to the upset to the landing in Detroit. It was riveting testimony. He spoke uninterrupted, except for the one or two times when someone needed clarification.

NTSB investigator John Ferguson, the Operations Group Chairman, was the first one to bring up the cockpit voice recorder. He asked Hoot directly if he had erased the CVR. "Not to my knowledge," Hoot replied. When asked if it was Hoot's habit to erase the recorder, Hoot said that he usually erased the voice recorder after every flight but didn't remember erasing it on this flight. He later added that he had not seen anyone else erase the cockpit voice recorder.[7]

Next up was Fred Rathke, the original Investigator-in-Charge. Rathke asked Hoot if there had been any intentional or unintentional movement of the flap handle. Hoot indicated that there had not been any movement of the flap handle.[8]

After a few questions from one of the Boeing representatives regarding the control difficulties Hoot had experienced after the alternate flap extension, FAA attorney James Dillman began his questioning. Dillman started off with a lengthy exchange over the weight of the aircraft and whether or not Hoot could remember the exact weight prior to and after the climb to FL 390. He then asked a series of questions that seemed aimed at making Hoot look reckless, or, at the least, unconcerned about the possible dangers of flying at the upper altitude limits. He asked Hoot if he knew how much bank angle he could safely use at 39,000 feet.

Hoot said that he wouldn't normally make any banks in excess of five or ten degrees at that altitude, but he was confident that he would be safe making a bank of at least thirty degrees. Later analysis would show that the plane could have made as much as a forty-three degree bank and still be within limits.

Dillman persisted with his assumption that the crew had been going too fast for the weight and altitude. "Captain, could I ask you, in the maneuver that you experienced, do you believe it probable that an overspeed warning would have occurred?" When Hoot answered "yes," a long discussion ensued as to what procedure Hoot would use to curtail an overspeed condition. Hoot responded by saying that he would "slow the airplane down."

Seeming to realize that he wasn't getting the answers he wanted and obviously frustrated, Dillman moved on to a topic he was more comfortable with—the Federal Aviation Regulations. That's where Dillman spent most of his time, accusing pilots of not abiding by this or that regulation and then penalizing them for their indiscretions. Dillman asked Hoot if he was familiar with a section of the Federal Aviation

Regulations dealing with cockpit voice recorders. Specifically, Dillman wanted to know if Hoot was familiar with the requirement to preserve cockpit voice recorder data following an accident or incident.

Hoot said that he never even thought about it. When Dillman followed up by asking Hoot for his interpretation of the regulation for preserving CVR data, Hoot said that he believed it was for post-humus investigations. When asked to clarify, Hoot said the following: "That's a post-accident, but there's nobody left to tell you."

Dillman paused as he considered Hoot's response. "Is it your understanding that in an accident which did not involve fatalities that you were free to erase the cockpit voice recorder?"

Hoot leaned forward in his seat. "Are you insinuating that I erased, intentionally erased the cockpit voice recorder?"

"I'm not insinuating anything, sir," Dilllman said defensively. "I'm asking you your opinion of the regulation."

Ken Cooper objected to the question, stating that Hoot was not being offered as a Part 121 expert. This was followed by a heated exchange between Dillman, Kampschror, and Marshall Hydorn as to the importance of the questions. "I fail to see what relevance this questioning has in an investigation of this accident," Hydorn stated bluntly. "It's an enforcement line of questioning."

Kampschror agreed and steered the questioning back to Hoot's general understanding of the regulation. Dillman pointed out that the regulation specifically provides that the administrator of the FAA may not use cockpit voice recorder data in enforcement or civil action and wanted to know why it was Hoot's routine to erase the cockpit voice recorder after every flight.

"In part," Hoot explained, "it's an accepted practice, and as far as I am concerned, at the time was done by everyone. It's done by an awful lot of people. When they put the cockpit voice recorder on the airplane, I'd say 100 percent of people always erase it after every landing when they park their brakes, and having been off the airplane and come back on, that's one of the things I did. It's a regular flow pattern; it's a routine I go through on a checklist. It's like shedding off—taking the tape out of your tape deck on your car, doing something like that. And I do that every time, and so do—and when I was on the aircraft before, that's what everybody always did."

Dillman wasn't satisfied with the answer. "Well, regardless of what other people do, Captain, could you tell me why you do it?"

"Because I might say something unkind about some of the people in management, and they might throw that tape out and send it someplace." Hoot's honest response highlighted the real reason why pilots routinely erased the CVR. Despite assurances by regulators that CVR recordings could not be used for disciplinary purposes, pilots weren't ready to put those regulations to the test.

Before he was through, Dillman referenced a newspaper article that reported Hoot had admitted erasing the CVR. Hoot denied that he had made any such statements and claimed that the story was inaccurate.[9]

By the time Hoot and his lawyer, Ken Cooper, left the makeshift witness stand, Hoot felt confused. He still hadn't processed the implications in the line of questioning regarding the supposed CVR erasure. Rather than it being a forum for gathering important information that might lead to answers as to the cause of the upset, Hoot felt as if he had just been cross-examined by a hostile prosecutor in a criminal trial.

As Hoot was exiting the hearing hall, an ALPA representative asked him if he was willing to give an interview. Hoot said that he would. He was escorted down a hallway to where reporter Joules Bergman, the Science Editor for ABC News, was waiting. After answering a few questions, Hoot went straight to the airport and caught the next flight back to Las Vegas.

•┄•┄•

Next up for questioning was first officer Scott Kennedy. If he was nervous, he didn't show it. The fact that he was the first officer on the flight had more to do with his seniority number more than anything else. Scott was an experienced pilot with twelve years of service for TWA and more than three years as a pilot in the Army. Most of Scott's flight time with TWA was on the Boeing 727.[10]

After giving a brief rundown on his aviation background and his work history with TWA, Scott was asked a series of questions regarding the flight on the fourth, specifically related to the flaps/slats operation. What were the flap retraction speeds? Did he notice any abnormal operation regarding the retraction of the slats? Was the flap handle in the up detent?

They were pertinent questions aimed at ruling out the possibility of mechanical failures with the flap/slat system. The examiner, NTSB investigator John Ferguson, then asked a series of questions related to the flight conditions the night of the accident. Did they encounter any icing? Did they experience any turbulence at FL 350 or after the climb to FL 390? What was the aircraft weight at FL 350? At FL 390?

Once again the line of questioning was aimed at ruling out possible contributing factors that might have played a role in the incident. Scott's answers effectively dismissed the contributing factors raised by the questioning.

In describing the rollover event, Scott explained the reasons why he didn't react to Hoot's command to extend the spoilers. "I heard the captain say something like, 'get her up,' or it could have been 'get them up,' or something like that, but I thought he was talking to the airplane.

It's not uncommon when you're riding a horse or when you're flying an airplane or driving an automobile to talk out loud, and I thought that's what he was doing."[11]

Scott said that just prior to the incident he was doing a groundspeed check. He testified that his attention was focused inside the cockpit and that he didn't feel any buzz or buffeting. His first indication that there was a problem was when he looked up and noticed that the airplane was turning to the right and that Hoot was trying to stop the turn with the yoke and rudder.

Scott gave a narrative of the dive and recovery from his perspective. He mentioned how he and the flight engineer had talked to Hoot during the recovery, telling him to ease the plane over due to their excessive nose high attitude. After the recovery, Scott and Gary Banks were immediately pressed into action, running a series of emergency checklists, including the system A hydraulic fluid loss checklist, the alternate flap extension checklist, and the manual gear extension checklist.

Ferguson then asked Scott about the evacuation of the passengers. "Now, I'd like to discuss the evacuation. How were they evacuated? Who gave the order to evacuate? How was that given?"

Scott told Ferguson that there was no evacuation. He referred to it as a deplaning. The possibility of injuries would have been much greater had the passengers been evacuated by the emergency slides, Scott explained. It was when following this line of questioning that the issue of the cockpit voice recorder came up.[12] "Now the cockpit voice recorder indicates an erasure. Did you erase the recorder?" Ferguson asked Scott.

"No, sir. I did not," Scott answered.

"Did you see anybody erase it?"

"No, I do not know who erased that, if, in fact, it was erased."

"On the aircraft that you were on, did the pilots usually erase it?"

"I have seen it done, and I have also seen it passed, so I wouldn't say that it is unusual to see it done."[13]

After a few questions from Kampschror and Jim McIntyre, FAA lawyer Jim Dillman took the microphone. Dillman was especially interested in inquiring who was and who wasn't in the cockpit. "Was there anybody else in the cockpit during this event?" Dillman asked Scott.

"Besides whom?" Scott answered, confused by the question.

"Besides yourself, the captain, and the flight engineer?"

"No, sir."

Scott also stated that he did not leave the cockpit at any time nor did he see any other crew member leave the cockpit.

Dillman then moved on to questions related to the CVR. He began by asking Scott if he had noticed Hoot erasing the CVR on any of the legs prior to the New York to Minneapolis leg. Scott indicated that he did not.

Dillman next asked Scott if it was possible to erase the CVR unintentionally by accidentally brushing up against the CVR erase button. Scott wasn't sure but said that he didn't think so. It wasn't brought out in the testimony, but in order to erase the CVR, the erase button must be pressed and held for at least two seconds, preventing accidental erasures.

Dillman's line of questioning was fair and reasonable. He was trying to prove or disprove Hoot's testimony that it was his practice to erase the CVR after every flight. And he wanted to also address the possibility of an accidental erasure.

Before the end of Scott Kennedy's testimony, he faced one other question related to the CVR. This question came from ALPA safety investigator Jim McIntyre. "Would you, as a first officer, normally be involved with the CVR anyway?"

"No, Sir," Scott said emphatically. "I don't touch that thing." And with that, Scott Kennedy's testimony ended. After a short recess, Gary Banks took the witness stand.[14]

———•—•———

After the usual background questions, NTSB Investigator John Ferguson moved to questions about the upset. While Scott Kennedy had testified that he hadn't noticed any buzz or vibration, Gary Banks said that he had felt something abnormal. "Well," Gary began, "I was at the engineer's panel, facing the panel, and not particularly looking at any one thing. The first that I remember of anything happening was a very-high-frequency vibration, I thought, but I was—I'd never felt that before, so I couldn't really relate it in my mind to anything, and events happened very quickly thereafter . . ."[15]

Gary explained his initial confusion over seeing an all-black HDI (horizon direction indicator also known as an ADI, or attitude direction indicator). It was dark outside, and he said it felt as if the plane was rolling over to the right; his initial reaction was to check what he was sensing with the instrumentation, but there was no horizon indicated on the HDI. He mentioned how he felt as if he were about to black out as the g-forces increased. He also talked about his feelings of helplessness at not being able to help in any way.

After the recovery from the dive, Gary described his actions with regard to running the various checklists while also finding time to brief one of the flight attendants. The descriptions he gave of the events prior to, during, and after the upset were detailed and spoken without any hesitation.

The subject of the cockpit voice recorder came at the end of Ferguson's questioning. "The cockpit voice recorder indicates an erasure. Did you observe anyone erasing the cockpit voice recorder?" Ferguson asked Gary.

"No," Gary replied.[16]

Next came a few questions from the ALPA representative, Jim McIntyre. He was followed by FAA lawyer James Dillman. After a few questions about fuel logs and whether or not the fuel was balanced, Dillman started his line of questioning regarding the rumor, or speculation, that Gary had left the cockpit prior to the upset. Gary said that no one had left the cockpit. When asked how the meal trays were returned to the flight attendant, Gary said he believed that a cabin attendant came up and took them.[17]

For the scenario the NTSB and Boeing engineers were considering, Gary would have to leave the cockpit, with the upset occurring shortly after his return. Gary's testimony, for the time being, had ruled out that possibility. Frustrated, Dillman gave the floor to Kampschror, who returned to the topic of the cockpit voice recorder. "Mr. Banks, I believe you were asked, were you not, after landing, during the cleanup of the cockpit, whether or not you'd observed anybody erase the cockpit voice recorder. Your response was no; is that correct? Did you yourself erase the cockpit voice recording?"

"No," Gary replied.

"Have you had any prior experience with this being done on other flights?"

"Absolutely."

"Who normally does it? In your experience, who has done it?"

"Both captains and first officers."

"Is it always done at the direction of the captain, or does the first officer do it independently?"

"First officer sometimes does it independently."

"Have you yourself done it on previous flights?"

"No. It doesn't bother me one way or the other."[18]

———— •◦• ————

Of the five parties to the investigation, the Boeing representatives had remained silent for most of the session, except for a brief exchange with Hoot concerning the use of trim after the alternate flap extension. They had not asked a single question or made a single comment during Gary's or Scott's testimony. They quietly gathered their papers and slipped away from the proceedings unnoticed.

For the media who had gathered to report on the hearing, one overriding theme emerged: The cockpit voice recorder had been erased. Jim McIntyre sat silently as the room cleared. He sensed that it had not gone well. He hadn't had an opportunity to introduce any contradictory evidence regarding the CVR, such as the possibility that there may have been other explanations for the supposed CVR erasure. Marshall Hydorn, an ALPA representative, had been able to elicit testimony concerning the fact that since the CVR records over itself every thirty minutes, there would not have been anything meaningful on the tape anyway since the entire episode from start to finish took more than forty-five minutes. All they could do now was wait and see what the media response was going to be.

They didn't have to wait long. The CVR erasure was the leading story in print and on television newscasts.

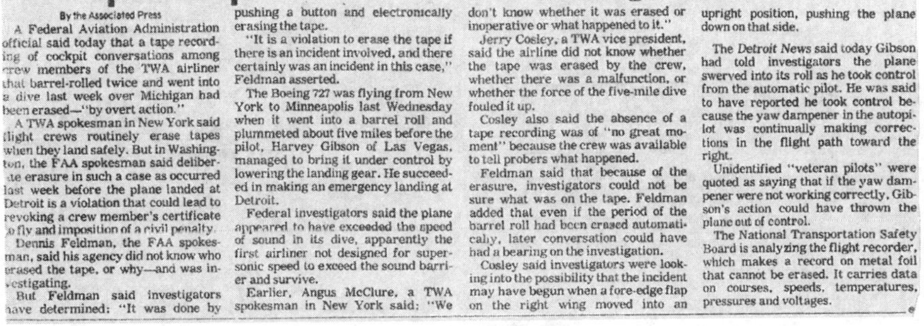

Cockpit Tape Erased in Diving Airliner

By the Associated Press

A Federal Aviation Administration official said today that a tape recording of cockpit conversations among crew members of the TWA Airliner that barrel-rolled twice and went into a dive last week over Michigan had been erased—"by overt action."

A TWA spokesman in New York said flight crews routinely erase tapes when they land safely. But in Washington, the FAA spokesman said deliberate erasure in such a case as occurred last week before the plane landed at Detroit is a violation that could lead to revoking a crew member's certificate to fly and imposition of a civil penalty.

Dennis Feldman, the FAA spokesman, said his agency did not know who erased the tape, or why—and was investigating.

But Feldman said investigators have determined: "It was done by

pushing a button and electronically erasing the tape.

"It is a violation to erase the tape if there is an incident involved, and there certainly was an incident in this case," Feldman asserted.

The Boeing 727 was flying from New York to Minneapolis last Wednesday when it went into a barrel roll and plummeted about five miles before the pilot, Harvey Gibson of Las Vegas, managed to bring it under control by lowering the landing gear. He succeeded in making an emergency landing at Detroit.

Federal investigators said the plane appeared to have exceeded the speed of sound in its dive, apparently the first airliner not designed for supersonic speed to exceed the sound barrier and survive.

Earlier, Angus McClure, a TWA spokesman in New York said; "We

don't know whether it was erased or inoperative or what happened to it."

Jerry Cosley, a TWA vice president, said the airline did not know whether the tape was erased by the crew, whether there was a malfunction, or whether the force of the five-mile dive fouled it up.

Cosley also said the absence of a tape recording was of "no great moment" because the crew was available to tell probers what happened.

Feldman said that because of the erasure, investigators could not be sure what was on the tape. Feldman added that even if the period of the barrel roll had been erased automatically, later conversation could have had a bearing on the investigation.

Cosley said investigators were looking into the possibility that the incident may have begun when a fore-edge flap on the right wing moved into an

upright position, pushing the plane down on that side.

The Detroit News said today Gibson had told investigators the plane swerved into its roll as he took control from the automatic pilot. He was said to have reported he took control because the yaw dampener in the autopilot was continually making corrections in the flight path toward the right.

Unidentified "veteran pilots" were quoted as saying that if the yaw dampener were not working correctly, Gibson's action could have thrown the plane out of control.

The National Transportation Safety Board is analyzing the flight recorder, which makes a record on metal foil that cannot be erased. It carries data on courses, speeds, temperatures, pressures and voltages.

Figure 12 AP Article

For Hoot and the other two crew members, it was a turning point. It was eight days post incident. They were heroes no more. As unbelievable as it might sound, the crew would not be questioned about the upset by any NTSB or Boeing investigator for the remainder of the investigation.

Chapter Six

Shifting Winds

As suspicions grew about possible crew involvement with TWA 841, the FAA descended on TWA's Kansas City training center for a thorough review of the pilot training program. FAA inspectors pored over training materials, monitored classroom instruction, and observed simulator training.

"When you have something that happens and you don't know why yet, you have to look at everything with the remotest association," FAA spokesman Joseph Frets was quoted as saying. "And we're not pointing the finger at TWA. We're not insinuating anything. We just want to know what happened."[1]

The FAA review extended to include Hoot, Scott, and Gary as well. Hoot was required to attend an FAA program on high-altitude awareness. That was followed by simulator training where Hoot was tested on his knowledge of high-altitude performance and maneuvers such as emergency descents and Dutch Roll. Once Hoot demonstrated that he had no problems with high-altitude flying, he was subjected to more simulator training. Hoot wasn't due for recurrent training. He could have protested to the union, but he didn't want to stir up trouble. So he reluctantly agreed to undergo additional simulator flying. When he learned that his simulator instructor was going to be Captain Falluco, the Manager of Flight Training, he realized it was going to be more than just a normal simulator check. He was there to be evaluated. On one of the simulator evaluations, an FAA examiner sat in the observer's seat. If there were any doubts as to the importance being placed on Hoot's evaluation, the FAA examiner's presence verified it. One mistake and his entire career could be put in jeopardy. Hoot was feeling stressed but confident as the session began. Soon he was too busy dealing with engine fires and other assorted emergencies to worry about what Captain Falluco or the FAA examiner was thinking. Hoot went through the simulator training successfully, but he didn't appreciate the added scrutiny and the added stress.

Newspaper coverage of the accident had turned decidedly against the crew in the immediate days leading up to and after the public depositions on April twelfth. Several papers continued to report, erroneously, that the captain had admitted to erasing the CVR. One news story from the Associated Press picked up by newspapers across the country quoted an FAA spokesman as saying that the CVR was erased by "overt action."

The negative press was fueled by comments credited to so-called knowledgeable sources or unnamed FAA or NTSB officials. A reporter for the *Washington Post* wrote the following account of the supposed CVR erasure. "Several Federal Aviation Administration officials, interviewed on a background basis, say they continue to believe, but have no proof, that the erasure of the cockpit voice recording was done intentionally, not by habit, because it would have told investigators something the crew did not want them to know."[2]

In 1979, social media didn't exist. There was no Twitter or Facebook where individuals could voice their opinions regarding the crew's alleged actions, but there were plenty of reporters willing to state their opinions. Many in the media continued to report that the tape was completely blank. One reporter for the *Chicago Tribune*, a Michael Kilian, mocked the crew in an article titled: "Unwinding the (expletive) cockpit tape mystery." In the article the author attempts to fill in the missing recording with fictional dialogue of the crew first reacting to the dive and then discussing erasing the CVR.[3]

The article was accompanied by a cartoon that also spoofed the cockpit voice recorder erasure. In the cartoon a man and woman are standing in line to see a film. The marquee shows the film title as "Hoot Gibson: Thirty Seconds Over Flint: Best Performance In A Double Roll." The man looks up at the marquee and says to his wife, "I was kind of hoping for a talkie . . ."

Figure 13 Cartoon that accompanied Michael Kilian's article

The controversy over the CVR erasure did have one unexpected outcome. The long-standing practice of erasing the CVR after each flight came to an abrupt end, with some pilots jokingly referring to the CVR erase button as the "Hoot Gibson" button.

From the moment the first negative articles appeared, the crew became a target. Unscrupulous reporters went looking for anything they could find to discredit the crew. A reporter for the *National Enquirer* went so far as to follow Gary Banks' mother-in-law to a restaurant where, he would later report, that he overheard a conversation indicating that there had been a fight in the cockpit. The editor for the tabloid, thinking that he had a major scoop, had three different reporters approach each of the three crew members at their places of residence. The idea was to question each crew member at the same time so that there would be no way for them to communicate with each other beforehand.

At the appointed time, the three reporters descended upon the three crew members. One reporter disguised himself as a physician, going as far as carrying a physician's bag, in an effort to gain first officer Scott Kennedy's trust. The reporter told Scott that he was treating a passenger who had been on the flight and started questioning him about the possible fight in the cockpit. Kennedy wasn't buying any part of the man's story. He looked him in the eye and said, "I know Gary Banks said no such thing. Please leave."[4]

The *National Enquirer* didn't get the scoop they were hoping for, but that didn't stop them from publishing the unfounded rumor. Once the NTSB investigators got wind of the story, they treated it as if it had come from a trusted source and immediately began pursuing the story themselves. TWA's upper management also heard the rumor. Ken Ensslin, TWA's Director of Flight Safety, called Gary Banks in for questioning without notifying anyone from ALPA. Gary was understandably guarded when he entered the room to find Ken Ensslin and TWA attorney Jim Mollenkamp waiting for him. Gary denied the allegations.

"What about a fight in the ramp office at JFK?" Gary was asked. "There were no fights at any time on this trip," Gary assured them.

As the investigation moved into its third week, outsiders became impatient for answers. One industry analyst was quoted as saying, "Considering they have a live crew, no dead passengers, a whole aircraft— it's difficult to see why it's taking so much time. If the aircraft had gone in [crashed], there would have been enough time by now to reassemble the pieces, conduct the autopsies and figure out what went wrong."[5]

Hoot had no way of knowing everything that was being said or written about him, but he had seen a number of negative articles concerning the CVR. He couldn't understand why so much attention was being given to the supposed CVR erasure. In his mind, the CVR was a tool for accident investigations where the crew did not survive. "If they want to know what was going on in the cockpit, all they have to do is ask me," Hoot would say. But the investigators weren't talking to the crew.

After passing his simulator evaluation, Hoot was returned to the line. He was more than a little anxious as he gathered up his paperwork for his first trip since the incident. He had been gone for a couple of weeks and wasn't sure of the reception he would receive. The flight to Chicago was uneventful. Not a word was spoken about TWA 841.

The next leg of the trip was to New York with a new set of flight attendants. After running the required checklists, Hoot pushed back from the gate and was about to taxi out for departure when the number-one flight attendant rang the flight attendant call bell in the cockpit. "We have to go back to the gate," she told Hoot.

"Why?" Hoot asked. "What's going on?"

"We have a flight attendant who refuses to fly with you."

The lead flight attendant explained to Hoot that, when she was announcing the names of the pilots, a flight attendant in back came running forward and demanded to be let off the flight.

Hoot reluctantly taxied back to the gate, where the flight attendant and several first-class passengers disembarked. It was an uncomfortable hour-long delay before the airline could locate a replacement flight attendant.

When Hoot returned to his home in Las Vegas, he was physically and emotionally exhausted. He was certain that once TWA management learned about the Chicago incident, he would be terminated. His fears intensified when he saw a message on his phone from TWA. The message, however, was not from TWA management. It was a message from scheduling advising him that he was scheduled for L-1011 upgrade training.[6]

Hoot had mixed feelings about the news. He was glad to learn that his job was safe, at least for the time being. But he had some real concerns about his physical and mental state. He was still having difficulty sleeping. And the constant distractions related to TWA 841 were making it hard for him to concentrate. After giving it some thought, Hoot decided that going to L-1011 school was a good thing. He wouldn't have to fly the line and face the possibility of another flight attendant or passenger revolt, and immersing himself in learning a new airplane might help take his mind off the negativity surrounding him.

Knowing that he would be trading the stress from TWA 841 for the stress of training, Hoot laced up his running shoes and headed out the door. Jogging was something Hoot did on his days off as well as on layovers. He ran the same route around his neighborhood nearly every day when he was home. As he made his way around the block, he thought about the incident in Chicago. Maybe it was just an overreaction by one ill-informed flight attendant, he thought. That's when he noticed something peculiar. The streets were unusually quiet. The neighbors he would routinely wave to as he passed by were absent. He looked out ahead of him and saw one or two neighbors abruptly end what they were doing and head inside, closing the door behind them. That's when it dawned on him that maybe Chicago wasn't an isolated incident. He had no way of knowing it then, but things were about to get a lot worse.

Chapter Seven

Fear of Flying

The experiences of the passengers aboard TWA 841 after the incident were as varied as were their reasons for being on the flight. For many, prior plans and schedules left little time for reflection. Passenger Peter Fehr, an obstetrician, got a couple of hours of sleep after arriving home before heading to the hospital where he was scheduled to perform surgery. None of his co-workers were aware of what had happened aboard TWA 841. When he arrived at

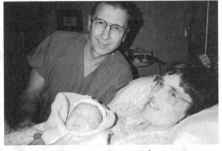

Figure 14 Passenger Peter Fehr

the hospital, he changed into his scrubs and prepared for surgery. He didn't say anything to his surgery team about his experience the night before. He needed to focus on the task at hand.

Passengers Douglas Page and his co-worker Lou Dougherty were scheduled for an 8:00 am meeting on April fifth. They didn't arrive at their hotel until after 6:00 a.m. because they had to wait for the rental car agency to open. Doug

Figure 15 Passenger Douglas Page

called the client and asked if they could change the meeting to a later time, saying only that they had gotten in late the night before.

Holly Wicker and her coworker, Sheryl Fisher, were met at the airport by the children's adoptive parents. The anxious parents had waited at the airport throughout the ordeal. Holly accompanied the infant Asha and her new parents to Children's Hospital in Minneapolis for a scheduled examination of the baby. Holly had been examined by paramedics back in Detroit and had turned down their offer for a more thorough examination at the hospital. She also turned down another offer to be examined while waiting in the nearby emergency room.[1] When she arrived home she complained to her husband about pain she was having in her neck and back. After getting a few hours of rest, Holly made an appointment to see her doctor that afternoon.[2]

News about TWA 841 hadn't broken in Minneapolis when passengers first arrived early on the morning of April fifth. That would change by the end of the day. By the time the evening news aired, TWA 841 was a national news story. Walter Cronkite reported on the incident for CBS news. Newspaper coverage began a day later. "Passengers tell of ordeal in plane that rolled over," was a headline in the *Minneapolis Star Tribune* on April 6, 1979. "Passengers Recount Death Thoughts," was one of the more sensationalistic headlines. Theories as to the cause of the near crash began appearing as early as April seventh. "Plane's Dive is Laid to Malfunctioning Wing Flap," was the title of a *New York Times* article.

Early news accounts of the incident were fraught with errors. Several papers gave out erroneous passenger and crew counts. Other reporters, learning that a slat was missing from the leading edge, reported that the pilot had tried to slow the plane down in the dive by extending the flaps. Despite the many inaccuracies, the news coverage did convey the seriousness of the incident. For the first time passengers were learning that they were only seconds away from crashing. That knowledge heightened anxieties that many were already feeling. A number of passengers reported having nightmares and trouble sleeping. Holly Wicker had a recurring nightmare of a hand and arm of nothing but veins and bones reaching up for an oxygen mask.[3]

Memories of the incident resurfaced in unexpected ways. One passenger, Sheryl Fisher, had a flashback when a strong wind rattled her trailer, reminding her of the vibration she felt prior to landing.[4] Another passenger, Frederick Rascher, was sitting in his car as it was pulled along an automatic car wash. He panicked when the car started rattling from the high pressure hoses. As the car darkened from the soap and water, he couldn't take it anymore. He jumped out of the car and ran through the spray until he was in the clear.[5]

Those with a more optimistic outlook considered the near-death experience a wakeup call. They took chances they might not have taken otherwise. They felt as though they had been given a unique gift of life. Bob Reber, who was on the flight with his wife Gwen and who had been a bit of a penny pincher before TWA 841, now didn't think twice about making a large purchase. "You just never know when all of a sudden, poof! And it's all over," Bob commented to Minneapolis writer Buzz Bissinger.[6]

Roger Peterson, after reading numerous newspaper accounts about the upset, felt as if he had been given a second chance. He wanted to share his story with a larger audience, so he contacted the "Tonight Show." They put him in touch with a producer for Tom Snyder's late night talk show, "Tomorrow." Tom Snyder was a popular interviewer in the vein of Charlie Rose. Roger was invited to appear on the show to talk about his experience as a passenger aboard TWA 841. The twenty-minute segment aired on April 18, 1979. Six months later Holly Wicker also appeared on the show.

Some passengers vowed to never fly again, including one passenger who lived in Australia and had to make frequent visits to the United States.[7] For those who found it impractical to get from point A to B by any other means, they resorted to taking pills or alcohol before boarding, all the while being hypersensitive to every sound and vibration they felt from takeoff to landing. Passenger Douglas Page, upon arriving back at IBM headquarters in California, told his superiors that he preferred to not have any further assignments that required travel by air. He would fly again for personal reasons, but he found that he preferred smaller aircraft and flight numbers that didn't add up to thirteen.

Other passengers used the incident as an excuse for making drastic changes in their life, like the passenger who divorced his wife, saying that the near crash made him realize that he no longer loved her.

While some passengers would go on to file lawsuits against the airline and the aircraft manufacturer, claiming mental and physical problems, most were happy to have just survived. Everyday occurrences like going to the park on a warm, sunny day or having dinner with friends could be enough to trigger an emotional response. Passenger Jeannine Rakowsky was watching her daughter's jazz group singing show tunes at a local mall when she suddenly burst into tears. Watching her daughter and knowing how close she had come to not being there made her realize how fortunate she was.

<hr />

On May 25, 1979, less than two months after the emergency landing in Detroit, TWA 841 passenger Patricia Carlson was driving home in northern Minnesota listening to the radio. It was the Friday before Memorial Day weekend. As the song she was listening to ended, the announcer came on with a breaking news story: A DC-10 taking off from Chicago's O'Hare International airport had just crashed, killing all onboard. The news startled Pat, forcing her to pull off to the side of the road until she was able to settle her emotions. Like all of the passengers and crew aboard TWA 841, Pat had experienced something that few people ever have. She knew what it was like to be on a plane as it was about to crash. She had a unique insight that caused her to look at other airline tragedies differently. Hearing about the DC-10 crash brought her right back to that April 4th night over Michigan. Other TWA 841 passengers would have similar reactions to the Chicago crash and other airline calamities that were to occur over the ensuing years.

The crash of American Airlines Flight 191 was at the time, and remains, the deadliest airline crash in U.S. history. Flight 191, with 271 passengers and crew, departed Chicago O'Hare International Airport at 3:02 p.m. central time. Its destination was Los Angeles, California. As the plane rotated for takeoff, the number-one engine separated from the left wing. The plane crashed near a trailer park just 4,600 feet off the end of the runway, killing all onboard. Two people on the ground were also killed.

As investigators combed over the wreckage and examined the separated engine, which had detached from the wing along with the engine pylon, their concern was that perhaps there was a structural problem with the engine pylons on the DC-10. Adding to their concerns was the fact that Flight 191 was the fourth fatal crash of a DC-10 since its introduction in 1971. There had also been several non-fatal incidents involving the DC-10. One airline, Overseas National Airways, lost two DC-10s within a year of receiving them. The rash of incidents and accidents and the possibility of a design flaw with the DC-10, along with intense media attention, forced the FAA to suspend the type certificate for the aircraft, effectively grounding some 300 airplanes.

The grounding of the DC-10 fleet on June 6, 1979, caught the attention of the TWA 841 investigators. They knew that a similar grounding of the 727 fleet would have serious repercussions throughout the aviation industry. In 1979, the Boeing 727 was the most popular aircraft in the world. The financial hit to the airlines and the economy would have been crippling. Airlines would have been forced to lay off thousands of workers as planes sat idle. Flight schedules worldwide also would have been disrupted, causing delays and cancellations.

Aside from the enormous financial hit that Boeing would have faced, an even greater threat loomed. If the public perceived that the 727 was an unsafe aircraft, Boeing would have been unable to repair the damages even if the grounding was brief. Such was the case of the ATR aircraft following an accident on Halloween night, October 31, 1994. The plane, an ATR 72, crashed in a farm field near Roselawn, Indiana, after encountering freezing rain and heavy icing. The investigation uncovered a design flaw with the aircraft that allowed ice to form aft of the de-icing boots. The aircraft manufacturer made design changes to the de-icing boots, and airline operators made changes to their procedures and training, but public perception had turned against the aircraft. Airlines operating ATRs in northern states were forced to move them to warmer climates.

The most recent grounding of an entire aircraft fleet happened as late as January 2013. The Boeing 787 Dreamliner was grounded because of problems with lithium batteries catching fire. As the investigation into what was causing the batteries to overheat and catch fire dragged on, airlines affected by the grounding insisted on compensation from Boeing for losses they were incurring. The Dreamliner grounding lasted five months. One airline, Poland's LOT airline, claimed that it had losses of more than 30 million dollars related to the five months they were unable to fly the plane.

A similar grounding of the 727 fleet was not an unreasonable outcome. The NTSB had a plane that had suddenly rolled over and plunged from an altitude of 39,000 feet to within seconds of crashing, and they didn't know why. If public and media attention were enough to force the FAA to ground the DC-10 fleet, the same fate could easily befall the 727. To help diffuse that possibility, FAA officials and NTSB investigators were careful to stand behind the plane. When reporter David Noland from *Aviation Consumer* magazine contacted the NTSB to request an interview, he was put in touch with Leslie Kampschror, the Investigator-in-Charge (IIC) for TWA 841. When asked about the integrity of the 727, Kampschror responded, "I'm satisfied that there was nothing wrong with the airplane." As for the crew's possible involvement, Kampschror was quoted as saying, "I assume they're hiding something, but I can't prove it. We're wrestling with that problem very hard right now." In the same article, an NTSB spokesman was said to have made the following statement: "I think those guys were fooling around up there, and I don't think we really know what they were doing yet."[8] Kampschror would later claim that he was misquoted. The article, however, clearly shifted blame away from the aircraft and onto the crew, with the NTSB credited as the main source.

Kampschror's suspicions of crew involvement were also on display in a quote that appeared in an article written by Minneapolis writer Buzz Bissinger. "This is the kind of case the Board has never had to deal with—a head-on collision between the credibility of the crew versus the airworthiness of the aircraft."[9]

As the Flight 191 investigation moved forward, parallels to the TWA 841 investigation became apparent. One of the first discoveries was that the cockpit voice recorder had stopped recording right at the moment of engine separation. It was later determined that the engine generator for the number-one engine powered the circuitry for the CVR. When investigators discovered a broken bolt at the crash scene, a news conference was held, with the lead investigator claiming that the broken bolt had been the cause of the accident. A metallurgist later discounted that claim. The broken bolt didn't even come from the plane. The DC-10 had crashed near an old airport and maintenance hangar. One other important similarity involved the slats. Even with the loss of the engine, the plane should have been able to continue to fly and safely return to the airport. But after the loss of power from the number-one engine, the first officer, who was flying, reduced the power on the two remaining engines and slowed to a lower speed as per company procedures. Unfortunately, when the number-one engine separated, it also took out the hydraulic lines that operated the slats on the left wing. Since hydraulic pressure was lost, the slats on the left wing retracted. The left wing stalled as a result of the slower speed, and the plane was unrecoverable from that point.

The DC-10 was eventually cleared when investigators discovered that the engine that had separated had undergone an improper maintenance procedure. The maintenance procedure, which saved 200 man-hours, involved removing and replacing the engine and pylon as one unit using a forklift. Ultimately, a combination of factors led to the pylon mount being overstressed, resulting in the failure.

Chapter Eight

Born to Fly

The first few weeks after the incident proved to be a confusing and frustrating time for Hoot. He couldn't understand the reluctance of the investigators to speak with him, and that included the TWA and ALPA investigators. When he learned that the NTSB had released information saying that the plane had bottomed out of the dive at around 5,000 feet, he told whoever would listen that it was closer to 50 feet. He had pulled a tree branch out of the right landing gear. Hoot was told to let the investigation run its course and not challenge the investigators. It seemed an odd way to run an investigation, Hoot thought.

Hoot had been with TWA since 1963. By the time of the TWA 841 incident, Hoot had accumulated more than 23,000 hours of accident- and violation-free flight time, 15,000 hours of which were as a pilot for TWA. While he may have had a reputation as a partying bachelor outside of work, he was considered a true professional in the cockpit and was well respected among his peers.

Hoot grew up on a small farm in Illinois about seventy-five miles west of Chicago. The eldest of three children, Hoot took his first airplane ride around the age of five when a barnstormer landed in a field on his father's farm. It was a two-seater biplane, with the pilot sitting in the back. Hoot sat on the lap of a woman who would later become his first-grade teacher. As a teenager, Hoot rode his pony to the local airport three to four miles away. He washed airplanes in exchange for airplane rides. A local crop-dusting pilot offered to take Hoot flying in exchange for

Figure 16 Hoot in third grade

helping him with his crop-dusting work. Hoot had the unenviable job of standing in a field with a flag raised above his head. The crop duster would fly over Hoot and then start spraying the four or five rows of whatever crop was growing. Hoot then scurried over four or five rows for the next pass. Hoot would later joke that inhaling the crop-dusting spray had stunted his growth, which pegged out at five-foot-six.

When he had no pilots to pester, Hoot would hang around the mechanics while they worked on planes. He convinced one mechanic to let him taxi an old Taylor Cub. Hoot claimed that he eventually got the Cub going fast enough that he was able to lift it off the ground for a few hundred feet, about the same distance as the Wright Brothers' first flight. That's when he got serious about wanting to learn how to fly. He soloed at age fourteen, having lied about his age.

Hoot's real name is Harvey Glen Gibson. He was named after his father. His family called him by his middle name of Glen. Hoot got his nickname after appearing in a school play dressed as an owl. His role was to run across the stage yelling, "Hoot, hoot, hoot!" He often grew tired of having to repeat the same story over and over and would sometimes mention rodeo star and cowboy actor Hoot Gibson as the source of his childhood nickname just to make the story more interesting.

Hoot had a knack for all things mechanical. Before he got bit by the flying bug, he was already driving his dad's truck, tractor, and any other motorized vehicle he could get his hands on. Not long after soloing, he began ferrying crop-dusting planes from one location to the next. He eventually earned money working as a crop duster himself while still in high school.[1]

Figure 17 Hoot's first marriage at age 18

Hoot married shortly after graduating high school. He was eighteen years old. He claimed that it was his mother's idea because she thought his high school girlfriend was pregnant. Hoot worked odd jobs and did his best to earn enough money to support himself and his new wife. He became a father by age twenty. Needing a more stable income, Hoot enlisted in the Marine Corps. He spent most of his two-year commitment in Hawaii with his young family in tow. Hoot was assigned to a hospital, where he became the personal driver of a navy Admiral. He also drove an ambulance and did odd jobs assisting the doctors and corpsmen. Hoot signed up for two years of active duty followed by five years of reserve. Though he was not a pilot in the Marine Corps, Hoot's love for flying was never far from his mind. He had two more sons during this time, but the marriage ended in divorce not long after he left the military. His third son, Kevin, was born after the divorce was finalized. Prior to his divorce, at a time when he was separated from his wife, Hoot had a brief affair with another woman that resulted in a fourth son.

After leaving the Marine Corps, Hoot took a job working in a factory in Aurora, Illinois. He spent most of the money he earned on renting planes. Hoot was looking for anything other than factory work when out of the blue he received a letter asking if he would be interested in becoming an Air Traffic Controller. The pay was good, so he signed up and soon found himself working at Chicago's Midway airport, which at the time was the busiest airport in the world. This was a time before radar. Controllers were forced to visualize where each aircraft was in space using only the aircraft call sign and an information strip containing the aircraft's altitude, speed, heading, and last known position. It was a stressful and mentally demanding job. During this time Hoot and a friend started an aircraft charter company flying Beech 18s. Hoot also found part-time work ferrying old P51 Mustangs to a restoration facility in Indiana. The charter company and ferry work allowed Hoot to keep his hand in flying.

When his employer, the FAA, found out about the charter company they gave Hoot an ultimatum—drop the charter company or resign. Their argument was that the charter company presented a conflict of interest. As a controller, Hoot was in a position to give priority handling to his own aircraft. It wasn't a hard decision for Hoot to make. He had already decided that he wasn't cut out to be a controller.

Hoot's charter company grew to become one of the largest in the Chicago area. When he was approached by an executive of Allstates News to start up a corporate flight department, Hoot agreed and set to work purchasing a DC-3 and writing the operations manuals for the fledgling enterprise. Hoot soon learned that Allstates News was, in fact, the parent company for *Playboy* magazine. Hoot, at the age of twenty-eight, was soon flying Hugh Hefner and a bevy of Playboy Bunnies around the U.S. When he was hired by TWA less than a year later, fellow pilots learned of Hoot's time at *Playboy* and his reputation as a partying girl-chaser took root.

The airlines have always been a cyclical industry of boom and bust. A pilot's career can be affected positively or negatively depending on when they are hired. In Hoot's case, his timing couldn't have been better. He was hired in the first class of flight engineer/pilots. The idea was that the flight engineer position was to be a stepping stone into the pilot seat. Prior to this time, the flight engineer position was a permanent position held by non-pilots. Hoot was hired as a flight engineer on the Lockheed Constellation.

It was a great time to be an airline pilot. The airlines were expanding, adding new jet aircraft at the rate of two or three every month. They needed pilots to fly these new aircraft. TWA quickly grew from a pilot force of five hundred to more than 2,000 in a few short years. Those hired at the beginning of this wave had their pick of aircraft and seat. Hoot was single, based in New York and Paris, and seeing the world. But he was working as a flight engineer on the Constellation and later the Boeing 707, and he wanted to be back in the pilot's seat. He also missed his children. So he transferred back to Chicago and was put on the fast track to captain on the DC-9 and soon after that the Boeing 727.

Hoot upgraded to captain on the DC-9 just four years after being hired. He moved to 727 Captain after a brief stint on the DC-9. Hoot

spent most of his time flying as a captain on the 727 in the years leading up to Flight 841. He married his second wife, Sandy, a flight attendant and a former Miss Missouri contestant, on New Year's Eve 1969. They married in Las Vegas. Hoot was thirty-five and Sandy was just twenty-one. For their honeymoon, Hoot and Sandy joined several other TWA pilots and their wives on a trip to Phoenix, Arizona, where they went skydiving.

Figure 18 Hoot in 1971

Hoot's marriage to Sandy added to his reputation for being eccentric. He had a beautiful younger wife. He flew aerobatics. He drove fast cars and souped-up motorcycles. And he lived an uncommon lifestyle for that time period. In the early 70s, pilots flying for a major airline lived in the city where they were based. Hoot saw no reason why he couldn't live wherever he wanted as long as he was able to make his schedule. Hoot was based in Los Angeles, but he thought the cost of housing was too high. So he started looking for a home in Las Vegas, where housing was more affordable. There were several flights a day between Los Angeles and Las Vegas. So Hoot purchased a house in Las Vegas and became one of the first airline commuters. He purchased a small trailer that he parked in the employee parking lot at LAX. If he or Sandy had an early-morning departure out of LA, they would commute in the night before and spend the night in the trailer. It wasn't long before other pilots followed Hoot's example.

On their days off, Hoot taught Sandy how to fly. Sandy eventually earned her commercial pilot's license. Sandy, however, had no aspirations of working as a professional pilot. She enjoyed working as a flight attendant during the heyday of air travel, when flight attendants were admired and envied. Her motivation for learning to fly was for the peace of mind it offered her, knowing that if something were to happen that she could do more than be just a helpless spectator.[2]

As TWA began adding larger jet aircraft like the L-1011 and Boeing 747, Hoot decided that he wanted to fly the big iron. He didn't have enough seniority at the time to hold a captain slot, so he elected to fly as a first officer on the Boeing 747. Hoot took a slight cut in pay with the move, but his seniority and choice of international flights made the switch worthwhile.

Hoot and Sandy divorced in the summer of 1978. Their age difference played a major factor in the breakup. Hoot may have had a reputation for being a colorful character, but he was no different from anyone else when it came to the hurt and pain of divorce. He went through a prolonged period of melancholy and blamed himself for their eventual split.

In his spare time, Hoot enjoyed nature, whether that be by hiking in the mountains of Utah, enjoying the desert landscapes around Las Vegas, or lounging on the beaches of California. He also enjoyed less-exotic hobbies such as coin collecting, a hobby he picked up from his father.

In the three months leading up to the April 4 TWA 841 flight, Hoot had been out on medical leave with a broken ankle. Hoot told the Los Angeles-based chief pilot that he had broken his ankle as a result of a motorcycle accident. He said that he had been riding behind a truck and took a nasty spill when some gravel fell from the back of the truck. The story that made the rounds at TWA, however, was that Hoot was speeding and lost control, adding more fuel to his daredevil reputation.

As it turned out, the entire story was just a cover for the real reason he had broken his ankle.

<hr />

Single and with lots of time on his hands, Hoot picked up odd jobs flying on the side. One of his favorite part-time flying jobs was with a company that provided air tours of the Las Vegas strip. The tour company used two different aircraft for the tours, depending on the number of sightseers. A helicopter was used for one or two people. A Ford Tri-Motor was used for larger groups. Hoot was qualified to fly both.

Figure 19 Hoot in the Ford Tri-Motor

Hoot's experience flying a wide variety of aircraft, including helicopters, caught the attention of the Las Vegas Police Department. They approached Hoot and asked him if he would be interested in helping them with search-and-rescue operations. Searching for lost hikers and stranded motorists was a common occurrence in Las Vegas and the surrounding area. When there wasn't a need for search and rescue, Hoot sometimes flew the department helicopter. He also began working with the officers in the narcotics division. Drug smugglers would land in the dry lake beds around Las Vegas, unload their cargo, and depart before the authorities could catch up with them. They would bury large drums of gasoline in the sand, which they would use to refuel the planes. The head of the narcotics division asked Hoot if he could help them identify the aircraft that were being used. Hoot would measure the width between the tire tracks and look for other tell-tale signs such as a tail wheel track that might help him identify the aircraft. The DC-3, a tail dragger, was a popular aircraft for drug smuggling back then due to its cheap cost. So were other older aircraft like the Beech 18 and the DC-6, aircraft with which Hoot had flying experience. Hoot also had a knack for spotting good locations where the 50-gallon fuel drums were likely buried.

One day Hoot found himself on the same Southwest Airlines flight as Las Vegas Sheriff Ralph Lamb. Sheriff Lamb, who was the basis for the lead character in the short-lived television series *Vegas,* starring Dennis Quaid as Sheriff Lamb, asked Hoot to sit with him to discuss business. The Sheriff asked Hoot if he would be interested in becoming more involved with the narcotics division. The Sheriff knew that Hoot was an airline pilot and could travel for free. He wanted Hoot to fly to various seminars and drug classes as a representative of the department. Hoot told the Sheriff he would help the department in any way he could.

Hoot had gained an interest in the drug business after working as a volunteer at a detention center in Las Vegas. He counseled young offenders and tried to set them straight. He saw firsthand the damage drugs could do. So he was open to doing more to help fight the drug problem when Sheriff Lamb approached him with the idea. Soon Hoot was spending his time off flying to various training seminars, where he learned the ins and outs of the drug-smuggling business.

His flying background, along with his military experience in handling weapons, made Hoot a valuable asset to the department. Hoot enjoyed spending his off hours with the narcotics officers. They treated him as an equal. His friendship with the officers in the department eventually led to Hoot participating in more dangerous operations. Hoot was asked to pose as a pilot looking for work hauling drugs. He'd hang out at local bars and put the word out that he was a pilot looking for work, saying that he was willing to fly anything anywhere for the right price. If he did find a potential contact, he would invent some excuse why he couldn't fly the flight. Instead, he would offer to find another pilot or offer to train someone in the drug operation to fly the plane.

As the undercover work progressed and Hoot became more involved in setting up actual drug flights, the potential for serious injury or death increased. He sometimes found himself dealing with very dangerous people in very dangerous situations. One time while doing air surveillance in a small plane at night, the officers on the ground wanted to know how many vehicles were at the location under surveillance. Unable to get close enough for a good view without alarming the drug smugglers, Hoot shut both engines off, swooped down over the area to get a better look, then climbed back up and restarted the engines.[3] In another instance, Hoot and a number of undercover officers intervened during a large drug deal. The drug smugglers took off running in all directions. Hoot took off running after a Hispanic man. Hoot was running along a cement wall while the suspect was running on a path below him. Hoot made his move to tackle the guy. He jumped from the wall, and, instead of tackling the suspect, Hoot landed on a patch of ice and ended up breaking his ankle.

Hoot knew he couldn't call TWA and tell them that he had broken his leg in a drug bust. He wasn't even supposed to be working outside of his airline job. So he made up the motorcycle story. He was out for three months. It was the same three-month medical leave that preceded his return to 727 captain and ultimately TWA Flight 841, his first flight back after suffering his broken ankle.

Later, when Hoot became a regular on television news programs reporting on TWA 841, his connections at the DEA suggested that it might be better if he lay low for a while. They didn't want any drug runners recognizing Hoot. But it wasn't long before Hoot was back working on another drug operation. For Hoot, it was a way to forget about TWA 841. The narcotics guys were on Hoot's side from day one.

Hoot wasn't paid for his services. He was compensated with gifts, usually expensive guns, which Hoot held onto into retirement. Over time Hoot's gun collection grew rather large to include machine guns, pistols, shotguns, and various rifles. His most prized gun, however, was a silver-plated pistol with his name engraved on the side, given to him by his friends in the narcotics division.

Hoot's involvement with the Las Vegas Drug Enforcement Agency continued throughout his employment at TWA. He eventually worked with a number of other law-enforcement agencies, including Border Patrol, Customs, the FBI, the Mexico State Police, and the El Paso City Police Department.

Chapter Nine

A Fly on the Wall

Prior to the implementation of the cockpit voice recorder (CVR) and flight data recorder (FDR), accident investigators had little to go on other than the plane wreckage when trying to determine the cause of a plane crash. As commercial air traffic increased and the number of fatal accidents rose, the debate over the value of these devices as investigative aids began. Few people argued with the need for a flight data recorder. Information related to airspeed, heading, altitude, and vertical acceleration (g-forces) could help investigators better understand what was happening to an aircraft prior to and during an accident. The CVR, however, was a different story. Most pilots were adamantly opposed to the device. They viewed it as an invasion of privacy in the workplace. What other work group would authorize the taping of everyday conversations? they argued. Pilots were afraid that comments made in the cockpit could later be used by management in disciplinary actions. They worried that mistakes uncovered by a CVR could lead to airman certificate actions.

The Air Line Pilots Association (ALPA), the dominant union representing airline pilots working for major airlines at that time, saw the introduction of the CVR as a valuable investigative tool. The information contained on a CVR might prove beneficial in showing that pilots had acted properly when dealing with emergency situations. With the majority of its members opposed to the introduction of the CVR, ALPA had to strike a delicate balance between assuaging the concerns of its members while also trying to shape the regulations under consideration.

Figure 20 The CVR erase button located on the overhead panel

In this regard they did an admirable job. Since most accidents occur over a short time period, ALPA was able to get the recording length down to just the last thirty minutes of a flight as opposed to two hours as was first proposed.[1] Regulators also agreed to include language in the rules stating that cockpit voice recordings could not be used in any enforcement action against a crew. And finally, in order to give pilots some sense of control, they agreed to allow the addition of an erase button.

Once the CVRs started showing up in cockpits in the early 1960s, many pilots decided that they would erase the CVR at the conclusion of every flight. This became standard operating procedure in the immediate years following CVR implementation. It wasn't a written procedure, except in a few isolated instances such as at Northwest Airlines, which for a time included erasing the CVR on the secure cockpit checklist. Nor was it condoned in any formal way by the pilots union. It was simply an accepted practice. Most pilots didn't think twice about reaching up and pressing the erase button at the completion of all checklists.

In reality, the pilots' concerns were without merit. For one, no one was standing around after every flight waiting to pull the CVR tape to see what embarrassing comments the pilots may or may not have made. The tape recording over itself after every thirty minutes meant that no recording would last for very long. More importantly, CVR recordings provided valuable insight into what exactly was going on inside the cockpit in the final moments before a fatal crash. When that information was combined with the data obtained from a flight data recorder, investigators were better equipped to piece together the sequence of events leading up to an accident.

In most cases, the contents of the CVR are never heard by anyone, unless there is a fatal accident. The actual recording is heard only by the investigators, except in rare court cases. The public and family members are provided only transcripts of the CVR. But even reading a transcript of a pilot's last words can be a traumatic experience for the family. Voice recordings can range from words of resignation to expletive-filled shouts as the crew tries to avert disaster. It can also reveal moments of un-professionalism. The crew of a commuter plane on a ferry flight was joking about pranks they wanted to play on other pilots moments before they tried to perform a barrel-roll and ended up crashing in a farm field.[2]

The idea that a cockpit voice recording might prove valuable in a non-fatal accident or incident did cross the minds of regulators when they included in the regulations language requiring the preservation of cockpit voice recordings in the case of an accident or incident.

So what one person might see as a routine procedure performed by habit, hitting the erase button at the conclusion of a flight, another person might see as a deliberate action. The NTSB investigators obviously felt that the CVR erasure of TWA 841 was deliberate and thus regarded the crew with suspicion. Their suspicions were only heightened after Hoot told TWA investigators and later testified that it was his habit to erase the CVR after every flight.

Had investigators looked at the supposed CVR erasure with a more critical eye, they would have found sufficient evidence to support the possibility that there was no deliberate erasure of the CVR. The first piece of contradicting evidence concerns time. When the plane finally came to a stop on the taxiway at Detroit, the plane was immediately surrounded by emergency vehicles that had been waiting by the side of the runway. Mechanic Mel Brown had plugged into the maintenance intercom to speak with the crew within minutes. One of the first things he told Hoot was that the plane was leaking fuel and that they needed to get the passengers off the aircraft. So even if one were to assume that the crew had decided to erase the CVR to cover up damaging evidence, there wasn't time for them to have had such a conversation. They were too busy coordinating with the flight attendants, emergency crews, the tower, and mechanic Mel Brown to devise some cover-up. Hoot testified that he was busy dealing with the emergency and that the CVR never even crossed his mind.

In August of 1981, during his deposition in the civil trial, Hoot was asked about the CVR erasure. Here is his response.

Well, I would just darn near believe that I didn't erase it, but I don't deny that. The reason that I don't think I did erase it is I recall, after landing, you go through a flow pattern, you know, manipulating switches. When we landed, so many things were in an unusual position that we decided to leave them there for the people who were going to inspect the airplane to have a better idea what had happened.

For years—I don't know when I got qualified in the airplane—'69, I guess, as a captain—what I've always done is—every time that we pull into the gate and park the airplane, park the brakes and shut down the engine, I go through and turn off, like windshield heat and all the switches.

You know, you go up and down and turn off all the switches for what we call securing the cockpit for the time that we're on the ground. What I normally do is, with this finger, I usually flip the guard up on the emergency light system. We had turned the emergency lights off because when we take the power off the airplane, the emergency lights automatically come on and it would drain [the batteries].

So, what I normally do is—when I flip this guard up, I just automatically hit this switch [the erase button] next to it with my thumb. It's just one motion. I've been doing this since I've been on the airplane. Only this time, it was confusing because I already had the emergency light switch in the on position where it is normally not in the on position, and I've never put that switch in that position before.[3]

Hoot's response is revealing for a number of reasons. First, he states that he wanted to leave the switches in their current position to help the "people who were going to inspect the airplane to have a better idea [of] what had happened." That is not consistent with a crew trying to cover up some misdeed. Then he describes how his normal flow was disrupted when he came across the emergency lights switch. Erasing the CVR was part of a flow that he did on a routine basis, and that flow was interrupted.

The next piece of evidence that tends to support the crew's testimony that they didn't erase the CVR is the nine minutes of actual audio that were on the tape. There is a difference between a blank tape (silent) and a CVR tape that has been bulk erased. When a CVR is bulk erased, a tone is emitted. In the case of TWA 841, the CVR tape had twenty-one minutes of the bulk-erase tone and nine minutes of clear audio. The CVR records not only the communication of the cockpit crew members through a centrally mounted microphone, but it also records radio communications as well as intercom communications, such as calls to and from the flight attendants.

The CVR transcript provided below was taken from the NTSB official report. The report distinguishes who is speaking by using FD to represent the fire department and CKPT to represent the cockpit. Investigators made no attempt to determine whether it was Hoot or Scott who was talking.

According to the official transcripts, the nine minutes of audio starts with communication between the fire department (FD) and the cockpit (CKPT).

> FD: Hello cockpit
> CKPT: Yeah.
> FD: Ah, did you call operations and request a bus?
> CKPT: No, but we will.
> FD: Okay, thank you.

The official record is that the conversation above was between the cockpit and the fire department over the emergency frequency. More than likely, however, this conversation was between the cockpit and mechanic Mel Brown, who plugged into the maintenance intercom upon arriving at the plane. Mel Brown gave a statement saying that he communicated to the crew that there was a fuel leak and that the fire department requested the aircraft be deplaned as soon as possible. This conversation is not on the CVR. Emergency responders are trained to communicate with the aircraft by the aircraft call sign. It would be highly unusual for them to use the phrase "hello cockpit." A typical call from a mechanic or other ground personnel wanting to communicate with the cockpit would be "ground to cockpit." Additionally, it's unlikely that the fire department would be inquiring about calls to operations. So if this communication was between Mel Brown and the cockpit, it would indicate that the CVR erasure, if there was an erasure, occurred sometime after Mel Brown informed the crew of the fuel leak and the need to deplane the passengers.[4]

Next there is communication between the crew members picked up by the cockpit area microphone (CAM) and from the plane to TWA operations (TWA OPS) using the radio.

> CAM: What's the ramp frequency here?
>
> CAM: Ah, he's right, he wouldn't know. I'll get it. (This conversation supports the NTSB's account that it was the fire department asking about calling operations since they would not know the frequency. However, it is also likely that there was some confusion over whose voice they were hearing.)
>
> CAM: Detroit, one twenty nine one.

CAM: I wonder if there's anybody in there?

CAM: Ah, I hope so.

RADIO: Ah, ramp TWA, this is eight forty one.

TWA OPS: Yeah, go ahead.

RADIO: Ah, we've been asked to deplane the passengers, ah, because of a slight fuel leak here. The fire department has asked us to get 'em off and ah we'd like some kind of transportation, a bus for them, please. What we're going to do is drop the aft air stairs and let them walk off, ah, without excitement, we just want to get them off easily, but we need to get them out of—off the taxiway here.

TWA OPS: Yeah, are you still, you still on the runway or . . . ?

RADIO: No, we're on a turnoff from the runway. We're clear of the runway.

TWA OPS: Okay, we'll see what we can do here, is there any way that you can keep in contact with us here?

RADIO: Ah, I'm talking to you from the airplane right now.

TWA OPS: I mean can you stay on this frequency, though.

RADIO: Yes I can.

Next comes some revealing conversation between the crew members. Up to this point they had been busy coordinating with the fire and rescue personnel, mechanic Mel Brown, and the flight attendants. Now for the first time they have a few seconds to catch their breath. (Note: Text in brackets is questionable audio; an asterisk denotes inaudible sounds.)

CAM: (Sound of seat movement)

CAM: Want help?

CAM: Well, we won't need that any more.

CAM: [Looks like] a hydraulic fluid loss, huh.

CAM: That's what we were told—hydraulic.

CAM: Did you feel kind of helpless in that seat back there? (This question was most likely directed at Gary Banks, who was sitting in the flight engineer's seat.)

CAM: Well, I'll tell you.

CAM: [Believe me.]

CAM: Yeah.

CAM: [Definitely.]

CAM: Yeah.

CAM: If it happened here, hard to see what's happening. You guys were trying to pull it up, like—

CAM: Yeah.

CAM: Saying get it up, pull it up, like—

CAM: That's, ah—emergency descent, as a flyer who wasn't flying it.

CAM: [Thing] did all right, well done.

CAM: (Sound of cough)

CAM: What are you eating? You got one of those cough drops?

CAM: Huh, yeah by * [right out of the] * okay?

CAM: Son of a gun.

CAM: * I'll get you one.

CAM: Throat a little dry?

CAM: Yeah, a little dry and my mouth's a little, little dry. (Hoot claims that he is the one requesting a cough drop from Scott.)

CAM: Okay, I'll stay here and stay on the radio.

If the crew had done anything that might have led to the upset, they certainly weren't indicating any complicity in this audio. The next thing audible on the tape is more conversation concerning the arrangement of transportation for the passengers to the terminal.

TWA OPS: Eight forty one, from Detroit ramp.

RADIO: TWA's eight forty one, go ahead.

TWA OPS: Yes, sir, looks like you're pretty close to Eastern's terminal there, you think it's conceivable that we can walk the people over there? I'm gonna have a hard time gettin' a bus.

RADIO: Okay, if you could bring somebody over as a guide, I think that would be fine. They wouldn't mind walking that far.

TWA OPS: We'll do that.

CAM: Okay, what they intend to do is they cannot get a bus so they're going to bring a guide out and walk them to the Eastern Terminal.

CAM: Ah, whichever one of these it is, but in any case they're going to walk them.

CAM: * they won't let them on the airplane?

CAM: What's that?

CAM: They won't leave them on the airplane?

CAM: No, I don't imagine they will now that they're off.

CAM: Do you want me to call them back and see about that?

CAM: Oh, no *

CAM: Hoot.

CAM: Yeah.

CAM: * for all the help the people did great. They did exactly what they were told to do.

CAM: That's because you guys took over and did it.

CAM: There were times on there when I had problems [just looking to see if it was over with *]

CAM: *

RADIO: Ah, ramp, TWA eight forty one.

TWA OPS: Go ahead.

RADIO: Do you need a—any further contact here? If not I'll turn the radios off.

TWA OPS: Ah, no, except, ah, can you give me anything, any indication on the airplane or anything dispatch, planning and everybody else is calling, ah can, is there information that you can give me?

RADIO: No, sir. We can't. I'm sitting in the cockpit and I can't tell you, I don't know what the situation is. You'll have to talk to maintenance.

TWA OPS: Yeah, well I mean, ah, you lost hydraulic is that it?

RADIO: We assume that's what happened but we can't tell you that—what I say until [you] talk to maintenance.

TWA OPS: Okay, you can sign off then.

CAM: (Sounds of electrical interruption)

RADIO: Detroit ramp do you read?

RADIO: Detroit ramp do you read?

Those were the last words discernible on the tape. There is nothing in the transcript that supports the supposition that the crew was trying to cover something up. If anything, the transcripts exculpate the crew. Unfortunately, the transcripts were never published or discussed by any members of the media, many of whom continued to report that the tape was completely blank.

The idea that the crew might have deliberately erased the CVR in order to cover up something came on the heels of the Watergate scandal some six years earlier. One of the more intriguing aspects of the Watergate scandal involved audiotapes of White House conversations between President Nixon and his top aides. When the audiotapes were finally released, it was discovered that portions of the tapes had been erased. Whether or not the erasures were intentional became the source of much debate.

Hints that the CVR was going to play an important role in the TWA 841 investigation came very early on. NTSB Chairman James B. King is said to have made the following comment to several TWA accident investigators after learning of the alleged erasure, "If we accomplish nothing else, we want to teach pilots a lesson about erasing voice recorders." It may very well have been that this mindset led King to order the public depositions of the crew just eight days after the incident.

Chapter Ten

Miss Piggy

A *t the time of the TWA 841 upset,* the Boeing 727 was
the most popular aircraft in the world, with more than
1700 aircraft operating worldwide. Boeing had accomplished this feat
in just sixteen short years from when the first planes started rolling off
the assembly line.

The history of the Boeing 727 dates back to the late fifties when
the concept of a short-to-medium-range commercial airliner was first
considered. Prior to this time, aircraft used by commercial airliners
were re-purposed military aircraft. Having a military contract with a
guaranteed number of orders on hand was the only way to start a new
aircraft program. But Boeing had the foresight to recognize that there
was going to be a need for a smaller aircraft to serve local markets.
Large jet aircraft like the Boeing 707 and the DC-8 were ideal for long
overseas flights and for coast-to-coast travel, but they required much
longer runways and were not fuel efficient on shorter-stage lengths.
Turboprop aircraft like the Lockheed Electra, which was a popular
short-range aircraft at the time, couldn't compete with the comfort and
speed of jet aircraft. What was needed was an aircraft that could carry
100 to 150 passengers on stage lengths between 500 to 1,500 miles into
airstrips with runways as short as 5,000 feet and do so economically. It

was with those goals in mind that the 727 program was born. Another important distinction of the Boeing 727 from the aircraft that preceded it was that it was one of the first aircraft designed with input from the end users—the airlines themselves.

Figure 21 Boeing 727-100 with all high-lift devices deployed

In order to meet the demanding goals set forth for the aircraft, engineers had to start from scratch. One of the first problems the engineers had to overcome involved the wings. Taking off and landing on short runways required a high-lift wing capable of sustaining flight at low speeds. The solution was to incorporate leading edge and trailing edge flaps and slats that increased the camber of the wing, thus providing more lift. After takeoff, the leading- and trailing-edge devices could be retracted. Once the aircraft reached its cruising altitude, a swept-back wing would allow the aircraft to fly at high speeds by delaying the onset of shock waves that form as airflow over the wings approach the speed of sound.

Next the engineers tackled the need for quick acceleration and better-than-average climb performance. Their answer was a tri-jet

Figure 22 Boeing 727-100 tri-jet

configuration with three engines placed on the tail of the aircraft. Two engines were mounted on the sides of the tail. The third, center engine was submerged in the tail. An air intake duct mounted at the base of the vertical fin would then route air to the engine through an S duct. The use of a three-engine configuration gave the 727 several advantages over competing two-engine designs like the Douglas DC-9 and the French-built Caravelle. A three-engine airplane could take off with lower visibility and ceiling minimums, a one-hundred-foot ceiling and one-quarter-mile visibility versus a three-hundred-foot ceiling and a half mile for a two-engine aircraft.[1] A three-engine aircraft could fly over-water routes like New York to San Juan. Two-engine aircraft were restricted on over-water routes due to a requirement that two-engine aircraft be within one hour of a suitable landing field with the loss of one engine. Three engines provided better takeoff performance at hot, high-altitude airports like Denver. And three engines offered better engine-out climb performance with the loss of one engine on takeoff, providing a safety advantage over two-engine designs.

To help with lift at low speeds, Kreuger flaps were installed on the leading edges near the fuselage. The Kreuger flaps extend out and downward, greatly increasing wing camber. To augment roll control, spoilers on the upper wing surface were rigged to operate in conjunction with control wheel deflection. The spoilers could also be used for in-flight speed brakes, and all spoiler panels could be used during a landing for increased drag, aiding in slowing the aircraft after touchdown and reducing stopping distance.

The unique design of the aircraft, however, also created problems. The 32 degrees of wing sweep were efficient at higher altitudes but less efficient at lower altitudes. In order to improve roll control at low speeds, it was necessary to have both inboard and outboard ailerons. To prevent over control and a twisting of the wings at higher speeds, the outboard set of ailerons were automatically locked out whenever the flaps were retracted.

Figure 23 split rudder

Another problem associated with the swept-back wing was Dutch Roll. Dutch Roll is a condition caused when an aircraft with a swept-back wing yaws to one side or the other. In a yaw to the right (tail moves left), the left wing is positioned more perpendicular to the relative wind, creating more lift and a roll to the right. When the pilot tries to correct the roll by applying left rudder and left aileron, the condition is reversed, and the aircraft rolls to the left. Without some kind of yaw damping, the aircraft can become uncontrollable. The Boeing 727 was especially susceptible to Dutch Roll because of its high degree of wing sweep and a large tail and rudder surface area. To counter the severe Dutch Roll characteristics of the 727, Boeing engineers made several important design decisions. First they decided to split the rudder into an upper and lower configuration, with each section controlled by a separate hydraulic system. This allowed partial rudder control in case of hydraulic failure of one system. Unlike the elevators and ailerons, each of which are hydraulically operated and have the capability of manual reversion, there is no manual reversion capability for the rudder. Rudder inputs by the pilots are transferred by cables from the rudder pedals to the hydraulically operated rudder power control units (PCU) in the vertical fin. Both the upper and lower rudder were equipped with independent yaw dampers that restricted rudder travel to four to five degrees of travel once the flaps were raised. This was accomplished by reducing the hydraulic pressure to the rudders from 3,000 psi to 800 psi. Should a pilot lose a yaw damper at altitude, the recommended procedure was to immediately descend to 26,000 feet or lower. Loss of both yaw dampers was considered an emergency situation.

One feature of the yaw damping system was the lack of rudder pedal feedback whenever the yaw dampers commanded rudder movement. If a yaw damper sensed a yaw and commanded rudder movement to counter that yaw, there was no corresponding feedback to the pilot's rudder pedals. The only indication a pilot would have that a yaw damper was controlling rudder movement would be an unexpected movement of the nose.

Should a yaw damper fail in flight, there were no warning lights or audible alerts to notify the crew of the failure. The only indication of a failed yaw damper was a fail flag in the rudder position indicator, which could easily go unnoticed during normal operations. A failed yaw damper could also lead to a split rudder situation, where either the upper or lower rudder was displaced disproportionately to the other. Considering the importance of the yaw damper to the lateral stability of the Boeing 727, the lack of a better warning system was considered by some to be a design flaw.

Figure 24 Boeing 727-100 3D model

Despite the many challenges Boeing faced in bringing a new aircraft to market, they had met their goals. The 727 was a modern-looking aircraft with a sweptback wing and a high vertical fin and horizontal stabilizer. The fuselage was wide enough to accommodate three abreast seating on each side of the aisle. The plane was capable of taking off on very short runways, climbing to altitude quickly, where it could cruise at speeds of up to mach .9, descend quickly using wing spoilers, and then land on runways as short as 4,500 feet. Once on the ground the plane was totally self-sufficient, with an auxiliary power unit (APU) for power and air and an aft stairway that allowed for passenger boarding and deplaning.

The first test flight, flown by Boeing test pilots Lou Wallick, Dix Loesch, and Marvin Shulenberger, occurred on February 9, 1963. The aircraft performed well, but in an ironic twist, the pilots had some difficulty retracting the leading-edge slats. The hydraulic actuators could not handle the air loads and had to be redesigned.

In what might be considered an aggressive flight certification schedule, the first aircraft were delivered to launch customers United Airlines and Eastern Airlines just a few months after the first test flight. N840TW, the plane used for TWA Flight 841, was delivered to TWA on July 13, 1965. It was the 160th Boeing 727 to roll off the assembly line.[2]

By April of 1979 the Boeing 727-100 had been replaced by the 727-200, an aircraft that was 20 feet longer than the earlier model. The shorter 727-100, in comparison, had a short, stubby appearance. The short fuselage paired with a large rudder surface made the plane overly sensitive to rudder input. Pilots who flew the early 727 claimed that the aircraft was underpowered at high gross weights and seemed to wallow through the air, especially at high altitudes. The portly appearance and undesirable flight characteristics led to the 727 acquiring the ignominious nickname of "Miss Piggy," or simply "The Pig." Aircraft N840TW was nicknamed "Sky Pig."

Despite the unflattering nickname, the 727 was considered to be a solidly built aircraft. The high degree of wing sweep allowed for a thicker, stronger wing. The landing gear and wheel brake system were straightened to absorb the abuse of repeated takeoffs and landings on very short runways. The fact that the plane did not break apart during the nearly 6 G pull out of TWA 841 is a testament to just how well-built the aircraft really was.

From an airline operations standpoint, the 727 exceeded all expectations. But not long after the first 727s began rolling off the assembly lines, the tide began to change in the commercial airline industry. As more and more airports started receiving jet service, complaints about noise rose. As fuel prices escalated, airlines began looking at ways to reduce their fuel costs. Additionally, pilot contracts and the threat of strikes kept wages high. It wasn't long before airlines started looking for alternatives to a noisy three-engine aircraft that also required three highly paid pilots.

Chapter Eleven

Putting the Pieces
Back Together

W*hile Hoot was dealing with the fallout* from being suspected of erasing the CVR, TWA was readying aircraft N840TW for a return to service. Airlines don't make money from airplanes sitting on the ground. Repairs began almost immediately after FAA and NTSB personnel had taken photographs of the plane and documented the damage suffered in the unprecedented dive. The list of damaged items included the following:

1. #7 leading edge slat and #6 flight spoiler missing (The NTSB misidentified spoiler #6 as spoiler #10.)
2. #4 flight spoiler damaged
3. Landing gear doors and mechanisms damaged
4. Right-hand inboard flap carriage damaged
5. Right-hand main gear side brace and actuator support beam broken (The support beam broke when the right main landing gear over extended.)
6. Lower fuselage skin wrinkling fore and aft of wing attach point

In addition to the items listed above, investigators noted evidence of hydraulic fluid leakage aft of the #7 slat, evidence of hydraulic leakage in the rudder, and a fractured tee-bolt for the #7 slat. There was also evidence that the #7 slat had not been aligned properly.

Jim McIntyre was one of the many people who had descended on N840TW the day after the incident. In addition to working as a pilot for TWA, Jim was also a captain in the navy reserve. He was an accomplished individual with a disciplined and determined approach to his work. Jim scoured every inch of the plane, looking for the tiniest defect, knowing that the damaged aircraft and missing parts were clues to what might have happened to TWA 841. As he walked around the aircraft, moving control surfaces and testing the strength of various sections of the plane, he noticed something unusual with the right outboard aileron. It had about an inch-and-a-half of free-play. The outboard ailerons on the 727 are locked out when the flaps are retracted. Jim looked at the flaps and noted that they were up. He checked the left outboard aileron; it wouldn't budge. It was locked out. He called over a mechanic who agreed with him that there should not have been any free-play. Upon closer inspection, they discovered that a bolt on the aileron-to-actuator had fractured. The fractured bolt and aileron free-play was added to the list of damaged items. Its importance to the investigation would grow over time.

The biggest clue as to what might have caused TWA 841 to enter into an uncontrollable rollover and dive was the missing #7 slat. But there were other clues that called for further investigation. For example, why did the right landing gear over extend but not the left? What was the significance of the free-play in the right outboard aileron? And what role, if any, did the failure of the lower rudder yaw damper play? Piecing together the clues from the damaged aircraft was going to be a daunting task. In most accidents, investigators start with the wreckage and the debris field and work backwards from there. What was the pitch angle of the aircraft when it hit the ground? Was the wreckage confined to a

Figure 25 N840TW on the tarmac at Detroit

small area, or was the debris field spread out over a large area, indicating a possible in-flight breakup? There was no wreckage with TWA 841. But somewhere in Michigan there was a debris field.

The search for that debris field and the missing parts from TWA 841 began a little less than two weeks after the incident. Notices appeared in the local Michigan newspapers, and radio spots aired on local radio stations. "Want Help in Finding Pieces of Jetliner," was one such headline. "Of primary interest to the Federal Aviation Administration and the National Transportation Safety Board is a six-foot aluminum slat that came off the right wing of the plane."

One half of the missing slat would turn up a few days after the notices were released. Farmer Vern Deshano came across a piece of the missing slat while working the fields on his farm, located about eight miles north of the Tri-City Airport in Saginaw, Michigan. He and his father had been spraying a fence line with weed killer when he saw a large piece of honeycomb material. Vern didn't know anything about the near-fatal crash or the search for missing parts, but he was certain that the foreign object he had found had come from a plane. The field was just a few miles from the Saginaw airport. Planes were always passing overhead as they made their way to and from the airport.[1]

Vern took the piece of metal back to the barn, where he learned about the plane that had nearly crashed and the search for missing parts. Vern called the local paper and then placed a call to the Tri-City airport. Accident investigators from the NTSB arrived a few days later with metal detectors and searched the nearby fields for additional parts.[2] Several other missing parts, including the second half of the number seven slat, were found spread out in a debris field about the size of a football field. Investigators took pictures and mapped the debris field for further analysis. The parts found in Vern Deshano's field were analyzed by the NTSB for several weeks, after which they were placed in a six-by-four wooden box and shipped to Boeing.

During the repairs of the incident aircraft, investigators tested both the normal and alternate flap system for any malfunctions. The flaps and slats performed normally, as did the indication system. These tests were performed with the #7 leading edge slat still missing, as it had not yet been replaced.

Had anyone anticipated the controversy that would surround the investigation, the plane would have remained in the hangar in Detroit, untouched, except by investigators looking for clues. No one had the foresight to suggest that perhaps it would be prudent to preserve the aircraft for further investigation and testing. It could be argued that TWA, ALPA, and the NTSB investigators made a mistake by not insisting that the aircraft remain available for future testing until a definite cause of the upset could be determined, even if that meant that the plane might be out of service for an indefinite period of time. The safety implications justified such a course of action. This was a near-fatal airline accident that occurred during one of the safest phases of flight—cruise. Statistics have shown that airline fatalities that occur during cruise account for only eight percent of all fatal accidents, with takeoffs and landings accounting for the highest percentage of fatalities. Only the descent phase has shown a lower percentage of fatal accidents, at four percent.[3]

Ironically, had the plane crashed in Vern Deshano's farm field in Auburn, Michigan, the bits and pieces would have been taken to a hangar, rearranged, and placed where each part was located on the plane, and then examined with a fine-tooth comb. In this instance, they had a mostly intact aircraft. Few accident investigations are so lucky. But any opportunity to preserve that valuable evidence was lost as soon as mechanics began repairs. The landing gear and gear doors were replaced. Both yaw dampers and both rudder actuators were replaced. The damaged electrical boxes in both gear wells that contained the connections for the gear safe indicators, as well as operation of the CVR erase function, were repaired without any testing to see whether the erase function was even operable.

The missing number seven slat was not repaired in Detroit. Instead, the hydraulic lines were capped off. The goal was to get the plane repaired to the point where it could be ferried to the TWA maintenance facility in Kansas City, Missouri, for more extensive repairs. The preliminary repairs were completed just twelve days after the upset.

Had the aircraft been the scene of a crime, these actions would have been equivalent to destroying evidence. But no one from ALPA or the NTSB objected. As a result, evidence that would have been extremely helpful to investigators was replaced, repaired, and/or destroyed.

As TWA worked to repair the damaged 727, the interested parties to the investigation met at Boeing's headquarters in Seattle, Washington, to conduct simulator tests. Accident investigations involving aircraft make use of the party system, whereas the NTSB investigation team is aided by a group of interested parties such as the aircraft manufacturer, the airline, and union personnel representing pilots and mechanics. It is often argued that the party system is flawed because each individual group is influenced by its own self-interests. The union representatives want to protect the pilots. The aircraft manufacturer wants to protect its reputation as well as safeguard itself from lawsuits or costly maintenance fixes. The flip side to that argument is that each interested party has expertise that they bring to an investigation and can assist the Board in making their overall safety recommendations.

Since a 727-100 simulator was not available, Boeing programmed a 727-200 simulator to match as closely as possible the conditions present when the upset with 841 began. Additionally, investigators hoped to duplicate the flight data recorder (FDR) traces by hooking up an FDR similar to that found on 841. By this time, investigators had zeroed in on the number seven slat as the most likely cause of the rollover and dive. Pilots flying the simulator were briefed beforehand that the number seven slat would be extended in isolation.

In the first dozen or so simulator tests, pilots were able to easily regain control of the aircraft with little or no altitude loss. Taking into account that the simulator pilots knew in advance that the slat was going to be extended, tests were run involving different combinations of control inputs and pilot response time. In some instances, pilots delayed taking corrective action until the plane was nearly inverted. In other tests, pilots used excessive corrective control inputs of the ailerons and or rudders. The goal was to find a set of circumstances that would lead to loss of control and also match the FDR traces from TWA 841.

In the instances where pilots were able to get the aircraft into an uncontrolled dive, they were able to regain control when the number seven leading edge slat was retracted, simulating its departure from the aircraft.[4] This would seem to bolster the theory that the slat had caused the accident. Slat comes out and the aircraft rolls out of control; slat breaks off and control is regained. However, in some of the tests where the plane was allowed to continue into a vertical dive, pilots were able to recover when the gear was extended and the number seven slat remained extended. This outcome raised the question as to what exactly it was that saved the plane from crashing. The gear coming out and changing the center of gravity and the aerodynamics of the dive? The slat breaking away from the plane? Or was it a combination of the two?

In none of the simulator trials were the investigators able to duplicate the FDR traces from 841. This was not totally unexpected. Simulators have a limited range of motion. Attempts to duplicate a complex maneuver such as a 360-degree roll and spiral dive at more than 40,000 feet per minute were unlikely to provide meaningful results. Still, investigators hoped to at least duplicate the traces at the onset of the upset.

Over the course of several days, with pilots from each interested party participating, 118 simulator tests took place. None of the simulator trials were able to accurately duplicate the TWA 841 FDR traces. There were two simulator tests that led to a loss of control and also had some correlation to the 841 FDR traces. In one instance, the pilots had to delay taking corrective action for 16.5 seconds. Interestingly, if the delay was sixteen seconds, control was regained with only a 6,000-foot altitude loss. In the second test that produced a correlation to the 841 FDR traces, the pilots delayed action for twelve seconds and then disconnected the autopilot and rapidly applied left aileron and full left rudder until the plane had rolled 285 degrees to the left, which was about 45 degrees past inverted. This was followed by a loss of altitude and an uncontrollable roll back to the right. The plane continued to roll to the right, despite full left aileron and full left rudder, until the slat was retracted and the pilot regained control.

In both instances the pilots did not react in a manner that any pilot would be expected to react in a similar situation. In the first test, the crew would have had to sit idle for 16.5 seconds as the plane entered an un-commanded roll of about 117 degrees to the right. In the second instance, the crew would have had to over-control with a bank to the left to the point of going inverted.

When the logic of what was being proposed was questioned, NTSB investigators offered what they felt was a plausible explanation. The two men at the controls were experienced pilots and unlikely to let an aircraft reach such extreme attitudes without some corrective action. So they decided that both pilots must have experienced spatial disorientation. They based this on the fact that it was night time and there was no defined horizon. The captain also stated that just before the upset he had been going through his chart bag, which the investigators saw as another opportunity for him to become spatially disoriented. Of the two scenarios, they thought it unlikely that the crew would allow the plane to bank to the right for nearly seventeen seconds without taking corrective action. They even took the extra step of phoning Hoot to ask him directly how long he had waited before taking corrective action. TWA accident investigator Gene York made the phone call.

Hoot's response was that it couldn't have been more than ten seconds. Based on Hoot's response and the unlikeliness that any pilot would delay taking corrective action for more than 16.5 seconds, the investigators zeroed in on the second scenario, involving a bank to the right followed by an over-correction to the left. They did this despite Hoot's sworn testimony and his comments made during the phone call that there were no banks to the left. Additionally, the investigators never questioned any of the flight attendants or passengers as to whether or not any of them remembered a bank to the right followed by a bank to the left that put the aircraft inverted and then an abrupt turn back to the right.

Another problem with the simulator tests was that the simulator used in the tests was a Boeing 727-200 and not a 727-100. The fuselage on the 727-200 was twenty feet longer than the 727-100, giving it different performance characteristics in roll and yaw from the shorter 727-100.[5] Additionally, the simulator tests did not consider what effect the free-float in the right outboard aileron might have had on lateral control.

Unsatisfied with their initial FDR test results, investigators conducted heading gyro tests in an effort to determine the effects of pitch and roll angles on gyro performance. Using the data collected from the two simulator tests that most closely correlated with the FDR traces from flight 841, they mounted the heading gyro from the 841 aircraft onto a movable platform and then tried to duplicate the maneuvers from the two simulator tests. The results showed no correlation to the 841 FDR traces and only a slight correlation to the FDR traces from the roll-reversal simulator test.

The truth of the matter was that the FDR data was of limited value. The foil data recorders found on aircraft like the 727 were not designed to handle a maneuver as radical as what had occurred on TWA 841. Additionally, the FDR on TWA 841 was fourteen years old. The combination of a radical maneuver involving yawing and sideslip, inverted flight, a spiral dive, instrument errors, gimbal errors, and worn-out mechanisms resulted in a jumbled mess that even the experts had difficulty sorting out. One example involved the heading trace, which showed a movement backwards in time. Not even the manufacturer of the recorder could explain this anomaly.[6]

The flight data recorder on TWA 841 recorded to foil just four parameters: heading, altitude, airspeed, and g-loads (also referred to as vertical acceleration). Today's aircraft are equipped with digital flight data recorders that record many more parameters such as pitch attitude, engine settings, and flight control positioning. Recorders on fly-by-wire aircraft can record hundreds of parameters. Most people following aircraft accidents today are accustomed to seeing exact computer reenactments of a flight's final moments. These reenactments are made possible by taking information from the digital flight data recorder (DFDR) data. This wasn't the case in 1979. So it isn't hard to see why the investigators found it so difficult to duplicate the FDR traces from 841.

———— •○• ————

On May 12, 1979, the newly repaired N840TW was towed from the maintenance hangar in Kansas City, Missouri. Waiting to meet the aircraft were TWA captain George Andre and Boeing flight test engineer Lou Wallick, The two men, along with a TWA flight engineer, were scheduled to take the aircraft up for a test flight.

The three pilots were well aware of the history of the aircraft. They knew that this wasn't going to be a standard checkout. Boeing's taking the step of sending one of their top test pilots was more than enough proof of that supposition. Lou Wallick was one of the original test pilots during the Boeing 727 certification flights. He flew the very first flight of the Boeing 727. He was the acting director of flight testing. A former naval aviator with some 3,000 hours in the Boeing 727, most of which were accumulated in flight testing, Lou Wallick was perhaps the most qualified 727 pilot on the planet.[7]

Andre and Wallick started the test flight as they would with any aircraft coming out of a major overhaul. They performed a slow-speed evaluation and a high-speed evaluation; they checked the stall warning systems, landing gear operation, flight controls, and use of the alternate flap system. They performed the various flight tests at both low and high altitudes.

Suspecting that the number seven slat was involved in the TWA 841 upset, Captain Andre and Wallick extended and retracted the slats several times. During one of their tests, one involving the alternate flap system, the number seven leading edge slat failed to retract. The airplane immediately rolled to the right. Andre had to apply approximately 25 degrees of opposite control wheel deflection to keep the plane level. This happened at an altitude of 15,000 feet and a speed of 235 knots. Once they regained control, Andre realized that he had exceeded the speed for slat extension and retraction. When he slowed to below 230 knots and cycled the flaps/slats again, the number seven slat retracted normally.

The scare, however, made the three pilots even more cautious for their next test, which involved extending flaps and slats at cruise speed at flight level 390. After leveling at 39,000 feet, Andre selected flaps to two degrees. As the leading edge devices extended, the aircraft began to buffet severely. Andre would later describe the buffeting as "startling."

When they were back on the ground, Andre wrote up several minor problems he thought should be addressed before the plane could be returned to service. The maintenance squawks were cleared, and Andre flew another test flight three days later. The second test flight was uneventful. TWA, however, wasn't ready to release the plane back into service. They wanted to put a few more flights on the books before putting paying passengers in the back. The plane was scheduled for several training flights before it was finally released for passenger service.[8]

George Andre would recount his experiences with aircraft N840TW four years later while being deposed for a civil suit filed by one of the TWA 841 passengers. At that deposition, Andre offered his own opinion about TWA 841. He testified that he did not believe that the crew had intentionally extended the flaps or slats and that it was his opinion that there had to be a mechanical malfunction to cause the slat to extend. He also posed a theory that, up to this point, had not been debated, at least not in any official capacity. Andre surmised, based on his own experience and the results of the many simulator tests indicating that the aircraft was easily controllable with the number seven slat extended in isolation, that the slat must have extended in a skewed position. He explained that if the slat were skewed, as opposed to a normal extension, this deviation would account for the deceleration shown on the FDR traces and the loss of control. He also stated that he had seen a telegram from a Boeing engineer just two days after the incident indicating that lateral control was dependent on whether the slat was in the normal or skewed position, which Andre inferred meant that control might be lost if the slat were skewed.

It was a theory held by others in the investigation, but it was also a theory that would have been difficult to prove. Boeing did consider the possibility that perhaps the slat over-extended in such a way as to allow more of the slat surface to be perpendicular to the relative wind, like a hand stuck out of a moving vehicle and held palm down. Their analysis, using wind tunnel data, showed that the additional drag caused by this worst-case scenario did not reach the level of drag indicated on TWA 841.[9] Additionally, even if the slat had been extended in a skewed or over-extended position, something still had to cause the slat to extend.

Chapter Twelve

The Boeing Scenario

I*n addition to the simulator tests,* NTSB and ALPA investigators pored over maintenance and safety reports looking for past instances of leading-edge slat problems on Boeing 727 aircraft. ALPA's investigation revealed that since 1974 there had been more than 400 service-difficulty reports concerning mechanical problems with 727 slats. The defects included broken bolts, broken mounting devices, and inoperative actuators. ALPA investigators found reports of a number of cases involving a single leading-edge slat extension and separation. What the reports didn't say was whether or not these extensions of a single-leading edge slat were scheduled or unscheduled, meaning positive command input vs. un-commanded extension.

ALPA investigators did uncover one instance in 1976 of a reported unscheduled slat extension. The slat extended as a result of a broken slat actuator support fitting. The aircraft in question was equipped with a different slat actuator than the one found on TWA 841, but the ALPA investigators considered it proof that a slat could extend due to mechanical failure. There was another case in 1978 that involved the unintended extension of leading edge devices at an altitude of 25,000 feet and a speed of 350 knots. In this instance, the captain felt a vibration that he attributed to a partially extended trailing edge flap. In his attempt to retract the flap using the alternate flap system, the leading edge slats were unintentionally extended. The captain immediately attempted to retract the leading edge slats, but the number six and number seven slats on the right wing remained extended, causing the aircraft to roll to the right. Considerable aileron and rudder input were necessary to keep the plane level. Once the plane slowed, the slats retracted, and the plane landed without incident.[1]

The data showed that, at the very least, it was possible to have a single leading-edge slat extend either as a result of a problem with the slat actuator, the locking mechanism, or a failure during the retraction phase. Boeing had even conducted flight and wind tunnel tests in 1975 to determine the effects of asymmetric extension of wing leading-edge slats. The tests were conducted because of reported slat actuator locking failures.[2] Furthermore, the tests were conducted to evaluate control characteristics associated with an unscheduled extension of a single leading-edge slat. The tests revealed that leading edge slats number two and number seven caused the most adverse roll characteristics but was controllable when a significant amount of lateral control was applied. The flight tests were conducted at a speed of .80 mach and up to an altitude of 35,000 feet.[3]

The wind tunnel tests that preceded the flight test had shown that the rolling moment of an isolated slat at high speeds was severe and could lead to loss of lateral control. Test pilot Lou Wallick was certainly aware of that data when he began the test flight. The list of test conditions for the test flight included climbing to 39,000 feet and then accelerating to a cruise speed of mach .90. Wallick, however, made the decision to cut the flight test short after experiencing extreme buffeting during the high-speed test at 35,000 feet. Test director, Mahan, who was onboard the flight, later wrote in his report that the pilots elected to quit further testing due to "extreme cowardice."[4]

In none of the cases involving a single slat extension did the aircraft become uncontrollable. Wind tunnel tests revealed that the aircraft became uncontrollable only when the angle of attack and airspeed reached a specific threshold. In the case of TWA 841, it was determined that the aircraft would become uncontrollable at an angle of attack greater than 6 degrees and a speed greater than .83 mach.

Despite the lack of supporting evidence from their initial testing, the NTSB investigators felt confident in moving forward with their theory that the entire episode was caused by the number seven slat being extended in isolation. They next turned to Boeing for answers as to what might have caused the slat to extend.

Boeing's response was that in order for a single slat to extend on its own, multiple failures of the slat actuator system were required. There were two methods for keeping the slats in the retracted position: a mechanical lock and 3000 PSI of hydraulic pressure. For any unintentional extension there would have to be a failure of the locking mechanism as well as loss of hydraulic pressure. Additionally, aerodynamic loads on the slats help hold them in the retracted position. There was another possibility that involved a broken or separated piston rod from the slat actuator or a fractured piston. The physical inspection of what was left of the slat actuator after the incident could not conclusively rule out that possibility. The damage to the slat actuator also precluded the investigators from categorically ruling out a failure of the locking ring. Portions of the locking ring were missing. Additionally, the part of the locking ring they did have indicated a lack of wear, which may have indicated that it was not working properly.

Since the crew didn't report any problems with the system A hydraulics prior to the incident, and there were no indications of un-commanded slat movement, mechanical failure was ruled out, leaving crew manipulation as the most likely cause of the incident, according to Boeing. The

Boeing investigators did state that they considered two other possibilities that could have caused the upset: yaw damper failure or an autopilot failure. They indicated that both of these were ruled out through flight simulator tests and that the tests showed no correlation with the TWA 841 FDR traces.

Boeing engineers proposed three different scenarios in which physical manipulation of the controls could cause a single slat extension. The most obvious one was moving the flap handle. When the flap handle is moved to the two degrees position, slats 2 and 3 on the left wing and slats 6 and 7 on the right wing also extend. In this scenario, someone on the flight deck accidentally catches the flap handle on their sleeve or some other article of clothing that then causes the flaps to extend. Upon noticing this, the crew would quickly retract the flaps, but the number seven slat would remain extended because of a misalignment. This scenario was ruled out as highly unlikely. The flap handle rests in a detente. Moving it requires that it first be raised and then moved aft. If it was so easy to accidentally extend the flaps and slats by catching the flap handle on an article of clothing, then it would be happening all the time.

The next scenario involved the alternate flap system. First the crew would turn on the alternate flap switch on the overhead panel; then they would move a toggle switch for the slats to the down position. Once that was accomplished, all of the leading edge slats would extend randomly over a period of about twenty seconds. This scenario was ruled out because investigators could not think of any reason why the crew would try such a procedure at 39,000 feet during cruise.

A third scenario was proposed that involved a complex set of moves by the crew. In this scenario, the crew moves the alternate flap arming switch on the overhead panel to the "on" position. Next they pull the leading edge control valves circuit breaker on the bulkhead near the

Figure 26 The Flight Engineer panel. The circuit breaker panel is to the right of this image.

flight engineer's station to disarm the system. The next step is to move the alternate arming switch back to "off." At that point, the leading edge slats are isolated from the hydraulic system, and the flaps can be selected to two degrees without the slats extending, which they would do in normal operation. The stated goal of this procedure was to improve performance by reducing the angle of attack. If someone were then to push in the pulled circuit breaker, slats 2, 3, 6, and 7 would then extend. At that point one of the two pilots, noticing this sudden change in configuration, would retract the flaps and slats, but the number seven slat remains extended because of the misalignment.

It's not entirely clear who came up with this theory. There is evidence that NTSB investigator John Ferguson, the Operations Group Chairman, came up with the theory very early on in the investigation. David Noland, a writer for *Aviation Consumer* magazine, gave a deposition in the civil suit indicating that he had heard about the procedure from several airline captains he had interviewed. Kampschror also gave a deposition in the civil suit indicating that he had used the procedure himself while flying the F84F single-engine military aircraft. A more likely source of this scenario, however, is Boeing. Most of the Boeing employees assigned to the TWA 841 investigation were engineers and not pilots. The procedure for isolating flaps and slats is a Boeing maintenance procedure.[5]

Regardless of who came up with the theory, it made sense to the NTSB investigators. They had evidence they believed indicated that the incident happened within close proximity to the flight engineer leaving and returning to the cockpit. They based this on the written statement from passenger Holly Wicker as well as supposedly from the captain himself in the statement he gave to the two FAA inspectors the night of the upset. They were also certain that the crew had intentionally erased the cockpit voice recorder to destroy incriminating evidence. It was the most plausible theory in their minds, and they would spend the better part of the next two years trying to prove it.

Hoot was on a trip flying as an L-1011 captain when he first heard about the flight engineer, circuit breaker scenario being proposed by Boeing and the NTSB. "Who in their right mind would even attempt something like that on a passenger flight at flight level 390?" Hoot asked Jim McIntyre, who told him about the proposed theory. Hoot didn't think anyone would take the scenario seriously. Jim McIntyre didn't share Hoot's skepticism.

In late September 1979, Boeing submitted their report on the incident to the NTSB. The report included the following statements:

> From the Boeing Company's review of the physical evidence supplied, its knowledge of the 727-100 characteristics, and information supplied by the NTSB, a likely sequence of events occurring on the TWA Flight N840TW was as follows:
> A positive system command was initiated within the slat extension system that extended leading edge slats.

A positive system command was initiated to retract the leading edge slats.

The rolling moment caused by the asymmetry of the extended #7 slat was not appropriately controlled by the flight crew, although it was within the capability of the airplane to do so at normal speeds.

The report also included a summary portion that laid out the scenario implicating the crew. From that point on, it became known as the Boeing Scenario. The report was written by Boeing engineer Robert Davis, who had been assigned the task of writing the report in June of 1979 after having been recently promoted to the position of technical adviser. Davis was not a pilot; he was unfamiliar with the flight controls of the Boeing 727, and he was not aware of the testimony of the flight crew.[6] At a technical review held in Washington on October 31, 1979, TWA and ALPA both objected to the summary portion, claiming that it contained conclusions that were erroneous, misleading, and inappropriate. Boeing subsequently requested that the summary portion be removed from the report. That never happened, and the summary section remains in the public docket.

On October 15, 1979, *Aviation Consumer* magazine ran an article written by David Noland on the TWA 841 incident. In the article, the magazine lays out the Boeing Scenario, which the author claimed came directly from interviews with Leslie Kampschror. "Did the Captain's 'fooling around' cause that TWA 727 to roll over and dive from 39,000 feet last spring? (Captain "Hoot" Gibson managed to recover the airplane from the terrifying dive in the nick of time and make a safe landing.) . . . According to the NTSB's chief investigator on the accident, L. D. Kampschror, there is no evidence of any mechanical malfunction.

'. . . Boeing tells us it's impossible for the slats to pop out because of aerodynamic loads . . .'"[7]

Figure 27 Flaps two degrees and no slats

Noland then goes on to explain the Boeing Scenario, adding that "there has long been an 'unofficial procedure' among some 727 pilots." Quotes by Kampschror and the other unnamed source were soon picked up and reprinted by other media outlets. The cat was now out of the bag. The TWA 841 rollover, spiral dive, and near-fatal crash was caused by the crew fooling around in the cockpit. No one in the media took the extra steps to find someone, anyone, who could say that they knew a 727 pilot who had ever used the procedure outlined in the article. No reporter mentioned that this was Hoot's first trip as a 727 captain in more than eighteen months, and that it was highly unlikely that any professional pilot would attempt such a procedure under those circumstances. Nor did any reporters mention that there is a written procedure for dealing with popped circuit breakers, and pushing them in without doing further investigation would have been against the airline's written policy.

Kampschror wasn't happy when the article came out. He called writer David Noland to criticize him on what Kampschror claimed was a mischaracterization of what he had said. David Noland hadn't recorded the interview, but he stood by what he wrote.

When Jim McIntyre first read the article, he fired off a letter to NTSB chairman James King asking that Kampschror be removed from the investigation, claiming that Kampschror was biased. The tension between McIntyre and Kampschror became so heated that Kampschror himself asked to be removed.[8] Both requests were denied.

It was at this point that the harmonious relationship between the interested parties fractured. Boeing and the NTSB concentrated their efforts on crew manipulation as the initiator of the slat extension, while TWA and ALPA shifted their focus to trying to prove that the slat had extended due to a mechanical failure.

Accident investigations are not supposed to work this way. While all of the parties shared information, the interaction between the TWA and ALPA investigators and Investigator-in-Charge Leslie Kampschror was strained.

Neither group spent much time questioning the crew. The NTSB and Boeing determined that the crew could not be trusted. Other than the sworn testimony the crew gave in depositional hearings; the crew was never questioned in a less-formal setting. And while Jim McIntyre and Harold Marthinsen kept in contact with Hoot, the TWA and ALPA investigators decided that they didn't need to question the crew about the upset, either. Everyone was convinced that the entire incident was caused by the unexplained extension of the number seven leading-edge slat. What more could be gained by talking to the crew? Hoot claims that he was told to not make any noise. "If you want our help," his ALPA advisers told him, "then let us handle this." This lack of crew involvement would later prove to be one of the major failings in the investigation. By not questioning the crew more thoroughly, important details and clues that might have led investigators on an entirely different track were missed.

The splintering of investigative groups weakened each group's ability to conduct a thorough investigation. Both ALPA and the NTSB had limited resources. ALPA, for example, did not have the ability to conduct engineering and aerodynamic testing to validate their theory that the slat extension was the result of a fractured piston on the slat actuator. They couldn't even get their hands on an actual Ronson actuator to examine it. Instead, they were forced to rely solely on engineering diagrams of the actuator. Additionally, the TWA/ALPA investigators were pilot volunteers still working full time for the airline. The NTSB, for all intents and purposes, had handed the entire investigation over to Boeing. It was their aircraft, and they had the expertise and financial ability to conduct whatever testing the investigators required. TWA was willing to do only whatever testing their maintenance and engineering staff were already equipped to perform.

While the Boeing and NTSB theory that the crew extended the leading edge slats through positive control input explained the extension, the theory did not match any of the testing done to date, nor did it match the crew's sworn testimony. The ALPA theory of a cracked piston had its own set of problems. For one, they could not find a single case of a cracked piston in the service history of the Ronson actuator. Ronson, the manufacturer of the piston, claimed that it was extremely remote for such a crack to occur because of a design limit of 3,784 pounds per square inch, which represented a 3,200 percent safety margin.[9] Additionally, in order for the slat to extend due to a cracked piston, the crack had to occur near the base of the piston, near the locking keys, which would allow the slat to extend. Once the slat was extended as a result of the cracked piston, the ALPA investigators had to explain how the damaged slat would have been able to withstand the high g-loads and not separate until later in the dive. They also had to explain how the system A hydraulics could maintain pressure with a cracked piston. System A hydraulic pressure was required to extend the landing gear, which was extended by the crew late in the dive. These were not easy problems to explain away, and they had no way of proving anything. Furthermore, they were not in a position to do testing independent from the investigation. Despite their reservations, they had to work with the NTSB.

In fairness to Mr. Kampschror and the NTSB, when ALPA presented their hypothesis that the slat may have extended as a result of a cracked piston near the locking keys, Kampschror asked Boeing to run tests to determine if the claims were valid. Boeing ran a series of tests that ultimately resulted in the conclusion that it was highly unlikely for a crack to develop with a piston, but even if it did, it would not result in the extension of the slat, according to Boeing.

The investigative groups made no attempts to explain some of the other unanswered questions about the upset, such as what caused the yaw damper failure, and what role did it play in the upset? What caused the plane to want to bank to the left after the recovery? Why did the right landing gear over-extend but not the left? And what was the significance in the free-play found in the right outboard aileron?

For their part, TWA and ALPA investigators did agree to investigate the validity of the Boeing Scenario. They contacted their counterparts from other airlines asking if they had ever heard of or knew of any flight crews using such a procedure. They asked fellow pilots. No one came forward. One could argue that the reason they couldn't find any pilot willing to admit to having knowledge of the procedure was because it was an unauthorized procedure. A pilot claiming to have done this procedure would also be admitting that he had exceeded the limitations of the aircraft and could face possible disciplinary action, including termination. In order to avoid this conflict, investigators indicated through various channels that pilots could come forward anonymously. Union leaders were asked to solicit input from members who might know something about the procedure. TWA instructors and management pilots were instructed to ask around to see what they could find. They were told to offer immunity to any pilot who came forward. Not one pilot from any airline claimed to have knowledge of the procedure known as the Boeing Scenario.

Chapter Thirteen

Libel

When *various news outlets learned* of the leaked story about the Boeing Scenario and the accusations that the pilots had been "fooling around" in the cockpit, things got much worse for Hoot. He was constantly reminded that he had taken on the role of villain. Hoot learned that some of his former flight students had torn out the pages in their logbooks that had Hoot's signature. Hearing stories like that hurt.

One of Hoot's favorite pastimes was to hang out at the local airport and talk to the young pilots just starting out in their careers. But when he went to the airport after the incident, he saw those same young pilots turn away from him. He heard them whispering behind his back. Hoot felt embarrassed and ashamed and stopped going altogether.

Hoot's notoriety extended beyond the aviation community. On a number of occasions, someone would stop him in a grocery store or clothing store and say something along the lines of, "Aren't you that pilot that's been in the news?" When Hoot would say that he was, they would usually smirk and walk off. Friends and neighbors asked Hoot if he had been suspended or if he was still working as a pilot, assuming that he had been penalized or terminated due to the accusations. It reached the point where Hoot would routinely shop out of town while on trips just to avoid having to go to the local stores in Las Vegas. Few people would make a comment directly to his face, but when he did overhear a negative comment, Hoot would confront the person and try to set the record straight. Most people didn't want to hear Hoot's side of the story. They had already made up their minds based on the news reports.

When a TWA L-1011 captain was fired, word spread that Gary Banks had finally confessed to pushing in the circuit breaker and Hoot had been terminated. As it happened, Hoot was flying as captain on the L-1011 at the time and the captain who was fired lived in Las Vegas. Some ill-informed pilot took what few facts he knew and drew an incorrect conclusion, which then became the source of the rumor. The rumor of Hoot's termination was picked up by a few reporters who then called TWA for confirmation.

"'Hoot' Gibson of plunging jet fame is still in the saddle," was the title of one newspaper article that ran after the reporter discovered that the termination story was false.[1] Unfortunately, similar to the reaction of those hearing the numerous other false stories surrounding this incident, many people still believed that the crew had been terminated.

Hoot learned through ALPA that a ground instructor at Eastern Airlines was relating to pilots attending recurrent training everything the NTSB was alleging about the upset. That Hoot had caused the upset. That Hoot had then tried to cover up his actions by erasing the CVR. Hoot briefly considered filing a lawsuit against Eastern Airlines. Fortunately, Hoot had some allies at Eastern. One pilot sympathetic to Hoot's plight went to the Vice President of Flight Operations at Eastern and complained about the instructor. The subject was soon dropped from further recurrent classes.[2]

The condemnation of the crew wasn't a topic restricted to pilots. Other airline employees were just as quick to denounce the crew and

TWA over the alleged misconduct. They spread the unfounded rumors at every opportunity. One example of this came out during the deposition of Timothy Wicker, the husband of TWA 841 passenger Holly Wicker. Timothy was a co-plaintiff in the civil trial against Boeing and TWA. The deposition was held a little more than one year after the upset and before the NTSB had completed their investigation. The attorney representing TWA, Donald Chance Mark, asked Mr. Wicker what information he had on the incident other than what he had been told by his wife Holly or read in the newspapers.

"I have spoken to several people in the airline industry in general," Timothy Wicker said, "not with any point to specifically finding out the base cause of the accident. But just to find out what they heard about it."

". . . Can you tell me generally what you have learned in talking with people in the airline industry?"

"The general consensus of the people I spoke with was that the cause of the accident was not related to a problem with the aircraft itself but rather with the crew."

After some follow-up questions, Timothy Wicker expanded on his earlier answer. "I have had people tell me that the crew screwed up. Yes, I have had people tell me that the crew was fooling around trying some different things and these actions, which were presented to me as irresponsibility, caused the accident."[3]

The idea that the incident had been caused by crew misconduct had become so prevalent that aeronautical universities began describing the Boeing Scenario to students. Hoot feared that his reputation was tarnished beyond repair.

Unlike Gary and Scott, Hoot didn't have a family to turn to during this difficult period. His brother and sister lived thousands of miles away, as did his mother. He desperately wanted to tell his side of the story, so he vented to a neighborhood boy who was staying with him at the time while the boy's parents went through an ugly divorce. He had been divorced from Sandy for less than a year and hadn't seen her since the divorce, but he called her and invited her out to dinner. Sandy was still working as a flight attendant for TWA. Hoot didn't know what rumors she had heard. He wanted Sandy to hear it straight from him that he hadn't done anything to cause the upset. Sandy told him that he needn't worry. She knew that he would never do anything that might be considered unsafe.[4]

One rumor circulating was that TWA had granted the crew immunity for revealing the truth about the incident and that the crew had admitted to having performed the Boeing Scenario. This rumor caught the attention of the Justice Department, which looked into the possibility of charging the crew with perjury.

Everywhere he turned, it seemed as if someone was out to harm him in some way. Hoot didn't know whom he could trust. He began to feel as if his every move was being monitored. He felt certain that he was being followed. He didn't know who or why, but he reached the point where he would enter a building through one door and exit through another. Was it paranoia? Perhaps. Then again, some members of the press had already resorted to chicanery in an attempt to entrap the crew.

In an effort to put an end to the vicious rumors circulating about his alleged misconduct, Hoot volunteered to take a lie detector test, truth serum test, and even undergo hypnosis. But no one took him up on his offer.[5]

Those who knew Hoot and the other two crew members personally never doubted them. Others, even some of the TWA and ALPA investigators, weren't totally convinced. They had read through the reports and agreed that it was highly unlikely that a slat could extend on its own. Discussions over whether the crew did or did not act in some way to cause the incident were a common occurrence behind closed doors.

One TWA investigator, Gene York, who knew all three crew members and had talked to them at length about the incident, purchased a voice stress analyzer at a spy shop in downtown Manhattan. He paid for the $8,500 device with his own money. His motivation was to prove that the crew was telling the truth.

When he brought the voice stress analyzer to one of the ALPA investigative meetings, he was told rather bluntly to "get that thing out of here." They wanted no part of it. Their reluctance may have been an indication of some lingering doubt, or it could have been simply that any information that might have been derived from such a device couldn't be used in any official capacity in the investigation.

All of the rumors circulating during this period painted the crew in a negative light. There were no rumors about the plane malfunctioning. One story that spread quickly was that Hoot had committed suicide. Hoot even received a call from TWA wanting to make sure that he was still alive.

At work and while in the public eye, Hoot put up a brave face. Behind closed doors, however, was another matter. He would often sit alone in a dark room, his eyes welling up, wondering when and if it was all going to end.

When Hoot expressed his frustration with the investigation to Jim McIntyre and shared how the false accusations were affecting him, Jim proposed a novel idea. He suggested that Hoot file a lawsuit against the NTSB for libel. Jim had his own misgivings about the direction the investigation had taken. He had already requested that Kampschror be removed. He believed the accusations of crew involvement to be unfounded.

Hoot gave the idea some thought. He asked friends for their opinion. The more he thought about how the NTSB had excluded him from the investigation, the angrier he became. He called Jim McIntyre and asked him if he could recommend a lawyer. Jim gave him the name of attorney Landon Dowdey. Landon had worked with ALPA on a number of certificate action cases against pilots.

Hoot contacted Landon Dowdey and gave him a $5,000 retainer in early November of 1979. They discussed the merits of the case and what parties should be included in any possible lawsuit. Hoot gave Landon a quick rundown on how he had been vilified in the press. Landon's list of possible defendants included Boeing, the NTSB, the FAA, NBC, the *National Enquirer*, and Leslie Kampschror. It was the start of a long relationship between Hoot and Landon Dowdey.

Chapter Fourteen

Preliminary Findings

B*efore a cause or probable cause of an accident* is determined, the NTSB investigators present their findings to
a five-member NTSB Board. The Board members are political appointees
who serve five-year terms. The Board votes on whether or not to accept
the investigators' findings and recommendations. The presentation of
the findings is given in an open forum according to the guidelines of the
Sunshine Act[1], thus the meetings are often referred to as Sunshine meetings.

On Thursday, January 17, 1980, the NTSB investigators met in
Washington, D.C., with the five NTSB Board members for the first
Sunshine meeting. The purpose of the meeting was to discuss the investigation to date as well as to expand on a preliminary report concerning
the incident. In attendance was nearly everyone associated with the
investigation. The meeting began with Leslie Kampschror explaining
that the investigators had been confronted with a number of rumors and
that as part of their investigation they felt obligated to investigate them.
The first rumor they discussed was the fight in the cockpit. Kampschror
admitted that they had heard the story third or fourth hand and that
after checking out some of the details they determined that the rumor
had no credence. He added, almost as an afterthought, that they also
had the sworn testimony of the crew that no such fight had occurred.

The second supposed rumor concerned the Boeing Scenario. Kampschror had this to say on the subject: "Quite a number of Boeing 727 captains have contacted us and passed this rumor [on] to us. In our questioning of them, they said that they had never indulged in this practice, and they do not know if anybody had or would even advocate such a practice. Theoretically there could be some improvement of the aircraft performance if this is done. Boeing engineers believe that there would not be any significant improvement in aircraft performance. However, it is possible to do this. You can set up the system to extend trailing edge [flaps] independently of movement of leading edge devices. The flight crew testimony indicates that they had not been involved in any such activity."[2]

Here Kampschror is admitting to the Board that not only have they not found anyone to admit to having performed this procedure but also that even the Boeing engineers were saying there wouldn't be any performance improvement if the procedure was performed.

Next Kampschror brought up the rumor of the flight engineer leaving the cockpit and returning just prior to the upset. He started out by indicating there was a conflict in the flight engineer's sworn statement and the signed statement provided by one of the two FAA inspectors who had interviewed Hoot the evening of the incident. He then tried to dismiss the rumor as not being relevant because everyone was in agreement that the flight engineer was in the cockpit when the incident occurred.

Board member Francis McAdams wasn't having any of that. He questioned Kampschror about the discrepancy. "In your presentation, I don't know whether you said the absence of the flight engineer from the cockpit was a rumor. As I understand it, it wasn't a rumor, it was a signed statement by an FAA inspector that the flight engineer had left the cockpit just previous to the incident—or, he returned to the cockpit just previous to the incident, according to a statement given to the FAA by Captain Gibson. My question is, when you received the statement from the FAA, did you go back to Captain Gibson and refresh his memory in some way, and say, 'We do have this statement from the FAA, and it indicates the flight engineer was absent from the cockpit'?"[3]

Here McAdams is asking a common-sense question. Kampschror responded by indicating that he had not gone directly to the captain but instead had asked the ALPA representatives to look into the matter. When their response came back that Captain Gibson didn't recall making such a statement, Kampschror decided that going directly to the captain would result in a "stalemate."

"Well, you don't know that until you ask the questions," McAdams fired back. "When the flight engineer was confronted with the statement from the FAA inspector about what Captain Gibson said, he may have said, 'Yes, as a matter of fact, I did leave the cockpit, take the trays back to the galley.' And then he may have been asked. 'What did you do when you got back to the cockpit?' and 'How soon after your return to the cockpit did this incident start?' and questions of that sort. So I think there seems to be a slight gap in what we know at this time, until it's tied down."[4]

The arguments between Kampschror and several of the Board members continued over the relevance of the flight engineer's absence and the credibility of the crew. "We felt at that point that the physical aerodynamic evidence was the best evidence," Kampschror stated. "To get into and try to resolve issues of credibility at that point would, in the end, perhaps prove very little."

McAdams pressed for more. "It seems to me that we have already established the credibility of the crew; we have already done that. Now, here, we have another issue, and we still don't know what happened in the cockpit, and we don't know what actions the crew took and we say that. So, I feel there is a gap with respect to this particular issue. I don't know how the other Board members feel about it, but that's the way I feel about it."

Board member Patricia Goldman added her thoughts to the discussion. "Well, when you say it has no relevance to what happened, one of the scenarios that we explored would be the scenario which required some action while he was out of the cockpit, wouldn't it?"

James Danaher, the Deputy for Operations of the Accident Investigation Division, spoke on behalf of the investigators. "If I could add a few more remarks, it should be borne in mind that this statement by the captain, given to the FAA inspector, was—the context in which it was given and manner should be kept in mind. First of all, it was an interview of the crewman by an inspector, or, two inspectors, who then went out and wrote a summary of it. It is not time-correlated with any measure of precision, more say—more so than to say that, some time, prior to the occurrence, the flight engineer left, reportedly, to take trays back to the galley. And it was believed that the context in which that was given had no real relevance to activities that subsequently occurred in the cockpit and to the aircraft."

"Well, it is time-related," said McAdams. "I think, because according to the statement, it says the second officer had just returned to the cockpit after taking the trays back to the galley. 'The aircraft started a slow rolling.' And it seems to me he's saying, as the flight engineer returned to the cockpit, the incident started.

"Whether or not it has anything to do with the accident, we don't know, but it could because there is a scenario that perhaps the flight engineer did do something upon his return to the cockpit which may have caused the upset. And it seems to me it would be a very simple thing to find out and put this thing to rest, find out whether he was out of the cockpit and what he did when he returned to the cockpit."[5]

The arguing over who said what regarding the flight engineer's absence from the cockpit continued until Board member Patricia Goldman stated the obvious. "Well, there are other people who were potential witnesses who might be questioned as to that potential conflict."

"Did the flight attendants give any testimony with respect to this?" McAdams asked the staff. "Do we have any signed statements from the flight attendants or from passengers?"[6]

Kampschror responded by saying that he did not have any sworn testimony from the flight attendants regarding this specific issue. The failure to question the flight attendants or the passengers concerning this important topic raised some serious concerns. There are only two possible reasons for such an oversight, neither of which reflects favorably on Kampschror. One, Kampschror simply never considered it. The second reason is he considered it but decided that the answers he might receive could derail his theory of the upset. If Kampschror had sworn testimony from the flight attendants and passengers stating that the flight engineer never left the cockpit, then the NTSB's theory of the incident would be shot down. But if he did nothing and left it as an open conflict between the crew's testimony and that of the FAA inspector's, he could always fall back on the crew's questionable credibility.

As much as Kampschror didn't want to get into a discussion about the pros and cons of the scenario they were trying to pin on the crew, McAdams continued to question him on the theory. "I'm a little confused. This is not actually a rumor. This is what could have happened, as I understand it, if you wanted to extend the flaps for some reason or if you only wanted to extend two degrees, the slats or two degrees, the flaps. You could get the 2, 3, 6, and 7 slats out, the two degrees of flaps.

"Now, this is not a rumor. This is one of the ways, as I understand it, that this accident could have happened. And because of previous damage to the number 7 slat and because of air load, when the 2, 3, 6, and 7 slats were extended the 7 slat did not come back in. So this is not a rumor, this is one way that this accident could have happened."

James Danaher responded to McAdams's comments. "As a point of clarification and, perhaps, amplification, to put things in perspective, this rumor, so to speak, didn't come to the investigation staff as a bolt out of the blue or sudden revelation. The cracking of trailing edge flaps, in a circumstance where the airplane may not quite be performing as it's supposed to in the book, and perhaps it's because of the loading of the aircraft—or some other combination of circumstances—pilots, for years have experimented with cracking a little bit of trailing edge flaps to get the aircraft, quote 'on the step,' to optimize performance. This is a trick or technique that pilots have used for years.

"This, in the present context, gets—it has intuitive appeal because it provides a potential motivation for crew behavior, that is, possible extension of these flaps or leading edge slats which had an undesired result. And it provides a convenient and appealing basis for explaining a hypothetical behavior. At the risk of being obvious, that's the context that this information should be considered in because, normally, if one thinks why would a crew be manipulating controls when they are at cruise, in an established state, en route, quite a distance from their ultimate top of the letdown—as I say, this has the appeal in that it provides some basis for a scenario."

After defending the scenario and then stating that it was common practice in the industry, Danaher added the following, "But our exploration of it, by questioning the crew and informal discussions with other 727 pilots, did not gain any acknowledgment that this practice is, indeed, engaged in with any regularity or significant frequency at all."[7]

Danaher's testimony, which was full of contradictions, summed up the investigation to date. The investigators were convinced that the crew had done something to cause the accident, but they couldn't prove it. They had come to that conclusion, despite sworn testimony to the contrary and their own testing, because they assumed that the captain had deliberately erased the CVR. So they became selective on what they accepted as being truthful and what they considered deceptive. If they found a statement from Hoot that fit their theory, like Hoot's statement that he was putting charts away, they adopted it. If he said something that was contrary, as in there were no turns to the left, they ignored it or tried to explain it away.

Of the five NTSB Board members present, the one who seemed to have the most difficulty with what the investigators were saying with regards to the crew's actions was Francis McAdams. McAdams was the only pilot on the Board. He had been with the NTSB since its inception in 1967. Before that he had been an aviation safety inspector for the CAB. He wasn't about to sign off on something that didn't make sense.

Figure 28 NTSB Board member Francis McAdams

As the discussion continued concerning the theory that the plane banked right and then violently back to the left as the captain over-controlled it, McAdams once again pointed out the incredulity of their theory. "Well, it would seem to me to be very difficult for three crew members, with a great deal of experience, if, in fact, this aircraft did roll to the left, which I think we now have established. And it rolled past the inverted position to the left . . . I don't believe any crew member would not realize that. Now, maybe, one crew member might be spatially disoriented, but would all three be spatially disoriented to the extent they wouldn't recognize this rapid roll to the left, rolling in seven seconds to the inverted position?"[8]

Kampschror replied by saying that it was just one of several theories. Later in the meeting, during a discussion concerning the recovery from the upset, Chairman King made a comment that would seem, at best, insensitive. The brief exchange began with Richard Tobiason, the Chairman of the Performance Group, stating that the crew most likely would not have been able to recover from the dive had the slat not failed.

"And you are telling us that, in this particular case if the slat hadn't failed the chances of its recovery then become marginal, at best?" King asked Tobiason.

"Yes, sir."

"And certainly random?"

"That is correct."

"And for our purposes, we would have recovered probably all the instrumentation and had an easier case to work with, which is, indeed unfortunate. It would have made a very big hole in the ground."[9]

Here Chairman King is insinuating that their job would have been a whole lot easier had the plane crashed—the presumption being that the CVR would have been recovered, with all of its incriminating evidence.

The discussion then turned to the NTSB conclusion and how it was to be worded in the final report. Kampschror once again outlined the facts of the case: Mechanical failure had been ruled out, including a mechanical failure resulting in the inadvertent extension of a leading edge slat, a mechanical failure of the yaw damper, or a mechanical failure of the autopilot roll mode, the latter two having been ruled out through testing and an inability to get a satisfactory correlation with the FDR readout. That left open several scenarios involving intentional or accidental manipulation of the controls, and after looking at all the various methods that might lead to a single slat extension, their conclusion was that the accident had to have been caused by "flight crew action."

By now everyone seemed to be in agreement with this conclusion, including Board member Francis McAdams, who earlier had seemed to reject much of what was said. "I think it's set forth fairly clearly in the report as now written. The only problem I have is that I think the most probable cause, then, is the extension of the slats due to flight crew action. All we are adjured to find is the most probable cause. And I think, based on what I have heard in this room this morning, the most probable cause is the extension of the slats due to flight crew action. And I think that is said very clearly in the report itself. And I think that is probably what happened. And I think that that is what we should conclude."[10]

There was further discussion on the nuances of how this section of the report should be worded. Then chairman King chimed in with what could be considered their CYA language. "I think what we said is, since the weighing of the evidence involves a rejection of the possibility of an unscheduled extension of the number 7 slat, the Safety Board believes the following comments are appropriate: We believe the flight crew's erasure of the Flight 841 CVR is a fact we cannot ignore."[11]

Here chairman King is stating, as fact, that the crew had erased the CVR. He, and everyone present, completely ignored the sworn testimony Hoot gave stating that he did not remember erasing the CVR, and that he wasn't even thinking about the CVR once they were on the ground. He also ignored the testimony of the other two crew members stating that they did not erase the tape nor did they see anyone else erase the tape. At no point during this meeting was there a discussion concerning the possibility that perhaps there was another explanation for part of the CVR being blank, such as an improperly working CVR.

Shortly after making the comment about the flight crew's erasure of the CVR, Chairman King tried to backtrack and come up with less-incriminating wording, indicating that in no other accident had the crew's credibility been questioned. "Now, I don't think, ordinarily in accident cases we go into credibility. I don't think we ever have before, although here, in this case, with the amount of physical evidence that we have, it would appear that the flight crew did not recollect all of the things that happened in the cockpit."[12]

This response would seem to indicate that the NTSB had sufficient evidence to point to crew involvement. In truth, they had no proof that the crew had done anything improper at any time.

In an effort to defend the Board's conclusions regarding the CVR erasure, Board member McAdams recounted a story he believed to be factual. "As I understand it—and I may be wrong, but I thought there had been published reports that the captain had said to a reporter, I believe, that he had deliberately erased the CVR in fear of FAA enforcement action."[13]

Kampschror dispelled that rumor by indicating that the captain had stated that he had been misquoted. But it demonstrated the tunnel vision the investigators and the NTSB Board members had with regard to the supposed CVR erasure. The mindset that the crew was trying to cover something up tainted the investigation from the moment the claim first began to circulate.

For the next two hours they debated over the exact wording to be used in the final report. They still had to account for the discrepancy between the crew's statements and their findings. It was like listening to a roomful of lawyers tasked with writing a product disclaimer. "Our weighing of the evidence" . . . or how about, "Ultimately, our weighing of the evidence" . . . no, wait, try, "because of the absence of information from the CVR, the Board has accorded more weight to the physical evidence than to the flight crew's testimony." Strike that. How about, "Not having information from the CVR to put into balance, we believe the probative value of the physical evidence outweighs that of the flight crew's statements." It went on like this for nearly an hour before they decided to take a break.

After the break, the discussion on how to phrase the final report continued, but now they were trying to iron out the exact wording to be used in describing their probable cause findings. And once again Board member Francis McAdams had trouble following the logic of their findings. "So, the question is, what do we use in this case? Do we use the testimony of the crew? Do we use the simulator runs? Do we use the FDR? Do we use only one of them or a combination . . . ? And it's not clear to me what we are using for evidence to say that this man misused the flight controls. It just doesn't jump out at me."

"Well, we could probably use some other word," Tobiason answered, "because 'misuse' probably has some implication that someone is trained and therefore knows what to expect and what to do. Maybe there is a better word for that. But there are two scenarios: one fits the recorder and known flight test data; one best fits the captain's description of only rolls to the right but does not match his estimate of how long it took or the length of the delay it took to initiate corrective action. It would be hard to believe that you would wait 17 or more seconds to control something like this, if you had any understanding of what you're doing."[14]

Richard Tobiason was the Chairman of the Performance Group. He was the person most directly involved in trying to determine what had caused the upset and then what had occurred during the recovery. Richard Tobiason flew several of the simulator runs. He was the one who had requested that Hoot be questioned as to how long he had delayed before taking corrective action. His comments demonstrate the difficulty they were having in trying to piece together the sequence of events based on the conflicting evidence from the crew's statements, the FDR traces, and the simulator runs.

"Let's put it this way, Tobiason explained. "If you recognize a problem at 30 degrees or 40 degrees, you can get that airplane back wings level without any problem at all, and you don't use more than half the available control wheel motion anyhow. If you diagnose it properly, there wouldn't be any problem at all."[15]

Board member McAdams was now again on the fence. And once again he brought up the conflicts regarding the flight engineer leaving or not leaving the cockpit. "Well, we do have one issue, the issue of the difference between the crew's statement and the FAA inspector's statement. Now, what are we going to do about that?"

McAdam's comment started another argument over whether or not it was necessary to clarify that conflict. This led to a curious statement from James Danaher. "If I can speak for the staff, I believe that the conclusion as—was that, regardless of how he reacted to that, that it wouldn't lead to a sudden discovery and recollection of things that he failed to recall before."[16]

Danaher's comment only reinforced the notion that the investigators had decided on their theory of what had happened and having the crew dispute that theory wasn't going to be helpful to them, especially since they had already deemed the crew as untrustworthy.

McAdams wasn't buying the argument, and neither was Board member Admiral Patrick Bursley. He, too, wanted the conflict resolved by re-deposing the flight crew. After some further debate, Kampschror agreed to hold another deposition concerning the flight engineer's absence from the cockpit. They then argued about who else besides the flight crew should be deposed. The flight attendants? The FAA inspectors? It was during this line of questioning that McAdams brought up another glaring omission from the investigation. "While we're at it, talking to the flight attendants, we ought to find out what their reaction was to this whole maneuver. Did they feel a buffet? Did they have any idea what the airplane was doing? The flight attendants are pretty well trained during their training as to what airplanes do. I think they get primary aerodynamics and that type of thing. They might have some information that might be helpful."[17]

McAdams was stating the obvious. How could the investigators not have already questioned the flight attendants and passengers concerning what they felt or didn't feel before and after the incident? The only statements from the flight attendants concerning the emergency were written statements submitted to TWA a few days after the incident, which were then handed over to the NTSB.[18] There is no evidence that anyone from the NTSB spoke directly to any of the four flight attendants.

The question by McAdams piqued the interest of Vice Chairman Elwood Driver. "I would just like to follow up on this. You are going with the second officer then to ask him if he was out of the cockpit or in the cockpit, are you not? You are going to go deeper than just that one question?"[19]

Chairman King tried to downplay the need for additional depositions in a meandering, nonsensical statement. "I think the one thing that should be clearly understood by everyone present is that this going back to discussion is merely to be certain that our own investigation is complete. We traditionally open and close doors. So, what we are doing is opening and closing a door that the Board is not satisfied has been satisfactorily opened and closed. It is not to suggest that there are any divine revelations upon any of the door openings or closings. It is merely to close out a complete investigation. So, I don't think there should be anything implied by what we are doing. It is not intended to be so. There are some inconsistencies, and we would like to do follow-up questions."[20]

Figure 29 NTSB Chairman James King

The comment seemed to be aimed at the spectators in attendance. McAdams, however, wasn't swayed by King's reasoning. "Well, another thing that may be of some benefit to this so-called—we're going to take depositions. This case did not go to hearing. Witnesses weren't called in, normal types of witnesses that we would call in a hearing. And I think that's one of the difficulties with this case right now, the fact that we probably should have had a hearing. Any time there is controversy involved between flight crew statements and the physical evidence, I think one of the best ways to resolve that is through the medium of a public hearing."[21]

ALPA had been requesting that a public hearing be held long before this meeting, but that information wasn't brought forward. Instead, Kampschror tried to defend his decision of not holding a public hearing. "Just one further thing for the record," Kampschror began. "Again, the best evidence in this case, in my estimation, is the physical aerodynamic evidence to refute the flight crew's testimony. And that's what we have attempted to rely on in the report exclusively."[22]

This was followed by the most profound statement made by anyone the entire day. It was given by the one person on the Board willing to challenge the report as written—Francis McAdams. "You see, Mr. Chairman, we have a case here where if we were going to act on it today, we would be citing the crew as the cause of the accident. And the crew has not had the opportunity to examine the witnesses who get up and support the physical evidence. They have not had that opportunity.

"Now maybe they will have it as a result of this meeting today. So I think going back for two depositions will serve a double purpose, a very beneficial purpose. And it might solve the problem that we have been wrestling with all day."

"Which problem have we been wrestling with?" King asked.

"The problem of what happened," said McAdams.

"I'm sorry," King replied. "I had had several problems that I'd been working on. All right. Is there further discussion on the report?"[23]

Any hopes that the TWA and ALPA investigators may have had for an opportunity to challenge the NTSB's theory of the accident in a formal setting were quashed. There would be another deposition of the flight crew and the flight attendants, but Kampschror would set in advance guidelines that the only question to be resolved at the depositions was whether or not the flight engineer had left the cockpit.

Chapter Fifteen

Where Was the Flight Engineer?

A s *the date neared for the depositions* on the question of
the flight engineer's whereabouts prior to the upset,
Hoot made an appointment to see a psychologist. He had several reasons
for making the visit. For one, Landon Dowdey was moving forward
on the possible libel suit, and well-intentioned friends and fellow pilots
were advising him that he needed to have documented evidence that he
had suffered as a result of the false accusations made by Boeing and the
NTSB. As it stood, they argued, Hoot hadn't experienced any fallout
from the investigation. Not only hadn't he been fired, but he had been
promoted. Hoot needed to show that the false accusations had caused
him harm. The truth was that Hoot really did need to talk to someone
about what he was experiencing. He hadn't received any psychiatric
counseling after the incident. He was plagued with anxiety and had
trouble sleeping. There is also a high probability that Hoot, along with
Scott and Gary, were suffering from post-traumatic stress disorder
(PTSD). Hoot took the advice and scheduled an appointment with a
local doctor in Las Vegas.

Hoot saw Dr. Eva Von Rheinswald several times in the weeks preced-
ing the second deposition. Two days before the depositions, on January 27,
1980, Hoot asked Dr. Rheinswald to hypnotize him. Hoot was hoping

that he might be able to remember more details about the upset under hypnosis. He especially wanted to be asked whether or not Gary Banks had ever left the cockpit. Hoot was certain that Gary had never stepped out of the cockpit at any time, but he was willing to do whatever he could to determine if he might remember things differently under hypnosis.

As it turned out, no new details emerged from the hypnosis. But one thing that did result from Hoot's visit with Dr. Rheinswald was the recommendation for follow-up visits. Hoot started seeing the doctor on a regular basis. He also agreed to see a psychiatrist who worked for the AOPA (Aircraft Owners and Pilots Association). The combined visits provided Hoot the psychological and psychiatric counseling he desperately needed. He paid for the visits out of pocket. The less TWA knew about the counseling, the better, was Hoot's thought.

The depositions to decide if Gary Banks had left the cockpit and returned just prior to the upset were taken in Kansas City, Missouri, just twelve days following the first Sunshine meeting. NTSB Board member Francis H. McAdams, who was the driving force for having the depositions, did not attend. Instead, he issued a statement directed at NTSB Chairman King:

> As I have repeatedly stated, in view of the fact that not only the credibility and professionalism of the crew but also the airworthiness of the B-727 are an issue in this proceeding, the crew should be given the opportunity to comment upon all of the evidence on which the Board will ultimately base its final determination of cause. The crew has never been afforded this opportunity . . . It is obvious that the crew's knowledge of the facts of the accident is the best evidence unless there is other evidence that overwhelmingly controverts that of the crew. This is not the instant case, since the crew's knowledge has not been

tested against the physical evidence. In this respect, the evidence we now have, without supporting or controverting testimony of the crew, is in large part circumstantial and based on speculation.[1]

Despite McAdams's efforts to broaden the scope of the depositions, he was overruled by Chairman James B. King.[2] To ensure there was no confusion as to the scope of the depositions to be taken that day, NTSB Chairman Martin Speiser began with the following statement: "The scope of the deposition proceedings will be limited to testimony concerning the movement of the flight crew from their assigned positions in the cockpit during this flight."[3]

The first person deposed was FAA inspector Ronald Montgomery. He was one of the two FAA inspectors to interview Hoot at 1:00 a.m. the evening of the incident. Montgomery testified that neither he nor FAA inspector Roger Gordon took notes. Montgomery worked for the FAA as an air carrier safety inspector. His primary duties at the FAA centered on airworthiness issues. He was not a pilot.

John Ferguson, a member of the NTSB investigative team, began the questioning of Montgomery. After the standard preliminary questions related to Montgomery's background and employment history, Ferguson broached the subject at hand. "Now referring to your typed statement, the second paragraph and it's . . . about 10 lines down, the sentence begins, 'The second officer had just returned to the cockpit after taking trays back to the galley.' Do you see that?"

"Okay."

"Is this a direct quote or a paraphrase of what the Captain said?"

"Nothing there is a direct quote. It's all a summary of what I heard. That statement is the gist of what he said in our presence, the two of us, as I heard it."[4]

Montgomery told Ferguson that he had made a handwritten summary of their interview late the next day. A typewritten summary was prepared by Montgomery's secretary the following day.

Next on the witness stand was Roger Gordon, the second FAA inspector present at the interview with Hoot the night of the incident. Like Montgomery, Gordon was an airworthiness inspector and not a pilot. Gordon had also prepared a handwritten report that was later transcribed by a secretary the next day. His report, as it related to the flight engineer's activities prior to the upset, was slightly different from Montgomery's. In his report, Gordon stated that the captain had said that the meal trays had been removed from the cockpit but didn't indicate how they were removed.[5]

Later during questioning it became clear that the two FAA inspectors wrote their reports independently of each other and neither was privy to the contents of the other.

Unable to clear up the conflicting statements by the two FAA inspectors, Roger Gordon was excused and lead flight attendant Mark Moscicki was called to the stand. Mark had been working in first class. He explained that it was his practice to start at the back of first class with the meal service and work his way forward, at which point, after completing the first-class meal service, he would then offer meals to the flight crew.

Mark testified that there were only six passengers in first class on the flight and that he had finished the first-class meal service rather quickly. He estimated that approximately forty-five minutes had elapsed from the time he served the flight crew until the upset occurred.

John Ferguson then asked Mark about the meal trays. "Did all the crew members eat together?"

"I don't recall."

"Did you pick up the trays from the cockpit after the crew was finished?"

"No, at that moment I don't know if I collected all three or not."

"Did you collect any?"

"I don't recall."

"Do you know if any of the cabin attendants picked up the trays?"

"No, they didn't. I know that some were brought back out by the flight engineer and delivered to me."

"And delivered to you, where? At the galley?"

"Not quite at the galley. He had started out, maybe was getting toward the rear of the first class cabin. I met him and took them away from him."[6]

So there it was. The speculation related to whether or not the flight engineer left the cockpit or didn't was now answered. Gary Banks left the cockpit long enough to walk back to the end of first class and hand the meal trays to Mark.

Kampschror and Ferguson must have been feeling fairly confident at that point. Their confidence wouldn't last long. Jim McIntyre indicated to Speiser that he had a few questions for the witness.

"Would you, if you could try, and I know it's difficult, would he have given you the trays at least, pick a figure and we can work from there, 30 minutes prior to the incident or 20 minutes, or what?" McIntyre asked Mark.

"I would say at least 30 because after that point there was time enough to finish cleaning up the entire aircraft; also time for me to sit down and feed my crew dinner, which I had finished a good five minutes before the incident happened."

Jim followed up with another important question related to the timing of events. "When the flight engineer came back, approximately

30 minutes prior, did he spend any time with you or did he just hand you the trays and return immediately to the cockpit?"

"He spent no time with us whatsoever. He handed me the trays and went back to the cockpit immediately and never came out again."

"You saw him reenter?"

"Yes, I did."

"O.K., you never saw him come back out?"

"Absolutely not."

"Did you feel or sense any climb on the part of the aircraft from the point at which you served the meals or he brought the trays back, prior to the onset of the accident?"

"No, none whatsoever."[7]

Jim McIntyre wasn't a lawyer, but in a few short minutes he proved that he certainly could have been. Not only was he able to slip in a question beyond the scope of the depositions (the question related to whether or not Mark had sensed the aircraft climb), but he also completely destroyed the NTSB's theory that the accident had been initiated when the flight engineer returned, saw the popped circuit breaker, and then pushed it back in.

Gary was out of the cockpit only long enough to walk about fifteen feet to the end of first class and then back to the cockpit. In that time, Hoot and Scott would have had to discuss the unauthorized procedure regarding the extension of the trailing edge flaps and then execute the procedure, including searching for and locating the right circuit breaker, all before Gary had made it back to the cockpit.

Jim also established that at least thirty minutes had transpired from the time Gary returned to the cockpit and the onset of the event, which was counter to the NTSB's theory that the onset occurred shortly after Gary's return.

Other witnesses were waiting to testify, most importantly Gary Banks, but before he could testify, there was testimony from Carlos Machado-Olverdo and Francine Schaulleur. The two flight attendants worked the flight along with Mark Moscicki and Carol Reams, who wasn't present at the depositions. Both flight attendants were working in the back of the plane. They corroborated much of what Mark had said concerning the timing of events. Both also testified that they were not told in advance the purpose of the depositions or what questions they might be asked.

Francine hadn't seen anyone leave the cockpit, but she did testify that she'd stepped inside the cockpit for a few minutes to eat her dessert. Carlos, who was born in Ecuador but had been living in the U.S. for the past fourteen years, didn't see anyone leave the cockpit either. He testified that after finishing the service in coach and then picking up trash, he headed to the front of the plane to eat his meal. He was sitting in the forward jump seat closest to the cockpit door when the upset began.

When the moment came for Gary Banks to put the matter to rest for good, he testified that he didn't believe that he had left the cockpit for any reason. But he also admitted that it wasn't unusual for him to step out to hand the trays to the flight attendant. He also had no recollection of flight attendant Francine Schaulleur's entering the cockpit to eat her dessert.[8]

Gary's inability to remember leaving the cockpit to hand the trays back to Mark lent credence to the idea that it was an insignificant event. Had it been more closely related in time to the upset, he might have connected the dots between the two events.

Flight attendant Mark Moscicki didn't know in advance the purpose of the depositions. He didn't hesitate when he testified that Gary had handed him the trays as Gary walked back to the galley. It was his honest recollection. Gary, on the other hand, couldn't recall details like Francine entering the cockpit.

Still, there were two more crew members who might be able to shed more light on the subject: Scott Kennedy and Hoot. Scott was next to take the stand. Shortly after Scott was sworn in, Jim McIntyre stood up and stated that Scott Kennedy had a prepared statement he wanted to read before testifying. Speiser wanted to see the contents of the statement before allowing it to be read into the record. After reviewing the prepared statement, he ruled that it was outside the scope of the deposition proceeding. Scott's wife Sandra was in attendance. She sat in the front row holding two-month-old Clinton Kennedy on her lap. When Speiser announced that the statement could not be read, she shook her head to show her displeasure. A woman sitting next to Sandra tapped her on the shoulder and silently admonished her.[9]

Scott, who had hoped to use the opportunity to deny the allegations of crew misconduct in a formal setting, was also displeased with the ruling. To him it was just another example of the NTSB's attempts to silence the crew, but he didn't protest and simply took his seat.

Scott wasn't able to provide anything helpful that might clear up the conflicting statements regarding the flight engineer's movements. He didn't remember anyone leaving the cockpit. He didn't remember anyone entering the cockpit. He couldn't remember if he had eaten his meal on that leg or not.

FAA attorney James Dillman, who had been present at Scott's original deposition back on April 12, accused Scott of colluding with the other crew members to alter their testimony. That prompted an objection by the ALPA attorney. Dillman's line of questioning was accusatory in nature. After repeated objections by McIntyre and the ALPA attorney, Dillman backed off, and Scott was excused.[10]

Hoot was the last to testify. Kampschror began the questioning. "Captain Gibson, do you recall any of the statements that you made on the 4th and 5th of April?"

"Yes, sir."

"Do you recall specifically any statement about the movement of the flight crew members to and from the cockpit just before the control problem began at 39,000 feet?"

"Not to and from the cockpit."

"What do you recall with relationship to the movement of flight crew members?"

"Pardon me; I said that the flight engineer just returned to his seat after sending the trays back."

"Do you recall specifically having related that to the FAA inspectors?"

"I don't recall a whole lot about that . . . interview. I recall that that was one of the things that I mentioned during the talk that I had with them, yes."

"Could you repeat that, please? That the flight engineer had sent the trays back?"

"Yes, I did mention that to him, yes."

"By sending the trays back, what does that mean?"

"Well, I don't know if he had left the cockpit or how he done it, but he handed the trays back or stepped out of the cockpit and handed them to the cabin attendant."[11]

Hoot stated that he was confused when he talked to the FAA inspectors and that he had given them incorrect information concerning the timing of events. But his overall impression was that there was no correlation between the flight engineer handing the trays back and the upset. The two events simply were not connected.[12]

Hoot would later tell friends that he had been anxiously awaiting the depositions. He wanted to know who it was that had started the rumor about the flight engineer leaving the cockpit. Hoot made the comment that he wanted to do "bodily harm" to that individual. So he was a little embarrassed to find out that it was his own comments given to the two FAA inspectors that in part led to the misunderstanding.

Gary Banks never confirmed or denied that he left the cockpit that night. He told Hoot on numerous occasions that he was certain that he did not. Part of Gary's reluctance to admit to having left the cockpit may have to do with the culture that existed at that time between the captain and other crew members. Cockpit crews today are taught crew resource management where crew members are treated more equally. There have been many accidents caused by first officers unwilling to challenge an autocratic captain. In 1979 you didn't leave the cockpit without asking for permission to do so from the captain. You didn't leave the cockpit without wearing your uniform jacket and hat. Doing so could be interpreted as a sign of disrespect. But even Hoot acknowledged that when he was a flight engineer he sometimes took meal trays back to the galley without checking with the captain first.

After the depositions on January 29, 1980, the NTSB never again referred to any scenario involving the flight engineer leaving and then returning and pushing in circuit breakers. The subject was dropped from all further reports.

Chapter Sixteen

Fabricating Evidence

Jim McIntyre's follow-up questions to flight attendant Mark Mosciki at the January 29, 1980 depositions put an end to the Boeing Scenario, but it didn't stop the NTSB from pursuing crew manipulation as the probable cause of the rollover and dive. The NTSB investigators were convinced that the incident began with positive command inputs from the crew that caused slats 2 and 3 on the left wing and slats 6 and 7 on the right wing to extend, and then positive command inputs to retract the slats but with the number 7 slat remaining extended due to a misalignment. But none of the evidence supported that theory. Simulator tests showed that a slat extended in isolation was an easily controllable condition. And the FDR trace comparisons they had between the TWA 841 FDR readout and the simulator and heading gyro tests didn't match. With their main theory disproved, they were forced to conduct additional testing. Their next series of tests involved hooking up a heading gyro and FDR to a tilt table in order to have a full range of motion on all three axes.

TWA and ALPA investigators participated in the tilt table tests. They also continued to attend technical review meetings with the NTSB and Boeing. Jim McIntyre and Harold Marthinsen kept up a steady stream of correspondence with Investigator-in-Charge Leslie Kampschror and

Boeing's lead engineer Prater Hogue. Their correspondence was professional and respectful, always using the salutation of "Mr. Kampschror" when referring to the lead NTSB investigator. In ALPA's private correspondence, however, they referred to Kampschror as Kamps, LDK, or simply K.

Several months passed with little activity other than the tilt table tests, which did not provide any meaningful results. TWA and ALPA investigators also made little progress on their theory of the incident, which involved a cracked piston in the slat actuator. After reviewing hundreds of service reports involving slat actuators, they couldn't find a single instance of a cracked piston in a Ronson slat actuator.

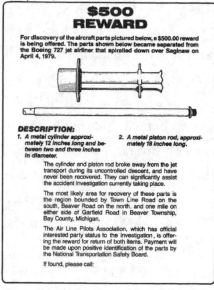

As fall approached and the investigation stalled, Jim McIntyre decided that the only way to prove that the incident was caused by a crack in the slat actuator piston was to locate the piston. He knew that the piston had to be out in a farm field close to where the other parts were found. He had the ALPA air safety team pay for newspaper ads asking for help in locating the missing slat actuator parts. He also had brochures printed offering a $500 reward to anyone finding "a metal cylinder

Figure 30 The brochure that was handed out in the search for the missing slat actuator parts

approximately twelve inches long and between two and three inches in diameter." The flyers contained a drawing of the cylinder and piston rod along with a contact number.

Jim and several volunteers drove to Auburn, Michigan, and went door to door near the area where the original parts were found, handing out the brochures and asking if anyone had come across any of the missing parts. Their efforts paid off when one farmer handed over a piece of metal he had found on his land, which turned out to be a piece of the right outboard aileron trim tab.[1] The part was sent to the NTSB in Washington, but it didn't provide any useful information. No additional parts turned up.[2]

With no new leads, Jim McIntyre suggested that the NTSB conduct a flight test. Jim argued that a flight test could provide an opportunity to compare FDR readouts at the onset of the upset under varying flight conditions. If the NTSB was adamant that all four slats came out, Jim argued, then let them put all four slats out to see what the FDR shows. If the acceleration traces matched, then the NTSB theory would have some merit. Kampschror agreed to conduct the flight test.

Agreeing to conduct a flight test is one thing; finding an aircraft and someone willing to pay the estimated $50,000 cost was another matter. ALPA didn't have an aircraft or the means to pay for one. The NTSB didn't have the funds. TWA declined, saying that they weren't in the test-flight business. That left Boeing as the entity to both pay for and supply the aircraft. Boeing had a 727-100 already set up as a test aircraft. It was a Boeing 727-100 equipped with the same type of FDR as found on 841. Test engineers also installed additional flight data recorders that recorded more parameters and with greater fidelity than the Lockheed FDR. These additional parameters included: aileron wheel position, roll angle, roll rate, aileron position, spoiler position, upper and lower rudder position, as well as several engine-performance parameters.

Since this was a flight test, no attempt was made to simulate the dive portion of the 841 flight. Instead, the focus was on trying to recreate the steps the Boeing engineers believed the crew performed that led to the upset and then to compare the FDR traces. The flight test was conducted on October 2, 1980 with Boeing test pilot Lou Wallick once again at the controls. FAA test pilot Earl Chester was the copilot.[3] Also onboard was an NTSB investigator by the name of Robert Von Husen. Von Husen had been hired in April of 1980 to replace Richard Tobiason, the former head of the Performance Group, and who had taken a job with NASA. Von Husen, who was not a pilot, was working his first accident investigation. He sat in the cockpit in one of the jump seats.

Investigator-in-Charge Dean Kampschror was present for the test flight. He sat in on the preflight briefing, but he elected to not take part in the actual test flight. Hoot was there also. He had flown to Seattle the previous day. He visited Boeing's headquarters and ended up having lunch with the President of Boeing. But when Hoot asked if he could ride along on the test flight, he was told that he could not. The excuse they gave him was that it was due to insurance reasons. Hoot offered to sign a waiver, but Boeing wouldn't budge. He was, however, allowed to be present for the preflight and post-flight briefings.

Hoot stood off to the side as the engineers gathered to discuss the test flight. He listened as they described the planned maneuvers. He wanted to jump in and tell them that they were wasting their time, but Jim McIntyre, who was also present, had warned him not to interfere. Still, Hoot couldn't believe that not one engineer had asked him a single question. The one person in the room who had actually experienced the upset and no one was interested in his input.

The test flight was to be known as E209. The first series of configuration changes were performed at a mid-altitude of 25,000 feet. The various configuration changes included the Boeing Scenario of trailing edge flaps to two degrees without any leading edge slats, two degrees of flaps with leading edge slats 2, 3, 6, and 7 extended, and flaps to five degrees with all leading edge devices extended. The same configuration changes were then performed at flight level 390 at a cruise speed of .8 mach.

Figure 31 Flaps two degrees with slats 2, 3, 6, and 7 extended

With the plane level at 39,000 feet, the pilots set up the Boeing Scenario of trailing edge flaps to two degrees and no slats. The airspeed bled off as soon as the flaps extended. Next they pushed in the circuit breaker and allowed spoilers 2, 3, 6, and 7 to extend. The aircraft began to buffet severely. The plane porpoised as the autopilot tried to maintain altitude. They repeated the maneuver with the autopilot off. The aircraft pitched up sharply when the slats extended, and the buffeting was just as severe as it was with the autopilot on.

When the plane landed, Hoot listened in as the engineers described the extreme buffeting they encountered when slats 2, 3, 6 and 7 were extended at 39,000 feet. One engineer described the buffeting as shocking and startling. Hoot heard them talking about the speed decay with flaps only, indicating a decrease in performance. This, of course, was counter to the claim that the crew had performed this procedure in an attempt to improve performance. It sounded to Hoot as though the flight test had disproved once and for all the Boeing Scenario. He was ecstatic.

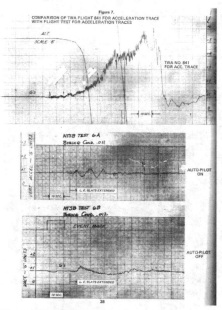

Figure 32 FDR acceleration trace comparison for TWA 841 and Boeing test flight e209 autopilot on and off

Kampschror and the other NTSB employees said little as the two FDRs were removed from the test plane. When they brought the recorders back to Washington, D.C., they were disappointed to learn that there were no similarities to the FDR readouts from TWA 841, especially the acceleration trace readout. Nothing matched up. Kampschror turned to Boeing for answers. Boeing responded by saying that they needed more time to analyze the data.

There was a lot riding on the FDR comparisons. The NTSB needed hard evidence to support their theory on the cause of the TWA 841 upset. No one was feeling more pressure to find similarities between the readouts than Robert Von Husen, the newest member of the investigation team. He had been given the task of writing the report comparing the FDR readouts from the test flight with the readouts from TWA 841. When Von Husen first looked at the preliminary report of the acceleration trace comparison prepared by FDR specialist Billy Hopper, he didn't see what he had hoped to see. He had been sitting in the cockpit when the pilots extended the flaps and slats at cruise. He had felt the buffeting. But the buffeting was not as accurately reproduced as he felt it should have been. Specifically, the frequency of the buffeting and the level of oscillation did not match those of 841. The acceleration trace for TWA 841 was high frequency and low amplitude. The acceleration trace from E209 was more spread out and at a much higher amplitude.

At a deposition Von Husen would give a year-and-a-half later in a civil suit filed by several of the TWA 841 passengers, Von Husen described his initial reaction to seeing Billy Hopper's FDR analysis of the October test flight. "When I was onboard the test flight at Boeing, I experienced the buffet levels. I also received from Boeing outputs of their flight test instrumentation. And the flight test instrumentation showed buffet of frequency . . . higher than what was shown on the flight data recorder as Mr. Hopper read it out. And the flight test instrumentation agreed more closely to what I thought I felt during that flight."[4]

In an effort to find some correlation between the flight test acceleration trace readouts and the accident aircraft's acceleration trace readouts, Von Husen came up with a new analysis technique. This technique involved making cellulose impressions of the foil traces and photographing the impressions under high (200 power) magnification. The photographs were then combined together and time and amplitude scales were calculated and drawn over the composite traces.[5] In this manner, Von Husen determined that the high frequency g-trace oscillations associated with airframe buffet on the flight test aircraft FDR and the accident aircraft FDR were identical at a frequency of 6 cycles/second and an amplitude of +/- 0.05g.

At the deposition Von Husen gave in the civil trial, TWA attorney Donald Chance Mark asked Von Husen about this new technique for reading the acceleration trace. "What precipitated the preparation of that document [addendum to the Performance Group Chairman's report]?"

"I was concerned that the readout that was made by the—the gentleman's name was Mr. Hopper that read out the flight data recorder for the accident aircraft as well as for the flight tests, may not contain all of the information that I desired from those flight data recorders because of possible limitations in the methodology that he was using to make the readouts."[6]

As a new employee with the NTSB, Von Husen wanted to make a favorable impression. Not only was he overwhelmed with trying to make sense of the new data, but he was also burdened with the task of reviewing his predecessor's work. A visual comparison between the two acceleration trace readouts showed no similarities. When viewed under a microscope, the usual method for examining FDR readouts, drawing a meaningful comparison was difficult because the microscope could view only very short-time segments. Those limitations are what led Von Husen to develop a completely new method for comparing FDR readouts. To add credibility to his new technique, Von Husen stated that when he examined the acceleration traces produced for other flight conditions such as when the throttles were reduced or when flight spoilers were applied, he found that they did not match the oscillations he noted when the flaps and partial slats were extended. Von Husen would detail his findings in an addendum to the Performance Group Chairman's report dated May 27, 1981.

Von Husen's addendum report also included Boeing's new analysis of the test flight data, which now showed a similarity between the test flight and TWA 841. Boeing claimed that the test flight aircraft had a different autopilot than the one used on TWA 841, which factored heavily into the test results. They also claimed that a test switch in one of the monitoring instruments had been left in the test (hold) position by maintenance personnel. When factoring in those two anomalies, their calculations showed that the acceleration traces would have matched more closely.[7]

The addendum report with Boeing's new analysis of the flight test landed on Jim McIntyre's desk just one month before the NTSB was scheduled to hold its final Sunshine meeting. Jim had no particular allegiance to ALPA or TWA. His primary goal was to see that the investigation was conducted honestly and fairly. He had worked tirelessly, along with Harold Marthinsen, to discover the truth. But when he reviewed the new technical documents submitted by Boeing, he responded by firing off a letter of protest to NTSB Chairman James King. In the letter he comes close to accusing both Boeing and the NTSB of fabricating evidence.[8]

> *The primary purpose of the flight test was to compare the FDR trace with that of the accident aircraft. The latest analysis of the autopilot by Boeing appears to throw into question the validity of the test flight results. Because the FDR traces were different, Boeing now wants to contend that this difference was due to (1) the failure of a flight test engineer to notice that a switch was in the wrong position and (2) a difference in autopilots—a factor not considered significant prior to the flight test. In fact, the report simply proves that the flight test did not meet the stated objective, i.e., "to obtain data which could be used for comparison with the accident Flight Data Recorder (FDR) and to assist in establishing the configuration changes that may have occurred on the accident airplane prior to loss of control."*
>
> *The original readouts of the acceleration traces from both the accident FDR and the flight test FDR indicated different acceleration frequencies, thus indicating a possible difference in configuration between the two. Because this contradicted the*

staff's preconceived ideas regarding the extension of all leading edge devices, a new method of readout was developed. The new readout method, according to the staff, now shows the same frequencies for the accident FDR and the flight test FDR.

Our own analysis will show that the results of the new readout merely render any conclusions regarding the acceleration trace frequency comparison as worthless.

Jim also addressed another development concerning a new passenger statement. The depositions of January 29, 1980 regarding the movements of flight engineer Gary Banks prior to the incident had indicated that Gary had indeed left the cockpit to hand the trays back to the flight attendant, but this had occurred at least thirty minutes prior to the upset, which put a big hole in the entire Boeing Scenario. The idea that there was a correlation between the flight engineer leaving and then returning to the cockpit came primarily from the written statement of passenger Holly Wicker taken on the day of the incident. She had stated that the incident occurred within minutes of the person whom she believed to be the flight engineer returning to the cockpit after handing the meal trays to a flight attendant. This was in direct contradiction to the testimony of Mark Moscicki. The NTSB, for some unexplained reason, had thrown away the only two written statements they had, including Holly's. In a deposition Holly gave for her civil trial against TWA and Boeing, Holly repeated her claim of seeing the flight engineer hand over the meal trays to the flight attendant and then return to the cockpit just prior to the upset. When Kampschror read the transcripts from the deposition, he contacted Holly Wicker and asked her to provide another written statement in which she repeated her claim concerning the flight engineer. Jim McIntyre was furious that Kampschror had requested the new statement.

This [new statement] appears to be a further blatant attempt to refute prior testimony, gained from sworn, sequestered witnesses, who were thoroughly cross-examined in public depositional proceedings conducted by the NTSB staff in Kansas City on January 29, 1980.

By contrast, this unsworn statement of [a] witness, a two year old recollection with no contextual reference, was apparently solicited from only one person who happens to be actively engaged in litigation against TWA. If, as ALPA stated, witness statements are pertinent to this investigation, why only this one with no opportunity to examine and cross-examine? Can it be a further example of the selective gathering of information to support a prior conclusion by the NTSB staff? We believe the Board members should thoroughly question the circumstances surrounding the inclusion of this witness statement in the "evidence."

Jim summed up the three-page letter with the following (the underlined phrases are repeated from the original letter):

It should be noted that we seem to have here, as in other parts of this investigation, difficult circumstances to explain. First, we have a conclusion based on multiple assumptions. That is, the oscillation was <u>most probably</u> caused by higher rate <u>and</u> the higher gain was <u>probably</u> caused by a test switch being left inadvertently in a test position and they <u>believe</u> the autopilot on the accident aircraft would not have allowed this oscillation. In fact, we do not know if any of the above are true because no test has been conducted on an aircraft with the same autopilot characteristics as the accident aircraft . . .

> *It is our belief, with respect to the autopilot, that any conclu-*
> *sion based upon the information supplied would be correct only by*
> *chance because of the multiple assumptions that have been made.*
> *What we seem to have is an attempt to show a correlation, based*
> *on assumptions, between flight test and simulator data and then*
> *somehow relate this to the accident data. We seriously question*
> *the validity of any such methodology.*

Von Husen's findings from his comparison of the acceleration traces between TWA 841 and the Boeing flight test would be challenged in testimony given in a civil trial as well as later petitions for reconsideration. Harold Marthinsen was asked about Von Husen's analysis in his testimony for the civil trial of passenger Holly Wicker. Harold Marthinsen was a no-nonsense individual who took a scientific approach to his work. He never let himself get caught up in opinions or speculation. When Boyd Ratchye, the lawyer representing Boeing, cross-examined Harold over his testimony on the FDR analysis, things didn't go well for Ratchye.[9]

"What criticism do you have of Mr. Von Husen's work on his comparison of the g-tracings of the Boeing flight test and TWA 841?" Ratchye asked Marthinsen.

"Well, I don't believe his conclusions are valid," Marthinsen replied.

"What criticism do you have of the methodology that he adopted?"

"I don't have any criticism of the methodology."

"Is it your opinion that there is no similarity in the buffet signature between TWA 841 and the buffet signature of the Boeing aircraft used in the flight test?"

"No, I would say there is similarity, but that similarity is only a function of a frequency response of a flight recorder."

"What does that mean for me, a layman?"

"Well, the flight recorder can only recall a certain level of frequency, and virtually anything that is put in the airstream on an airplane at that mach number and altitude is going to produce frequencies in excess of what the recorder can record."

"How do you know that?"

"Tests that were done by TWA."

Harold's testimony left the Boeing lawyer flustered and frustrated. He hadn't expected to hear such contradictory evidence. So he kept trying to undo the damage he inadvertently caused. "Is it your testimony, then, that the frequency of the buffet on the Boeing test flight was not identical to the frequency of the buffet on the TWA 841?"

"Well, we don't know what the actual frequency was. All we know is what the recorder recorded. And it recorded the limit—its limit."

Ratchye had a habit of asking the same question over and over again in an effort to get the response he wanted. Flabbergasted by Harold's contradictory testimony, Ratchye asked the question again using different phrasing. "Is it your testimony, then, as an engineer that the frequency of the buffet on the corrected tracing for acceleration on the Boeing flight test differs from the recorded frequency for the acceleration trace on TWA 841?"

"Well, let's back up and make sure—first of all, the Board made a readout of the flight test data and of the accident aircraft. It was those two readouts, the flight test readout and the accident readouts, that we compared. And we found that there [was] no similarity. The Board subsequently devised a new method—well, let me put it this way. After we submitted our report to the Board and showed them that there was no correlation, the Board then devised a new method of reading out flight recorders, a method which had never been used in the past. In fact, as far as I know, it is the only time that it has ever been used. And in that method, they determined that the frequency from the accident airplane was the same as the frequency from the flight test, where the No. 2, 3, 6 and 7 slats were deployed. And [what] I am telling you is that the frequency of the recorder is all they measured. They measured the limit of the recorder response, nothing more."[10]

By now the Boeing lawyer realized that he had dug himself into a hole. So he switched to a different topic—the comparison of the amplitudes of the acceleration traces. "Does your same line of reasoning apply to the NTSB's findings on the amplitude of the buffet?"

"Well, subsequent to our submittal to the Board, Boeing did some additional work in which they allege that there was a switch that was inadvertently in the wrong position. That was the cause of the large excursions of the g-trace."

"Do you accept that finding by Boeing?"

"I don't accept it. I still have a problem with [it]—I don't see any comparison between the accident g-trace and the flight test. The flight test still has a large G excursion, which is not consistent with the accident airplane."[11]

In another reference to the dissimilar acceleration traces between TWA 841 and the E209 test flight, Don Mark, the lawyer representing TWA in the civil trial, introduced a handwritten note referencing a phone call from Von Husen. Mark brought up the note during the videotaped deposition of Boeing engineer Jim Kerrigan, reading a portion of it for Kerrigan to comment on:

> Then the words appear, "present E209 data would not be convincing that all four slats extended at once. Any additional information Boeing can submit would be greatly appreciated."[12]

The handwritten note was dated April 13, 1981, nearly six months after the test flight. It clearly demonstrates that the NTSB knew they had a problem and that they were relying on Boeing to explain away the discrepancy.

Much of what the NTSB claimed to be the physical evidence, i.e., the flight data recorder readouts, would be challenged in later petitions for reconsideration. Here is what one author of a petition for reconsideration had to say concerning Von Husen's improvised analysis technique:

> A forensic test should, as a matter of common sense, satisfy three criteria: the underlying scientific theory must be considered valid by the scientific community; the technique itself must be known to be reliable; and the technique must be shown to have been properly applied in the particular case.[13]
>
> The Board's comparison of the normal acceleration traces (in the second paragraph on AAR page 13) did not meet the above criteria, and did not qualify as sound forensic technique. There is a limited frequency response of the acceleration channel of such flight data recorders. Thus, unrelated vibrations of unequal frequency beyond the response limit of the recorders would appear on recorder foils as the same vibration frequency.[14]

The ALPA petition further challenged several other assumptions made by both Boeing and the NTSB:

> The NTSB's comparison between recorded data from the flight test and recorded data from the accident aircraft proved inconclusive. In an effort to explain these weaknesses, the Board included false information in their report. The third paragraph

on page 13 of the NTSB report stated: It was determined that during the flight tests . . . a test switch . . . in the DADC . . . had been left in the test (HOLD) position.

The source document for that information was a letter (dated May 11, 1981, included in the NTSB docket) from Boeing's H.P. Hogue to NTSB's Kampschror. A close examination of that letter shows that the manufacturer never actually observed the switch in that HOLD position. Prior to the flight test, proper verification of configuration of crucial test components should have been planned by the test engineers. Normally, the test records would have included specific documentation of component configuration variables. However, the manufacturer presented no such documentation of the position of that DADC test switch for the October 1980 flight test.

During the flight test there proved to be a periodic, un-damped oscillation, of the FDR g-trace that developed after leading edge slats 2-3 and 6-7 extended. Such an oscillation was not seen on the FDR g-trace of the accident aircraft. The manufacturer was unable to explain this dissimilarity. Then in an effort to correlate this dissimilar result from the test, the manufacturer made an assumption about the configuration of the test aircraft. These were the actual words reported by the manufacturer to the NTSB: There can be little doubt that this switch was in the test position the day E209 [the Boeing test flight] was flown. The manufacturer's use of such an assumption in test analysis should have provoked the skepticism of the NTSB investigators. Suspicion should have prompted the Board to ask: What other variables were mismanaged during this one crucial test condition?

The disagreement with the acceleration trace analysis wasn't the only problem ALPA had with Von Husen's addendum report. In order to make a more compelling argument for the NTSB's theory, Von Husen knew he needed more data than what he was able to extract from the acceleration trace comparison. So he next zeroed in on the airspeed trace. His analysis showed that the speed decay occurring on the test aircraft after the plane was configured with flaps two degrees and the extension of slats 2, 3, 6 and 7 was very similar to the speed decay shown on the FDR for TWA 841 just prior to the upset. The speed decay from other configurations such as spoiler deployment, thrust reduction, and flaps to five degrees with all the slats extended had differing speed decays. To Von Husen and Kampschror, this was irrefutable proof that prior to the upset the plane had been configured with flaps at two degrees and slats 2, 3, 6 and 7 extended.

The ALPA investigators had a problem with this part of Von Husen's analysis as well, but they were given only a few weeks to comment on the findings before the second Sunshine meeting. They simply didn't have the requisite time to conduct a thorough analysis. Once again it would be testimony given in the civil trial that would challenge this part of Von Husen's work.

Here's what one TWA expert witness had to say on the subject when asked about it by TWA lawyer Donald Chance Mark. "You noted some differences between that airspeed trace and the Boeing airspeed trace?" Mark asked the witness.

"Yes, sir."

"And what were those differences?"

"Well, the differences were that in the 841 it was what I would refer to as a sinusoidal trace, that is, it had the very smooth deceleration very similar to a sine wave that was tilted as opposed to the Boeing test flight trace [which] was more of a constant. It had [a] similar appearance, sinusoidal appearance, but not quite as smooth as 841's."[15]

Harold Marthinsen also gave testimony on the airspeed trace analysis. Boeing Lawyer Boyd Ratchye brought up the subject. "Did the flight test measure speed decay in different configurations?" he asked Marthinsen.

"The airspeed was recorded for all the flight tests," Marthinsen answered.

"Well, that's a little different thing. Did the flight tests record speed decay on extension of the spoilers, upon extension of the four leading edge slats, and upon pulling back the throttles?"

"Well, as I say, the airspeed was measured for all of those flights. You could determine what that decrease in speed was, if you were so inclined."

"Mr. Marthinsen, wasn't the speed decay of the aircraft at cruise on the flight test aircraft, with the extension of the four leading edge slats, the identical speed decay measured in TWA 841 upon the onset of the incident?"

"I don't know that. I never made that determination. And again, I don't see the relevance of it."

"As an aerodynamicist, do you draw no conclusion from the comparison of the speed decay on TWA 841 at the onset to the speed decay with all four slats extended?"

"No."

"Why is that?"

"I have just told you several times. There are too many variables involved. (Here Marthinsen is referring to prior testimony.) There is not enough information from the flight recorder alone to determine what the configuration change was from the speed decay alone."[16]

TWA pilot George Andre, who had flown a test flight of the accident aircraft after its repair, was also asked about the speed decay during questioning by Boeing attorney Boyd Ratchye during Andre's deposition in the civil trial. Ratchye wanted to know if Andre agreed that the speed decay comparison between E209 and TWA 841 was evidence that the two aircraft were similarly configured.

Andre's answer rattled the Boeing attorney. "Well, if we want to ignore some other [facts] . . . For one thing, the speed decay on TWA 841, the time that it begins is almost identical with the time that the altitude starts, starts to decrease. That would indicate that the speed decay is starting at the same time the airplane is going out of control, and in the scenario you are proposing—there would have been, this period of constant heading and constant altitude with the only thing in the flight recorder trace being a speed decay. There also would have been the buffet present on the airplane that all 89 people on the airplane would have noticed. All those things are missing . . ."[17]

ALPA's challenge of the validity of Von Husen's analysis did not persuade Chairman King, who allowed the questionable FDR evidence to be presented to the Board. The FDR evidence presented by Kampschror at the second Sunshine meeting would play a crucial role in the Board's final vote.

After months of testing and analysis comparing the FDR traces from 841 with those from the numerous simulator, gyro, and E209 flight tests, NTSB investigators were ready to present their findings to the Board. To help seal the deal, the NTSB prepared a graphical comparison of the heading traces from TWA 841 and the actual and calculated traces from the simulator tests, which now showed an almost identical comparison. In order to obtain the graphical readouts, investigators applied gimbal error corrections, turning performance calculations, magnification of FDR trace patterns, and mathematical equations for heading gyro errors, all of which were programmed into the Safety Board's scientific data reduction and plotting computer.

The NTSB findings, however, bore absolutely no resemblance to what the crew had reported. For the new calculated data to fit their theory, the NTSB had to completely discard most of what the crew had testified to and then find fault with what was left. One example concerned 841's airspeed at 39,000 feet. Hoot had said that they were cruising at .80 mach. But for the plane to become uncontrollable, the speed had to be greater than .83 mach. So the NTSB investigators concluded that the speeds had to have either been higher than what was reported or a side slip was introduced, which would have lowered the controllability parameters.

To the ALPA investigators and others with some knowledge of the facts, it appeared as if the Boeing engineers and NTSB investigators had massaged the data to the point where they could have made the plotting computer give them whatever plot they wanted. The ALPA investigators, however, were working hard to counter any claims by Boeing and the NTSB by releasing their own findings of probable cause.

Chapter Seventeen

Eye of the Storm

As *much as Hoot would have liked* for all the attention surrounding TWA 841 to just disappear, he found it difficult to escape. Coworkers wanted to know what was happening. His friends asked him about the investigation. The news media continued to report on the latest developments. Even his neighbors would ask him for updates. He would have preferred to just go back to flying the line as an anonymous pilot, but that was impossible. Lawsuits filed by a number of TWA 841 passengers assured that Hoot's involvement with TWA 841 was likely to continue well into the foreseeable future.

Then there was Hoot's own libel suit. His legal battle against the NTSB and Boeing was taking a toll on him both mentally and financially. Hoot had paid his attorney, Landon Dowdey, a $5,000 retainer to explore the possibility of a libel suit. That money was quickly absorbed. He wrote another check for $4,000 in late November 1979 and another for $1,754 in January 1980. Hoot was doing well as a captain for a major airline, but he didn't have the financial resources to fight a long, drawn-out battle against the government at an estimated rate of $5,000 a month. Even though Scott and Gary were included as plaintiffs in the lawsuit, they were not contributing toward the legal costs. They didn't earn what Hoot earned as a captain. They both had families to support.

Scott, who initially had reservations about the lawsuit, eventually got behind the effort. He gave Hoot a check for $5,000, but he told Hoot he couldn't afford to give more.

Union leaders at TWA brought up the legal battle the crew was involved in at one of their regular meetings. At the meeting, held in early November of 1980, it was agreed that the MEC chairman would present a formal request to ALPA national asking for help with the crew's legal costs. They agreed to limit the request to $50,000. They also agreed to solicit a $10 contribution from every TWA pilot to be placed in a legal action fund.[1] With more than 4,000 pilots on the seniority list, the small contribution had the potential to put a major dent in Hoot's legal bills. Unfortunately, no one took the next step to actually solicit the contributions. So even though the idea was put to a vote and approved, no money was collected.

The mounting legal fees and constant reminders of TWA 841 left Hoot feeling exhausted and depressed. That depression spread into other parts of his life. Hoot's relationship with his children, for example, was one of limited contact. Hoot had made attempts at establishing a relationship with his children over the years, but many factors worked against him. As a pilot employed by a major airline and being based at different locations throughout the world, maintaining regular contact was impractical. There was no Internet or social media back then. He couldn't Skype his kids. Then there was his strained relationship with his first wife and her new husband. Hoot always felt as though he was imposing when he called, so he called less frequently.

Hoot's youngest son, Kevin, who was born after Hoot's divorce from his first wife, could count the number of times he had spent with his dad on one hand. One of his earliest memories of his father was when Hoot came to visit when Kevin was seven or eight years old. Hoot took

Kevin flying in a friend's Cessna. Hoot didn't know it, but ever since that first airplane ride, Kevin had aspirations of following in his father's footsteps. He was planning on asking his dad for help after he graduated. But after the incident, Kevin could see that his dad was distracted. So he decided to hold off talking to his father about his desire to become a pilot. A year later, Kevin was staying with friends in Phoenix, Arizona. He decided to call his dad. He didn't mention anything about wanting to learn how to fly, just that he wanted to visit and spend some time with Hoot. Both of his older brothers had spent time living with Hoot and Sandy in Las Vegas. But Hoot brushed him off. He told him that it wasn't a good time. Kevin said he understood and hung up the phone. Kevin wouldn't hear from his dad again in any meaningful way for another ten years.[2]

Wanting to get away from the investigation and all of the negative stressors in his life, Hoot decided to visit Utah, where he owned property. It was late September, his favorite time of year to visit Utah. He had two weeks of vacation. He thought the mountains and cool air would do him some good. Hoot owned a cabin nestled in the mountains at an elevation of 9,000 feet.

Accompanying Hoot on his trip to Utah was a new girlfriend. Upon arriving at his place in Utah, Hoot discovered that his cabin as well as the truck he kept on the property had been vandalized. When he tried to move the truck, he found that he couldn't get it into reverse.

That evening he and his girlfriend were invited to a party. Hoot, who wasn't a big drinker, had a few drinks. The next day he had a bad hangover. He hadn't acclimated himself to the high altitude, and the alcohol only made things worse. Needing supplies and aspirin, he decided to drive into town to do a little shopping. Since he couldn't get the truck into reverse, he had to parallel park, which turned out to be a bad move because he ended up blocking a driveway. Hoot hopped back into his truck to move it but found a vehicle had parked in front of him. The only way out of the situation was to drive around the parked car in front of him. So Hoot carefully maneuvered the truck around the car and through what Hoot believed to be a shallow ravine. Instead, the shallow ravine turned out to be a six-foot ditch. The truck was so deeply entrenched in the ditch that it was now leaning on its side.

The only way to extricate the truck from the ditch, according to the person who responded to Hoot's call for help, was with a forklift. After several failed attempts, the forklift driver finally raised the truck out of the ditch, but in so doing, he damaged the transmission. Now the truck wouldn't move in any direction. The whole ordeal sent Hoot's blood pressure off the charts. Hoot had a history of high blood pressure, a problem associated with his fluctuating weight. He was also short of breath due to the high altitude, so he decided to make a visit to a clinic just down the road. That's when his troubles really began.

Hoot told the nurse that he had a headache and was feeling flushed. She took his blood pressure and temperature. Both were on the high side. A few minutes later, a Dr. Bezek saw Hoot in an examination room. Thinking that he should give the doctor some background on his medical history, Hoot told the doctor about his difficulty controlling his blood pressure. He mentioned that he was having trouble sleeping and said that he had problems with anxiety. When Dr. Bezek asked Hoot what was causing his anxiety, Hoot told the doctor about TWA 841 and the false accusations and how that was affecting him.

Hoot told Dr. Bezek that he had taken blood pressure medication during extended periods of time off, such as when he had broken his ankle. He mentioned having had a few drinks the night before and feeling lightheaded. Hoot was given a prescription for his insomnia and another for medication to lower his blood pressure.

A few days later Hoot flew to Seattle for the Boeing flight test. When he returned to Las Vegas, he found a message on his phone from the Los Angeles-base chief pilot about a problem with his FAA medical. Hoot learned that he was being grounded for medical reasons. The TWA chief medical examiner, Dr. Robert Anderson, had suspended Hoot's medical certificate because of reported high blood pressure. As a captain flying for a major airline, Hoot was required to maintain a first-class physical. Hoot found out later that the doctor he had visited in Utah had contacted an FAA flight surgeon friend about Hoot's high blood pressure and anxiety issues. The flight surgeon then passed on the information to TWA.[3]

Hoot flew to Kansas City in an attempt to clear things up with Dr. Anderson. Instead of lending a sympathetic ear, Dr. Anderson wanted Hoot to sign up for the TWA alcoholism-treatment program. Hoot had no idea why he was being asked to sign up for the program. He was not an alcoholic; he rarely drank. Hoot would discover much later that Dr. Anderson had founded and managed the alcoholism-treatment program at TWA. Hoot refused to sign up for the program, indicating that he didn't have a drinking problem. This angered Dr. Anderson, who then ordered Hoot to undergo a series of medical tests.

In November, Hoot flew to California for cardiovascular tests. In December of 1980, he flew to Washington for a series of psychiatric and psychological tests. He would complete one evaluation and then a few weeks later be told that he had to go somewhere else to take more tests or undergo an extensive physical. Hoot didn't know it at the time, but despite passing whatever physical or psychiatric test he was given, many of the doctors were writing negative evaluations. Hoot would learn much later, after filing a freedom-of-information request, that the doctors were twisting his words and making subtle substitutions for what Hoot had actually said in order to bolster their negative findings. A few doctors suggested that Hoot's medical problems were related to his unwillingness to come clean with TWA and the NTSB over causing the upset.

When Hoot's first class medical certificate expired, he went to his regular FAA physician and had the medical renewed. When Dr. Anderson found out about the new medical, he was furious. He claimed that Hoot had received his medical fraudulently. He accused Hoot of flying while on blood pressure medication and not revealing that information to TWA or the FAA. He claimed that Hoot was mentally unstable. Hoot was facing serious charges. ALPA became involved. Hoot would eventually get Landon Dowdey involved, but Landon was advised that it would not look favorable for his client if he embarrassed TWA.

Hoot became increasingly frustrated. He made numerous requests to obtain his medical records but was unsuccessful. Hoot flew to Oklahoma City, where all FAA medical certificates are issued. He took a cab to FAA headquarters and went directly to the office of Dr. Audie Davis, the head of the FAA medical department. Hoot introduced himself to the secretary and gave her his name and pilot certificate number. The secretary disappeared, and a few moments later Dr. Audie Davis entered the room and introduced himself. He invited Hoot into his office.

Hoot had no idea what to expect as he took a seat in the doctor's office. If anyone could make his life miserable, it was this man. The doctor told Hoot that his medical records were in Washington, but he did have a number of recently filed medical reports and physicals. After flipping through a folder filled with doctor evaluations and the results of the many physicals and psychiatric tests Hoot had taken, Audie Davis looked up from the folder. "So who did you piss off?" he asked.

Hoot shrugged. He told the doctor about the run-in he'd had with the TWA medical examiner. He then recounted his failed attempts to regain his medical certificate and his inability to acquire his medical records. Dr. Davis told Hoot that as far as he was concerned there was no reason that he shouldn't be allowed to fly. He assured Hoot that he would call Dr. Anderson personally to straighten out the matter.

Hoot left Oklahoma feeling that he had made some progress. That confidence, however, was short lived. When Dr. Anderson received the call from Dr. Audie Davis, Dr. Anderson perceived it as an attempt by Hoot to go over his head. He argued that Hoot had psychological problems and was not fit to fly. Audie Davis disagreed and said that he intended to issue Hoot a new medical certificate. That set off a new round of objections by Dr. Anderson, who contacted the FAA in Washington with his concerns.

It would take an additional two months before Dr. Anderson's objections were finally overruled, and Hoot was once again cleared to fly. It had been six months since his visit to the doctor in Utah. Dr. Anderson would leave TWA not long after this ordeal to take a position with an airline in Canada. Unfortunately for Hoot, his dealings with Dr. Anderson affected Hoot negatively even after the doctor's departure. The word was out that Hoot had been under psychiatric care and was being evaluated for mental instability, accusations Hoot couldn't easily deny because of the many tests demanded by Dr. Anderson.

Hoot's disdain for Dr. Anderson surfaced during one of his depositions for the civil trial. He was being questioned by attorney Harry

Sieben, the lawyer representing Barbara and Susan Merrill. Attorney Sieben wanted to know why Dr. Anderson had insisted that Hoot sign up for an alcohol-treatment program.

"Before he gave the physical, he said, 'Hey, you've got to go for treatment'?" Sieben asked Hoot.

"No," Hoot replied. "He said that he wanted me to sign up on this alcoholism program. If anybody in the whole world is not an alcoholic, it's me."

"Did he give you any reasons at all as to why he wanted you to sign up for an alcoholics program?"

"No. He didn't give any reason. I figure that—"

"Did you ask him why?"

"Yes, but I didn't get any answers."

"What did he say?"

"I figured he had some reasons, but I'm not going to say what I thought they were."

"What do you think his reasons were? I'd like to have you tell me."

"I'd like to tell you."

"Do you have some theories of your own on what his reasons were?"

"I have some theories, but I'm not going to say."

"Well, what are your theories?"

TWA attorney Don Mark spoke up. "I think he indicated he wasn't going to say."

"But I'd like to have him say," Sieben insisted.

"I'm not going to say," said Hoot.

"Just so the record is clear, you're refusing to tell me that?"

"At this time."

Attorney Don Mark found the heated exchange amusing. "Maybe if you beat him with a rubber hose, he'll tell you later," Mark commented.[4]

Hoot's battle to regain his medical certificate had one unforeseen outcome. In an effort to keep a record of what Hoot felt was an attack on his character, he began saving every detail related to his case. He told one friend that he wanted to keep a record because no one would believe him otherwise. He had already amassed a collection of newspaper articles and stories about TWA 841. To that he added the numerous letters he had either written to or received from doctors concerning his medical suspension. Hoot became a document hoarder. He carried notebooks with him so he could jot down notes when an important thought came to him. If a notebook wasn't readily available, he'd jot down his thoughts on a piece of scrap paper.

He was too busy to organize the documents. He kept them piled up in a closet, eventually purchasing plastic containers to store the mountains of letters, articles, investigative reports, correspondences from ALPA, and the numerous three-ring binders of random notes. Later, when lawsuits and civil trials arose, Hoot requested and received thousands of pages of depositions and trial testimony. The documents became so voluminous that he eventually filled an entire storage shed from floor to ceiling.[5]

When Hoot returned to flying after regaining his medical certificate, he received a cool reception from his fellow pilots. More than a few pilots were startled to see Hoot back on the line. Hoot learned that a number of rumors had been circulating during his absence: The FAA had taken his certificate. He had been terminated by TWA. He'd had a nervous breakdown. The suicide rumor resurfaced. One story that had made the rounds was that Hoot had been admitted to a mental institution.

Hoot assured all who asked that he was fine. He would try to make a joke of it, but the truth was that he felt uneasy with the odd stares he would sometimes get when he walked into operations. It reached the point where he would avoid operations altogether, except to retrieve his paperwork or to check his mailbox.

Feeling the need for a sympathetic ear, Hoot decided to make a side trip to Duluth, Minnesota. Duluth was home to Jeannine and Bob Rakowsky, two first-class passengers aboard TWA 841. Jeannine Rakowsky had sent Hoot a Christmas card thanking him for allowing her and her husband Bob the opportunity to spend another Christmas with their family.

Hoot received the card several weeks after Christmas. Jeannine didn't have Hoot's address, so she sent it addressed to "Captain Hoot Gibson" in care of TWA. The card arrived during Hoot's drawn-out battle to regain his medical certificate. The simple gesture went a long way towards restoring Hoot's confidence. So he thought he'd look up Jeannine and thank her personally.

Jeannine picked Hoot up at the airport and took him out to dinner, where they met up with Jeannine's husband Bob. Hoot shared his frustrations with the investigation, the attacks on his character, and the accusations of mental instability. Jeannine and Bob listened intently as Hoot described how the investigators were trying to pin responsibility for the near disaster on the crew.

After dinner, Jeannine and Bob insisted that Hoot spend the night at their house rather than stay at a hotel. Hoot ended up sleeping on the couch in the family room. The next day Floyd and Patricia Carlson, traveling companions of the Rakowskys on TWA 841, joined them for lunch.

Hoot became emotional as he recounted all he was going through, coming close to tears on a number of occasions. Talking about his troubles with people who had a shared experience with him and who were supportive seemed to help. He felt a sense of calm as he said his goodbyes. Despite the chaos and turmoil swirling around him, Hoot had found a moment of respite. He had happened upon the eye of the storm in the most unlikely of places—Duluth, Minnesota.

Figure 33 Hoot with Jeannine and Bob Rakowsky

Chapter Eighteen

Circumnavigation

J im McIntyre and Harold Marthinsen had spent the better part of two years trying to uncover the truth about TWA 841. Their goal was to find out what had happened and to make sure that it didn't happen again. Despite their best efforts, however, they were unable to claim with any certainty what had caused TWA 841 to roll over and dive some 39,000 feet. They suspected a failure in the slat actuator, but their exhaustive review of maintenance service reports uncovered only one report of an un-commanded slat extension, and that incident involved a different slat actuator than that found on TWA 841.

Jim kept Hoot up to date with the investigation with regular phone calls. He also forwarded copies of all correspondence between himself and other investigators. Jim's updates always ended with an upbeat message about how TWA and ALPA were looking after the interests of the crew and how they were challenging Boeing and the NTSB on their theory of the accident.

Hoot was grateful for Jim's words of encouragement, but they did little to lessen Hoot's anger and frustration over the accusations leveled against him. It wasn't until Hoot read ALPA's report on the investigation that he let himself believe there could be a different outcome than the negative one he envisioned.

On March 27, 1981, ALPA presented their findings from the investigation. The report detailed the many inconsistencies and illogical assumptions made by Boeing and the NTSB. For example, the report pointed out that as far back as the simulator tests the comparisons between TWA 841's FDR and the simulator FDR readouts were suspect.

Addressing itself to the incongruities of the simulator results with headings shown by the flight data recorder, the Boeing report explained: The "poor" correlation is due to gimbal errors caused by the abnormal attitudes encountered by N840TW. When these errors are accounted for, a reasonable correlation is obtained for some of the simulated slat malfunction/separation conditions.

Examination of the graphic representations of the simulated scenarios in figures 25, 26, and 27 leaves considerable doubt as to whether there is any correlation whatsoever, reasonable or otherwise, between the simulation tests and the flight data recorder. The "overcontrol scenario" represented by figure 26—that is, to correct a 60 degree right bank, the pilot's 'full roll control to the left' was 'commanded continually,' causing the aircraft 'to roll left over 220 degrees' before rolling once again to the right—according to the report, "comes closest to matching the flight recorder data during the initial portion of the maneuver." But "closest" is only close by comparison with the gross dissimilarities exhibited by the other scenarios.[1]

The well-thought-out document pointed out gaps in the investigation such as the failure to explain the aircraft's tendency to roll left during the recovery, failure to explain the cause of the lower yaw damper fail flag and its possible significance, and failure to adequately address the effects of the free travel of the right outboard aileron.

The report also addressed the dissimilarities between the October 1980 flight test FDR readouts and TWA 841's FDR readout.

A flight test on a Boeing-owned 727 was conducted on October 1, 1980 with a stated objective of establishing an FDR trace signature for comparison between the TWA Flight 841 FDR and the scenario of intentional extension of 2 degrees of trailing edge flaps only. By resetting circuit breakers and adding leading edge slats 2, 3, 6 and 7, the conditions of the test flight approximated those of Flight 841 prior to the accident onset. The test results produced points of significant dissimilarity between the normal acceleration traces of the flight test recording and that of Flight 841 crew and passenger testimony.

In the debriefing of the flight test, the Boeing test pilot observed that extension of 2, 3, 6, and 7 slats produced a sharp pitch-up change of 6 degrees (autopilot off). The autopilot corrected for this tendency. However, the FDR traces for this test condition, both autopilot on or off, clearly shows a marked G increase at the point where the buffet indication begins. There is no such G increase at the similar point on Flight 841's FDR g-trace.

A second dissimilarity between TWA 841 and the Boeing test flight is indicated by the frequency of buffeting sensed by the FDR normal accelerometer. The test condition with 2, 3, 6 and 7 leading edge slats extended, shows approximately one cycle per second (Hertz). This is identical for both autopilot on and off conditions at this configuration. The initial period of buffeting recorded on TWA 841's FDR is at more than double that frequency. Figure 6 clearly shows these dissimilarities and that the test configuration was not the same as that existing on Flight 841 prior to the upset.

Descriptions by the test pilots of the nature of buffeting when 2, 3, 6 and 7 slats were extended were "sharp," "startling" and "moderate intensity." No such descriptions of buffeting prior to the roll appear in the testimony of the flight crew, cabin crew, or passengers on Flight 841.[2]

From the beginning, Jim McIntyre had been the crew's staunchest supporter. He had demanded that Boeing remove the Boeing Scenario from the summary portion of the Boeing report. When he felt that lead investigator Leslie Kampschror had lost impartiality, he asked that he be replaced. He challenged Boeing's and the NTSB's analyses of test data and questioned the methodology used to obtain both calculated and assumed data. For Jim McIntyre, the TWA 841 investigation was a textbook case on how not to conduct an accident investigation. Jim summed up his feelings and conclusions in a letter forwarded to NTSB chairman James B. King.[3]

We believe preexisting fatigue, corrosion, and component failures with the No. 7 leading-edge slat and right outboard aileron mechanisms caused the No 7 leading-edge slat to extend. We further believe the free play in the right outboard aileron played a significant role in controllability of the aircraft and initiation of the maneuver.

The NTSB should restate in the strongest possible language, it's long-established policy against parties, witnesses, and staff expressing opinions and conclusions as to the probable cause of an accident while the investigation is in progress.

The NTSB should establish a suitable forum for the full and impartial examination of all the evidence and witnesses pertinent to the investigation. Such a forum could be either a public hearing or an expanded depositional proceeding presided over by a member of the Board.

The current NTSB procedures place an unwarranted burden on the Investigator-in-Charge and the limited composition of the technical staff. In this case, hypotheses not supported by fact have been presented as hard evidence without an opportunity for full cross-checking and validation by all the interested parties. The Investigator-in-Charge, in effect, becomes the sole arbiter of the evidence and analysis presented by the staff to the Board. Often the scope of the evidence is outside the staff's technical expertise and competence. This results in the interested party with the greatest resources and manpower actually conducting the investigation, in many instances.

The FDR played a significant part in the investigation, yet it presented innumerable difficulties. First, the accuracy and fidelity of FDR data are not fully understood. Three years ago, at the request of ALPA, the Board undertook a scientific evaluation to determine the accuracy of recorder data. Yet to date, the results of this study have not been completely analyzed. Furthermore, only limited investigation of possible recorder errors was conducted. For instance, the effect of gimbal errors which produced the large heading change to the left in the TWA 841 case was apparently a mystery to the staff. It was only after ALPA produced other similar flight recorder readouts of aircraft which had rolled that the staff agreed to the gyro tests at Kansas City. The Board should have cataloged all the known potential errors so that future investigations are not hampered.

Second, the limited number of output parameters on the subject FDR [has] presented severe difficulties in determining the actual maneuver performed by the aircraft. Recorders with many more parameters, including pitch and roll attitude, have been in airline use on wide-body aircraft for years. Yet new-production aircraft are still entering service with FDRs of the same type as that used on the subject aircraft. We feel it would be desirable to retrofit this type of recorder to aircraft which will be in fleet use for an extended period of time.

Jim's letter to Chairman King was followed by another letter a few days later by J.J. O'Donnell, the president of ALPA.[4]

Dear Jim,

Once again I call your attention to the case of TWA 841 which is now pending Board review.

In spite of the certain fact that there has not been one substantial shred of evidence of any crew error or wrong doing whatsoever, this flight crew has suffered from a malicious, unfounded rumor circulated in the national media and throughout the industry that the crew somehow caused this mishap by initiating a non-standard, incorrect procedure in the cockpit. In spite of all efforts to correct this totally false hypothesis - however it began - the rumor persisted and, in fact, the incorrect "procedure" has been and may still be described in various airline training programs. Almost needless to say, this rumor has seriously hurt the flight crew's reputation and has caused each of them enormous personal grief. This is especially anguishing when through extraordinary professional skill the crew was able to save this aircraft and the passengers from an almost certain disaster.

Now, at last, the Board will have a chance to address this case. I especially call your attention to the ALPA investigators' analysis of the evidence and their recommended findings which were submitted to you on March 30th.

I ask each of the Board members to give this case most serious consideration and to finally set the record straight publicly and permanently.

Sincerely,

J.J. O'Donnell, President

When Kampschror first read the ALPA report and the accompanying letters, he considered suing for libel, commenting that the ALPA investigators had taken liberties with the evidence.

———— ✦ ————

Landon Dowdey read the ALPA report and the two letters to Chairman King but doubted that it would persuade anyone from changing their opinion of crew involvement. For Landon, that was a matter for the courts to decide. He had worked tirelessly for a year and a half putting together the biggest lawsuit of his career. It was David against Goliath, and Landon stood to benefit personally and professionally.

Being the savvy lawyer that he was, Landon decided to file the lawsuit the day before the two-year anniversary of the upset. It was a strategic move made to highlight the investigation as the longest one in NTSB history. It also guaranteed maximum exposure for his clients. He sent out press releases to all major publications and major television networks advising them that he would be holding a press conference with an important announcement related to the TWA 841 investigation.

The press release produced the desired result. As the appointed time approached, the room reserved for the press conference overflowed with reporters and television camera crews. Landon took on a serious demeanor as he approached the podium. He began by chastising the NTSB for failing to conduct a fair and impartial investigation. He told those in attendance that his clients were being unjustly blamed for the upset and that those false accusations had caused irreparable harm. He then summarized the specifics of a twenty-million-dollar lawsuit against Boeing, the NTSB, and lead investigator Leslie Kampschror.

Landon anticipated that the lawsuit was going to be a leading and ground-breaking news story. It isn't every day that a lawyer takes on the federal government and a large corporation. He could sense from the questions asked that the reporters in attendance were grasping the enormity of his announcement. He took a number of questions and then motioned for Hoot, who was standing nearby, to come to the podium. Landon had given them a sensational story; now he was going to give them a face to go along with that story.

Hoot took a few nervous steps forward. He wasn't one for public speaking. While Landon had spent hours going over the details of the lawsuit with Hoot, he hadn't spent any time preparing Hoot for the press conference. When a reporter for a national news organization asked Hoot if he had an opinion as to whether or not the 727 was a safe aircraft, Hoot thought about his response and then answered that despite what had happened to him, he felt that the 727 was safe. Hoot was being honest. To him, any aircraft that could withstand a spiral dive like the one he had endured and still keep flying was a safe aircraft.

Landon, however, was furious. Here they were filing a twenty-million-dollar lawsuit over a flawed investigation, an investigation wrongfully blaming the crew for something they didn't do, and Hoot tells the press that there's nothing wrong with the plane. To Landon it was the worst thing that Hoot could have said. The comment took all the wind out of their sails. Had Hoot said that the 727 was unsafe as long as no one could explain what had happened, it would have been front-page news. It would have been national news. After Hoot's comment, Landon felt that they would be lucky if they got any attention at all.

As it turned out, Landon's concerns were not warranted. Over the next several days and weeks the lawsuit did make the national news. It wasn't front-page news as Landon had hoped, but it was a public-relations victory for Hoot, Scott, and Gary. It was the first time the public heard from the crew. It allowed the media to show that there was another side to the story than the one being touted by the NTSB and Boeing.

The specifics of the lawsuit were that the theories proposed by Boeing and the NTSB were false and unsupported by the facts and the evidence, and were furthermore discredited by the ensuing tests. Those unsupported theories and assertions were then published, placed into the public record, and widely circulated through industry channels and the media. The plaintiffs were deprived of any opportunity to examine or cross-examine witnesses or otherwise verify the reliability of the facts, data, and methods used in the investigation.

Kampschror's interview with *Aviation Consumer* magazine became an example of how the NTSB prejudged their conclusions before all the evidence was in. The suit claimed that the premature conclusions proposed by the NTSB were motivated by an attempt to side-track any meaningful investigation of the airworthiness of the Boeing 727.

As for the damages experienced by the crew, the suit listed the unproven and unsupported claims made by Boeing and the NTSB that the crew: intentionally erased the cockpit voice recorder in an attempt to conceal information related to their conduct, performed an unauthorized procedure that led to the upset, and failed to take appropriate action to regain control of the aircraft. The circulation of these false claims resulted in defamation and injury to the professional and private reputations of the three crew members. The false accusations had led directly to economic and emotional loss, mental pain and suffering, anxiety, and other emotional and physical consequences. The suit stated that the damages experienced by the crew were ongoing and likely to continue into the future.

The twenty million dollars asked for in the suit was to be broken down with ten million for Hoot and five million each for Scott and Gary. The suit charged that the NTSB and Boeing had failed to perform their duty to conduct a fair and impartial investigation. The suit further alleged that Boeing and the NTSB spread misinformation throughout the aviation industry and the media.

The well-written lawsuit cited numerous reference cases to support their right to sue. Also, its numerous references pointed to specific regulations that were either ignored by the NTSB or improperly implemented. It was a well-composed and -presented case of defamation. Only time would tell if it would go any further than the room in which the suit was announced.

———————◆·◆·———————

A month after Landon's press conference, Hoot received a bill from Landon Dowdey for $42,885. On top of this bill were other bills totaling several thousand dollars to cover travel-related expenses for lawyers assisting Landon. Hoot didn't have the money. He arranged a payment plan with Landon. To raise funds, Hoot sold his interests in two acrobatic planes. He also sold his new car and opted to drive a beat-up '68 Buick.

Along with the legal bills from Landon came words of caution about their chances for success. Landon was careful not to sound overly confident. His list of concerns included First Amendment protections for freedom of speech, technical difficulties in taking action against government employees, issues related to the Privacy Act, and problems showing evidence of complicity.

As Hoot's payments to Landon slowed and it became clear that no money would be forthcoming from ALPA or TWA, Landon agreed to a contingency fee. His take if they were to win would be one-third the total payout, or close to seven million dollars.

Chapter Nineteen

An Improbable Probable Cause

At the completion of every accident investigation the NTSB investigators present their findings to a five-person Board, who then vote on a probable cause. The phrase "probable cause" is a legal term that offers the NTSB a level of latitude when deciding especially difficult cases where a clear-cut cause cannot be determined. Such was the case with TWA 841.

On June 9, 1981, a second Sunshine meeting was held in Washington, D.C for the purpose of voting on the probable cause of the TWA 841 upset. Two of the five Board members were absent: Chairman James King and Patricia Goldman. That meant that the probable cause finding would be voted on by just three Board members: Vice Chairman Elwood Driver, Admiral Patrick Bursley, and Francis McAdams. It had been more than two years since the incident, making it the longest-running NTSB investigation to date.

Sunshine meetings are open to the general public. The meetings are held in a large auditorium at NTSB headquarters to accommodate the interested parties, the press, and the public. Kampschror, however, had informed Harold Marthinsen that it would be best if the flight crew did not attend. Kampschror had avoided any confrontation with the crew throughout the investigation and saw no reason to have one now. But there was no way that Hoot, Scott, and Gary weren't going to attend.

When the three crew members arrived at the auditorium, they were barred from entering. So the three paced up and down the hallway as spectators poured in. No one seemed to recognize the crew, or at least no one acknowledged them. Soon the auditorium was filled, with every seat taken. Scott's wife Sandra was there and allowed into the room. But the three crew members were forced to listen to the start of the proceedings from behind a closed door. Once the meeting was well underway and there were no additional people trying to enter, the security staff disappeared and Hoot, Scott, and Gary let themselves in. They stood against the back wall.

Usually by this point in the investigation, the probable cause is firmly established. The NTSB staff present their findings, the Board votes, and the final wording of the NTSB report is finalized. That wasn't the case with this investigation. Kampschror and his staff had determined a probable cause, but as he and his staff began presenting their findings, it became apparent that there were still problems with their theory of the accident.

Figure 34 IIC Leslie Kampschror (third from the left with back to the camera) presents his findings to NTSB Board members (from left to right) Francis McAdams, Chairman Elwood Driver, Admiral Patrick Bursley

Kampschror admitted that they'd had difficulty matching the FDR readouts between TWA 841 and the flight test aircraft. The frequency of the acceleration traces didn't match, nor did the magnitude of the oscillations. He explained that they magnified the acceleration traces by 200 times and discovered that the frequency response between the incident aircraft and the test aircraft were identical at six cycles per second. He then discussed the test switch being left in the on position, which, he explained, caused the discrepancy in the magnitude of the oscillations.

The one person who found the report problematic was Board member Francis McAdams. He challenged the logic and the wording of the report, stating bluntly on more than one occasion, ". . . I couldn't find anything in the report as written that clearly showed me the sequence of what we think happened to this aircraft."[1]

Not finding a clear explanation of what had caused the upset as it was written, McAdams attempted to summarize his understanding of the report. "As I understand it, at 39,000 feet, a little over Mt. Gay, the report seems to state that there was a buffet that occurred. Shortly after the buffet—and I think we believe that the buffet was due to the extension of the [trailing edge] flaps 2 degrees and the full extension of the 2, 3, 6, and 7 slats. Then, according to the way I read the report, the slats were scheduled to retract and they did retract; the 2, 3, and 6 retracted. The number 7 was isolated in the extended position.

"As a result of that, the aircraft started a roll to the right. At approximately 35 degrees, the roll was stopped and the aircraft was rolled back to almost the wings level position. At this point, the aircraft was laterally controllable. It then began another roll to the right which could have been caused by either distraction on the part of the captain or a relaxation on the controls, and the aircraft again rolled to the right to approximately 35 degrees where the roll was momentarily stopped.

"Again, at this point, at the second roll to the right, the aircraft was laterally controllable. It then rolled to the right uncontrollably through a 360-degree roll. The reason for the continuation of the second roll to the right, as I read the report, was the captain either over-controlled the aircraft—in other words, put too much lateral control into the aircraft with aileron and rudder, which induced a side slip condition and at that point, with the side slip condition, the angle of attack and the airspeed, then the aircraft became uncontrollable.

"Is that what we are saying in this report?"[2] Being a pilot himself, McAdams wanted to understand for himself how the pilot of TWA 841 lost control after momentarily controlling the plane back to wings level and then letting the plane become uncontrollable as the report had stated. In an earlier portion of the report, McAdams had read a reference suggesting the possibility that control was lost because the pilot induced a side slip, and the combination of the side slip, angle of attack, and airspeed led to loss of control.

Kampschror, however, was quick to point out that the side slip condition was only one of several possible scenarios and that they had no way of determining whether or not there was side slip. ". . . We speak in terms of probability," Kampschror explained, "but we do believe that a side slip condition developed. We are not absolutely certain of which controls and the manner in which they were applied to produce that side slip. But if the aircraft is put in the approximately 4.8-degree side slip condition at that particular point, in considering that lateral control margins are reduced from what we had used in the flight simulator, reduced to margins that were, in effect, developed in flight tests, then we believe that the aircraft—that the rolling moment produced by the number 7 slat became predominant and the aircraft was no longer laterally controllable at that point."[3]

McAdams's summary also highlighted an important shift in the NTSB's theory of the accident. Ever since the simulator tests were held back in May of 1979, the NTSB had settled on two scenarios that would lead to loss of control. The first was the over-control scenario, where the plane banks right 60 degrees, and then the pilot tries to recover by rolling 285 degrees to the left. The second scenario was known as the delay scenario. In this scenario the pilots take no action for 16.5 seconds until the plane reaches a right bank of 117 degrees. These two scenarios were derived from simulator tests where the plane lost control and also showed some correlation to the heading trace from TWA 841 at the onset of the incident.

Both scenarios fell short from a logic standpoint. Each scenario required pilot actions that were so out of the norm that they were not believable. Now the NTSB was proposing that the plane banked right to about 35 degrees, the pilot corrected to near wings level, allowed the plane to roll again to 35 degrees, paused momentarily, and then lost control due to spatial disorientation. The new theory also stretched credulity, but it wasn't as extreme as the earlier theories.

At first glance the new theory seemed plausible. It was nighttime, the crew was surprised by the sudden roll, Hoot became distracted or disoriented or both and simply lost control, or, as McAdams had suggested, he introduced a side slip that then led to the loss of control. No attempt was made to explain how the NTSB came up with this new theory, a theory that made more sense than the previous theories but was not backed up by the evidence. First there is the testimony of the captain, who always maintained that the plane banked to the right and never to the left. Then there is the lack of supporting evidence on the FDR. The TWA 841 heading trace indicates several rapid heading changes prior to the upset. In one case the heading changes from 289 degrees to 294 degrees in less than half-a-second. That rate of change equates to about 10 degrees a second. An aircraft flying at the speed TWA 841 was flying would have to be in a 70-degree bank to produce a 10-degree per second heading change. In addition, a plane banked at 70 degrees pulls nearly 3 G's. There is no correlating G increase found on the TWA FDR.

So how did the NTSB explain these discrepancies? The answer is they didn't have to. The last-minute change to the NTSB's theory wasn't introduced until the probable cause hearing. At no time during the hearing were these obvious discrepancies brought up for discussion. The answer as to how the NTSB resolved the conflict regarding the lack of a correlating g-trace was buried deep in the final report. The new theory hadn't been derived from actual testing at all; it came from a new analysis of the FDR traces that now included a calculated trace using gimble error calculations. In other words, the new theory didn't match the FDR evidence so they discarded that evidence as being unreliable due to gimbal-error. In its place they provided a new calculated heading trace that better fit their theory. No explanation was provided as to why there would have been gimbal errors prior to the upset.[4]

As McAdams read the report, the only explanation that made sense to him was that loss of control was caused by pilot-induced side slip, and he wanted the report to reflect that finding. None of the other scenarios made sense to him. He also didn't like the use of the word "untimely" when describing Hoot's actions to control the initial upset. In questioning the NTSB staff, it was revealed that their analysis showed that the recovery to wings level had occurred in less than four seconds and that the response to halt the second roll was also four seconds. That seemed more than "timely" to McAdams.

McAdams also felt that under the circumstances Hoot's response to the situation he found himself in was appropriate. "It seems to me that time interval, with what he has got underneath him, it may have been an appropriate response," McAdams said. "He did retard the throttle. He did use full left rudder, and then everything fell apart because of the aerodynamics of the situation."[5]

Here McAdams is supporting the crew's actions. He is saying that Hoot's response to the situation as it occurred was the appropriate response but that his response induced a side slip condition that led to loss of control.

Kampschror did not like what he was hearing. He had written a report that blamed the crew for causing the upset, and now McAdams was claiming that the crew had acted in a way that was appropriate to the situation. "To me, the failure to introduce the control forces necessary to maintain wings level flight in that particular second, when he was near wings level flight was—involved a lack of timeliness," Kampschror argued.[6]

As McAdams and Kampschror debated whether or not the crew's actions, more specifically Hoot's actions, were timely or untimely or appropriate or inappropriate, Hoot and his fellow crew members listened, knowing full well that the entire argument was moot because the maneuver being argued over never happened.

This fact was not lost on McAdams, who may have spotted Hoot and the crew standing against the back wall. "You see, the problem that we are faced with, and why I think it is necessary to have something in the analysis, not only in the synopsis, but in the analysis, is that we are rejecting the testimony of the crew based upon flight tests, analysis of the flight data recorder, and the tilt tests. That is, in fact, what we are doing. We are rejecting what the crew has said happened. I think we have got to lay out somewhere in clear terms so that it's clearly understood why we are rejecting the sworn testimony of the crew."[7]

Rather than address McAdams's statement concerning the rejection of the crew's testimony, Chairman Driver suggested that they break for lunch. Hoot, Scott, and Gary took the opportunity to meet with some of the ALPA members in attendance, including Jim McIntyre. McAdams's line of questioning was in part favorable to the crew, even though McAdams apparently was buying the crew's involvement in initiating the upset by extending the flaps and slats. McIntyre suggested that a favorable vote on the report was not a done deal.

Before the meeting resumed, Hoot stopped by the men's room. He was standing at a urinal when Leslie Kampschror walked up to the urinal next to him. They had a brief, innocuous conversation, the contents of which Hoot has long since forgotten. What Hoot does remember, however, is that it was the first and only one-on-one conversation he had with Leslie Kampschror throughout the investigation.

After the lunch recess, the discussion started where they had left off, with Kampschror and his staff defending their findings to the Board. One area up for debate was the exact wording of the probable cause statement. McAdams was still having trouble with the staff's reluctance to conclude that the loss of control was a result of side slip.

William Hendricks, the Chief of the Aviation Accident Division, spoke in defense of the report. "I think we would have to say that based on what our analysis is, that we are unable to explain fully why the loss of control occurred. Based on the captain's statements, this is one of the most plausible—"

McAdams interrupted Hendricks mid-sentence. "We are in this curious situation where we are accepting the captain's testimony for certain things that happened to this airplane, and we are rejecting his testimony for other things that happened to the airplane. What I'm trying to get us to say in one place is what we think happened, irrespective of the captain's testimony, and we put it in one place. This is from our readout of the FDR; the simulated test, the flight tests and the tilt table test. This is what we think happened irrespective of what he said happened. You can't accept his testimony for one thing and reject it for another. We are making an analysis from documentary evidence. I think that is where we should stay."[8]

Kampschror and his staff seemed reluctant to change anything in the report. They had spent two years investigating this accident, and the report as written, at least to their way of thinking, was as clear as it was ever going to be. But McAdams was still having problems. He wanted to know why Kampschror and his staff wouldn't agree to include more detail about why the accident had occurred, especially in light of the fact that they were discrediting the crew's sworn testimony. James Danaher, the Deputy Director of Operations for the NTSB, gave a simplistic answer. "Because it is complex and there are a number of factors."

"Our whole analysis, everything we have done here today, is to explain that why," McAdams said. "I want to see it one place. I want to understand it myself; what we are saying as to why this accident happened. I have yet to see it in one place, and I have looked and looked."[9]

During the lunch break, McAdams had written an account of the accident as he understood it. It was a departure from the staff report. In McAdams's version, the crew's actions after the initial onset were appropriate for the situation.

McAdams read his account into the record. ". . . The crew, being unaware that the number 7 slat was extended, attempted appropriately to counter the right roll with full left rudder and aileron. However, this action induced a right side slip which increased the local mach number and angle of attack at the number 7 slat.

". . . I have put in there that the action of the crew was appropriate under the circumstances in the time they had and not knowing what was wrong with this airplane. The most appropriate action in the world would have been full aileron and full rudder. Unfortunately—and they had—the only way they would know what was happening with the airplane was to check their instruments. They would have no real feel in the wheel as to—that the aircraft was beginning its second right roll.

"When it did this very rapid roll, I think then they acted appropriately in the input of full rudder and aileron. Unfortunately, the input of full rudder and aileron induced this side slip, mach and angle of attack, and the aircraft became uncontrollable.

"I have left out the part of it, 'Contributing to the Captain's inappropriate use of the flight controls was distraction due probably to his efforts to rectify the source of the control problems.' I am not convinced that he was distracted. I think he was doing as best he could, what he should have been doing, which is to try to counter this unexpected right roll, two right rolls. I think he did what he had to do. Unfortunately, aerodynamically, it didn't work."[10]

McAdams rewrite of the report caught everyone off guard. He not only gave credit to the crew, but he discarded wording that was detrimental to the crew. This set off a round of discussions between the Board members and the NTSB staff on whether or not to adopt McAdams's version. McAdams was pinning everything on the accident as having been caused by the introduction of side slip, but that was only one possibility and one the NTSB had no way of proving.

The discussion continued with an important comment and observation from Board member Bursley. "Just as we were having difficulty before lunch in groping for a characterization of the captain's actions that didn't seem unduly critical of his situation, I think we can go the other way in buying off, in terms of an endorsement of his reaction to his situation. And I have the feeling that from a tilt that was bothering us before lunch of hitting him a little too heavy, given the complexity of his circumstances, we may be going in the other direction of positively endorsing some actions which, as I read in the analysis, while people weren't prepared to say what he did was wrong, they were not prepared to stand up in their chairs and cheer about it, either. I get the sense that Member McAdams's suggestion is taking us over in that direction."

McAdams rubbed his eyes in frustration. "Well, if someone can tell me straight out that the actions that he apparently took—and this is according to all of our documentary evidence—was the application of full left rudder and full aileron under the circumstances; was that inappropriate to try to counter whatever was wrong with this airplane, was it inappropriate?"

"Perhaps not under those precise circumstances," Kampschror said, "where the roll rate is high; where he has perhaps diverted his attention to something else and has come back to the instruments to realize the aircraft is rolling very rapidly. Then he must apply the counter controls with the same degree of rapidity. That's why I go back to the wings level situation where he should have stabilized the aircraft with the appropriate control inputs, and he should not have diverted his attention elsewhere at that particular moment when the aircraft's wings were level. That's why his actions were untimely."

McAdams wasn't following Kampschror's logic. "You mean you are talking—now his actions are untimely at the point where he recovered from the first right roll?"

"Yes, sir," Kampschror said.

The debate between Kampschror and McAdams became heated as McAdams challenged Kampshror to explain his reasoning. "In other words, at this point, when he had recovered the aircraft, you are saying then he should have reduced throttle and what else?"

"And remained on the instruments and stabilized the aircraft to determine exactly what the lateral condition in terms of the capability was."

"How do you know he wasn't on instruments? You say he was distracted at the time, because he was trying to troubleshoot what was wrong with the airplane, which is a natural reaction. One way to troubleshoot it is to check our instruments. This is not distraction. This is what he should have been doing."

"He was trying to control the aircraft, sir. He had to do that by instruments. He should have directed the other flight crew members to find out what was wrong."

"In three or four seconds, with an airplane that was doing very, very weird things? You are putting an impossible burden on this man."

"It wasn't doing particularly weird things. The aircraft was controllable under those conditions."

"It wasn't controllable for very long. How long did it stay wings level? What is the time interval before it started off into a very rapid roll to the right?"

"Perhaps as little as one second."

"That isn't very long to be controllable."[11]

At this point Vice Chairman Driver interrupted the discussion to suggest a short recess. The exchange between McAdams and Kampschror highlighted the many problems with the NTSB's findings. They couldn't prove anything. They had no idea why or how the plane went from being controllable to uncontrollable. They couldn't say what control inputs were used and to what degree.

To the observers in the auditorium, it seemed as though there was no way the Board could vote favorably on the report as it now stood.

There were too many unanswered questions. But after the short recess Kampschror spoke up in defense of his report. "I have serious problems with Member McAdams's proposed probable cause. We think clearly the aircraft was controllable when the number 7 slat isolated in this position. This probable cause would infer that the aircraft was not controllable under those conditions."

"I don't say it was controllable," McAdams interjected. "After the input was put into it, then it became uncontrollable."[12]

The arguing over what the crew should or shouldn't have done continued on until the absurdity of what they were arguing over was demonstrated by a comment by William Hendricks. "I just have one observation, if I might. If you take that the way it was written there [referring to McAdams's rewrite]—I understand the intent of it—but it is a two-part probable cause. If you just took the second part as written, it would say the probable cause would be the operation of the flight controls to counter the second roll resulting from slat asymmetry, saying, in other words, you shouldn't use flight controls to counter the roll, the second roll."

It was late in the afternoon. Board member Francis McAdams seemed to be fighting a one-man battle. His attempt to rewrite the probable cause only confused the matter further. The other two Board members seemed ready to sign off on the report as it was and be done with it. Lacking support from his counterparts, McAdams capitulated. His only consolation was an agreement by Kampschror to change the wording of the probable cause to include the following: "Contributing to the captain's untimely use of the flight controls was distraction due probably to his efforts to rectify the source of the control problem."

And with that simple change of wording, the three Board members voted to accept the findings of probable cause, and the meeting was brought to a close.

Jim McIntyre and Harold Marthinsen sat stunned. They couldn't believe anyone could have voted on a probable cause finding that relied so heavily on unsupported assumptions. As spectators began spilling out of the hearing room, Jim and Harold along with several ALPA and TWA representatives gathered in the hallway. Scott Kennedy's wife joined the group. As the first officer on TWA 841, Scott wasn't subjected to the level of negative publicity Hoot endured, but he was equally upset by the accusations of crew involvement. Sandra Kennedy wanted to hear what Jim McIntyre and the rest of the group had to say.

They were gathered in a circle when lead investigator Leslie Kampschror approached. The relationship between the TWA and ALPA investigators and Kampschror was contentious. With the investigation now at a close, Kampschror felt free to speak his mind. "You guys put up a tough fight," Kampschror said, "but we can't have the traveling public thinking these old airplanes are going to fall out of the sky."[13]

Hoot wasn't around to hear the comment. He and the other two crew members had been surrounded by reporters immediately after the meeting. Later, when he was told what Kampschror had said, Hoot committed the quote to memory. In later years, long after many of the details of what had happened had faded, Kampschror's words would rise to the surface anytime someone would ask him about TWA 841.

The official probable cause finding reads as follows:

> The Safety Board determines that the probable cause of this accident was the isolation of the No. 7 leading edge slat in the fully or partially extended position after extension of the No's 2, 3, 6, and 7 leading edge slats and the subsequent retraction of the No's 2, 3, and 6 slats, and the captain's untimely flight control inputs to counter the roll resulting from the slat asymmetry.

Contributing to the cause was a preexisting misalignment of the No. 7 slat which, when combined with the cruise condition airloads, precluded retraction of that slat. After eliminating all probable individual or combined mechanical failures or malfunctions which could lead to slat extension, the Safety Board determined that the extension of the slats was the result of the flight crew's manipulation of the flap/slat controls. Contributing to the captain's untimely use of the flight controls was distraction due probably to his efforts to rectify the source of the control problem.

When a reporter asked Hoot for his reaction to the meeting and subsequent findings, he had this to say, "It was like an out-of-body experience. It was like I was dead or something—the Board and staff members argued over things they hadn't even asked me."[14]

At a deposition a few months later, Hoot was once again asked about the Board's findings of probable cause. Attorney Harry Sieben read the summary section from the NTSB accident report and then asked Hoot whether he agreed or disagreed with the NTSB's findings. "It's like a fairytale," Hoot responded. "It's like out of a novel someplace."

While Board member Francis McAdams voted to adopt the probable cause finding, he had serious reservations. Wanting his objections in the public record, McAdams wrote a dissenting opinion.

> *Although I voted to approve the Board's report which concluded that the extension of the leading edge slat was due to flight crew action, I do so reluctantly. The report as written, based on the available evidence, i.e., the analysis of the flight data recorder, the simulator tests, the flight tests, and the tilt table*

tests, appears to support the Board's conclusion. However, I am troubled by the fact that the Board has categorically rejected the crew's sworn testimony without the crew having had an opportunity to be confronted with all of the evidence upon which the Board was basing its findings. At the time of the first deposition, the following evidence was not available to the crew or to the Board: the flight data recorder analysis, the results of the simulator and flight tests, and the tilt table tests. Although the crew was deposed a second time, their testimony was limited to one issue, i.e., the physical location of the flight engineer at the time of the incident. I had recommended that since the Board was ordering a second deposition it be conducted de novo so that the crew would have been aware of all the evidence. The Board did not agree. Furthermore, I do not agree that a probable cause of this accident, as stated by the Board, was "the Captain's untimely flight control inputs to counter the roll resulting from the slat asymmetry." In my opinion, the Captain acted expeditiously and reasonably in attempting to correct for the severe right roll condition induced by the extended slat.

Chapter Twenty

Turbulence

T he final NTSB report received the media coverage that Landon Dowdey had hoped for with his press conference announcing the twenty-million-dollar lawsuit. "NTSB report blames six-mile dive on crew," was one headline. "Jeliner's Crew Blamed for Dangerous Dive," was the title of another UPI story. In the article Hoot is quoted as saying, "Nobody's ever talked to us since they took the initial deposition. We may as well have been killed because nobody's acknowledging we're alive."[1] The passengers on the flight obviously had a keen interest in the NTSB's final conclusions. They had been following the investigation more closely than most. Many of them also wondered why they hadn't been interviewed by anyone from the NTSB. So when the final report was out and the crew was officially implicated, more than a few passengers felt anger, not directed towards the crew who had saved their lives but aimed at the investigators.

One passenger, Jeannine Rakowsky, the first class passenger Hoot had visited in Minnesota, was so upset with the findings that she felt compelled to express her opinion to local reporter H. G. Bissinger, who had been covering the incident from the beginning. In a letter dated June 11, 1981, she wrote the following:

Dear Mr. Bissinger,

After reading your article in yesterday's issue of your news-paper regarding the NTSB ruling placing blame on the flight crew which resulted in the dive of TWA Flight 841 on April 4, 1979, my husband and I felt I had to write this letter in response to this absurd, contradictory, and untrue ruling.

Why didn't someone interview the first class passengers? After a phone call from Mr. C. Hayden Leroy shortly after the flight, we heard nothing from any investigator.

The Board made their ruling on the premise that Flight Engineer Gary Banks, after returning to the cockpit, punched a circuit breaker back in. I can recall every second of that flight. I can hear the cabin bell ding that called our flight steward to the cockpit. If Gary Banks told me that he did in fact return those dishes, I would tell him he was mistaken. We saw no member of the flight crew come out of the cockpit at any time during the flight.

We get the distinct impression that the NTSB wishes the plane had crashed. If that had happened, it would have been ruled pilot error and the monkey would have been off their backs. I refuse to feel guilty that we survived so a few so-called professional flight investigators would have an easier job.

The Board's total lack of acceptance of sworn testimony from the crew is unjustifiable. What is ironic is their statement that if they had not ruled against the pilots it would have cast doubt on the airworthiness of the aircraft.

NTSB's James Danaher was quoted saying Captain Gibson might be viewed as "something less than a hero." To whom? Him? Captain Gibson (pilot) and Kennedy (copilot) are much more

than heroes to us, and I totally disregard any inane remarks to
the contrary.
    Sincerely yours,
    Jeannine (Mrs. Robt.) Rakowsky
    Passenger-Survivor
    Seat 3-F, TWA Flight 841

In retrospect, it's hard to fathom why the investigators didn't bother to re-interview any of the passengers. Fourteen passengers were interviewed by phone shortly after the incident. The man who conducted the interviews, Human Factors Group Chairman Haden Leroy, never pursued follow-up interviews.[2] He didn't record the initial interviews. And he lost his notes concerning the interviews. Two written statements were on record, one by Holly Wicker indicating that she saw who she believed to be the flight engineer, walking the meal trays back to the galley and then returning to the cockpit. That statement and another written statement from a second passenger were handed over to Kampschror, who later admitted to having thrown them away.

Going back and re-interviewing the passengers seems like an obvious first step regarding the question of whether or not Gary Banks left the cockpit. It could have also answered questions related to their theory. The flight test conducted in October 1980 showed that when the flaps were extended to 2 degrees, along with the extension of slats 2, 3, 6 and 7, the plane porpoised as the slats were being extended and there was noticeable buffeting, described by some onboard as startling. Surely that would have been felt in the back of the plane. It was nighttime and it's unlikely that any of the passengers could have visually noticed the flaps being extended, but the flaps, hydraulically operated, made an audible sound whenever they were extended or retracted. Why not ask the passengers if they heard any abnormal sounds prior to the upset? It would also have been beneficial to ask the passengers if any of them had noticed a bank to the right followed by a bank to the left followed by a roll to the right.

As it turns out, Kampschror did in fact contact several passengers for a follow-up interview. This information was disclosed during Kampschror's testimony in the civil suit filed by several passengers. He admitted that he had contacted several passengers in search of specific information. He followed those conversations by sending forms to two of the passengers on which they could provide written statements. When he got the written statements back, he decided that they didn't contain any useful information, so he threw them away. A closer examination of his actual response is revealing: "When I got them back," Kampschror said, "I could tell that their recollections of events did not include the immediate—what first came to their attention, at least in terms of what I would want from—or was seeking . . ."[3]

In other words, the passenger statements didn't corroborate his theory, so he discarded them. It's also possible that the statements, in fact, may have provided information damaging to the NTSB theory. Here is more testimony from the same deposition. TWA attorney Chance Mark is asking the questions. He is referring to the human factors report prepared by Haden Leroy. "Is it true that the report prepared by Mr. Leroy indicates that the move detailed the passengers' recollections of the aircraft maneuver and those recollections were that the aircraft rolled off to the right and assumed a very steep dive?" Don Mark asked Kampschror.

"That is one of the recollections, apparently," Kampschror replied.

"Did the passengers also indicate that there was initial vibration?"

"Yes. The report says nine passengers related the initial vibration or shaking to various degrees of turbulence."

"Did any of the passengers that were interviewed indicate that the buffet was startling?"

"I don't think any of the passengers mentioned buffet."

"Did any of the passengers mention a startling condition?"

"I don't see any mention of a startling condition here."

One can argue that Kampschror's decision to discard the passengers' written statements was tantamount to destroying evidence beneficial to the crew.

ALPA's executive Board met a little over a month after the NTSB Board's findings of probable cause to discuss their next course of action. Their immediate response was to draft a letter to the President of The United States and members of Congress informing them of what they saw as "deficiencies of the NTSB related to the investigation of aircraft and incidents" and to offer suggestions for improvement. They also discussed what steps they would take to file a petition for reconsideration.

A week after the ALPA Executive Board meeting, ALPA President J.J. O'Donnell wrote a letter to NTSB Chairman James King calling for a warning letter to be sent to all operators of 727 aircraft. The purpose of the request was to point out the lack of logic behind the Board's findings.

> . . . *If the Board seriously accepts and believes that the series of events described in your report did in fact occur, several positive Board actions would now appear imperative.*
>
> *Considering that the 727 is the most widely used airline transport aircraft in the world, it would now be logical for the Board to recommend to the FAA that the FAA notify all B-727 operators on an urgent basis that it has been determined that*

normal application of counter controls to stop a high altitude roll
may result in loss of control of the airplane.[4]

The fact that the crew was being blamed for the upset was largely known in aviation circles long before the release of the official report, but now the public at large was hearing it for the first time. The story was covered by major publications like the *New York Times* as well as much smaller local newspapers that reprinted stories from UPI and the Associated Press. To counter the growing negative publicity, as well as demonstrate their disagreement with the NTSB findings, ALPA honored the crew with an award for meritorious and honorable service for saving the aircraft and the lives of everyone onboard.

Figure 35 Jim McIntyre presents Scott and Hoot with a meritorious service award.

The awards did little to quell the anti-crew sentiment expressed by pilots outside TWA. The NTSB's final conclusions were circulated widely among pilot groups. Pilots who had sided with the crew wrote letters of support. Other pilots, many who believed that the NTSB got it right, wrote letters critical of the crew for what they believed to be a black mark on the profession. One such pilot, a 727 first officer for United Airlines named Walter Bates, wrote a letter to ALPA National indicating that he sided with the NTSB. "Their evidence is hard and conclusive while you offer only opinions," he wrote. He went on to say that he personally flew with two captains who routinely employed the technique of extending trailing edge flaps while inhibiting the leading edge slats. He didn't provide any proof other than to say that the motivation for using the technique wasn't to improve performance but to allow the flight attendants to have more time to do their service and to provide a flatter deck angle for the food carts to move up and down the aisle.[5]

The ALPA investigative team considered the letter, which had a condescending tone, as having come from a disgruntled pilot who didn't agree with a press release issued by ALPA that supported the crew. No one followed up on the letter to verify the first officer's accusations. The letter, however, would find its way into the civil litigation as proof that some pilots knew of and had used the so called Boeing Scenario to extend the flaps without extending the slats. The lawyer representing Boeing would later criticize Harold Marthinsen for not turning the letter over to the NTSB even though the letter arrived after the conclusion of the investigation.[6]

One consequence of the NTSB ruling was that pilots who may have been on the fence as to whether or not the crew had been responsible for the near-vertical dive were now convinced that the crew had, in fact, caused the upset and then tried to cover it up. For Hoot, knowing that other pilots now believed the NTSB's findings was more painful than the actual ruling.

Hoot responded to the loss of support by writing down a list of mistakes that he had made and recommendations to pass on to other pilots who might find themselves in a similar predicament.

1. Always have the number of your union rep with you at all times.
2. Never talk to anyone before talking to your union rep.
3. Don't let anyone know where you are staying after an incident.
4. Make sure the front desk does not give out your room number to anyone.

5. Don't let mechanics touch anything in the cockpit.
6. Never talk to the press.
7. Never agree to give a deposition in front of the media.
8. Seek medical and psychiatric care immediately after an incident or accident.
9. Assign someone to counsel the crew on what to expect going forward.
10. Crew members should be kept in the loop throughout the investigation.

⸻⬩⸻

Two months after the NTSB ruling, Hoot found himself in a courtroom giving the first of several depositions he would have to give over the course of the next year and a half. A number of passengers had filed lawsuits seeking damages, claiming medical and psychological problems as a result of the high G dive and recovery. The attorneys representing the passengers each had a chance to question Hoot. Hoot was the captain. He was the pilot who the NTSB had ruled had caused the whole thing. One by one they tried to find a crack in Hoot's already-tarnished armor. His broken ankle in the months prior to the upset was an area of interest to the attorney representing passenger Alan Mahler, an Obstetrician-Gynecologist who claimed that he was unable to work after the incident due to vertigo.[7] Did Hoot have enough strength in his recovering leg to apply sufficient force on the rudder?[8] Was Hoot taking pain medication? Was Hoot taking medication to help control his high blood pressure? Hoot had testified that he had trouble sleeping, so had he taken sleep medication? The question about sleep medication led to a humorous exchange between Hoot and attorney James Schwebel.[9]

"Would you ever take any medications to assist you in going to sleep?" Schwebel asked Hoot.

"I never have," Hoot replied.

"Where did you sleep the evening of April 3rd, 1979?"

"Columbus, Ohio."

"What hotel?"

"I have no idea."

"Do you usually sleep in a room by yourself or do you share it with other crew members of the flight crew?"

"By myself, unless I get—well, never mind."

"Unless you get lucky?"

"Yes. I usually sleep by myself, though."[10]

Not long after giving his first deposition related to passenger lawsuits, Hoot received a call from someone at CBS asking him if he would be interested in participating in a documentary about TWA 841. Hoot said he wasn't interested. He didn't want anything to do with a documentary. A few days later he received a call from a TWA official who told Hoot that TWA had given the okay for the documentary and that they wanted him and the rest of the crew to cooperate with the filmmakers. The TWA official convinced Hoot that the documentary could help him and TWA. So Hoot agreed to talk to producers Paul and Holly Fine, a husband-and-wife team who worked for CBS producing stories for "60 Minutes" and other CBS programs.

From the start, Hoot sensed that Paul and Holly wanted to tell the story from the crew's and passengers' perspectives and not the story being touted by the NTSB. Most of the material for the documentary was to be based on an article published in the *St. Paul Pioneer Press* by writer H.G. Bissinger. The article was titled *The Plane That Fell From The Sky*.[11] The documentary was to have the same name. Hoot was familiar with the article. He had agreed to be interviewed by Bissinger and felt that the finished article was fair, factual, and well done. Hoot told the filmmakers that he was onboard. He signed some paperwork and agreed to provide whatever help he could.

It would take more than a year before he, Scott Kennedy, and Gary Banks would be brought together to do something none of them could

Figure 36 Producer Paul Fine films a scene for the documentary "The Plane That Fell From The Sky."

have imagined. The crew, along with thirty-nine of the eighty-two passengers, was asked to reenact the flight on camera using an actual aircraft, a mock-up, and a simulator.

Hoot wasn't sure how he would react when it came time to reenact their April 4th flight. Filming began on a studio sound stage in December of 1982. When the cameras started rolling during filming in the simulator, it was as if he was right back in the cockpit struggling to regain control again. It was a surreal experience that upset him more than he had expected. Everything that had transpired over the past three years came rushing back in a flood of emotions.

Hoot, Gary, and Scott, along with nine passengers, were asked to do some additional filming in Las Vegas several months later. At some point during the second shoot, buttons with the words "I flew with Hoot" began circulating among the passengers and crew. Hoot hadn't seen the buttons for years. The buttons had been made by the sister of a TWA captain. Hoot had been giving acrobatic rides in an open cockpit bi-plane. The buttons were handed out to the nauseous riders at the completion of the flight. A friend of Hoot's who showed up for the filming decided to bring a handful of the buttons with him to hand out to passengers. The buttons became a highly sought-after item.

The "I flew with Hoot" buttons later became the inspiration for a different version of the buttons that some TWA flight attendants wore on their uniforms. In the later version, the button had the "I flew with Hoot" phrase superimposed over a picture of an upside down TWA 727.[12] Whether the buttons were derogatory in nature or a sign of

Figure 37 Passenger Roger Peterson and Scott Kennedy during a break in shooting of the CBS documentary "The Plane That Fell From The Sky." Passenger Holly Wicker is standing in the background, center of the image.

support is debatable. When TWA management found out about the buttons, they threatened to take disciplinary action against any flight attendant wearing one.[13]

While most of the passengers who participated in the documentary were supportive of Hoot and the rest of the crew, there were a few who were still on the fence. They had agreed to participate in the documentary in hopes that they might learn new details about what had happened. Passenger Floyd Carlson summed up the general consensus among many of the passengers when asked by a reporter whether or not the passengers agreed with the NTSB findings. "Some of them definitely blamed the crew, and I guess there were a lot of them that didn't really know what happened and were there (in Los Angeles) to try and find out."[14]

Hoot had no way of knowing it at the time, but his participation in the documentary would eventually lead to some important revelations about what really happened to TWA Flight 841.

Chapter Twenty-One

Questioning the Investigators

Hoot's initial disappointment over the findings of probable cause was quickly replaced with a determination to correct what he and others knew was a faulty conclusion by the NTSB. He was determined to set the record straight, and there was no better way to accomplish that task than by winning his twenty-million-dollar lawsuit. The libel suit, however, was tied up in the Las Vegas court system. The first judge assigned to the case was forced to recuse himself because he had adjudicated Hoot's divorce from Sandy. A further delay occurred when both Boeing and the NTSB filed submissions for summary judgment to have the suit dismissed.

With his own lawsuit stalled in the courts, Hoot turned his attention to the lawsuits filed by passengers against TWA and Boeing. Many of the same people involved in the TWA 841 investigation, including investigators from Boeing and the NTSB, were required to give depositions related to their involvement with the investigation. Hoot planned to attend as many depositions as his schedule permitted. One deposition he was especially interested in attending was the deposition of Leslie Kampschror.

In early January of 1982, Hoot traveled to Washington D.C., to be present for the testimony of Leslie Kampschror and several other NTSB employees. Hoot stayed with Landon Dowdey at his residence during the depositions, sleeping on the floor. Both men were eager to hear what Kampschror and the other investigators would have to say under oath.

The depositions were held in a windowless conference room at NTSB headquarters. Since the majority of the lawsuits filed by passengers had been filed with the Minneapolis court system, the insurance company for TWA had hired a Minneapolis law firm to handle the civil suits. The man assigned the monumental task of defending TWA was a young lawyer by the name of Donald Chance Mark.

Hoot and Landon arrived early at the start of Kampschror's deposition. They were already seated when Kampschror entered the room. Hoot's only conversation with Leslie Kampschror during the entire course of the investigation was his brief exchange in the men's room during a break at the second Sunshine meeting. If there was one person whom Hoot held responsible more than any other for what Hoot saw as a flawed investigation, it was Investigator-in-Charge Leslie Kampschror. Now here he was sitting arm's length away from the man. Many thoughts ran through Hoot's mind as Kampschror took his seat, but Hoot is not a confrontational person. He remained respectfully quiet.

Three days had been set aside for Kampschror's testimony and that of several other NTSB investigators. The first day of testimony covered the early stages of the investigation, Kampschror's background, and how he came to be the Investigator-in-Charge. Hoot listened intently as Kampschror described his background as an ex-military pilot. His educational background included a law degree and a degree in Aeronautical Engineering, both from the University of Illinois. Kampschror had the demeanor and appearance of a corporate lawyer, which in many ways he was. His legal background, however, was mostly related to real estate transactions. He had a narrow face and dark hair cut businessman-short.

He appeared to have aged more than the two years it had been since Hoot first laid eyes on him. In many respects, Kampschror was well qualified for his position. He had been with the NTSB for ten years. He had worked in the accident investigation division for two of those years prior to the TWA 841 incident. And he had been the Investigator-in-Charge on at least four accidents prior to TWA 841. His experience, however, was lacking in other areas. For example, he had no experience in airline operations. He was a pilot with about 5,000 hours of flight time, but he did not hold a type rating on any aircraft, nor did he have a multi-engine rating. His training as an accident investigator consisted of a four-week course.[1] The day ended with very little being said about the actual investigation.

That evening Hoot and Landon had dinner together. They talked about the day's testimony and the status of the libel suit. Nine months had passed since they had filed the suit in Las Vegas. Hoot expressed his frustration with the slow pace of the legal system. Landon assured him that they were still on track. In some ways, Landon told Hoot, the extra time was a benefit because it gave them more time to prepare.

The next day, January 13, 1982, would turn out to be a memorable one. Not so much because of the testimony but more so because of what happened later that afternoon. It began as a rather pleasant January day. The temperature was mild for January. The sun broke through a thick cloud layer as Landon and Hoot walked to NTSB headquarters.

When they entered the room where the testimony was to take place, Hoot looked for Scott Kennedy. He had talked to Scott the previous night. Scott had told Hoot that he was planning on flying in for the second day of depositions, but he was absent as the depositions got underway.

Attorney Donald Chance Mark once again started the day's questioning. Using the NTSB's own procedural handbook as a reference,

Mark challenged Kampschror over how several key aspects of the investigation were handled, starting with the crew's televised depositions. "Mr. Kampschror, directing your attention to page 4 Exhibit No 17. Would you be kind enough to read the last sentence of subsection 2 for me?"

Kampschror adjusted his glasses and then read the noted section. "The location of the proceeding is determined by administrative convenience, that is, location of the witnesses, etc. It may be held at several different locations on non-consecutive days. The site shall be chosen carefully to create an informal environment and not take on either appearance or formality of a hearing."[2]

Kampschror argued that the manual that Mark was referencing was published after the TWA 841 investigation and that the section he had just read wasn't in the manual that was in effect during his investigation. But during a lunch recess Mark asked Kampschror to retrieve the manual that was in effect during the TWA 841 investigation and showed that the exact wording was also found in the older manual.

Mark read into the record another section from the same investigator's handbook. "The investigator should remember that guesses, rumors, or half-truths have no place in an accident record. Statements must be verified or be capable of verification. Theories are useful only in absence of facts and must be well substantiated. All evidence must be recorded accurately."

Mark had brought up what he knew to be lapses in the investigation, but he failed to demonstrate those lapses in his questioning. He had Kampschror read the statement that depositions should be taken at a site chosen to create an informal environment, but he failed to describe the media circus surrounding the crew's depositions eight days after the incident. He pointed out that investigators should avoid guesses, rumors, and half-truths but then failed to highlight that much of the investigation had been based on rumors, half-truths, and speculation.

In fairness to Don Mark, since Kampschror's testimony was being videotaped, Mark knew that he could challenge that testimony later when it was presented in front of an actual jury. It would then be up to NTSB attorney Steven Rolef to defend Kampschror. Mark's strategy was to have Kampschror himself discredit his performance as the Investigator-in-Charge by showing that he hadn't followed his own investigative guidelines.[3]

Later that afternoon, Scott Kennedy entered the deposition room and took a seat next to Hoot and Landon. "Sorry I'm late," he told Hoot. "My flight was delayed because of the snow." Hoot was surprised by the remark. It was the first that he had heard anything at all about snow.

The afternoon session continued where Don Mark had left off when highlighting the many lapses in the original investigation. He got Kampschror to admit that he had not found a single person who could testify that they knew of or were familiar with any commercial airline captain who had used the procedure of extending trailing edge flaps independent of the leading edge slats.

Toward the end of the day the discussion turned to the scheduling of the next day's depositions. Those plans, however, were put off when an NTSB official interrupted the proceedings to say that Mr. Kampschror was needed elsewhere. No explanation was given for Kampschror's sudden departure, but it was obvious by the amount of commotion going on in the building that something serious had occurred.

Attorney Don Mark gathered his papers and headed back to the hotel. He was shocked to see at least a foot of densely packed, wet snow on the ground. It was also bitterly cold with the temperature having dropped considerably from the morning. Adding to the surreal sight of the heavy snowfall were the sounds of sirens that seemed to be coming from all directions.

It wasn't until Don Mark got back to his hotel room at the L'Enfant Plaza that he learned that there had been a tragic airline accident just a few miles from where the depositions were taking place. A Boeing 737 operated by Air Florida had departed Washington National airport in heavy snow. Unable to gain altitude, the plane struck a bridge and crashed into the Potomac River, killing seventy-eight people, including four motorists on the bridge. Don turned on the TV and watched as rescuers on the shore and overhead in a helicopter tried to rescue survivors from the ice-covered waters. The drama played out for television audiences in much the same way that the USAir Flight 1549 ditching in the Hudson would play out in the media some twenty-seven years later.

Hoot, Scott, and Landon crowded into Landon's car and headed back to Washington National airport to drop off Hoot and Scott so they could catch flights home. On the way to the airport they stopped near the bridge where the Air Florida jet had crashed. It was a stark reminder of what could have been the fate of TWA 841.

Little was said as they blended into the crowd of onlookers. Seeing the floating pieces of wreckage and the television crews interviewing witnesses brought back memories of their own ordeal. It was the second major airline accident to occur since TWA 841. Hoot and Scott both hoped that the investigation into the Air Florida accident would go better than theirs.[4]

It would be nearly three months before the depositions for the civil trials would resume. Hoot couldn't attend the remainder of Kampshror's testimony, but he made it a point to be there for the deposition of Robert Von Husen. Von Husen was the NTSB accident investigator who had made the determination that the acceleration traces from the October

1981 flight test matched those of TWA 841 with regard to the vibration and deceleration prior to the onset of the near-crash. His findings helped bolster the NTSB's conclusions. Hoot was eager to hear what Von Husen would say under oath when those same findings were challenged.

Attorney Don Mark once again began the proceedings. Mark started off by asking Von Husen to explain how he had come up with his analysis considering the limited recording parameters of the FDR, the gimbal errors, and the tumbled gyros. Von Husen's response, however, was cut short by NTSB attorney Steven Rolef, who advised his client to not answer. Rolef was aware of Hoot's libel suit against the NTSB. He was aware that Hoot and Landon were in attendance. He wasn't about to let Von Husen slip up with his answers, so he continued to object to a multitude of pertinent questions.

Hoot grew frustrated by the constant objections. During a lunch break, Hoot caught up with Von Husen and took him aside. The conversation soon became heated, and Hoot said some things that Von Husen perceived as threats. Von Husen told his lawyer about his conversation with Hoot. When the lunch recess was over and the depositions were about to begin, attorney Steven Rolef made a formal request that Hoot be asked to leave.

Don Mark objected to the request, stating that Hoot had a right to be there. That led to an argument that resulted in Hoot's interaction with Von Husen making its way into the public record. The lawyer for the Wickers, Charles Hvass Jr., interjected himself into the proceedings. He asked Von Husen to state for the record what Hoot had said. Von Husen indicated that the conversation had started off friendly, but that Captain Gibson had asked to speak to him privately. That was when the conversation veered off in a different direction. "To the best of my recollection," Von Husen said, "the conversation eventually evolved to the fact that Captain Gibson told me that he felt that we had not considered the testimony of the crew sufficiently in this investigation and that we had in fact—I am not quite sure of the exact wording, but it was something along the line like hung the crew or hung something on the crew, and that they would pursue us, essentially, as long as we were alive, so to speak."[5]

After some discussion about whether Von Husen felt threatened and whether or not he could testify with Hoot present, Charles Hvass turned to Hoot and asked him for his side of the story. "Is there anything about this conversation that you recall differently?" Hvass asked Hoot.

"That is pretty much the way it went," Hoot said. "There are just a few very minor differences in that . . . I think what I said in actuality was that I felt that we—I felt that the NTSB had, what he said, hung us. That is pretty much the same thing. I felt the NTSB had hung us for something we had not done and that it had disregarded the testimony pretty much like he said. And I said since we didn't do it, I am sure that you would understand that we intend to fight this, you know, I didn't say until he dies, I said until I die, and I added a little thing. I said I promised I wouldn't come back from the grave, or something."

"You mentioned grave," Von Husen said from the witness stand, "but I wasn't quite sure how it was used."

Hoot continued with his version of the conversation with Von Husen. "I said I was going to pursue this as long as I live, if it took that long, because we have got convicted of doing something we did not do. And I just intended to fight it as long as I lived, if it took that long. I said something about—but I promised I wouldn't come back from the grave."

"Were you in any way intending to intimidate this witness?" Hvass asked Hoot.

"In no way at all," Hoot replied.

And with that Hoot was permitted to stay for the remainder of the testimony. But it was a rare instance where Hoot's frustration with the investigation into TWA 841 found its way into a formal setting, an opportunity that had not presented itself at any time prior.[6]

The depositions of Von Husen, Kampschror, and several other NTSB investigators spread out over many days and weeks. At one point or another, just about every individual who had been involved with the TWA 841 investigation provided testimony about their involvement. Years later it would take months to sift through the thousands of pages of testimony, but in so doing a true account of what had happened would slowly begin to emerge.

Chapter Twenty-Two

Costa Rica

eing single gave Hoot flexibility not afforded his married co-workers. He didn't hesitate to switch domiciles if the move improved his bidding seniority and time off. During the course of his career Hoot was based in New York, London, Paris, Chicago, and Los Angeles. His roots, though, were always in Las Vegas. He had a home there. He had married Sandy and settled down in Las Vegas. The dry climate and low cost of living appealed to him. The heat? Not so much.

Hoot was a pioneer in the practice of commuting to work via airplane. In order to get better schedules and more time off, Hoot bid back to the right seat of the 747. He worked just ten to fifteen days a month, flying international routes. As far as Hoot was concerned, he could live anywhere in the world as long as he showed up on time. In early 1982, Hoot found a place to live that he loved even more than Las Vegas—Costa Rica.

Hoot had discovered Costa Rica by chance. He had volunteered to take a charter flight to a destination he thought was in Puerto Rico. When he arrived at the airport, he learned that he would instead be flying to Costa Rica. He had no idea where Costa Rica was located and had to look for it on the large wall map in operations. It took him some time to find the tiny Central American country sandwiched between

Nicaragua and Panama. Hoot fell in love with Costa Rica during that visit. He thought it was the most beautiful place he had ever seen, with its pristine beaches, mountains, and lush tropical fauna.

When he returned to his home in Las Vegas, Hoot started toying with the idea of living in Costa Rica full time. Hoot loved the outdoors. Costa Rica, with a year-round average temperature of 60 to 80 degrees, seemed ideal. He traveled to Costa Rica on his days off. On one visit Hoot found some beachfront property at a price that was too good to pass up. Hoot purchased the property, which included a home, several acres of land, and a parcel of land that had a small landing strip.

Figure 38 Hoot in Costa Rica with one of his Dornier twin engine aircraft

Hoot had big plans for his time in Costa Rica. Having had some experience running a charter company, Hoot saw an opportunity for a similar company in Central America. He applied for a Costa Rican pilot's license. After successfully completing the required tests for his Costa Rican pilot's license, Hoot started the Trans Costa Rica charter company. He purchased two Dornier twin engine short takeoff and landing (STOL) aircraft, which allowed him to operate in and out of just about any airport or grass strip he was likely to encounter. He hired local pilots to do the majority of the flying. Hoot trained the pilots and gave them their check rides. His company flew passengers and cargo throughout Central and South America and the Caribbean.

The land Hoot purchased also contained a money crop in the form of jojoba (pronounced ho-ho-ba) beans. The beans produce an oil that is used in skin-care products. So when he wasn't looking after his charter company, Hoot could often be found riding his tractor, tending to his forty-five acres of jojoba beans.

Hoot was doing well in Costa Rica. His business was profitable, and his health was improving. Hoot had always been a jogger. He spent a lot of time jogging up and down the beaches of Costa Rica. He met a woman while in Costa Rica, whom he married. But the relationship lasted only a year. Hoot and his third wife, Gloria, eventually patched up their differences and remained friends. Gloria, who was an attorney, would eventually help Hoot draft a petition for reconsideration to the NTSB. But that was still a few years down the road.

Working the jojoba bean fields and managing his charter business kept Hoot's mind occupied. He could go months without ever giving TWA 841 a thought. But then a letter would arrive in the mail and bring it all back. Friends and supporters back home would send him letters of encouragement, thinking he was holed up in some hut in the jungle trying to avoid society. Several close friends flew to Costa Rica to see for themselves that Hoot was okay.

Hoot received letters from Donald Chance Mark, the attorney representing TWA in the civil trials, updating him on the progress of the upcoming court cases. Hoot held on to every letter, a habit he picked up after his run-in with the TWA medical examiner and his troubles regaining his medical certificate. He hoped that the documents he haphazardly stashed away would be of some value in the future. He just didn't know when or how.

While Hoot lived in Costa Rica, he kept his home in Las Vegas. He let fellow pilots use the house as a crash-pad. In early May 1983, Hoot flew back to Las Vegas to check up on his home and belongings. After catching up with friends there, Hoot headed off to Minneapolis, Minnesota where he was scheduled to testify in the civil trial of Timothy and Holly Wicker.

Chapter Twenty-Three

Lawsuits, Lawyers, and Liability

W*hile attempts by TWA and ALPA* to force the NTSB into holding a public hearing on TWA 841 were unsuccessful, an opportunity to re-examine the investigation in a formal manner did present itself in early May of 1983 with the civil trial of Holly and Timothy Wicker against Boeing and TWA. TWA had hoped to avoid a trial altogether. Settlement talks were held with the plaintiffs' attorney weeks before the trial was scheduled to begin. Boeing, however, bolstered by the NTSB findings of probable cause, refused to contribute any funds towards a settlement. That left attorney Donald Chance Mark no other choice but to proceed with the trial.

The attorneys had agreed in advance that the Wicker trial would be used to establish liability for all future trials. Twelve of the eighty-two passengers had filed lawsuits along with two spouses. Any subsequent trials would be conducted solely for the purpose of determining the amount of damages. Both Boeing and TWA had a lot riding on the outcome. If one or the other were found to be solely liable, they could potentially face hundreds of thousands of dollars in damages (millions in today's dollars).

The fate of the trial would be up to six jurors, three men and three women. An alternate juror was also present throughout the duration of the trial. The jurors were not sequestered. They were, however, instructed to not read or view any news related to the trial, which was no easy task considering the amount of publicity surrounding the trial. They were also instructed not to discuss the trial with anyone prior to deliberations.

For the crew of TWA 841, the civil trial offered an opportunity to set the record straight. As one writer covering the trial put it, "This trial gives the pilots another chance to tell their story and the possibility that the jury will come to a different conclusion than the NTSB did."[1]

Depositions for the civil trial began in June of 1980, a little more than a year after the incident. The actual trial began on May 10, 1983 in Minneapolis, Minnesota. The civil trial included depositions and testimony from both Boeing and NTSB investigators who worked on TWA 841. Testimony from the NTSB investigators, however, was limited by a section of the Federal Aviation Act designed to protect government investigators from having to testify in civil litigation arising out of an accident. The limitations placed on the testimony of NTSB investigators included the preclusion of any references to the Board's accident report. Only factual information from the investigation would be allowed. It meant that the jurors would be deciding the case based solely on the evidence presented at trial.

Attorney Charles Hvass, who represented the two plaintiffs in the case, was first to give his opening statement. Holly Wicker was suing over medical problems she had suffered as a result of the spiral dive. Prior to the upset, Holly had an infant resting face down across her knees. When the dive began and the g-forces increased, the baby began to slide down Holly's legs and away from her. The baby also appeared to be turning blue.[2] Holly, whose reported weight at the time was 195 pounds, claimed that as she bent over to perform mouth to mouth on the baby she strained her back and neck. Those injuries left her bedridden and unable to care for her three children, the oldest of whom was only ten. Holly worked as an adoption coordinator. Two of her three children were adopted, one from Costa Rica and one from India. Holly Wicker's husband, Tim, who was not on the flight but listed as a plaintiff, was suing for loss of consortium (companionship).

Charles Hvass was a tall, imposing figure who knew his way around a courtroom. Hvass worked for a law firm started by his father, who was also a former B24 pilot in WWII. In addition to Holly and Timothy Wicker, Hvass also represented nine other TWA 841 passengers who had filed suit against Boeing and TWA. Hvass held a private pilot's license with an instrument rating. That experience would come in handy during the course of the depositions and trial. This wasn't his first aviation case, but it was his highest-profile case by far.

As can be expected in a trial such as this, Hvass spent a great deal of time in his opening statement contrasting the Wickers' life before and after the incident. Before TWA Flight 841, the Wickers enjoyed an active lifestyle that included bike rides with the kids, canoe trips, hiking, skiing, and sailing with Holly's family in Vermont. Hvass told the jury that not long after TWA Flight 841 Holly started to complain of back and neck pain. She was admitted to a hospital, where she remained for more than three weeks. The hospital stay was followed by physical therapy and more doctor visits. Holly was told to remain in bed and to avoid physical labor. Her husband, Timothy Wicker, was forced to take over the cleaning and cooking while still working full time. The couple relied on friends and baby sitters until they decided to send the children to Vermont to stay with Holly's parents. The children were away for nearly three months.

Attorney Charles Hvass summed up the purpose of the trial with the following statement: "You have two basic areas of questions you are going to have to answer at the end of this trial. The first is who is responsible? Why did TWA 841 fall from the sky? The second question you are going to have to answer is what are the damages to Holly and Tim Wicker, physically and emotionally? And you are going to have to measure those damages at the end of this case."[3]

As a lawyer representing clients against two deep-pocketed defendants, Charles Hvass was in an enviable position. He had plenty of evidence from physicians, physical therapists, neurologists, and other specialists indicating that Holly had sustained injuries as a passenger on TWA 841. He didn't have to side with either of the two defendants, Boeing or TWA. He could have just focused his attention on the medical aspects of the case and let the jurors decide who was at fault and to what degree. But he did take a side nonetheless. Hvass finished his opening statement by laying the groundwork for the case against the crew. He talked about how simulator tests had proved that the plane was easily controllable if the pilots had reacted more quickly than they did. He hinted that TWA was going to blame the accident on a mechanical malfunction. He then provided a theory of the accident involving a pulled circuit breaker and crew manipulation of the controls.

Hoot was in the courtroom for the beginning of the trial. He was sitting next to Scott Kennedy. Both were scheduled to testify later in the week. Hoot studied the jurors as Hvass walked them through the Boeing Scenario. He liked what he saw. The jurors appeared to be intelligent people capable of grasping the complex nature of the case. He relaxed and waited for attorney Don Mark to make his opening statement.

———•◦•———

Representing TWA was attorney Donald Chance Mark. Don was in his early thirties. He was young for such a high-profile case, but so too were the opposing attorneys. Hvass was thirty-three, and Boyd Ratchye, the attorney for Boeing, was in his early forties. Still, with his long, dark-brown hair and boyish grin, Don looked like he was fresh out of law school. Despite his youthful appearance, Don came across as a seasoned professional, which he was. By the time of the TWA 841 civil trial, Don Mark had already tried a dozen or so cases.

Don worked for an insurance defense firm. It was a mid-size law firm that specialized in product-liability cases. The firm was also notable for defending airlines facing claims by passengers injured in mishaps as well as pilots facing certificate actions. Don was assigned the TWA 841 case because of his prior experience in handling other aviation lawsuits. One of those cases involved a corporate aircraft accident that took the lives of several top officers of a sunflower seed company. The loss of the executives resulted in the company folding six months after the accident. Don represented the estate of the dead pilot. He had also handled a number of other general aviation accident claims. He was smart, experienced, and well acquainted with Minnesota laws and court procedures.

Had Don Mark had better vision, he may very well have become a pilot himself rather than an attorney. His father had been a pilot for Northwest Airlines. His mother had been a stewardess for Northwest. As a kid Don traveled extensively, taking advantage of the free passes afforded the immediate family members of airline employees. Wanting to follow in his father's footsteps, Don took preliminary steps to enter the Air Force Academy. That was when he learned that his lack of 20/20 vision would force him to seek a different path.

Don Mark spent the better part of two years preparing for this trial. He had spoken with the crew members. He believed them when they told him that the upset did not happen the way the NTSB and Boeing said it did. He had spoken with experts who questioned many aspects of the original investigation. Don Mark began his opening statement by praising the crew. "We believe that the testimony of this case after several weeks is going to conclude, demonstrate to you, that number one, it was only because of the professionalism of the flight crew of TWA 841 that first of all the aircraft survived, and it was only because of that professionalism and that heroism eighty-nine people were able to walk off that aircraft, including the plaintiff in this case, Mrs. Holly Wicker."[4]

He next announced that he intended to challenge the plaintiff's claims over the seriousness of her injuries. "We're also going to be producing through independent medical examination with respect to Mrs. Wicker, the injuries she's claiming, but even more importantly we're going to be producing testimony through her own doctors to demonstrate she doesn't have the injuries she claims she does suffer from. We're going to be producing testimony to demonstrate that she had pre-existing problems; that those are the problems she is now complaining of."[5]

Don then introduced Hoot and Scott Kennedy by asking each to stand up. It was Don's way of letting Hoot and Scott know that this time around was going to be different. They weren't going to be silenced any longer. They were going to get their day in court.

Next Don Mark told the jurors how Hoot, Scott, and Gary saved the plane from crashing due to their skill and experience. He described for the jurors how the crew successfully handled multiple emergencies and landed safely in Detroit, despite having no flaps and two unsafe gear lights. Then Don talked about the CVR and its erasure. He explained how the CVR recorded only the last thirty minutes and would have recorded over the actual upset and recovery portion of the flight. He talked about the emergency situation the crew still faced after the plane came to a stop. "Now, there will be testimony that Captain Gibson on prior occasions did typically erase the cockpit voice recorder, but Captain

Gibson is also going to tell you that he was extremely concerned about the safety of his passengers at the conclusion of this flight. The fact is he made the landing, and you will hear passengers testify that this was the smoothest landing they had ever experienced. As he made that landing and turned off the active runway onto a taxiway he was advised by the ground emergency personnel that he had something leaking out of the aircraft, and it was leaking fuel. He's going to tell you that the last thing on his mind was worrying about a cockpit voice recorder."[6]

Don did what any good attorney should do when confronted with potentially damaging evidence. He brought up the CVR erasure himself and planted seeds of doubt in the minds of the jurors before Boeing and Hvass could blame the crew for the erasure. He used the same tactic to counter potential harm from the Bates letter, which was the letter written by a United Airlines first officer claiming to have witnessed other pilots performing the unauthorized procedure of extending trailing edge flaps without slats. "Now, we expect there to be testimony offered by either the plaintiff or Boeing by way of deposition, I believe, of an individual named Walter Bates. He is a second officer flying for a competing airline. I think he flies for United. He's never served as captain. And he apparently wrote a letter to the Air Line Pilots Association about a year, year-and-a-half ago. And he apparently was commenting on his own with respect to what occurred on flight 841. When you hear that testimony, I want you to listen very carefully to it because that is also the basis apparently for Boeing's theory that there was crew involvement in this maneuver. I want you to listen carefully to what Mr. Bates has to say about this unauthorized procedure that evidently Boeing will be discussing. Mr. Bates never performed the procedure himself. Apparently Mr. Bates is an 18-year pilot. He's seen the procedure performed once, but yet when we deposed him less than two months ago he couldn't tell us what the procedure was, and even more significantly, he couldn't tell us who performed the procedure."[7]

———•◦•———

Boeing's strategy for the trial was for an all-out attack on the crew. The lawyer representing Boeing, Boyd Ratchye, was an experienced trial attorney, having worked a number of aviation cases, including cases involving other aircraft manufacturers such as Beech Aircraft. He was a no-nonsense lawyer who didn't hesitate in going after a witness using his deep, booming voice.

Boyd began his opening statement defending Boeing and the 727. "I will be speaking on behalf of Boeing for about 45 minutes, and this again is an opening statement, a road-map statement of what our proof is going to be and what we intend to prove when we present our case. Counsel is here with me from Seattle, in Minneapolis. It's a complex case. It will be a difficult case. Part of the reason it's a complex, difficult case is it's an extremely important case. Proofs will show that there are 1,800 of these airplanes flying. This one is flying today for TWA, the aircraft that was involved in this accident. While we have been speaking this morning, Boeing 727's have been taking off and landing and flying passengers to every continent. This challenge to the integrity of this aircraft is serious. As it's suggested, over four years ago there was a problem with the aircraft rather than the crew. And that's then what it really shakes out to be with these 1,800 aircraft: Was there a problem with the aircraft, or was there a problem with the crew?"[8]

Ratchye then took an unfair jab at Hoot. "TWA no longer has pilot Gibson flying the aircraft," Ratchye told the jurors. "He flies a different aircraft. He is not responsible to fly this aircraft."[9] The statement insinuated that TWA was purposefully keeping Hoot off the 727, when the truth was that Hoot had been promoted to captain on the L-1011, and after flying that aircraft for a short period of time Hoot had bid back to the Boeing 747 as a first officer for more time off and a better schedule.

At one point in his opening statement, Boyd Ratchye slipped up. He said something that almost caused a mistrial. The instructions to the attorneys were that the jurors were not to hear any of the conclusions of the NTSB Board. Boyd was talking about some of the experts he planned to call when he made this statement: "The conclusion of a man named Von Husen who is an expert on the National Transportation Safety Board was—"

Attorney Don Mark objected as soon as he heard the words "conclusion" and "Safety Board" uttered in the same sentence. The judge allowed Ratchye to continue, but Don Mark wasn't about to let the comment go unchallenged. When Ratchye ended his opening statement, and after the jurors were excused for recess, Don Mark asked for a mistrial. "At this time on behalf of TWA I am going to make a motion for a mistrial based upon the comments made by counsel for Boeing in the opening statement on behalf of Boeing. The comments were that it is the conclusion of Mr. Von Husen, and the experts have concluded, language to that effect. It was my understanding from the Court's rulings with respect to the National Transportation Safety Board and their related reports that there would be no conclusionary evidence or testimony or reference made during the course of the trial. It's my understanding that only the factual portion of the report would go in. It's my belief that this jury has now heard at least from counsel that the NTSB has concluded, or at least a member has concluded, certain facts which are not necessarily the case, but in any event we have now placed the stamp of the United States Government upon this trial, and we have in effect taken away from the jury their right to listen to all of this evidence and make their own decision."[10]

The judge didn't declare a mistrial, but he did admonish Ratchye for his choice of words and warned all of the attorneys about making a similar mistake. If nothing else, Don Mark demonstrated that he intended to put up a vigorous defense and represent his client to the best of his ability.

<hr />

First to present his case to the jury was plaintiff's attorney Charles Hvass. Hvass began by calling Holly Wicker's co-worker and fellow TWA 841 passenger, Sheryl Fisher. Sheryl was there to not only testify about her experiences as a passenger aboard TWA 841, but also as someone who had personally witnessed Holly's experience with back spasms and partial paralysis on the left side of her face, which caused her to sometimes drool when she drank.

Attorney Don Mark in his cross got Sheryl to admit that she and Holly Wicker were not only co-workers but also close friends who saw each other socially outside of work. It was a subtle suggestion of possible bias.

The first day of trial ended with Sheryl Fisher commenting that she, too, had seen whom she was certain was flight engineer Gary Banks hand meal trays to a flight attendant minutes before the upset.

The next day began with testimony from passenger Robert Reber. Robert testified that he had lost consciousness at some point in the dive but that he did remember the plane shaking just before the upset. He also described the strong g-forces he had felt. ". . . I was literally nailed to the seat. I couldn't move my arms, I couldn't move my legs, I couldn't move anything."[11]

Robert Reber's appearance was followed by the first of two technical experts Hvass had hired to work on the case. Robert Masmussen was a hydraulic expert and former employee of Honeywell, a Minneapolis-based aerospace company. Masmussen had also been involved with the space program from the Mercury flights to the Space Shuttle. He had even worked on the lunar lander.

Hvass used Masmussen's testimony as a means of explaining to the jurors the operation of the slat actuator and what may or may not have caused the slat to extend. Using illustrations and cutouts showing the individual slat actuator parts, Masmussen repeated the same claims made by Boeing and the NTSB, which was that there were redundant means to keep the slat retracted and that mechanical failure was highly improbable. It was Masmussen's conclusion that the slat was extended by crew action.

Don Mark countered Masmussen's testimony by getting him to concede that he had completed his analysis without having access to the actual actuator involved in the incident, nor did he have any firsthand experience with the damaged aircraft. All of his work had been done with illustrations, photographs, and data supplied by Boeing. Don also got Masmussen to admit that a fracture of the piston near the locking rings could cause the slat to extend even though the possibility of that happening was remote.

When Don questioned him about his research in preparing to testify, Masmussen admitted that he had come across numerous cases of slat actuator problems prior to TWA 841 and that Boeing had conducted a flight test to determine the controllability of the aircraft with an extended slat in isolation. Both Hvass and Masmussen were quick to point out that the earlier problems were with the Decoto slat actuator and not the Ronson actuator, but Don had accomplished what he had set out to do. He had introduced to the jurors an opposing theory, one that pointed to the possibility of mechanical failure.

Knowing that this case would involve a lot of technical testimony, visual aids were present throughout the trial. All three attorneys made extensive use of diagrams, illustrations, mock-ups, models, cutaways, photographs, and video. While the attorneys sometimes struggled with the over-sized diagrams and illustrations, the presence of the visual aids served the purpose of making complex systems and theories easier to grasp.

The last person called to the witness stand on day two of the trial was James Bailey, Hvass's second technical expert. Bailey was a pilot who also had previously worked at Honeywell. Like Hvass's first technical expert, Robert Masmussen, Bailey had an impressive background. He had served as a Corsair pilot in the Pacific during WWII. As a military pilot, Bailey worked alongside pilots like Frank Borman, Tom Stafford, and Neil Armstrong. He had also worked as a test pilot for Honeywell.

Bailey's role in the trial was to criticize the flight crew for not taking appropriate action in controlling an easily controllable situation. He was also there to explain basic aerodynamic terms and concepts, starting with an explanation of how the ailerons, elevators, and rudder work in controlling an aircraft. It was flying 101, but it was necessary for the jurors to understand those basics before the more complex aspects of the upset were introduced. Day two ended with Bailey still on the stand talking about stalls, high-speed buffet, and the coffin corner.

When Bailey resumed the stand on day three of the trial, the topic moved on to what Bailey would have done differently if faced with the same situation as the flight crew. A summary of the many mistakes the crew made, according to Bailey, was that Captain Gibson should have reacted sooner, he should not have pulled back on the yoke, and he should not have applied rudder.

Hvass's attempt to find fault with the crew led to an interesting exchange concerning whether or not he could introduce into evidence a particular book. In his preparation for the trial, Hvass could not find anything in any of the TWA training manuals or the 727 flight manuals that addressed the exact situation Hoot had been faced with on April 4, 1979. He couldn't point to a specific procedure that, if followed, would have prevented the upset. He did, however, find information in an aviation book about flying large jets that he believed was pertinent. So Hvass decided to introduce this book into the trial by way of Jim Bailey. He brought up the book while questioning pilot Bailey.

"Let me interrupt you for a second," Hvass said as he approached the witness. "Prior to coming here to testify you reviewed with materials supplied by Boeing, ALPA, NTSB, is that correct?"

"Yes, that's correct," Bailey responded.

"Did you also read a book entitled *Handling the Big Jets* by D. P. Davies?"

"Yes, I read the book."

"Did you recognize this book as an authority in the field of handling large jet aircraft?"

"It's a very fine book. I did discuss this book with a number of other people, airline people, and they will support that opinion."[12]

Hvass then moved on to the topic of what the crew should and shouldn't have done but soon circled back around to the Davies book. "In connection with your testimony you said that you had read *Handling the Big Jets* by Mr. Davies."

"Yes," Bailey replied.

Hvass retrieved the Davies book from the plaintiff's table. "The date on this book is—this is the third edition, 1971, and Your Honor, at this time, pursuant to rule 803.18, Rules of Evidence, I'd like to read two excerpts from the book, read them to the jury."

Don Mark objected. When the judge overruled his objection, Don asked that a record be made of his objection. At that point the judge asked the attorneys to approach the bench for a discussion out of the hearing of the jury.

Mark argued that the book was not an authoritative document. In his defense, Hvass made the following statement: "Your Honor, the TWA flight crew newsletter said it was valuable information for both the novice and experienced jet flyer."

". . . What's helpful to me are the expert's opinions," the judge explained, "not necessarily the opinions of the attorneys, but if this witness expert called by the plaintiff says it's authoritative in the field under 803.18, in my opinion he can read it, but I think you ought to repeat the question to him as a condition precedent to proceeding in this fashion, and we will note your continuing objection to this. Thank you."

After the attorneys returned to their respective places, Hvass had Bailey state that in his opinion the Davies book was an authoritative document. Hvass then read several sections from the book and followed that up with questions to Bailey asking for his opinion on whether or not he agreed with what was just read. To those in attendance, it appeared as though Hvass had scored a minor victory.[13]

Boeing attorney Boyd Ratchye also took advantage of the judge's ruling concerning the Davies book. He mentioned the book near the end of his cross-examination of Bailey. "I have one more matter to cover, and it's in again this Davies book, and I just want to inquire—you have indicated this is an authoritative text in the field."

"Yes, that's correct," Bailey replied confidently.

Ratchye read a section from the book that really didn't apply to the case at hand. The section he'd selected dealt with flap over-speeds and the use of flaps in holding patterns at high altitudes. Ratchye was trying to draw inference to the fact that use of flaps above the limitations set forth by the aircraft manufacturer was prohibited.[14]

For all the debate over whether or not the Davies book should or should not be allowed into evidence and the apparent damage to TWA and the crew by the judge allowing it, in the end it didn't matter thanks to some quick thinking by Don Mark. In one brilliant move during his re-cross-examination of Bailey, he undid hours of damaging testimony in one fell swoop.

With Bailey still on the stand, Mark picked up the Davies book and approached the witness. "All right, sir. First of all, with respect to this book, *Handling the Big Jets*, everybody's had an opportunity to read here, so with your permission I will do the same. There is a preface to the book, is there not?"

"Yes," Bailey replied, not sure where this was headed.

"You are familiar with that, are you?"

"I think there is an acknowledgment and a few other things in there."

"All right. He thanks his wife and so forth, as they usually do."

"Yes."

"But then there is a preface after that, right?"

"Yes."

Mark opened the book and thumbed through the first few pages. "Beginning on—well, the page is not numbered, but it's the preface to the first edition, and it states as follows: 'I am anxious that this book should be received in the way in which it is offered, that is purely as an expression of my personal opinions. It is not an official ruling on the subject but is based on my experience of a variety of jet transports and includes the advice of many pilots specially qualified on specific subjects and the advice of engineering specialists. I am the first to admit that there are probably errors of fact in this book. I can only ask those who identify them to forgive me and let me know the truth as they see it. In some of the more contentious areas one of my biggest difficulties was to get two experts to agree on a particular point, and it was amusing to find myself acting as umpire in a field in which I was completely unqualified.'"[15]

To further diminish any damage done by Bailey's testimony, Mark established the following: Bailey had never flown a Boeing 727 as either pilot, co-pilot, or flight engineer, he had never flown any commercial jet, and he did not hold an Airline Transport Pilot (ATP) Rating.

After Bailey was excused from the stand, two more witnesses were called: Thomas Quill, a passenger aboard TWA 841, and Susan Armel, a neighbor of Holly Wicker's. Thomas Quill testified that his first recollection that something was wrong was when he felt the plane "veering off to the right" in a continuous pattern.[16] In cross-examination, Don Mark had Thomas Quill demonstrate the aircraft movement using a model. Don wanted to emphasize to the jurors that Thomas Quill's recollections did not include any banks to the left. Susan Armel testified to the numerous times she had witnessed Holly exhibiting signs of back and neck problems, including one instance where Holly had to leave a church meeting to ice down her neck. The judge then excused the jury for an early lunch recess. As the jury dispersed, the three lawyers met in the judge's chambers to discuss an issue raised by Don Mark. Earlier in the day, Don had read an article in the Minneapolis Star Tribune that contained statements attributed to Boeing Attorney Boyd Ratchye.

"Thank you, Your Honor," Mark began. "In this morning's *Minneapolis Star Tribune*, Thursday, May 12, 1983, there is coverage on the case, and the article is entitled *Reasons for Jetliner 6.5 Mile Plunge Argued*. We discussed earlier in chambers today that in addition to reporting the trial and the various exhibits and so forth that are expected to be offered, there is an entry in the article that states as follows: The lawyer for Boeing, Boyd Ratchye, said an investigation by the National

Transportation Safety Board concluded that the crew extended four slats, but when they were retracted only three returned. It goes on to say that the Safety Board, which did not have the missing pieces of the aircraft, concluded that the crew extended the slats, and there was no malfunction."[17]

Mark was furious. He wanted the article put into the record as evidence to show at some later time that the statements from Ratchye had occurred during the course of the trial. Ratchye denied having made any such statements. The judge didn't take sides, but he did prohibit the attorneys from speaking to the press about the case during the balance of the trial.

Up to this point the two plaintiffs in the trial, Timothy and Holly Wicker, had yet to testify. Tim Wicker took the stand as the last witness on day three. He verified Holly's condition before and after the incident and explained how her worsening health had affected him personally. The next day, May 13, a juror fell ill and Holly, who was scheduled to testify, had laryngitis. So the trial was postponed until the following Monday, May 16th.

When the trial resumed, the first witness called was not Holly Wicker but a friend of Holly's who was co-authoring a book with Holly about adoption.[18] She also testified about having witnessed several instances where Holly had exhibited severe back spasms.

Holly Wicker finally took the stand on what was the fourth full day of the trial. Holly began by explaining how and why she was on the flight. She next explained how she became injured and how those injuries had negatively affected her and her family. Holly's testimony was sincere and lacking in self-pity. She came across as truthful despite skepticism from those who felt that perhaps her injuries were not as severe as she claimed. The belief by some that Holly was only out for the money led to Holly's receiving hate mail. Unlike today's online bullying, Holly's hate mail was delivered directly to her house.[19]

Hoot was one of those in the Holly-as-malingerer camp. He couldn't understand how she could have been injured to the extent she was claiming. Hoot's negative opinion of Holly Wicker was partially the result of testimony she had given about a conversation she claimed to have overheard during the filming of the documentary *The Plane That Fell From The Sky*. Holly claimed that she had overheard Hoot make a comment to another passenger about the three crew members not being able to agree on the exact sequence of events inside the cockpit. It was also Holly's statement that had started the damaging flight engineer, circuit breaker theory. So he was skeptical of Holly's claims and motives.

Attorney Charles Hvass began by having Holly tell the jurors her version of events from the initial upset to the recovery. Holly started by saying that she first perceived something was wrong when she felt the aircraft shaking. She described the shaking as feeling like metal rubbing against metal. Her next perception was the tremendous pressure she felt against her body. Holly said that at the time she had the infant Asha lying face down across her knees. She next described how the baby began sliding down her legs.

"The pressure shoved me backwards towards my seat like—it's hard to describe, like this, but kind of down," Holly said as she tried to demonstrate her sitting position. "The baby felt like she was sliding down my knees. I felt like I was losing my control over her. She then began to turn blue, very blue."

"As Asha turned blue," Hvass asked Holly, "what did you do?"

"I tried to pull her up. I managed to get my other hand down to her, and I tried to pull her from my knees up to my chest, and I couldn't do it."

"How much did Asha weigh at that point?"

"She was malnourished. She weighed just a little over five pounds."

"And you couldn't lift her?"

"I couldn't lift her."

"When you couldn't lift her and she was turning blue," Hvass asked, "what did you do?"

"I bent over to my knees all the way down, and it was incredibly difficult. I thought I would never get there."

"When you got there what did you do?"

"I gave her two breaths, and something happened after the second breath. I don't know what it was. It was like a searing pain across my chest and the sensation that I had no air left, that there was nothing left to give her, and I was consumed with a fear that I wouldn't be able to breathe for her or myself."

". . . Did you feel any pain in your neck?" Hvass asked.

"I felt a sharp pain in my neck; I felt tremendous strain in my back."[20]

Hvass had shown through the testimony of other passengers just how strong the g-forces had been during the dive. Passengers had testified about being unable to lift their arms off their armrests. Holly's testimony about having to overcome those forces to help save Asha was compelling evidence that she had indeed suffered injuries to her neck and back.

Don Mark didn't challenge Holly directly about her injuries. Instead, he questioned Holly about previous injuries she had sustained, including those from a car accident that had resulted in Holly having to wear a cervical collar. He also questioned Holly about her decision to decline medical treatment in Detroit immediately after the accident.

Boyd Ratchye's cross-examination of Holly Wicker focused mostly on her testimony about having seen the flight engineer hand the meal trays to the flight attendant minutes before the incident. Holly had made that claim the night of the incident. She repeated it during her earlier deposition. And she made the claim again during the trial, adding that she recognized Gary Banks as the person she had seen and that she was certain that it was not one of the male stewards. Sheryl Fisher also testified to the same timing of events. The jurors, of course, did not have any knowledge that flight attendant Mark Moscicki had testified in January of 1980 that he had received the meal trays from Gary Banks at least thirty minutes before the upset. So was it simply a difference in opinion over the timing of events? That is what most people familiar with this particular controversy believed. But Holly added a detail that clearly delineated the incident into two separate versions of the same story. Holly indicated that she had seen someone whom she believed to be Gary Banks hand three meal trays to a female flight attendant.

Hvass's next and final witness was Holly Wicker's personal physician, Dr. Clifford Phibbs. Dr. Phibbs gave testimony on Holly's diagnosis and treatment. He talked about the various prescriptions for pain, headaches, and muscle relaxants as well as Valium for insomnia. He made a compelling case that Holly had suffered long-lasting injuries that were not easy to measure. When it comes to pain and discomfort, only the patient dealing with that pain can attest to the severity, Phibbs explained. In Holly's case, the muscle pain and back spasms were sporadic and unpredictable.

Don Mark zeroed in on the sporadic nature of Holly's complaints during his cross-examination of Dr. Phibbs. Holly had first come to Dr. Phibbs the day after the accident. At that time the initial tests done on Holly showed that she had a full range of motion in both her back and neck. X-rays taken at various times after the accident all came back normal. Neurological examinations were normal. Tests for detecting back spasms registered her responses as normal. Hvass did his best on redirect to diminish the damage, but Don Mark did exactly what he said he would do in his opening remarks—he used Holly's own doctor's testimony and reports to suggest that Holly did not suffer from the injuries she was claiming.

After four long days of testimony, Charles Hvass's portion of the trial was over. He had successfully laid out a case showing how and why Holly had been injured as a result of TWA 841 and how those injuries were still affecting her daily life. Don Mark, through his thorough cross-examination of witnesses, did an effective job of casting doubt as to the severity and cause of those injuries. The jury would ultimately have to decide who had made the most convincing case. But whether or not Holly Wicker should receive compensation was only one part of this two-part trial. The question to be answered next was who was responsible for those injuries? The answer to that question would take up the lion's share of the remainder of the trial.

Chapter Twenty-Four

Challenge and Response

Hoot liked Don Mark from the get-go. The fact that Don's father and mother had worked for an airline helped pave the way for a long-lasting friendship between the two men. But Hoot learned very early on that while it was TWA who was facing damage claims, the crew's actions before, during, and after the rollover would be the focus of the trial. If the opposing attorneys could show that the crew was at fault, then TWA would be guilty by association and solely responsible for all damages brought against the airline. Don explained to Hoot in no uncertain terms that he was going to be criticized once again by a whole new set of people. To help prepare Hoot for his depositions and trial testimony, Don spent time with Hoot in mock trials, taking on the role of the opposing attorney.

The mock trials proved to be a good idea. Hoot was defensive and unsympathetic. His responses were so bad that Don resorted to video-taping the questions and answers so Hoot could see for himself how poorly he was coming across. The tactic had the desired effect. When Hoot saw how combative he was with his answers, he immediately understood what Don was trying to accomplish. By the time of the videotaped depositions and his testimony at trial, Hoot was relaxed and confident.

Figure 39 Hoot with attorney Donald Chance Mark

Hoot was the first witness called by Don Mark. Don, through his questioning, led Hoot through the story of TWA 841 from liftoff at JFK to the emergency landing in Detroit. Along the way Don covered topics that he knew were going to come up in cross-examination: Hoot's time off for his broken ankle, his training to be re-qualified as a 727 captain, and Hoot's habit of routinely erasing the CVR after every flight. It was the same story Hoot had told before but with new details that hadn't appeared in earlier accounts, such as the fact that the plane yawed noticeably before the upset, and that he had briefly overpowered the autopilot prior to disconnecting it. Don Mark ended his direct examination of Hoot with the following exchange: "Captain Gibson, at any time did you manipulate any flight controls in an unauthorized manner prior to the upset of TWA 841?"

"Absolutely not," Hoot responded.

"Did anyone under your command manipulate flight controls in an unauthorized manner prior to the upset of TWA 841?"

"No, sir."

"That's all. Thank you, Captain Gibson."[1]

Attorney Charles Hvass had the first crack at Hoot for cross-examination. He wasted little time trying to poke holes in Hoot's story. He questioned Hoot on his testimony that he had moved his seat back a few inches prior to the upset in order to put his old charts away and retrieve the new charts for Minneapolis. Hvass tried to paint that ordinary task as somehow not performed with the "highest degree of care." His seat was back, which meant he couldn't react as quickly as he might have if his seat was closer. His attention was on getting his charts and not on flying the plane.

Hvass next attempted to paint Hoot as less than professional because he hadn't used the correct phraseology when he asked Scott to extend the spoilers. Then Hvass questioned Hoot about the CVR erasure. "You are aware that the FAA regulations then require that the cockpit voice recorder information be maintained whenever there is an accident, isn't that right?" Hvass asked Hoot.

"Yes, sir," Hoot replied.

"You didn't take any steps to maintain that cockpit voice recorder here, did you, Captain Gibson?"

"I never even thought about it."

"You knew this was a part 830 emergency that was going to have to be reported, didn't you, Captain Gibson?"

"At this point, I didn't think about that either."[2]

Hoot handled himself well during Hvass's cross-examination. He wasn't defensive or disrespectful. Hvass ended his cross-examination with an unusual line of questioning. "Captain Gibson, you are aware that you are required to report your permanent address to the FAA, is that right?"

"Yes, sir," Hoot replied.

"There is an FAA regulation on that?"

"Yes, sir."

"And when you took the stand yesterday, you told us your permanent address was on Territory Street in Las Vegas, is that right?"

"That's true."

"Isn't it true on January 7, you told the FAA that your permanent address was in San Jose, Costa Rica?"

"Well, that's where I am living now."

"That's all I have got. Thank you."[3]

Boyd Ratchye was next to cross-examine Hoot. His initial questions concerned the CVR erasure. Boyd made no effort to disguise his disdain for Hoot. "Now, I had understood you to testify that the CVR had as its purpose to aid in posthumous investigations," Ratchye began. "Is that your testimony this morning?"

"Yes," Hoot answered. "I said that's why it was put on the airplane."

"There is nothing in the regulation about posthumous investigations, is there?"

"Not that I read in the regulations, no."

"The regulation obligates you and TWA to save the cockpit voice recorder?"

"Yes, it does."[4]

Ratchye next spent a great deal of time on a training bulletin that had been issued prior to the time Hoot had returned on the 727 as captain. The training bulletin dealt with handling inoperative leading-edge devices or asymmetrical flaps. The procedure described the steps for extending the leading-edge devices but not the flaps. The point Ratchye was trying to make was that if you were to reverse the procedure you would reproduce the Boeing Scenario. But Hoot had no reason to even be aware of the bulletin since it wasn't a permanent procedure found in the training manual.

Mark countered Ratchye's line of questioning with his redirect examination. "With respect to the questions concerning the leading edge device inoperative and the trailing edge flap asymmetry," Mark asked Hoot, "those sections of the bulletin that you were given, prior to the unscheduled dive of 841 did you experience trailing edge flap asymmetry?"

". . . No, sir."

"And the purpose of the bulletin that you have discussed was what to do when you do experience trailing edge flap assymetry. Is that correct?"

"Yes, sir."

"Prior to the dive of flight 841, did you experience leading edge devise inoperative?"

"No, sir."

"That's all. Thank you."[5]

Many in the courtroom had expected a fiery exchange between Ratchye and Hoot. Here was Boeing's chief counsel finally getting a chance to cross-examine someone who had dared to challenge the integrity of the most popular aircraft in the world. But Ratchye was unable to elicit anything new or damning from Hoot. After several hours of cross-examination, he had failed to make a single significant point.

Scott Kennedy was next to take the stand. Don Mark's direct examination of Scott was centered primarily on having Scott recount the upset and recovery from his perspective. Scott told the jurors the same story he had recounted many times before. He was focused on the clock while making a ground speed check and was unaware that the plane was banking until he heard Hoot say, "Get 'em up."

When it came to the important questions concerning the CVR and crew involvement, Don gave Scott an opportunity to deny those accusations under oath.[6]

"As the passengers deplaned, what was the cockpit crew doing?" Mark asked Scott.

"We were doing the secure cockpit checklist and gathering up our items to get out of the plane," Scott replied.

"Was the secure cockpit checklist accomplished?"

"Yes, it was."

"You are acquainted with the cockpit voice recorder in the 727 aircraft?"

"Yes, I am."

"During the course of the flight, or at the conclusion of the flight, did you observe anybody erase that cockpit voice recorder, Mr. Kennedy?"

"No, sir, I did not."

"Did you in fact erase it yourself, sir?"

"No, no, I don't ever touch that thing."

Don ended his questioning of Scott Kennedy on the topic of the crew's manipulation of the flight controls. "Mr. Kennedy, on April 4, 1979, did you manipulate any flight controls in an unauthorized manner prior to the upset of TWA 841?"

"No, sir, I did not."

"On that day did you observe either Captain Gibson or Flight Engineer Banks manipulate any flight controls in an unauthorized manner?"

"No, sir, I did not."

"Thank you, sir. That's all."[7]

The cross-examination of Scott Kennedy by plaintiff's attorney Charles Hvass and the counsel for Boeing, Boyd Ratchye, followed a similar line where both lawyers tried to show inconsistencies in Scott's statements. The attorneys spent a great deal of time on exactly when Scott became aware that there was a problem. What was the bank angle when Scott heard Hoot say "Get her up"? Sixty degrees? Was the plane inverted as Scott claimed in an earlier statement? Why the discrepancies?

A common theme employed by both lawyers was that the crew weren't doing their jobs of monitoring the aircraft and did not respond quickly enough to the initial phases of the upset. Hoot wasn't paying attention because he was putting his charts away. Scott somehow didn't know the plane was rolling over because he was focused on making a ground speed check even though the yoke was right in front of him. And Gary, who had testified in a videotaped deposition that his mind was "idling" prior to the upset, should have been monitoring the instruments more carefully. And since there was ample evidence that a plane with a single slat extended is an easily controllable condition, none of the three crew members responded in a timely fashion to rectify the problem. As Hvass and Ratchye were apt to repeat over and over, the crew had not acted with the "highest degree of care."

After playing the videotaped testimony of Gary Banks, Don called to the stand flight attendant Mark Moscicki. Don had Mark recount the near-disaster from his perspective. Of particular importance to Don was Mark's recollection of receiving the meal trays from Gary Banks. But before he broached that subject, Don laid the groundwork for Holly Wicker's possible misidentification. "Can you describe for the jury, Mr. Moscicki, the uniform worn by TWA flight attendants on April 4, 1979?"

"Yes, I can. The uniform we wore then are identical to the uniform that we wear now. They are black. They have stripes on the sleeves. They were designed to be of a military fashion."

"Have you ever been confused by passengers on any flights that you have flown as being a pilot or cockpit crew member?"

"Very often."[8]

Next came the issue of the meal trays. Don asked Mark a series of questions related to when and how he had received the meal trays from the flight crew. Mark told the same story as he had told in his earlier deposition about meeting Gary Banks halfway between the galley and first class. When asked about the timing of that exchange, Mark couldn't remember how much time had elapsed from the time of the exchange to the upset. After a lunch recess, Don Mark had Moscicki read a portion of his deposition transcript where he had stated that at least thirty minutes had passed between the two events. Mark Moscicki also made a slight change to his earlier statements by claiming that Gary had brought back two trays and not three as previously stated.[9]

Flight attendants Carol Reams and Carlos Machado-Olverdo were next on the witness stand. Flight attendant Francine Schaulleur had died in an automobile accident prior to the trial. The testimony from the flight attendants placed all four in first class prior to the incident. Carol Reams was sitting in seat 2F. Carlos and Mark were both sitting on the aft-facing jump seats next to the cockpit door. Francine was in the galley warming a bottle of milk. Francine, who had given her deposition on this topic back on January 29, 1980, had said that she did not see Gary Banks leave the cockpit. She also testified that she did not receive the meal trays from Gary Banks. Both Carlos and Carol Reams testified that they did not see Gary Banks leave the cockpit at any time. Their testimony was a direct contradiction to the testimony given by Holly Wicker and Sheryl Fisher. It was a contradiction that the jurors would have to sort out. Both Charles Hvass and Boyd Ratchye alluded to the timing of events as being in close proximity to the meal tray exchange.

Throughout the trial both attorneys made attempts to compel witnesses to say that they had felt a sudden and startling vibration. They needed this, of course, to corroborate the testimony from passengers aboard the 1981 test flight. But despite their best efforts, no one described the vibration as sudden or startling. Attorney Charles Hvass brought up the vibration in his cross-examination of flight attendant Carol Reams. "Ms. Reams, when you talk about a vibration, I take it, it was a sudden onset?"

"Yes," Carol replied.

"Startling?"

"The onset wasn't so startling. The dive was."[10]

Later attorney Elisabeth Hoene, counsel for Boeing, made another attempt to get Carol to say that the vibration she felt was startling. "With respect to the vibration," Hoene began, "the shaking, whatever, can you describe how you sensed it? In other words, were you shaking? Did you feel it, you were being shook up and down?"

"No. No, I wasn't," Carol Reams replied. "It was a continuous and a very definite vibration, is the only way I can describe it."

"Did it feel like someone grabbed hold of the plane and started shaking?"

"Yes, yes, it did."[11]

Attorney Hoene would use the same line of questioning with each person she encountered on the witness stand who had been aboard TWA 841. The problem with her analogy, though, of comparing the vibration to someone "grabbing the plane and shaking it," was that she included no correlation to intensity or timing. A gentle but definite vibration could be described in the same manner. When passengers on the stand agreed with her analogy, they more than likely were referring to the vibration they felt during the dive and subsequent recovery.

Only one witness used the word "startling" to describe the shaking, flight attendant Carlos Machado-Olverdo, for whom English was a second language. Charles Hvass brought up the subject in his cross-examination. "At the onset of the incident, you heard funny sounds at the same time the airplane started shaking?" Hvass asked.

"Yes, sir," Carlos answered.

"What did you hear?"

"It sound like, you know, rumbling, shaking."

"Was it a sudden—"

"Yes."

"Was it startling?"

"Startling, you mean start and stop and start—"

"I mean startling, all of a sudden it was there and sort of grabbed your attention?"

"Yes, it was, yes."[12]

With the flight crew and cabin crew having given testimony contrary to the theory being put forth by Boyd Ratchye and Charles Hvass, Don Mark next set out to challenge the remaining pieces of evidence used to incriminate the crew. He did so through a methodical questioning of expert witnesses. Don's list of experts included pilots, an associate professor of human factors psychology, an aviation safety expert, and a hydraulics expert. But before he proceeded with that phase of his case, he tackled the question of Holly Wicker's claims of having been injured as a result of TWA 841.

Don's strategy was to show that Holly's complaints of back and neck pain were most likely the result of an earlier automobile accident. He hired his own specialist to examine Holly. The specialist, neurological surgeon Harold Buschstein, testified that he could not find anything wrong with Holly Wicker when he examined her other than some tenderness in the muscles of the back and neck. Dr. Buschstein found that Holly had full range of motion in her neck and back. He testified that Holly's complaints were subjective and that he could not find any measurable or determinable permanent injury.

Attorney Charles Hvass did a commendable job of lessening any damage done by Don Mark's expert witness. "You saw Holly Wicker, Doctor, for the purpose of what we call an adverse examination—is that correct?" Hvass asked Doctor Buschstein.

"Well, sometimes we call it an independent medical examination, seems to be the same thing," Buschstein replied.

"And the defense lawyers call it an independent medical examination, the plaintiffs call it an adverse examination—is that right? You weren't seeing Holly Wicker for purposes of helping her get better, were you, Doctor?"

"I was not a treating physician, no."[13]

Hvass then pointed out that the doctor had seen Holly only one time, his actual physical examination had lasted only five minutes, and he had not reviewed Holly's medical records since his examination. It was an effective cross-examination that greatly diminished Buschstein's testimony. Don Mark, however, was unfazed. His goal was only to sow a seed of doubt that perhaps Holly's injuries were not as severe as she claimed and that her previous automobile accident could account for her current complaints.

With the medical questions out of the way, Don took on the claim of crew involvement. Don challenged earlier testimony indicating that the crew was slow to respond. He put on the stand an expert in human factors who testified that the time Hoot took to analyze the initial buzz and motion of the plane was not only reasonable but appropriate. The same human factors expert commended the crew for the crew coordination they exhibited during the recovery and diversion to Detroit.

Don called to the stand the former Director of the Bureau of Aviation Safety for the National Transportation Safety Board, Charles O. Miller. Miller, who had left the NTSB in 1974, had been a vocal critic of the investigation into TWA 841. He was especially critical of the job done by Investigator-in-Charge Leslie Kampschror. Miller challenged the logic of the Boeing Scenario. He pointed out that Hoot had spoken with an FAA inspector within hours of the incident. Miller stated that in his experience statements given in such close proximity to an incident are often the most reliable. He made the following comment when asked about the written statement prepared by FAA inspector Roger Gordon.[14]

"Well, the first thing was, as I said earlier, that I believed the man under these conditions—it's inconceivable to me, as I think the jury heard before from another witness, it's inconceivable to me that the flight crew could have had time to make up a story of some—as stated earlier this morning, some unauthorized procedure, and under these conditions speak to an FAA inspector and give this kind of testimony to him. I just cannot in my experience justify or accept any argument that they took the time and were able to in this period of a few hours concoct a story and give this kind of statement to the FAA man."[15]

Don Mark, through his witnesses, had demonstrated to the jurors that the Boeing Scenario was an implausible theory. It didn't make sense from a logic standpoint. The idea that the incident began in close proximity to the flight engineer leaving and returning to the cockpit was contradicted by the testimony of the four flight attendants as well as passengers sitting in first class. There wasn't time or opportunity for the crew to perform such a procedure, nor was there time and opportunity to concoct a cover-up story. Further, Don called several pilots from various airlines, including United, and not one of them had ever heard of the procedure or knew of anyone who had. The one pilot who claimed to have had firsthand experience with the procedure, United Airlines first officer Walter Bates, could not explain how to perform the procedure and was unable to identify any pilots who had performed it.

Don's last task was to leave the jurors with an alternative explanation of what might have caused that number 7 slat to extend—part failure. Don accomplished this task with his next two witnesses. Don first called to the stand Beldon Rich, a hydraulics expert. Beldon Rich laid out two possible failure modes that could have led to an un-commanded extension of the slat.

Don's second technical expert, Eugene Morgan, a TWA project engineer responsible for technical support in the areas of hydraulics and flight controls, was the author of the TWA engineering report on Flight 841. Mr. Morgan had examined the damaged aircraft in Detroit and had participated in the investigation up till the point of his report, which was submitted on May 31, 1979. Don used Morgan's testimony to establish that the aircraft involved in the incident had been properly maintained. He also wanted Morgan's help in disputing some of the statements made by Hvass's technical expert, Robert Rasmussem.

The testimony and cross-examination of Don's two technical experts took two days. It was esoteric testimony that was sometimes difficult to follow. Both Hvass and Ratchye spent hours grilling Don's experts, pointing out that the previous slat actuator failures had been with the Decoto actuator and not the Ronson actuator found on TWA 841, and that the proposed failure modes were highly unlikely due to the design strength of the suspected parts. But Don pointed out to the jurors that the T-bolt that had failed on the number seven slat actuator wasn't supposed to fail, nor was the bolt that was supposed to lock out the right outboard aileron. Those parts failed. The Decoto slat actuator, which performed the same function as the Ronson actuator, had numerous failures. Despite Boeing's claims to the contrary, Don Mark made a convincing argument that no part was infallible.

Don Mark's last two witnesses were TWA 841 passengers Floyd and Patricia Carlson. Floyd Carlson had been sitting in seat 1C, an aisle seat. He had an unobstructed view of the cockpit door. Neither he nor his wife saw anyone leave the cockpit at any time during the flight. Neither Hvass nor Ratchye bothered to challenge their recollections. It was another unresolved conflict that the jurors would have to consider at a later time.

Chapter Twenty-Five

Weight & Balance

The last to present their case was Boeing. For Boyd Ratchye, the attorney representing Boeing, the goal was to not only minimize the liability to Boeing but to protect the integrity of the Boeing 727. His strategy for accomplishing that task was to call to the stand a long list of Boeing engineers and one outside expert, all of whom rehashed many of the same arguments made during the initial investigation: that there was no failure mode that could result in an un-commanded extension of a single slat, that there is no record of any failures of the Ronson 5 slat actuator that resulted in an un-commanded extension of a slat, and that the slat had to have been extended by positive command input.

Don Mark did a commendable job of challenging Ratchye's experts. In his cross-examination of Robert Davis, the author of the Boeing technical report, Don brought up the possibility of Boeing having to ground the entire fleet of aircraft for "safety purposes."

". . . And you currently have what, 1800 airplanes, did you say, 727's?" Don asked Davis.

"Approximately 1800, 727 aircraft flying," Davis replied.

"The economic impact on Boeing would be substantial if those airplanes were grounded, wouldn't it?"

"The economic impact would be primarily on the airline operators."

"Yes it would. It would also be on Boeing as well, wouldn't it?"

"Not directly."

"Well, don't you continue to service the airplanes and provide technical expertise?"

"Yes."

"And as a matter of fact, that sort of publicity would not be good for selling new airplanes, right?"

"No. Any type of publicity in our business associated with adverse effects of safety is not good."[1]

Don attacked the logic of Boeing's conclusions by having Boeing's own test pilot, Lou Wallick, admit that waiting seventeen seconds before taking any corrective action would be an inordinate amount of time to wait to correct a plane that was leaving its intended flight path.

Don challenged Boeing's analysis of the FDR by having Boeing engineer James Kerrigan read a memo written by Robert Davis, who had testified earlier, stating that the "vibration characteristics of the acceleration trace is not the intended function of the FDR." It was evidence from Boeing's own experts that the FDR was not a reliable source for drawing a correlation between airplane configuration and its effect on the acceleration trace recording.[2]

Don further challenged the validity of Boeing's conclusions regarding the FDR analysis by introducing into evidence another internal Boeing memo outlining the reliability and accuracy of the FDR. The memo to or by Robert Davis was dated August 6, 1980.

> Actual tests conducted approximately two years ago using the NASA Convair 990 aircraft Galileo II showed that both the Lockheed Air Services and Fairchild flight recorders were

not accurate in the area of vertical acceleration. Comparison of the readout data from these recorders with the output from the onboard computer system disclosed that the recorded data was considerably more exaggerated in magnitude than the actual forces encountered during the various flight maneuvers performed.[3]

The Boeing and NTSB analysis of the FDR acceleration trace was perhaps the single most significant piece of evidence offered by Leslie Kampschror and his team of investigators to convince the NTSB Board to vote on their probable cause finding. Yet Boeing's own findings showed that the flight recorder data was unreliable.

Ratchye's expert witnesses testified that they were certain that four slats had been extended on TWA 841 prior to the upset. Don Mark had his own set of experts who testified that they were certain that only one slat had been extended prior to the upset. It all boiled down to which experts the jury would believe.

If nothing else, the dueling experts demonstrated the unreliability of the physical evidence used against the crew. If two experts could look at the same FDR evidence and come up with two very different interpretations, what did that say about the soundness of the evidence? The hundreds of hours of videotaped depositions and courtroom testimony revealed much about how inconsistencies in the FDR trace comparisons between TWA 841 and the Boeing test flight E209 were explained away with assumptions and questionable analytical techniques.

The technical testimony regarding FDR traces and readings, autopilots, hydraulics, slat actuators, etc., took up the majority of the four-week trial. Charles Hvass had presented his case in the first four days. He spent the remainder of the trial cross-examining TWA's witnesses in an effort to discredit them. To the jury's credit, they paid attention throughout the trial, took notes, and even forwarded questions to the judge concerning some of the more esoteric testimony. The six jury members were college educated. They genuinely wanted to understand what had happened. They had listened to the crew tell their recollections of the upset. And despite Boyd Ratchye's and Charles Hvass's attempts to show inconsistencies in their statements, the jurors would later confide that they had believed the crew members' testimony. But they had a conflict that had to be resolved. Something happened to cause the plane to lose control. As the trial neared completion, the jurors anxiously awaited the closing arguments. They wanted someone to piece together a clear picture of what exactly had happened and who was at fault. At the end of four weeks the cause of the incident was no clearer to them than it had been for the three Board members who ultimately voted on a probable cause. But there was one major difference between the case presented to them compared to the case presented to the NTSB Board: The jurors had the benefit of hearing other experts contradict and challenge many of the technical findings of the NTSB.

———————

Closing arguments for the four-week-long Holly Wicker civil trial began on June 8, 1983. Boeing attorney Boyd Ratchye was first to make his closing argument. Ratchye, wearing his characteristic bow tie, summed up Boeing's entire defense in the first few minutes of his closing statement when he repeated a line from his opening statement a month earlier: "The question is really, was there something wrong with the aircraft, or was there something wrong with the crew."[4]

That statement was followed by a rehashing of prior arguments about the crew's lack of awareness and timely response. In his closing statement, Ratchye made claims about evidence, depositions, and testimony that were contrary to what had actually been said or presented during the trial. For example, when talking about the FDR evidence he claimed numerous times that the evidence was undisputed, uncontested, and unchallenged.

"They [the flight data recorder tracings] tell us what actually happened on the airplane, and they tell us in an irrefutable way. We have that information. It can't be deposed and changed, and the story can't be manipulated. It's hard scientific data."[5] If anything, the trial proved that the FDR readouts were anything but reliable.

Ratchye mischaracterized the testimony of prior witnesses. "The people who were aboard the aircraft [TWA 841] felt a sudden, sharp, and startling vibration," Ratchye told the jurors in dramatic fashion. Donald Chance Mark had pointed out through the deposition of Kampschror that the human factors report contained a very different description of the vibration and buffeting prior to the onset of the upset than the people aboard the Boeing flight test had reported. None of the TWA 841 passengers described the buffeting as "sudden" or "startling," except when answering leading questions. Both passengers and crew reported a very slight vibration that grew in intensity to a slight buffet.

In explaining the Boeing Scenario of how and why the crew allegedly extended the slats, Ratchye referred to the one and only statement from any pilot claiming to have knowledge of the procedure for extending trailing edge flaps independent of leading edge slats—the Bates letter. This was from the United Airlines pilot whose angry letter was sent to ALPA shortly after ALPA challenged the NTSB findings.

"I believe that here's what could have occurred," Ratchye began. "The crew's altitude, they are at 39,000 feet. Mr. Bates' procedure is known through the industry, that the crew in one way drops the nose by using the unauthorized procedure. In that period of time Flight Engineer Banks is out of the cockpit returning the trays. You may recall Mrs.

Wicker testifying that she observed him chatting with one of the flight attendants. He returns, is seated in the cockpit, punches the circuit breaker, and all four slats are extended."[6]

Here again Ratchye seems to be presenting a case that's different than what actually had taken place. Numerous witnesses, including Kampschror and NTSB investigator John Ferguson, the one who first proposed the theory after supposedly hearing rumors about the procedure, testified to having been unable to find a single commercial airline pilot who could state under oath that they'd performed the procedure. And the theory regarding Gary Banks' leaving the cockpit and returning just prior to the upset was contrary to testimony given by all four flight attendants.

"It's reasonable to believe that the Bates procedure for lowering the deck angle was known in the industry and was being adopted by this TWA crew," Ratchye told the jurors. "Now the reason I say that that's reasonable to believe is that it is consistent with the hard information, the hard, un-impeached, unchallenged information from the flight data recorder."[7]

As Ratchye neared the end of his closing argument, he once again questioned the crew's integrity and actions. "I think the FAA wants the information on the voice recorder, and what happened was TWA and the crew permitted that tape to be erased. What's important about that is we don't have the information. There could have been a lot of things going on, and certainly could have been a good deal of discussion that would have been useful for us to know. But it indicates, I believe, that the crew was not exercising the utmost care used by very careful persons. So what you have now, we have got this question, getting to the close on this question—we are just talking about TWA's negligence—what you have is you have a crew who is doing an unauthorized procedure. That's not utmost care. You have a crew who loses the aircraft. That's not the utmost care. And you have a crew who permits the tape to be wiped. That is not the utmost care." [8]

———•◦•———

Next to present his closing argument was attorney Donald Chance Mark. Mark began by again praising the crew. He recounted testimony that supported the crew's actions. He then tackled the cockpit voice recorder issue.

Figure 40 Artist rendering of Don Mark's closing argument

"I told you at the beginning that there would be a false issue in this case, and that has I think been borne true. I told you in my opening statement that there was going to be by the other parties a lot of time spent on the cockpit voice recorder and its erasure. I told you that in fact the cockpit voice recorder apparently was erased. You heard Mr. Kennedy, he didn't recall doing it. You heard from Flight Engineer Banks, he didn't recall doing it. You heard from Captain Gibson, he didn't recall one way or the other. He might have done it; he may not have done it. Captain Gibson testified it was his custom and practice to erase the cockpit voice recorder at the conclusion of the flight.

"Captain Gibson himself testified that this was a badly damaged aircraft as a result of the maneuver. It was an aircraft that he never in his wildest dreams thought he would be able to land successfully and safely. But he did. When he landed that airplane, despite all the problems they had with hydraulics, having to manually extend landing gear and the like, Captain Gibson's first thought was, we have been told that we have got sparks from the wheels, and we have been told that we have fluids leaking from the airplane. There is a chance of fire. He wasn't thinking about whether or not he was going to erase the cockpit voice recorder. He wasn't concerned about that at all. He was thinking about successfully deplaning passengers so no one would be injured in that phase of flight, and that's what he came here and told us about."[9]

Mark then reemphasized other important details about the CVR for the jury to consider. The tape would have recorded only the last thirty minutes of the flight; erasing the CVR is not a violation of the federal aviation regulations; and it was common practice for crews to erase the CVR after every flight, with one airline, Northwest Airlines, having erasure of the CVR written into their normal shutdown checklist.

Having thus dealt with the CVR issue, Mark then attacked the plaintiff's and Boeing's cases, calling the theories proposed by Boeing and the plaintiff the "3M conspiracy" theories. The first of Mark's 3M conspiracy theories was "manipulation" of the controls. ". . . We have been told that the flight crew of flight 841 manipulated the flight controls to cause this unprecedented dive. In Boeing's words they call it positive command input. What does that mean? That means that the flight crew did something. They did something that was wrong. What's the basis for that theory? Well, not one single commercial airline captain, not one has come into this courtroom and said that this crew did something wrong or that any flight crew has ever utilized such a procedure."

Mark countered the Bates letter and deposition by reminding the jurors that Bates was a first officer and not a captain; that the reasons given for the unauthorized procedure, according to Bates, didn't apply in this case; and that a United captain had testified that he had never heard of the procedure at United Airlines or any other airline. He then summed up the first of his 3Ms with the following:

"Now, that's argument number one, positive command input. This crew did something to jeopardize the lives of innocent people and to jeopardize their own lives, and I say that's a ludicrous theory. And the only reason they have arrived at that theory is they're trying to protect the integrity of this particular airplane . . ."[10]

The second M of Mark's clever 3M conspiracy mnemonic was "maneuver." "According to the parties, this airplane is controllable if there is control input made within seventeen seconds after the onset of the maneuver, and that's based upon all the testing apparently that they did. First of all, on the face of it, that argument is [in]consistent with the manipulation theory. It's inconceivable that any flight crew, if they had done such an unauthorized maneuver as manipulate flight controls, would then sit around for seventeen seconds and wait for the airplane to roll on its back. Those two theories don't make sense at all if you put them together. Yet Boeing and the plaintiffs say Captain Gibson and First Officer Kennedy should have responded sooner than seventeen seconds because if they had they could have saved this airplane."

Mark then moved on to the last M of his 3M conspiracy theories. "The next theory if you don't like those two is the maintenance. If you don't go along with the fact that this crew did something, if you don't go along with the fact that this crew didn't do something, how about this one: the airplane was improperly maintained."

The last part of Mark's closing argument dealt with testimony indicating that the plane was properly maintained and that it was a faulty part or parts that caused the upset of TWA 841, not crew action or inaction or improper maintenance. He criticized Boeing for destroying the parts from the aircraft and concealing the fact that the one part he had requested for testing had, in fact, not been discarded.

He talked about reports of problems with slat actuators, broken pistons and ruptured seals. He highlighted the fact that despite all of the flight testing that had been done to date there hadn't been one flight test involving an isolated no. 7 slat extension at 39,000 feet.

Taken individually, his exposition on faulty parts might not have carried much weight, but when presented in total he made a persuasive argument that there could be other explanations for what had caused the upset.

As Mark neared the end of his closing argument, he touched on the underlying reason for the trial, Holly Wicker's claims of being injured. He reminded the jurors of prior testimony that cast doubt on the severity of Holly's injuries. He didn't call her a liar, but he did give the jury causes to consider when deliberating on the amount of damages to be awarded.

Mark's final words to the jurors were the most impactful. "Perhaps the most poignant words that were uttered in this courtroom didn't come from the pilots, didn't come from any of the technical people but came from a lay person. Mrs. Jeannine Rakowsky testified in this case, and you recall she was being asked, what's your relationship with Captain Gibson? And they were asking about filming that went on in California. Did you see Captain Gibson in California? Yeah, I saw him. When have you last seen Captain Gibson? Do you recall what she said? When did you last have contact with Captain Gibson? She said, the last time we had contact with Captain Gibson was when I wrote him a Christmas card thanking him for allowing us to spend another Christmas with our family."[11]

•━•◆•━•

Had the closing argument by Donald Chance Mark been the last word in the trial, it's quite possible that the jury may have ruled differently than they did. But Mark didn't have the last word. That belonged to Charles Hvass, the plaintiff's attorney. Hvass played the role of tie breaker, assuming the jurors hadn't already made up their minds. He started his closing statement with a clever reference to the scales of justice. "Let's talk about the burden of proof first," Hvass began. "The burden of proof, you are going to hear the key words, what is the weight of the evidence? You have all seen a picture of Lady Justice or a statue of Lady Justice. She's standing with a sword in one hand, and in a right upraised hand are two scales, now, the old kind of scale, the one that's a beam with a pivot point in the middle and little chains that come down to a dish on either side. And when you put weight on one side of that scale or the other, the scale tips. The weights that you put on that scale is simply evidence. It's facts. It's not the number of witnesses, it's not the number of documents. It's when you mine through the evidence and you mine through the paper and you find in the testimony a truth that has weight. And when you have put that truth on one side of the scale or the other, if it tips over so slightly, then that truth has been established. And that's all we mean by the burden of proof."[12]

What followed next was Hvass tipping those same scales of justice he so eloquently described. Rather than let the jury decide on their own which side—that of Boeing's or TWA's—had presented the most persuasive arguments, Hvass gave the jury his own interpretation of the evidence. He tipped the scale in Boeing's favor by blaming the crew for causing the upset and then accused the crew of trying to cover up their actions by erasing the CVR. "We heard a statement that Captain Gibson gave testimony, it wasn't impeached, but I think, as you recall, we went through his prior statements, and we went through everything, and by the time we got done with it we discovered that there was no single story we could believe," Hvass told the jurors. "It was so bad that Mr. Miller, an expert witness for TWA, said, I can't tell you what the truth is as a trained investigator in all of the statements I have heard from the crew. He couldn't mine out those nuggets of fact to put on the scale because the testimony was so confusing."[13]

Hvass's condemnation of the crew continued, comprising the majority of his closing argument. "What I want to do is I want to start, and I want to look, and I want to say, what did the crew tell us? And as we look at what the crew told us, is there reason for us to look elsewhere? If there is no reason for us to look elsewhere, then stop right there. If there is no reason for Boeing and the NTSB and TWA to continue investigating after the accident happened, we just stop. We have the crew testimony, and that's what occurred. So what do we find when we begin the investigation, when we go to April 4, 1979? First look in the cockpit. Do we have an alert crew? We have Gary Banks, who first realizes the airplane is in trouble when it's pointed like this (indicates a diving plane). Mr. Banks doesn't want to be involved with the beginning of the incident, so he knows nothing about it. He saw no evil. First Officer Kennedy first tried to tell us that he realized the airplane was in trouble when it was here (indicates an inverted aircraft). But he's given us a statement about what happened in the cockpit, and in the cockpit he says, I was doing a ground speed check with the distance measuring equipment. I was looking over there. And the first thing he heard was the shout from Captain Gibson, 'get 'em up.' He didn't hear any evil before that. And he is looking right through a control yoke. What do we find? When we go to his statement we find that he finally admits that the first time he heard the shout the airplane was like this (indicating a banking aircraft). First Officer Kennedy has taken himself out of being somebody who can manipulate the flaps and slats because he didn't know what was going on.

"And what do we find with the person who is supposed to be flying the airplane? He is bent over the side of the seat, and his seat is pushed back, he is over here. And nobody's minding the store. And now we have a crew where nobody in the cockpit is flying the airplane. And that alone begins to make me say, what happened? It's a two edge sword. Either they're not doing anything wrong, and by turning away they didn't control the airplane, or somebody's not telling us the truth about what was going on in that cockpit."[14]

Hvass had this to say about the alleged cockpit voice recorder erasure. "Two days later we find out that the cockpit voice recorder is erased. Now, this has been called a bogus issue by TWA, but this is not a bogus issue. When we go to Exhibit 2, you have got 2-A, and you're going to have it back in the jury room, there is a tab about halfway down that says cockpit voice recorder. I want you to go to that, and you will find when you look at that tab that the conversation begins, beginning of recording following bulk erase. The cockpit voice recorder has been erased because somebody pushed the button. Now we get an explanation from TWA that it was forty minutes from the incident until they landed, and there was nothing on that tape. Did you hear any testimony from the crew that they were timing from the time of the incident until the airplane landed? Oh, no. When they landed, as far as they knew they had a thirty-minute tape on their hands. And it's going to tell us what happened in the cockpit. Okay? That's what they are thinking on the ground April 4, 1979, in Detroit. That's the thought process going on at the time, not some later justification by TWA."[15]

Later in his closing argument, Hvass tried to illustrate how Hoot was being less than truthful in his testimony. "But there was one little point that really gave me the character of what was going on with this crew. It wasn't very much. But when Captain Gibson first took the stand he was asked the question, pure and simple: Where do you live? And he wanted to make it sound for you very good and he said, Las Vegas, Nevada. But in fact we knew, and he told the FAA that he lived in Costa Rica. Now, I don't know why he didn't want you to hear that, and I don't know why he didn't tell you that, but this is the sign of somebody who is beginning to shade the truth. And when you are beginning to shade the truth, as you can see, everything goes from there."[16]

Had Hvass dug any deeper than the one statement referenced in Hoot's testimony, he would have discovered that Hoot maintained two residences. He lived in Costa Rica, but he also kept his residence in Las Vegas. There was no deceit on Hoot's part. Don Mark was fully aware of this misstep by Hvass, but since the statement came during closing arguments, and Hvass had the last say in closing, he couldn't correct the error.

When Hvass was finished criticizing the crew, he tipped the scales even further in favor of Boeing by defending them. "What do we do about Boeing? You heard a lot about T bolts, you heard a lot about slat actuators. Quite frankly, my witness Mr. Rasmussen, when I gave him the case I said, Mr. Rasmussen, here it is, I have sued Boeing and I have sued TWA, you tell me what you have got, you tell me what happened in this case. And I gave it to Mr. Bailey, my pilot, and I said tell me what happened. And they came back and they said I didn't find anything. So as I come to you, ladies and gentlemen of the jury, I am going to tell you this: The plaintiff has no evidence that Boeing did anything wrong. If you believe TWA's evidence, that's up to you. And I am not going to say no, that would be wrong, but I am going to tell you that as I did my investigation that's what I came up with, and that's the best I can tell you on that point."[17]

The rest of Hvass's closing argument concerned Holly Wicker's injuries and what he thought would be a reasonable and fair award for those injuries. He recounted how Holly had injured herself by trying to give mouth to mouth to the infant in her lap. It was a heroic gesture, Hvass maintained. He told the jurors that in his opinion that Holly should be awarded $400,000 and that her husband, Timothy Wicker, should be awarded $150,000 for his loss of companionship.

The jurors were given their final instructions and began deliberating that afternoon at 2:50 p.m. Considering that the trial had taken four weeks and had included days of complex technical testimony, it was no surprise that the jurors did not return a verdict on the first day of deliberations. They were excused for the evening and told to return at 9:00 a.m. on the next day. The jurors were advised against reading any related material or watching the news.

By mid-afternoon on the second day of deliberation, the jurors had their verdict. The six-person jury found that TWA (as the employer of the flight crew) was primarily responsible for the entire incident. However, they also found that Boeing was culpable. The judge's instructions in case the jury found both defendants negligent were to attribute a percentage to each totaling one hundred percent. The jury found that TWA was 70% responsible for the incident and that Boeing was responsible for the other 30%. Considering what lawyer Donald Chance Mark was up against, the jury decision was a successful outcome.

Holly Wicker was awarded a sum of $350,000. Her husband was awarded $44,000.[18] After the trial, Don Mark talked to the jurors and learned that they had initially considered splitting their verdict 50/50 between TWA and Boeing, with each equally liable. They did not believe Boeing's theory of crew manipulation. They found the crew believable. Had they thought that the incident had been caused by crew action, they would have found TWA 100% liable. The jurors did, however, feel that there was some merit to the possibility that a mechanical failure might have been caused by improper maintenance. They also thought the theory that the crew did not respond quickly enough was a possible explanation of why they lost control. For those reasons they felt that TWA was more liable than Boeing.

The fact that six everyday people, after hearing all of the evidence, had come to the conclusion that the NTSB's theory of crew manipulation was not plausible, was lost on the press and to anyone following the trial. If anything, the verdict reinforced the notion that the NTSB had got it right. That opinion would hold for many years to come.

One month after the trial, on July 14, 1983, CBS aired the documentary *The Plane That Fell From The Sky.* The documentary was well received. The story presented in the film was one of a mystery as yet unsolved. What had caused a commercial airliner to suddenly plummet more than 35,000 feet in just over one minute? The filmmakers chose to tell the story from the crew's viewpoint. They presented the NTSB's theory of the accident but also presented experts and commentary that contradicted that theory.

One person who happened to be watching the documentary was a retired aeronautical engineer for Grumman Aerospace by the name of Duane Yorke. Duane had been involved in aviation during the nascent days of jet aircraft design and testing. He was intrigued by the story. The entire incident reminded him of similar upsets that he was aware of during some of the very first test flights of high-speed, swept-wing jet aircraft. The day after watching the documentary, Duane Yorke decided to take a closer look at TWA 841. He requested and received all the reports and technical documents related to the investigation. Using the same evidence available to the original investigators, Duane Yorke began his own independent investigation. After several months of analysis he detailed his findings in a written report, which he then forwarded to the Accident Investigation Department of ALPA. It's not known if the report was addressed to a specific individual. What is known is that the report was received and filed away without much, if any, review.

Chapter Twenty-Six

Breaking Point

oot was in Costa Rica when he learned of the jury verdict in a communication from Don Mark. Don tried to put a positive spin on the news, telling him that the jurors had believed his testimony. Hoot was grateful for the work Don had done on his behalf but still felt as though he had been crucified all over again. He took the news like a death-row inmate might take learning that he had just lost his final appeal.

The news of the jury verdict had come on top of some equally bad news Hoot had received weeks earlier concerning his twenty-million-dollar libel suit, which had been dismissed by a U.S. District Judge.

Hoot had known that the libel suit was a long shot. Landon Dowdey had explained the many obstacles they had to overcome. He was aware that all three of the defendants in the case—Boeing, the FAA, and the NTSB—had filed for summary judgments to have the cases dismissed. Still, the news was a huge letdown.

The judge reviewing the lawsuit had sided with the defendants on almost every point. The judge agreed with Boeing's argument that Boeing had been asked to prepare a report by the NTSB and they had a privileged right to do so. He also agreed with the NTSB's and the FAA's arguments that they had a right to investigate accidents without fear of liability every time someone didn't agree with their findings.

Landon sent Hoot a letter promising to appeal, citing a number of procedural problems with the Judge's dismissal that he believed provided grounds for an appeal.[1] Hoot filed the letter away. Landon was on his own crusade at this point. Hoot went back to tending his jojoba beans.

Despite the bad news that came Hoot's way in early 1983, he did receive some good news. Hoot received word that the documentary *The Plane That Fell From The Sky* had aired. He had forgotten all about it. A few friends had written him and told him that the documentary had been favorable to the crew and cast doubt on the investigation. Hoot started receiving letters of support from people he didn't know who had seen the documentary. The letters were sent to TWA and "Hoot Gibson, in care of CBS" or "Captain Hoot Gibson." Hoot would get the letters months later, but he started to feel that maybe public perception was starting to turn in his favor.

The goodwill that came as a result of the documentary was offset by the renewed attention the story received as a result of the verdict in the civil trial. Hoot once again found himself dealing with questions about TWA 841. The stress and anxiety Hoot felt as a result of the intense media attention manifested itself in a long list of medical maladies he suffered from, including a perforated ulcer, hypertension, high blood pressure, insomnia, and a diagnosis of chronic anxiety syndrome, all of which threatened to sideline him indefinitely.

Hoot's job was also threatened in other ways. As a captain for a major airline, Hoot was required to go through recurrent training every six months. At the conclusion of this training is a check ride, where a pilot is evaluated on various emergencies. The check rides are a necessary part of the profession. They're needed because a pilot must demonstrate his or her proficiency and knowledge. But they're also stressful because a poor performance can have serious repercussions. In most cases a failed check ride results in additional training and a second check ride. Failure of a second check ride can lead to termination. In Hoot's case, he felt added stress each time he went in for training. He sensed that certain instructors were hostile toward him. They would criticize minor mistakes and make the check rides more difficult than they had to be.

The same could not be said about the pilots Hoot worked with on a daily basis. Hoot was one of the good guys. He was someone other pilots enjoyed flying with. Most of the TWA pilots disagreed with the NTSB's conclusions, especially after the documentary aired. Pilots went out of their way to offer encouragement. They left articles about dealing with stress and anxiety in Hoot's mailbox. They sent him inspirational poems about dealing with adversity. It was this camaraderie with his fellow pilots that kept him from calling it quits. And there were plenty of times when the idea crossed his mind.

Outside the TWA pilot ranks, it was another story. Hoot had an easily recognizable name, and more than a few passengers knew about TWA 841. He would sometimes learn from a flight attendant after a flight about some rude comment made by a passenger when they learned that Hoot was the captain on their flight.

Every flight Hoot took after the NTSB ruling had the potential for a negative encounter with someone who had read or heard about the probable cause finding or the civil trial. It didn't happen often, but when it did, Hoot's emotional well-being would plummet and remain low for days.

On one particular trip Hoot exited the cockpit and noticed a group of flight attendants gathered together in the galley area. As Hoot passed them one of the flight attendants shouted at Hoot. "I don't know how you got your job back after being fired," the flight attendant said loudly, "but I think this company is crazy to let you fly an airplane."

Hoot was stunned. He had been in a good mood. He was looking forward to a few days off. He didn't even remember speaking with this particular flight attendant. His heart sank as the woman continued her rant. "If I knew you were the captain, I would have informed the passengers and walked off the flight." Hoot wasn't looking for a confrontation with an angry flight attendant. He said nothing and continued to walk off the plane.

Hoot's reputation seemed beyond repair. Whenever there was a mishap at the airline involving a pilot, Hoot's name would be somehow attached. When a pilot taxied an airplane into a jetway at LAX, the agents were told that the captain was Hoot Gibson. The agents then spread the rumor to flight crews who asked about the incident.

Hoot was captain on a flight that experienced an engine failure on takeoff. The plane was fully loaded with passengers and fuel. Rather than wasting time to dump fuel, Hoot decided that they needed to get the plane back on the ground as soon as possible. He briefed the lead flight attendant that they were going to make an overweight landing and that there was a possibility of a brake fire or a blown tire because of their overweight condition.

Hoot made a successful emergency landing back at LAX. It was a smooth landing, and there was no brake fire or blown tire. Hoot deserved accolades for the way he handled the emergency. The flight attendant he had briefed, however, saw the whole incident differently. She told anyone who cared to listen that Hoot had taken off overweight and put everyone's lives in jeopardy. The flight attendant didn't know that commercial airliners have landing weights that are much lower than the maximum takeoff weight. Planes typically take off at weights that are above the landing weight. The fuel that is burned off en route reduces the weight of the aircraft for landing. Hoot could explain that fact until he was blue in the face, but that wouldn't have stopped some flight attendants from believing that Hoot had acted recklessly.

The negative comments regarding Hoot's flying ability or perceived recklessness were sometimes overheard by friends and supporters, who then found themselves in the position of having to defend Hoot's reputation. A few pilots who didn't approve of Hoot's bachelor lifestyle took pleasure in seeing Hoot taken down a few notches. When one of Hoot's friends, Glen Smith, a fellow TWA pilot and neighbor of Hoot's, overheard a couple of pilots making disparaging comments about Hoot getting what he deserved, Glen confronted them. "Keep your comments to yourself," Glen snapped. "You don't know what the hell you're talking about."[2]

While Hoot took the brunt of the negative publicity, Scott Kennedy and Gary Banks were also dealing with the negative fallout from the NTSB findings of probable cause. Scott had to put up with captains who would make snide comments, telling him to keep his hands off the alternate flap switch and to stay away from the circuit breakers. He also confessed to Hoot that he was still having trouble sleeping. Gary Banks, who had been furloughed from TWA, was suffering from a host of physical and psychological problems that had gone untreated due to his lack of health benefits. His bitterness towards TWA and the NTSB carried over into his personal life as his relationship with his wife deteriorated. Hoot tried to reach out to Gary but found that Gary was reluctant to discuss anything related to TWA 841. When Hoot had needed to give Gary information regarding the libel suit, he had to do so by letter. On one such occasion Hoot received a response from Gary's wife, Autumn Banks, which described how difficult it had been for Gary since the incident.

Dear Hoot,

I just wanted to let you know that Gary received your letter and he is in the process of responding. (He will also be sending ALPA a letter which hopefully will be published in their monthly newsletter.)

I know Hoot that you live with all of the accusations and criticisms daily, not only on the job but elsewhere. But I want you to understand too that by night Gary is still plagued by dreams and thoughts only known to someone else who has been through the same incident. Unfortunately, your letter has once again surfaced his nightmares which he doesn't even share with me. As his wife, it's difficult to watch it all happen again, but I'm here to listen and support him when he is ready. I tell you this because I know you care & also to thank you [for] the courage to see this thing to its conclusion. I'm sorry you've had to bear this all publicly, but you know that we've now all become victims of 841. Take care, dear friend; our thoughts & prayers are always with you.

Love,

Gary & Autumn (Nathan too!)

Autumn's eloquent letter told Hoot everything he needed to know about Gary's reluctance to talk about TWA 841. Unlike Gary, Hoot did receive limited psychiatric treatment, but the few visits he had were not enough. As a result, the long-term stress from the rumors and innuendos began to take its toll. Hoot complained to friends about feelings of nervousness and trouble sleeping, which he said continued to bother him. In time the possibility of not passing his FAA physical because of his mounting medical problems became a real concern. As much as he enjoyed his job, he felt he needed a break. So Hoot requested a leave of absence.

No one questioned Hoot or asked him to provide medical records when he requested his leave. There wasn't anyone in the flight department who didn't doubt that Hoot had been under a great deal of stress. TWA granted him his leave and told him that his job would be waiting for him when he was ready to return. Hoot put TWA 841 behind him and returned to Costa Rica.

Chapter Twenty-Seven

A Cold Case Gets a Second Look

N*ot long after the NTSB final report* of TWA 841, ALPA learned of six cases involving cracked pistons of Ronson actuators. The information concerning the cracked pistons was discovered in a coordination sheet prepared by Boeing a few weeks after the TWA 841 incident. The cracked pistons were reported in 1975 by Lufthansa Airlines. ALPA had insisted all along that the cause of the upset had been a cracked piston in the slat actuator. With this new information in hand, ALPA began the process of drafting a petition for reconsideration in the probable cause findings of TWA 841. The petition was submitted on January 11, 1983. Supplements to the petition were added in June and August of 1983, challenging the NTSB's analysis for drag calculations and their acceleration trace comparison analysis. The petition was the first of what would eventually become four petitions for reconsideration related to TWA 841.

Much like an appeal of a criminal or civil verdict, a petition for reconsideration is the means by which an interested party can have the NTSB review the findings of probable cause. Before the NTSB will even consider reopening an investigation, there must be new evidence or a showing that the Board's findings as to the facts, condition, and circumstances of the accident were erroneous. The chances of having an investigation reopened are remote but not impossible. A number of findings of probable cause have been corrected as a result of new evidence.

In most cases involving petitions for reconsideration, the NTSB is slow to respond if they respond at all, citing a lack of resources or an inability to devote time to closed investigations. After receiving the ALPA petition, however, the NTSB responded with great alacrity thanks in part to the level of interest in the case. In fact, the NTSB responded in record time, denying the petition less than a year after it was submitted.

In denying the petition, the NTSB cited that the cracked pistons in question had occurred on leading edge flap actuators and not lead-ing-edge slat actuators. The denial of the petition also stood by the original investigators' work concerning the drag calculations and accel-eration trace analysis.

ALPA's position was that it didn't make any difference whether the cracked pistons were from flap actuators or slat actuators. The simple fact that there were reported cases of cracked pistons proved their point that a piston could crack just as they had proposed. They had also sub-mitted a case involving an aircraft that had experienced a number 7 slat extension in isolation. The NTSB concluded, however, that it was not an extension but a failed retraction.

The denial of the petition was just another in a long list of setbacks for Hoot. The bad news barely registered. Hoot's primary concern was regaining his health. He went back to running his Costa Rica-based charter company and tending to his jojoba bean crop. Hoot was always a hands-on individual. He wasn't one to sit in an office and bark orders. He worked just as hard as his employees. When he wasn't working, he walked or jogged along the beach that lined two sides of his property.

As his strength returned and his mind cleared, Hoot looked for other money-making opportunities. In addition to his jojoba bean fields,

Hoot's property contained hundreds of coconut trees. Hoot came up with an idea to remove the husk of the coconut and cut into the shell with a lathe just deep enough to make it easier to crack open. He then shrink-wrapped the coconuts and sold them to supermarkets under the label *Cocolita Farms*.

Hoot's money-making ventures were profitable, but he missed the steady paycheck he received when working as a captain for a major airline. In early 1986, after three years of enjoying the sun and beaches of Costa Rica, Hoot felt that the time was right for a return to the cockpit. He notified TWA that he was ready to come off medical leave. The next question for Hoot was where did he want to go and what aircraft did he want to fly? Hoot decided that he wanted to fly the Boeing 747. He had enough seniority at the time to hold a junior captain slot, but he decided instead to take a first officer position. That way he could ease back into the flying routine without having the added stress and responsibilities of flying as captain. He would also have greater control over his flying schedule, something he needed in order to keep tabs on his Costa Rican affairs.

Of the many varied types of flying available to TWA pilots, one of the most coveted positions was the famed around-the-world flights. Leaving from either Los Angeles or New York, a passenger could travel to Asia, Africa, Europe, and back to the US without changing aircraft. As a senior first officer, Hoot was able to hold the around-the-world flights, which meant he could continue to live in Costa Rica and commute to work.

Hoot was commuting in from Costa Rica to begin one of his around-the-world flights when he ran into an old friend in operations. The friend was TWA pilot John Rohlfing. Rohlfing and Hoot had gone through DC-9 captain training together. They talked briefly before each headed their separate ways. Hoot didn't know it at the time, but his chance meeting with John Rohlfing would turn out to be a fortuitous one.

John Rohlfing hadn't seen Hoot in years and was genuinely happy to catch up with his old friend. John hadn't said anything to Hoot about TWA 841, but it was on his mind as he made his way through the terminal. Seeing Hoot made him think about the injustice Hoot and the other crew members had endured at the hands of the NTSB. John remembered Hoot as being a happy-go-lucky guy but not someone likely to take chances with an airplane, especially having just returned to the left seat.

John had been working for the union at the time of TWA 841, but since he didn't sit on the accident investigation committee, he was not privy to all that was going on with the investigation. He heard everything secondhand like everyone else, except for those rare occasions when he would run into Hoot down in flight ops or out on the line. He remembered Hoot as being reluctant to talk about the investigation, except to deny the accusations being leveled against him.

By this time John had moved up the ranks in the union and was now the chairman of the TWA/ALPA accident investigation committee—Jim McIntyre's position at the time of TWA 841. Jim had stepped down from his union position not long after TWA 841. There wasn't a whole lot going on with the accident investigation committee at that time, which was a good thing for TWA. But John was restless in his new position and looking for something substantial to dig into. So at the next committee meeting John brought up the idea of taking another look at TWA 841. To his surprise, everyone thought it was a good idea. They all agreed that the NTSB had got it wrong. Maybe it was time to take a fresh look at TWA 841.

After a quick vote the wheels were set in motion. TWA pilot and committee member Leigh Johnson was given the task of reviewing the TWA 841 investigation. John could not have picked a more competent individual. Leigh Johnson was a former aeronautical engineer at Boeing. He knew some of the Boeing engineers who had worked on TWA 841. He understood the culture at Boeing and the tacit demand on engineers to protect the integrity and reputation of the company when looking into mishaps and accidents involving Boeing aircraft. The fact that Leigh was also a pilot made him the perfect choice.

As an engineer and pilot, Leigh approached his new task in a methodical manner. He read everything he could get his hands on related to the original investigation. He talked to Hoot at length about his recollections before, during, and after the incident. When the demands of his schedule at TWA began to take away from the time Leigh needed to conduct a thorough review, John Rohlfing arranged for Leigh to have time off with pay so he could devote more time to the task. Like a detective digging into a cold case, Leigh was given free rein to follow leads wherever they took him.

After reviewing all of the documents available on hand at TWA related to TWA 841, Leigh flew to Washington D.C., to ALPA headquarters to review technical documents there. He made copies of everything, building his own case file. When John Rohlfing inquired about his progress, Leigh told him he needed more time. John gave him that time, using union funds to make up the difference in his salary.

After months of immersing himself in technical documents and reports, Leigh Johnson became convinced that the crew of TWA 841 had been falsely accused of causing the upset. It was incomprehensible to him how the investigators had failed to follow up on several important clues such as the failed yaw damper flag, the free-float in the outboard aileron, and the tendency of the aircraft to roll left after the recovery. He was dismayed by the total disregard of the sworn testimony of the crew.

Leigh was certain that the NTSB got it wrong, but he couldn't come up with a compelling alternative theory. That all changed when Leigh chanced upon a paper he found at ALPA headquarters that had been filed away with reams of other documents related to TWA 841. The paper was a technical analysis of TWA 841. The author of the paper was a retired aeronautical engineer named Duane Yorke. It was now early 1987, eight years after the TWA 841 incident. The document Leigh held in his hands was dated November 16, 1984, nearly three years earlier. One of the first things to catch Leigh's attention was the following statement:

> Limited slat strength in the extended position precludes the possibility of this item being the cause of the lengthy loss of control, especially at the extremely high indicated airspeeds and load factors (470 KIAS and 5.8 G's) encountered before recovery.[1]

Citing Boeing's own technical report, Duane Yorke referenced a section of the report that indicated that slat separation was most probable at 363 KIAS, which occurred at 32,000 feet. This meant that had the slat been extended at cruise at 39,000 feet, it would have separated much earlier in the dive and not towards the end of the dive as hypothesized by the NTSB. Had the slat separated earlier in the dive, and, according to the NTSB, recovery was made possible only when the slat separated, the crew should have been able to recover much sooner in the dive.

Duane Yorke's analysis next referenced the physical evidence of aircraft damage: the right gear broken side brace and actuator mounting beam; damage to the inboard flap track as the right gear over-extended;

and loss of system A hydraulics, also caused by the over-extension of the right landing gear.

This pattern of "differential damage" is consistent with a large left wing forward sideslip angle being present at the time of gear extension.

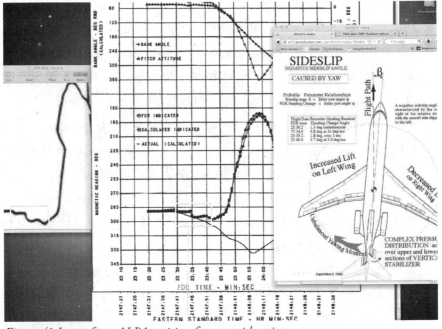

Figure 41 Image from ALPA petition for reconsideration

The existence of this apparently substantial sideslip angle at the moment of gear extension at such high speed and high "G" conditions requires a careful consideration of the possible causes of the sideslip condition. The NTSB report suggests that the entire maneuver was caused by the extension of the #7 leading edge slat at the cruise altitude and then the inability to retract that slat due to pre-existing misalignment due to a faulty T-bolt connection and other discrepancies. Recognizing the large sideslip angle present when the gear was extended would require this defective #7 slat to have remained attached to the aircraft to the extreme overload condition of 470 KIAS and 5.8 G's.

There is an unanswered question as to why the aircraft remained uncontrollable for an additional 32 seconds after the alleged cause of the problem had departed.

The most likely source of a large sideslip angle is a malfunction in the rudder system. At the beginning of the maneuver the Flight Data Recorder shows two sharp changes in heading. One of 1.3 degrees followed four seconds later by a change of 4.8 degrees. About 5 seconds then elapsed and the uncontrollable dive began. A large sideslip angle produces a large rolling moment in swept wing airplanes such as the 727. This rolling moment can in some flight conditions equal or exceed the rolling moment available from lateral controls. Rudder-induced rollover dives accounted for several fatal accidents when jets were first put into commercial service. More sophisticated control systems such as found on the 727 have reduced the probability of this type of event, but it still remains a possibility.

Three factors suggest a rudder-induced rollover in the case of Flight 841:

1. Substantial heading changes at the start of the maneuver
2. Substantial sideslip at the end of the maneuver
3. Continuous uncontrollability until the [lower] rudder was released at the end of the maneuver due to A-System hydraulics failure

The fact that the landing gear extension broke A-System hydraulic lines in the right wheel well is perhaps what really saved the airplane from what was otherwise an unrecoverable maneuver. The source of the signal that may have led to the rudder-hard-over is not clear since loss of A-system pressure would have returned the [lower] rudder to neutral in any case. Any evidence of the rudder causing the maneuver from a spurious or distorted electrical signal was probably lost due to the fact that these items were removed for separate tests rather than any in-place functional checks. It is also unclear as to the reasons that both rudder boost packages were changed before the aircraft was returned to service, but this is perhaps highly indicative of rudder problems.

Although the evidence suggesting a rudder-induced rollover is all circumstantial, it provides the most compelling explanation of the incident with the crew reports and the repairs made to the airplane.[2]

Leigh sat stunned after he finished reading Duane Yorke's report. The detailed report included technical drawings, references and citations, a time line contrasting the NTSB's conclusions with factual information, FDR data, and a sequential account of the dive and recovery. Suddenly it all made sense. The number seven slat was a red herring. It wasn't the cause of the incident; rather, it was a result of it. Investigators were so focused on the number seven slat as the initiator of the event that they discounted ample evidence that pointed elsewhere.

In the scenario presented by Duane Yorke, the rollover was caused by a yaw damper-induced rudder hardover, meaning that one or both rudders (upper and lower) were deflected by the yaw damper system, causing the plane to yaw severely to the right. As the plane yawed nose right, the left wing (because of wing sweep) produced more lift than the right wing. This resulted in the uncontrollable rollover.

Figure 42 Rudder hardover of the lower rudder

When Scott lowered the landing gear, a cooling line for system A hydraulics was ruptured, and hydraulic pressure for system A was lost. The lower rudder, which was powered by system A hydraulics, centered, thus allowing for the recovery. The number seven slat, which had shown possible signs of a locking mechanism failure, extended when system A hydraulic pressure was lost. The slat was then immediately torn from the plane, causing the loud explosion heard by passengers and crew.

Before he shared what he had discovered, Leigh decided to check into Duane Yorke's background. He made calls to former employers. Leigh learned that Duane Yorke had served as the Director of Supersonic Aircraft Development for the Grumman Aircraft Corporation. He also held an engineering degree from MIT.

Satisfied with Duane Yorke's credentials, Leigh presented the new theory of the upset to the TWA accident investigation committee. A vote was taken on whether to proceed with a petition for reconsideration. The decision to proceed was unanimous. Thus began a two-year process that would result in a document highly critical of the NTSB's work on TWA 841.

Leigh worked on the petition on his days off. Never having written a petition for reconsideration before, he first had to review other petitions for reconsideration to understand the format and expected content. Leigh turned to ALPA for help with composing the petition. He worked closely with Keith Hagy, who had replaced Harold Marthinsen as the Director of ALPA's accident investigation department. Keith offered ALPA's full support. He provided Leigh with examples of petitions for reconsideration that had resulted in the NTSB changing the probable cause finding. He also reviewed early drafts and made suggested revisions.

Leigh's petition was a well-thought-out and thorough document that included attachments, numerous illustrations, footnotes, and an index. It began with a simple, one-sentence statement: "The NTSB erroneously assumed that an extended slat caused the upset of TWA 841."[3] From there Leigh proceeded to rewrite most of the original accident report on TWA 841. The petition and accompanying attachments ran into the hundreds of pages. A summary of his findings include the following:

Failure of the NTSB to reference hydraulic leakage in the area of the lower rudder, which was possible evidence of a faulty lower rudder actuator.

Failure of the NTSB to reference skydrol (hydraulic fluid) bathing aft of the #7 slat, which was possible evidence of internal failures within the retract locking mechanism of the slat actuator.

False statement in the accident report stating that "tests of the CVR in the aircraft revealed no discrepancies in the CVR's electrical and recording systems." No such tests were performed.

No fault tests of the accident CVR or of any CVRs in other TWA aircraft. An example was provided concerning a UAL DC-8 accident at Salt Lake City, Utah. After discovering that the accident CVR was not working properly, United conducted inspections of all of their aircraft and found CVR anomalies fleet wide.

A possible explanation for the CVR erasure involving a power changeover from engine power to APU power.

NTSB's misidentification of the #6 flight spoiler identified as the #10 flight spoiler.

NTSB's error in reporting the difference in body length between the accident aircraft (a Boeing 727-100 at 116 ft 2 in) and the simulator used for flight testing which was a Boeing 727-200 at 136 ft. 2 in. As a result of the differences in body length, simulator tests resulted in inaccurate modeling.

Failure to simulate the effects of a rudder hardover.

Failure to account for more powerful engines on the flight test aircraft.

Failure of the investigators to note numerous prior instances and reports of slats that had been extended in isolation either by accident or by mechanical failure having departed the aircraft at speeds as low as 250 kts.

Criticism of the unscientific method used to show a correlation of the acceleration trace readings between TWA 841 and the test aircraft.

False information in the report concerning a test switch having been left in the HOLD position. There is no evidence to suggest that anyone actually observed this improper test switch positioning.

Failure of the NTSB to consider the effects of the free-float in the right outboard aileron and its possible connection as the initiator of the upset.

Failure of the NTSB to recognize and consider the limited frequency response of the accident aircraft FDR.

Failure of the NTSB to provide a wreckage distribution chart along with a trajectory analysis of separated parts. Doing so would have provided a more accurate picture of the sequence of part failures and separation. For example, the inboard half of the #7 slat was found in close proximity to the canoe fairing for the inboard flap, indicating that the slat most likely separated immediately after the gear was extended.

Failure of the NTSB to account for the right gear over-extension, which was evidence of a sustained sideslip condition.

Failure of the NTSB to explain the possible significance of the fail flag of the lower yaw damper.

Over-reliance on the manufacturer in conducting the investigation.

Failure to correlate the sudden heading changes shown on the FDR heading traces just prior to the upset as evidence of a yawing aircraft.

The Board erred when it effectively replaced the actual FDR heading data with its own calculated bank angle data.

The NTSB erroneously assumed that an extended slat had caused the upset. That assumption tainted all phases of their investigation.

The Board's total disregard for the testimony of the crew.

The Board erred in the report by stating factually that the Captain had erased the CVR when no evidence exists to support such a claim.

Failure of the NTSB to impound the rudder actuators and yaw damper transfer valves.

Failure of the NTSB to perform a proper tear-down analysis of the two main rudder actuators.

Failure of the investigators to review numerous reports of other yaw induced rolling incidents.

Reliance of the NTSB on circumstantial evidence over direct evidence: crew and passenger statements, damage to the aircraft, and FDR data.

Leigh's petition also contained several admonishments of the NTSB's actions concerning the crew. Leigh had this to say about the voice recorder: "The NTSB failed to accomplish the appropriate tear down analysis of the voice recorder system. Instead, Board members accused the crew of erasing the CVR. The Board combined innuendo concerning the CVR erasure, along with its assumption that the crew had attempted to extend flaps during cruise, to build a case in which the Board attributed the cause of the accident to crew actions. This combination of disparaging presumptions was the origin of a bias planted in the minds of the investigators; this bias fouled each phase of the NTSB's investigation." Instead of blaming the crew, Leigh argued, the Board should have commended the crew for their persistence.

In the recommendations section of the petition, Leigh presented a persuasive reason for the Board to review the petition. "Some members of the Board may contend that investigative errors that occurred a decade ago are now unimportant. Each member of the Board should carefully consider the nature of this case—investigators ignored direct evidence. Instead, the Board utilized circumstantial evidence created at the manufacturers facilities after the accident. The NTSB must acknowledge numerous investigative errors."

Lastly, Leigh included the following statement: "The falsely accused TWA crew deserves an apology from the manufacturer and from the NTSB."

As the petition was making the rounds among committee members and ALPA investigators, a TWA 727 in cruise over Ohio suddenly exhibited un-commanded aileron and rudder inputs with the autopilot engaged. The pilots had to use full right wheel input to maintain level flight. That incident prompted another pilot to recall problems he had encountered with the same plane involved in TWA 841 two years before 841's mishap. In the 1977 incident, the pilot, a TWA Check Airman, was receiving a proficiency check ride. Also onboard as observers were several TWA employees from engineering and pilot training. During the flight the pilot was directed to forcefully overpower the roll channel of the engaged autopilot so that the observers could evaluate the response of the autopilot system. At some point, while overpowering the roll channel and then disconnecting the autopilot, the autopilot did not fully disengage, and the pilot had considerable trouble maintaining control.

The pilot in the 1977 incident provided an affidavit recounting his problems with aircraft N840TW. A discussion ensued as to whether or not these two incidents were somehow related to TWA 841. Could a problem with the autopilot roll channel have caused the upset? Could an autopilot false disconnect and a condition known as control wheel ratcheting have been a factor in TWA 841? A simple explanation of control wheel ratcheting is a condition where the autopilot doesn't fully release after the autopilot is disconnected, restricting the ability of the pilot to make full control inputs.

There were arguments for and against including this new information in the petition. On the one hand, it presented new evidence. On the other hand, it didn't fit Hoot's testimony. Hoot never said anything about hearing binding noises in the controls or having difficulty turning the yoke. In the end, Leigh decided to include the new evidence. His feeling was that it was the NTSB's job to consider all that was presented. The control wheel ratcheting theory also could help explain Hoot's inability to regain lateral control at the initiation of the incident. The addition of this new evidence in the petition resulted in a nearly ten-month delay as Leigh had to rewrite large sections of the petition.

Chapter Twenty-Eight

Rudder Hardover

H*oot knew that efforts were underway* on a petition for reconsideration. He had talked to Leigh Johnson and knew about the rudder hardover theory. It made perfect sense to Hoot, who had always maintained that the aircraft had yawed to the right prior to the incident. But what really caught Hoot's attention was the affidavit from the pilot who had experienced control problems on the very same airplane that was involved in TWA 841. One of the pilots in that event was Captain Falluco, the manager of flight training. Captain Falluco had given Hoot his evaluation ride after TWA 841. Why didn't Falluco say something about having control problems with N840TW then? Hoot wanted to know. Hoot saw this new information as a deliberate attempt by TWA to cover up information that would have been helpful to the original investigators.

Hoot wasn't one to let his growing resentment towards TWA affect his performance. He did his best to do his job and not get into lengthy discussions about TWA 841. He'd answer questions about the incident and subsequent investigation when asked. He'd thank the flight attendants whenever one of them would come up to him and make a supportive comment. But the constant reminders took an emotional toll. To Hoot, it was as if he were being interviewed every time he went to work. He accepted the reality that he was forever tied to what happened on April 4, 1979. But along with the constant reminders about TWA 841 came a reemergence of his previous medical problems. Once again he found himself combating high blood pressure and stomach ulcers. He was fifty-five, a full five years away from mandatory retirement.[1] He had moved back into the left seat. He was a senior pilot making well over $100,000 a year, flying the most advanced aircraft available at that time, but he couldn't shake TWA 841.

Most of Hoot's interactions with co-workers were positive. Pilots would go out of their way to approach Hoot to shake his hand. But during his time away, new pilots had been hired at TWA. These pilots didn't know Hoot. All they knew about Hoot was what they had read or heard. Like most pilots not working for TWA, these newer pilots sided with the NTSB.

Hoot would walk into operations to get ready for a flight and sense that he was being stared at. He'd sit down to do his paperwork, and one or two pilots would end whatever conversation they were having and get up from the table and leave. It didn't happen often. But it occurred often enough that Hoot sometimes felt apprehensive when he was in a room with a lot of other pilots. He avoided social gatherings. He'd hear about a pilot having a get-together, but when asked to attend he'd find an excuse not to go.

Finally, Hoot had had enough. There weren't any bigger airplanes to fly. His health was deteriorating. His operations were going well in Costa Rica. He loved the peace and quiet there. When Carl Icahn bought TWA and started selling off the airline's most valuable routes and assets, Hoot grew bitter. In an effort to cut costs, TWA offered a number of senior pilots a buyout. So at the young age of fifty-five, Hoot officially retired from TWA. It was a decision he would later come to regret. It

Figure 43 Hoot with his 747 crew shortly before retiring

was only after it was all gone that Hoot realized what he had given up. He loved his job. He missed being in charge. He missed the challenge and responsibility of safely carrying 200-plus passengers halfway around the world. But his health concerns were persistent and about to get much worse.

Hoot's early retirement left him with a lot of time on his hands. He talked to his ex-wife, Gloria, about the new evidence uncovered by Leigh Johnson. He mentioned that he was considering writing his own petition for reconsideration and asked her if she would be willing to help. Gloria said yes. When Hoot presented the idea to Landon Dowdey, Landon also agreed to help.

Since the ALPA petition spelled out the new theory of the upset and detailed the numerous investigative errors made in the investigation, Hoot decided to focus on what he saw as an attack on his character. Hoot's early draft of the petition was full of disparaging remarks toward

Boeing, the NTSB, and Leslie Kampschror. "The investigator-in-charge (IIC) allowed the Boeing Corporation to usurp the Board's functions and made Boeing judge and jury of this investigation," Hoot wrote. Next Hoot made reference to the civil trial and overstated the jury verdict. "When examined, the jury concluded that the Boeing Corporation was negligent and that its negligence was a direct cause of the TWA Flight 841 accident."

When it came to the NTSB, Hoot didn't limit his criticism to Leslie Kampschror. "At the outset of the investigation, a pilot employed by the Board who participated in this investigation, John Ferguson, a former TWA pilot, engaged in 'crew room' conversation with other pilots regarding the accident. This occurred at Washington National Airport on April 5, 1979, which was prior to the Board's Washington, D.C., investigating team ever reaching the accident scene and obtaining any factual information or interviewing the flight crew. After requesting to borrow a 727 operations manual from one of the TWA crew members, Mr. Ferguson made the statement, 'We are going to hang Gibson by [his] balls.' Subsequently, I learned that this statement had been made by Mr. Ferguson from several pilots who were present when he made the statement."

Gloria toned down the language. She changed certain passages that Hoot had written in the first person and wrote them in the third person using the phrase "petitioner" or "the petitioner." She removed hearsay statements and discarded anything that could be taken as a personal attack. Landon's contribution was to cite specific rules and regulations that were broken or not followed by investigators. He also included legal references, which had the unwanted effect of making the petition read more like a legal brief. Landon also borrowed heavily from the libel suit, making many of the same arguments concerning unfounded accusations against the crew. "Because the Board's incorrect finding that probable cause of this accident was flight crew error, the Petitioner's professional reputation has been tarnished and he has suffered great emotional distress."

Unlike the ALPA petition, which mentioned control wheel ratcheting as a possible contributing factor, Hoot's petition cited control wheel ratcheting as a primary contributor to the upset. Hoot's petition argued that his inability to prevent the plane from rolling over was caused by a false disconnect of the autopilot roll channel, which resulted in control wheel ratcheting. Landon Dowdey, who was not a pilot, also felt strongly that control wheel ratcheting was a factor based on testimony Hoot had given in the civil trial in which he testified that he had briefly "overpowered" the autopilot before disconnecting it.[2] Wanting to strengthen the argument for control wheel ratcheting, Landon asked ALPA for help in identifying other instances of autopilot malfunctions. Eight incidents involving false autopilot disconnects were eventually uncovered and included in the petition. All of this took time. Months went by as various drafts of the petition passed back and forth among the three authors.

The plan all along was for ALPA's petition for reconsideration to be submitted first. Hoot's petition was to follow soon after and include the ALPA petition as an attachment. TWA was also working on a third petition using the same information uncovered by Leigh Johnson.

On October 9, 1990, three years after Leigh Johnson began to take another look at TWA 841, ALPA's second petition for reconsideration was ready for submission. John Rohlfing did not agree with Leigh's decision to include the references to control wheel ratcheting, but he was happy with the arguments presented in the petition. He was eager to present the petition to the NTSB. So eager, in fact, that he flew to Washington D.C., to hand deliver it. He didn't want to risk having the petition filed away like some unsolicited manuscript received by an overworked literary agent.

John made sure he had several copies of the petition with him when he and several other committee members arrived in Washington. They told the secretary who they were and why they were there. The men were then escorted into the offices of Ron Schleede, the Chief of Major Aviation Investigations at the NTSB.

John introduced himself and the other committee members and handed Ron Schleede a copy of the petition. After flipping through the document and appearing indifferent to its contents, Schleede set the petition down on his desk. He said something about being very busy and not having much time to look at it.

Rohlfing was incredulous. Here was a man whose job it was to make sure that accident investigations were competent and fair, and he was ready to discard three years of hard work without even looking at it. Rohlfing left Ron Schleede's office and asked if there were any Board members available. They eventually met with three NTSB Board members and handed each a copy of the petition. The Board members thanked the men for their work and promised to review the petition. The group left Washington with an uneasy feeling that maybe they had wasted their time. As it turns out, their concerns were warranted.

When Rohlfing returned from his visit to NTSB headquarters, he put TWA 841 on the back burner. There was nothing more he could do. ALPA's public relations department put out a low-key press release announcing the petition. Several newspapers picked up on the story. Buzz Bissinger wrote a lengthy follow-up article for the *St. Paul Pioneer Press* that included an update on the crew members. The new evidence was presented in aviation periodicals. "A New Look at TWA Flight 841," was the title of an article in *Air Line Pilot* magazine. The television show *Hard Copy* with host Bill O'Reilly dedicated an entire hour to the story.

The NTSB, however, was not moved by the renewed interest in TWA 841. The reality was that petitions for reconsideration have little chance of overturning earlier findings by the NTSB Board. The NTSB has limited resources to re-investigate old accident investigations. The same people who did the original investigation are often the same people receiving the petition, or they more than likely know the people involved in the original investigation and are reluctant to find fault with their counterparts' work. More often than not petitions for reconsideration are filed in cases where the NTSB has ruled that a particular accident or incident was caused by pilot error. Add to this the fact that TWA 841 had occurred more than eleven years earlier and had resulted in no fatalities or serious injuries, and it's easy to see why the NTSB had no interest in re-opening the investigation. Easy to see unless, of course, one cares about the truth.

One person who felt very strongly about the truth was Leigh Johnson. Not only did he want to clear the crew of TWA 841, Leigh wanted to alert the NTSB to what he considered to be serious investigative errors and scientific misconduct. He fully expected that his petition for reconsideration would receive the attention he felt it deserved.

The same was true for Hoot, Gloria, and Landon, and the authors of the TWA petition for reconsideration. They continued to work on their petitions with the hope that through their efforts the real story of TWA 841 would finally be told. The truth of the matter, however, was that the NTSB was not persuaded to reconsider their findings of probable cause.

There is, however, one sure-fire way to get the attention of the NTSB—raising a concern over safety. Nothing motivates the NTSB more than the insinuation that their inaction might result in an accident or may have already contributed to a fatal accident. As it turns out, it would take two fatal accidents and media attention before the NTSB would be pressured into taking another look at TWA 841.

⸺ • ⸺

The first of what would become a string of mysterious rollover-and-dive accidents occurred on March 3, 1991, less than five months after John Rohlfing had handed the ALPA petition for reconsideration over to Ron Schleede of the NTSB. United Airlines Flight 585 departed Denver's Stapleton airport for a short twenty-minute hop to Colorado Springs, Colorado. It was a clear but windy day. Windshear was reported at the Colorado Springs airport.

In command of the Boeing 737 was Captain Harold Green, fifty-two years old. He was assisted by First Officer Patricia Eidson, age forty-two. Green, an experienced pilot with close to 10,000 hours of flight time, was at the controls. As the plane neared Colorado Springs airport on a visual approach the plane suddenly rolled over and crashed less than four miles from the runway threshold.

Investigators suspected a problem with the rudder system. Maintenance reports on the accident aircraft revealed that on February 25 a flight crew had reported un-commanded rudder inputs. The crew pulled the circuit breaker for the yaw damper. Maintenance then replaced the yaw damper coupler. Two days later another flight crew reported un-commanded rudder inputs. This time maintenance replaced the rudder transfer valve. Unfortunately, the rudder components on United 585 were severely damaged in the crash, and only limited testing was possible.

Boeing had its own theory of the accident. Boeing hypothesized that the accident was caused by a rotor cloud, an atmospheric condition common in mountainous regions where high winds coming over mountain ranges create wind currents that form a tight rotation along a horizontal axis.

As the investigation dragged on, various rumors surfaced. One of the more ugly rumors involved a relationship gone sour between the captain and his female first officer. The captain, who was married and had a young daughter, was supposedly having an affair with the first officer. At some point during the flight an argument ensued that led to Captain Green attacking Eidson with a crash ax and then intentionally plowing the plane into the ground.[3] Unlike the rumors related to the crew of TWA 841, the United 585 rumors were not spread by the NTSB investigators, who categorically denied them as plausible based on the evidence they had. Pilot suicide, however, would be considered in other accidents where investigators were unable to determine a cause.

Besides the obvious similarity of a rollover incident, the crash also shared with TWA 841 a flight recorder that proved to be of limited value to investigators. Unlike the foil-type flight data recorder found on TWA 841, the 737 involved in the United 585 crash was equipped with a digital flight data recorder. But it was an outdated digital flight data recorder that recorded the same five flight parameters as the foil recorder found on TWA 841.

In 1987 the FAA issued new rules requiring that by 1989, all foil-type flight data recorders were to be replaced with digital flight data recorders (DFDRs). The FAA also requested that all FDR-equipped aircraft record up to 11 parameters by 1994. This request was later broadened to require all newly manufactured aircraft to be equipped with DFDRs that could record 28 specific parameters after October 11, 1991. The new rules, however, did not mandate the retrofitting of existing installations.

The Airline Transport Association (ATA), representing U.S. Major Airlines, filed petitions for relief from the new rules, stating that many of the aircraft in its members' fleets were scheduled to be retired from service as a consequence of the need to meet FAA noise requirements. So while there was plenty of evidence supporting the need for updated flight data recorders capable of recording 11 or more parameters, economics prevented their addition on older aircraft. As a result, the investigators working on United Flight 585 were hampered by the same limited flight recorder data that had frustrated the TWA 841 investigators.

While the 737 did not have a split rudder design like that of the 727, it did share many of the same components. Leigh Johnson felt that there were enough similarities between the two incidents that he contacted the head of the United Airline's ALPA accident investigation committee and gave him a copy of the TWA 841 petition for reconsideration.

Landon Dowdey was also certain that there was a connection. He saw the United 585 accident as a tragedy that could have been averted had the NTSB conducted a proper investigation into TWA 841. He worked feverishly to finish Hoot's petition. The final draft of the petition, completed two years after the process began, bore no resemblance to earlier drafts. The version submitted to the NTSB was a more tightly edited document that argued the following: The slat could not have caused the upset, the rollover occurred as a result of a yaw damper system malfunction, control wheel ratcheting was a major contributor to the accident, and the crew was not given an opportunity to confront or challenge the evidence used against them.

Landon Dowdey, who wasn't shy about using the press to further his cause, held a press conference to announce the petition. This time he made sure everyone was on the same page. The message Landon wanted the world to hear was that the TWA 841 flight crew was wrongly accused, that there was still a problem with the 727 autopilot/

yaw damper system, and that a similar problem with the 737 may have brought down United 585.

The press conference had the desired effect. Hoot's petition was the first one ever submitted by an individual. It reignited interest in the story and resulted in additional coverage in both print and the news media. "It's what occupies my mind totally, all the time, like an albatross," Hoot told writer Buzz Bissinger in a *Chicago Tribune* article.[4]

Seven months later TWA filed their petition for reconsideration on TWA 841, once again citing much of the same evidence uncovered by Duane Yorke and Leigh Johnson. The NTSB now had three open petitions for reconsideration. They also appeared to have no intention of acting on any of them.

Landon Dowdey, like Leigh Johnson before him, expected the NTSB to respond quickly to the petition that he had submitted on Hoot's behalf. When he hadn't heard anything from the NTSB after a year, he filed a petition in the nature of *Mandamus*, which was a formal request to a higher court to force a lower court, or in this case the NTSB, to act on a matter before them. The response from the higher court was that not enough time had elapsed to expect a response from the NTSB. So Landon had no recourse but to wait.

Hoot, whose spirits had been lifted by the attention the new petitions had initially received, once again lost hope that the investigation into TWA 841 would ever be reopened.[5] In all likelihood, not one of the three petitions had been looked at by anyone at the NTSB beyond a cursory review.

There are few mechanisms in place to prod the NTSB into acting. There are no rules or regulations stipulating that the NTSB must respond within a certain time period once a petition for reconsideration is filed.

There are also no rules stating that the NTSB is even compelled to respond to a petition for reconsideration.

While a malfunctioning rudder was considered to have played a role in the Colorado Springs accident, it was still just a theory. There were no overriding concerns regarding the safety of the 727 or 737 rudder systems that might have prompted the NTSB to take a closer look at TWA 841. It would take another fatal accident and the prodding of the press to get the NTSB to finally take action.

That chain of events began on September 8, 1994 with USAir Flight 427. It was a Thursday. Pilots Peter Germano and Chuck Emmet were approaching Pittsburgh International airport on a flight that had originated in Chicago. It was just before 7:00 p.m. There was still enough light for the passengers and crew to see the early fall colors on the trees below. Visibility at Pittsburgh was reported as fifteen miles, winds were 270 at 10 knots, and the temperature was 75 degrees Fahrenheit. First Officer Chuck Emmett was at the controls of the Boeing 737. They were in the approach environment, being vectored for landing on 28R at Pittsburgh. In front of them, also being vectored for an approach, was a Delta Airlines Boeing 727.

The partial transcripts below contain the communications between the pilots and air traffic control as well as between the two pilots.[6]

"UsAir 427, turn left heading one-zero-zero. Traffic will be one to two o'clock, six miles, northbound Jetstream climbing out of thirty-three for five thousand," came the instructions from the Pittsburgh approach controller.

Emmett turned to the downwind heading, and Germano, who was working the radio, told the controller that they were looking for the traffic. Two loud thumps were picked up by the CVR. "Whoa," said Germano as the aircraft encountered wake turbulence from the 727 ahead. The plane banked abruptly to the left.

"Hang on, hang on," Germano said to his first officer as the plane rocked back to wings level and then rolled again back to the left.

Emmett clicked off the autopilot and took manual control of the aircraft. He turned the wheel to the right and applied some right rudder but the plane continued to roll to the left.

"Ohhh shit," Emmett said as he struggled to right the plane.

The plane began to roll over and head for the ground, some five thousand feet away. Emmett pulled back on the yoke, which caused the airspeed to decrease and set off the stick shaker. Next the ground proximity warning "whoop-whoop-pull-up-pull-up" sounded. This was followed by "traffic, traffic," as the traffic collision avoidance system (TCAS) alerted the crew that they were getting too close to the Jetstream traffic. The last words heard on the CVR were Emmett yelling "Noooo . . ."

Now another aircraft had suffered an unexplained rollover and dive. And like United Airlines Flight 585 in Colorado Springs, the pilots were too close to the ground to recover. One hundred and twenty-seven passengers and five crew members perished in the crash.

Landon Dowdey was furious. How many more rollover accidents was it going to take before the NTSB would act? It had been nearly four years since ALPA had filed a petition for reconsideration and three years since Hoot's petition, and they still hadn't heard anything from the NTSB.

Landon wasted little time preparing a second petition in the nature of *Mandamus*. The new petition contained the following statement: ". . . The NTSB cannot delay action on a petition to reopen for so long a period of time as to compromise the efficacy of this court's statutory review obligations . . . Perhaps a year's delay, as in 1991, does not warrant this court's intervention. But over four years? That is the question now."

The petition then mentioned both the Colorado Springs accident and the USAir Flight 427 accident as additional impetus for the Board to act: "The Court should not allow the NTSB to delay exercising its statutory duties until the next fatal crash."

The new petition referenced a statement from the NTSB findings in the Colorado Springs accident. "The Safety Board understands that these same components are also used in the rudder controls of Boeing 727 model airplanes." There had been two rollover accidents in the span of three-and-a-half years. The rudder system was suspected in each accident. And the Safety Board was admitting that the 727 shared many of the same rudder components. Yet the NTSB failed to act on any of the petitions for reconsideration that had been filed for TWA 841.

Landon's petition for *Mandamus*, listing Hoot as the petitioner, did catch the attention of the press covering the USAir investigation. "Ex-Pilot Likens 1979 Spiral to '94 Fatal Crash," was the title of an article by the Associated Press. "Former Pilot Seeks to Reopen Case," was the title of a *Seattle Times* article. The negative press more than anything else prompted the NTSB to act. In January of 1995, the NTSB agreed to consider Hoot's petition for reconsideration. Ron Schleede was given the task of reviewing the petition. A little more than four months later, on May 4, 1995, the NTSB submitted their response. The petition was denied.

Hoot learned of the NTSB's response in a letter from Landon. He was angry but not surprised. Hoot's focus at that time was on what he felt was a ticking time bomb waiting to go off. Hoot was certain that there was a connection between his rollover incident and the two 737 accidents. He had been following both investigations closely, reading everything about them he could get his hands on. The more he read, the more he became convinced that the answer to all of these mysteries lay within the inner workings of the Boeing 727 and 737 rudder/yaw dampening system.

Hoot's concerns about the potential for another rollover incident were shared by the investigators looking into USAir Flight 427. If they couldn't determine what had caused the plane to roll over and crash, it would leave open the possibility of it occurring again. It wasn't difficult to imagine what impact that fear might have on the traveling public. There was a lot at stake.

The Boeing 737 involved in the Flight 427 crash was one of the newer planes operated by USAir. It had been purchased in 1987. Unlike the Boeing 737 involved in the United 585 crash, which recorded only five parameters, the USAir 737 recorded thirteen parameters. In addition to the five basic parameters of speed, altitude, heading, vertical acceleration, and mike keying, the following additional parameters were recorded: pitch, roll, and several engine parameters, including engine power. One parameter not recorded was rudder position.

In reviewing the data from the FDR, investigators noticed an abrupt heading change just prior to the upset. The heading change was to the left. The roll channel also indicated a roll to the left. This was followed by a reduction in pitch and a rapid decrease in altitude that ultimately ended in the crash. The additional parameters provided by the flight data recorder showed that the plane had experienced a rudder event that led to the plane yawing nose left and then a rollover and spiral dive that reached 4 Gs in just 28 seconds.

Along with the additional FDR parameters, the 427 investigators had one other important advantage over their United Flight 585 counterparts, the rudder power control unit (PCU) from Flight 427 survived the impact. Investigators sent it off for testing. While that process got underway, speculation and rumors took center stage. One early hypothesis involved the possibility that a thrust reverser had deployed in flight. This theory came about when workers scouring the wreckage site found a piece of the right thrust reverser that indicated it may have been unlocked at impact.

The Investigator-in-Charge, Tom Haueter, mentioned the thrust reverser part in a briefing. Tom cautioned reporters that it was too early to draw conclusions, but the press ran with the story anyway. "Thrust Reverser Suspected in USAir Jetliner Crash/Device Could Have Caused Nose Dive," was one such headline.[7] The thrust reverser theory was later ruled out when evidence was found indicating that the reverser was locked at impact.

Boeing once again had a theory of the accident that pointed away from a fault with the plane. Boeing's theory centered on the pilots. They hypothesized that perhaps the pilot had over-compensated for the wake turbulence from the Delta 727 and had stomped on the rudder. Boeing would spend a lot of time arguing this theory of the accident.

As is the case in any airline accident where a cause is not immediately determined, numerous theories arose. There was the bird strike theory. This theory carried enough weight that investigators combed through wreckage looking for signs of a bird strike. Nothing was found. Reporters looking into passenger histories discovered one passenger who had been scheduled to testify in a drug case. Could someone have brought the plane down to prevent the individual from testifying against them? A little fact checking with prosecutors, along with a lack of evidence of a bomb, ruled this theory out as implausible. One of the more bizarre theories was the fat man theory. In this scenario an overweight passenger inadvertently steps through a weakened section of the floorboard and breaks through, stepping onto the rudder control cable, displacing the rudder. The NTSB, not wanting to discount any theory that had even a remote measure of probability, conducted tests on a stripped-down 737. The tests showed that even the most obese passenger wouldn't have been able to displace the rudder by the amount needed to cause the upset.[8]

Everything was still pointing at the rudder, but tests of the rudder PCU by Parker Hannifin, the manufacturer of the PCU, found no discrepancies. The PCU functioned normally. Investigators didn't know what had caused USAir Flight 427 to crash, but they felt compelled to share what evidence they did have. So in January of 1995 they scheduled a public hearing. When Hoot learned of the public hearing, he made immediate plans to fly to Pittsburgh to be present there.

Hoot was in attendance as various witnesses and experts were called to testify. He watched with particular interest the animated reenactment. But Hoot was also eyeing the investigative panel, trying to sort out who was who. During a recess in the hearing, Hoot caught up with an ALPA representative who introduced Hoot to Herb LeGrow, the head of the USAir/ALPA investigative committee—the same position Jim McIntyre had held at TWA.

Figure 44 Hoot a few years before his visit to Pittsburgh for the USAir Flight 427 public hearing

Hoot asked LeGrow if it would be possible to speak to him after the hearing. LeGrow knew who Hoot was. He was familiar with TWA 841. He invited Hoot to join him for dinner.

That evening Hoot joined a group of about a dozen or so USAir/ALPA accident investigators at a Pittsburgh restaurant. Hoot was feeling anxious being around so many other pilots. His intention was to speak to Herb LeGrow privately, but he put his fears aside and did his best to fit in.

Sitting across the table from Hoot was USAir pilot and accident investigator John Cox. John was working with the Systems Group on the USAir 427 investigation. He was familiar with TWA 841 and had sided with the NTSB in the probable cause finding. So he was a little skeptical when Hoot started talking about the similarities between his event and that of USAir 427. John didn't see any similarities at all. TWA 841 was caused by an extended slat, and they were looking at a rudder problem. Jon Cox saw Hoot as someone who had flown in a different era. The planes, systems, and air traffic control were a lot more sophisticated now than they were back when Hoot was coming up through the ranks. But John was respectful and gave Hoot an opportunity to make his argument. Later, after Hoot had left, John caught up with Herb LeGrow. They talked briefly about whether or not they should take a look at TWA 841. John said he didn't think it was worth their time and effort. They had enough work on their hands trying to figure out what had happened to Flight 427.[9]

———◆———

By June of 1996 the investigation into USAir Flight 427 was stretching out into nineteen months, almost the same amount of time as the United 585 investigation had taken, which had ended with a final report saying that the plane had crashed for undetermined reasons. The NTSB was looking at the very real possibility of having to release a similar report on USAir 427.

The break in the USAir 427 investigation occurred on June 9, 1996. That's the date that Eastwind Airlines Flight 517 experienced a rudder hardover. Eastwind Flight 517 was a Boeing 737 en route from Trenton, New Jersey, to Richmond, Virginia. The two pilots were Captain Bryan

Bishop and First Officer Spencer Griffin. Eastwind Airlines was a startup airline that had only two airplanes, both Boeing 737s. As the plane neared Richmond, Bishop experienced un-commanded rudder movements that caused the plane to yaw and roll to the right. When Bishop tried to counteract the yawing and rolling by pressing on the left rudder, he encountered resistance. No matter how hard he pressed on the left rudder, it wouldn't budge. Bishop used the aileron and differential power to keep the plane from flipping over. Whatever was causing the jammed rudder released and allowed Bishop to right the plane. Seconds later the plane yawed and rolled a second time. The rudder once again released moments later. After turning off the autopilot and yaw damper, the pilots were able to land safely with no further un-commanded rudder inputs.

Members of the 427 investigation team flew to Richmond the next day. After speaking with the two pilots, investigators decided to conduct several flight tests to attempt to duplicate what had happened on Flight 517. Unlike the Boeing flight test, where Hoot was prevented from being on the aircraft during the test, the 427 investigators had the Captain of Flight 517, Bryan Bishop, fly one of the two test flights.

Results from the flight tests as well as tests of the rudder PCU turned up no smoking guns. What the incident did do, however, was convince the NTSB that there was a problem with the 737 rudder system. A new round of tests on the rudder PCU was requested.

Since the rudder PCU had passed all tests with flying colors, investigators decided to try a thermal shock test. The rudder PCU valve on the 737, also known as a dual concentric servo valve, was actually a valve-within-a-valve that had very tight tolerances. The idea was to super-cool the valve to simulate the cold temperatures at altitude and then shock the valve by injecting hot hydraulic fluid into the valve. Tests of a new valve from Parker Hannifin passed the thermal shock tests without issue. When the PCU from Flight 427 was tested, however, the valve jammed. A review of the data from the tests indicated that the jammed valve would have resulted in a rudder reversal, meaning had the pilot stepped on the right rudder to counter a yaw and roll to the left, the rudder would have actually moved left and exacerbated the problem.

Investigators had their smoking gun, or so it seemed. Critics of the test pointed out that the conditions required to reproduce the jammed valve do not occur during normal flight operations. For the valve to jam, the plane has to be at altitude for an extended period of time, and then there has to be some malfunction of a hydraulic pump that would result in the hydraulic fluid reaching 170 degrees Fahrenheit. None of the three incidents of suspected rudder-induced roll met the criteria required in the test. While it is true that later tests found it was possible to get the valve to jam without the thermal shock, these tests also were not realistic in that they required the pilot to push on the rudder in one direction and then rapidly apply rudder in the opposite direction.[10]

Still, the NTSB felt that they had solved the mystery of Flight 427. But they weren't quite ready to announce their findings to the world. Discussions began with Boeing, the FAA, and the NTSB on how best to handle this new information. What changes were going to be required to assure that this problem did not occur again? One early step was to issue airworthiness directives to all operators of 737s requiring rudder checks and other procedures for limiting the possibility of future rudder hardovers and reversals while an alternative PCU was developed. They implemented procedures for pilots to enable them to identify and handle un-commanded rudder inputs. The new procedures were to turn off the autopilot and yaw damper. Pilots were also advised to decrease pitch and increase airspeed.

At first glance the PCU problem discovered on the 737 ruled out any similarities with TWA 841. The Boeing 727 did not use the dual concentric servo valve.[11] The 727 had a split rudder design whereas the 737 did not. And Hoot testified that he had applied full left rudder. He didn't say anything about the rudder pedals not responding or being stiff. But what if the PCU valve wasn't the culprit? What if the problem all along was not with the PCU valve but some other component in the yaw dampening system such as the yaw damper rate gyros or couplers or some combination of the two?

A close look at these rollover accidents reveals similarities that point away from the PCU valve and to the yaw damping system. In the United Flight 585 accident, pilots reported un-commanded rudder movement in the days prior to the accident. That is a problem likely unrelated to the PCU valve. The day of the accident the plane experienced windshear that could have resulted in a cross-control condition. USAir Flight 427 encountered wake turbulence, which also could have led to a cross-control condition. In the case of TWA 841, had the right outboard aileron free-floated up prior to the upset as suspected, it would have caused the plane to bank to the right. The autopilot would have responded to the right bank by commanding a turn to the left in order to maintain heading. This, too, would have led to a cross-control condition. It's quite possible that the rudder hardovers experienced by all three crews were the result of the yaw damping system responding to a condition it wasn't designed to detect.

The fact that the Flight 427 investigators delayed making an announcement concerning their findings related to the PCU valve indicates a degree of uncertainty as to its importance. Investigators instead scheduled more testing. It was during this period that yet another 737 experienced a rollover, dive, and crash. Silkair Flight

185 was on a routine flight from Jakarta, Indonesia, to Singapore on December 19, 1997. Shortly after reaching its cruising altitude of 35,000 feet, the plane rolled over and began a spiral dive. The plane crashed into the Musi River near Palembang in southern Sumatra, Indonesia, killing all 97 passengers and 7 crew members. The time from the beginning of the dive to the crash was less than one minute. The plane was thought to have broken the speed of sound for a portion of the dive.

Investigators from the NTSB flew to Indonesia to assist the Indonesian National Transportation Safety Committee in investigating the crash. The plane was almost completely destroyed by the high speed impact, but both the CVR and FDR were recovered. The rudder PCU valve was also recovered and was sent to Parker Hannifin for testing.

When investigators reviewed the CVR, they discovered that the CVR had stopped recording some eight minutes before the crash. Six minutes later the FDR had stopped recording. Suspicion fell on the crew, especially the captain, for having purposely pulled the circuit breakers to both recorders. NTSB investigators suspected pilot suicide and began looking into the captain's background. What they found seemed to bolster their argument for pilot suicide: The captain was in debt to his brokerage account for more than $100,000, and his trading privileges had been suspended for non-payment. The captain had taken out a life insurance policy for three million dollars one week before the accident. The effective date of the policy was the day of the accident.[12]

In reviewing the captain's employment history, investigators discovered that he had been disciplined by the airline. In one instance, he was disciplined for pulling the CVR circuit breaker prior to a flight. He had also been demoted from the position of instructor. Captain Tsu Way Ming was a former military pilot for the Singapore Air Force. The day of the accident was the eighteenth anniversary of an accident that had killed three members of his squadron.

During the investigation into the captain's background, the rudder PCU was returned to Indonesian investigators, having passed all tests. The NTSB subsequently submitted their findings to Indonesian investigators with the conclusion that the captain had purposely crashed the plane, committing suicide. Indonesian officials, however, did not accept the NTSB findings and ruled that a cause could not be determined.

Back in the U.S., the NTSB investigators on USAir Flight 427 still hadn't released a final report on the accident. They had discovered the problem with the dual concentric servo valve almost two-and-a-half years earlier. Why such a long delay? The truth was that the evidence against the PCU valve was circumstantial. They couldn't prove that the rudder had jammed or reversed on flight 427. Then to make matters even more complicated, another 737 experienced un-commanded rudder movement one month before the NTSB team was set to present their findings to the Board.

On February 23, 1999 the pilots of a MetroJet 737 cruising at flight level 330 noticed the control wheel turning to the left. The first officer noticed that the rudder pedals were displaced to the right. When he tried to center the pedals, the rudder appeared to be jammed. The pilots immediately turned off the autopilot and the yaw damper, and the rudder pedals centered. This particular 737 had been retrofitted with a new servo valve designed to prevent rudder hardovers.[13]

Investigators looking into the incident determined that there were no similarities to Flight 427 and decided to move forward with their findings. In March of 1999 the last Sunshine meeting on USAir 427 was held. The final report on the accident was released, blaming a rudder reversal caused by the rudder PCU dual concentric servo valve.

The United 585 flight was also determined to have been affected by the same problem, and the report was updated to reflect the new findings.

Two seemingly unsolvable crashes now appeared to have been solved. Case closed. That was the story told to the public. But there were a number of people with knowledge of both investigations who felt that they hadn't solved anything. These people, some who were involved in the 427 investigation, believed that the evidence pointing at the rudder PCU was inconclusive and that there was still a problem with the rudder/yaw dampening system that made the airplane susceptible to rudder hardovers.[14]

Boeing agreed to make design changes that would eliminate the possibility of a rudder hardover or reversal. They switched to a different type of PCU valve. They also made design changes to the rudder/yaw dampening system.

———————

Family members of passengers aboard SilkAir 185 filed suit against the airline in Singapore. Those suits, however, were thrown out because the Indonesian National Transportation Safety Committee (NTSC) failed to accept the pilot-suicide theory, which would have implicated the airline. The families then filed suit against Parker Hannifin, the manufacturer of the dual concentric servo valve, which had also been implicated in the crashes of United Flight 585 and USAir Flight 427.

A Los Angeles-based law firm took on the case. They began by conducting their own independent investigation into SilkAir 185. Lawyer Walter Lack, the lead attorney, first looked into the accusations of pilot suicide. What he found contradicted much of what the NTSB had relied on to make their claim for pilot suicide. They discovered that Captain Ming had recently sold two properties and had a positive net worth. The life insurance policy that had looked so incriminating early on turned out to be a standard requirement for a new mortgage Ming had recently taken out.

When Lack's hired experts reviewed the FDR, they discovered that while the plane was relatively new, having been purchased less than a year prior to the accident, the plane inexplicably had an older model FDR. A review of the FDR, which recorded the last twenty-five hours of flying, indicated that the FDR had stopped recording on numerous occasions with some stoppages as short as four seconds and others as long as eleven minutes. In twenty-five hours of recording, the FDR failed to record some or all parameters for a total of sixty-six minutes.

An examination of the CVR audio that was recorded found that the cockpit conversations between Ming and his copilot as well as his conversations with the flight attendants were routine. Nothing the captain did prior to the flight indicated suicidal tendencies. Ming had called his wife before the flight to tell her what time to pick him up at the airport.

When the case finally went to trial in May of 2004, exactly twenty-one years to the month of the Holly & Tim Wicker trial, the judge ruled that the jury would not be allowed to hear any claims about pilot suicide. Instead, the trial focused on the rudder PCU. A microscopic examination of the rudder PCU, the only surviving part from the plane, revealed manufacturing defects and indications of metal filings inside the valve. When jurors were told of the propensity of the PCU valve to jam under certain circumstances due to the extremely tight tolerances, they sided with the plaintiffs and awarded the three remaining families in the suit a total of 44 million dollars. Parker Hannifin eventually settled with all of the SilkAir 185 families for an undisclosed sum.[15]

Chapter Twenty-Nine

What Really Happened?

If there was one aspect of the case that stood out in the TWA 841 investigation and made it different from any accident investigation before or since, it was the refusal of the NTSB investigators to involve the crew. This was an event that had many things going on immediately before, during, and after it occurred. It's easy to see how some details could have been left out or placed out of sequence in the crew's early accounts. Hoot told his story to the two FAA inspectors and then later that day at the mini-hearing held at the hotel. Then he gave a sworn deposition seven days later. That was it. In all three cases the stories were similar but not exactly the same. Details were added or left out with each telling. Had they questioned the crew more extensively, they might have been able to get a clearer picture of this very confusing event.

One detail that no one paid much attention to in Hoot's early re-telling of the upset involved the rudder. Hoot indicated on more than one occasion to more than one individual that the aircraft yawed prior to the upset. But this detail had been overlooked by just about everyone.

Here is the transcript of Hoot's deposition eight days after the upset. Kampschror was asking the questions:

Q. Please describe what happened from level-off at 390 to the beginning of the incident.

A. We leveled the aircraft off at—we climbed up there at Mach .80, leveled the aircraft off, and it was very smooth, quiet. There was very little air noise at that altitude. And the engineer set cruise power, made two or three adjustments to make sure that it was maintained at cruise, which it did, it was fine. And I think we had been at altitude about, it seemed to be, four or five minutes. And do you want me to describe what happened then?

Q. Please.

A. Okay. I had it on autopilot, and I was putting charts away and just rearranging my stuff in the cockpit, and detected a slight buzz, very—not even a hardly noticeable buzz, and I saw the yoke, the wheel of the airplane just starting to turn slowly to the left, and so I just continued to watch it. It was on autopilot. The autopilot was making a correction because the airplane at that time started a slow turn to the left, and the autopilot input was increasing to the left.

Q. The airplane was turning which direction?

A. The airplane was turning to the right. The autopilot was trying to correct, it was turning to the left, so I took the aircraft off the autopilot at that time, and—

At this point Hoot had not said anything about the plane yawing as he described the incident, but a few moments later, after a series of follow-up questions from Kampschror, he does.

A. Okay. Well, as it rolled over, when it became inverted, I had just a slight back pressure on it, and it did go off to the right.

I'm not sure how many degrees, but it went maybe 10 degrees off to the right on this heading before it rolled.[1]

That is the first official account where Hoot talks about the plane yawing to the right, but he didn't actually use the word "yaw." As difficult as it might be to comprehend, that was the last time anyone from the NTSB talked directly to the crew about the events leading up to the upset. Unfortunately, the ALPA and TWA investigators were equally guilty of excluding the crew from the investigation. Everyone was focused on what they believed was the initiator of the event, and that was the isolated number seven slat. No one considered it important to get more details from the crew, especially a crew suspected of deliberately erasing the CVR.

In fairness to the ALPA investigators, their efforts to get the NTSB to consider other possible causes of the upset were hampered by the narrow focus on the missing slat and accusations of crew involvement. This bias by NTSB investigators was evident as early as the depositional proceedings held eight days after the incident. In an article published in the *New York Times* the day of the depositions, the paper quoted an industry source as saying, "There's no question about the facts and the sequence of events."[2] The same article also contained a quote from an ALPA representative. ". . . An official of the Air Line Pilots Association said there was still a possibility that something had gone wrong with the spoilers or with the yaw dampers."

Hoot became increasingly frustrated with the way the investigation was unfolding. From Jim McIntyre and Harold Marthinsen, Hoot learned that the NTSB was claiming that the aircraft rolled right and then back to the left and that the crew had become spatially disoriented. That really irked Hoot. He was the one flying the plane. "Why the hell don't they ask me what the plane did?" Hoot complained to Jim McIntyre.

Hoot wanted the investigators to know that what they were claiming was untrue. He wanted to re-emphasize that the plane had never rolled left and that at no time prior to the upset did he become spatially disoriented. But when Hoot expressed his desire to speak to the investigators, Jim McIntyre informed him that he was unlikely to get anyone from the NTSB to listen. He advised Hoot to submit a sworn affidavit instead. The NTSB could still ignore it, but at least the affidavit would be placed into the official record, Jim explained. Here's how Hoot described the incident in the affidavit taken November 29, 1979.

I first realized that we had a problem when the control wheel started a slow turn about 10 degrees or more to the left, while the airplane remained relatively straight and level. As this was happening, there was a very gentle shaking or buzz. I had previously experienced a stall and mach buffet on other flights. It was neither of these.

Therein-after something seemed to let go and the airplane yawed and rolled slowly to the right, although the autopilot was still correcting to the left. At the same time the gentle buzz or shaking that I felt at the outset increased to a slight buffet.

Shortly after the aircraft began to roll, I disconnected the autopilot and applied full left aileron at about the same rate as the aircraft was rolling to the right. At about this time, I started coming in with left rudder fairly rapidly because the aircraft rate of roll was increasing. I remember looking back into the cockpit and seeing a bank angle on the HDI of around 40 degrees. I felt at this point that the aircraft was going to continue to roll over and I called out to the copilot. Throughout this sequence of events, I also held a gentle back pressure on the control wheel because the nose was dropping.

There was a clearly defined external horizon throughout the roll of the airplane. A moonlit deck was about 3 to 4 thousand feet below our cruise altitude. This broken-to-solid cloud deck extended several miles ahead of us and beyond the cloud deck I could see the shoreline of Lake Michigan and the glow of lights from cities across the lake.

At the start of the roll, I observed the outside horizontal reference and therefore had a clear indication of the direction of the roll. At no time during the initial phase did I ever suffer spatial disorientation. The aircraft roll was always to the right.[3]

The purpose of the affidavit was to afford Hoot an opportunity to dispute the NTSB's version of events and to do so in a way that would include those comments in the public record. In this account there is some detail that was missing from the first deposition. In this account Hoot does mention that the plane yawed prior to the upset.

Two-and-a-half months after the Board voted on a probable cause, pinning the blame on the crew, Hoot was required to give a number of depositions related to lawsuits filed by passengers. In these depositions Hoot was asked to describe the events leading up to the upset. While the general description of what took place was always the same, the details of what the plane was doing differed slightly from one telling to the next. Here is Hoot's description of the events just prior to the upset in his August 11, 1981 deposition.

The airplane was pretty much, you know, maintaining. Sometimes, in real high altitudes, the airplane is not quite as stable, directionally, as it is at low altitudes. The airplane was pretty stable. There was a little—I don't know if you'd describe it as a yaw. You could see that it was kind of sensing for the direction, but the aileron input was to the left.[4]

Later in that same deposition Hoot adds another important detail that hadn't appeared in any of his other accounts. He is still describing the events just prior to the upset.

. . . And somewhere in that same time span, the airplane yawed very noticeably quite a few degrees to the right. There was a thud or a bang or a sound that was more likely a compressor stalling in the right engine.[5]

A compressor stall occurs when the airflow to a jet engine is interrupted. Here Hoot is describing an aircraft that has yawed so severely to the right that it caused a disruption of the airflow to the right engine. The compressor stall was also heard by some passengers, with one passenger describing the compressor stall as sounding "like someone throwing rocks against the side of the plane."

So are Hoot's differing accounts of the events leading up to the upset an indication that he was lying? The lawyer for the plaintiffs in the civil trial made that argument. "He's changed his story so many times you don't know which one to believe," Charles Hvass told the jury in his closing arguments. The truth, however, is that it is common for someone to include or omit details when retelling a stressful, complex event. This is particularly true when the same event is retold months or years later.

Sometimes the further removed a person is from a stressful event the clearer their memory becomes. They'll remember details years later that hadn't seemed important right after the event. In late 1999, while waiting for a heart transplant, Hoot gave an interview to Kathleen Dowdey, the daughter of Hoot's personal lawyer Landon Dowdey. Kathleen had no aviation experience. Here is a part of the transcript from that interview.

> . . . I could see the nose of the airplane just a little bit and the control wheel, through the autopilot, was trying to stop it. This yawing back and forth. And I felt this a few times, and I thought, well, I don't know what's going on but I better disconnect the autopilot. Well right about that time the airplane yawed severely to the right, and then it came back and hesitated, and then it yawed to the right again and as it did, it went down, so the airplane is going down and banking to the right.[6]

In this account Hoot describes the yawing in much greater detail. His description perfectly matches the heading trace of the FDR, the same heading trace that the investigators had such a hard time understanding. Had Hoot been questioned more thoroughly, not only by the NTSB investigators but by the ALPA and TWA investigators, this recounting of the aircraft yawing might have caused them to consider other possibilities. Hoot was told on more than one occasion by representatives of both TWA and ALPA to leave everything up to them. Don't make a lot of noise, they would tell him. Additionally, Hoot was in training during most of the early phase of the investigation. He was taken out of the loop during the most crucial portion of the inquiry by both the NTSB and TWA.

In a deposition in the civil trial, Hoot was asked how much time he had spent talking to Harold Marthinsen, ALPA's chief accident investigator, about the specifics of the upset. "Well, we've talked about it different times," Hoot said. "I wouldn't know how much total time we've talked about it. In all of the times we've talked about it, it may only be 20 minutes, 30 minutes, you know, over the two-and-a-half years."

There were a few people who looked at the data objectively and concluded that something other than the slat could have been involved. The first serious look at the rudder as a possible cause appeared as early as the ALPA report that was submitted to the NTSB in March 1981.[7]

> The crew reported seeing a lower yaw damper [fail] flag after recovery . . . This flag is NOT associated with hydraulic failure. The flag appears if the rate gyro malfunctions or if there is a loss of electrical power to the rate gyro. A hardover signal from the yaw damper could cause a very sharp heading change, such as has been noted on the FDR at the initiation of the maneuver . . . Although proposed by ALPA, this consideration has never been pursued.
>
> Consistent with the sharp yaw indicated by the FDR heading trace is the compressor stall noise heard by numerous witnesses, including flight deck crew members, flight attendants and some passengers. It would be expected that a heading change of the magnitude shown by the FDR would cause a momentary disturbance of the airflow . . . would cause the typical "bang" of a compressor stall . . .
>
> Throughout the investigation, the evidence of this yaw has been ignored, even though its existence could help explain the true cause of the uncontrollable roll.[8]

It's obvious from the record that the investigators were presented with evidence of yaw damper involvement very early on. Some of the very earliest newspaper accounts, perhaps not considered a reliable source but a source nonetheless, mentioned the aircraft yawing before the upset.

"Harvey 'Hoot' Gibson, the pilot, has told National Transportation Safety Board investigators that he turned off the jetliner's automatic pilot when there was an indication in the cockpit that the yaw damper was continually correcting to the right. The yaw damper system senses minute right or left movements of the airplane and operates the rudder to keep the plane on course. Investigators say Gibson told them that the plane was on autopilot and as he took over the manual control, the plane suddenly yawed to the right, rolled completely over twice and dived earthward at a steep 60-degree angle."[9]

At least one passenger reported having the sensation of the plane "veering" to the right. Passenger Thomas Quill was sitting in seat 22F, which was the right side window seat in the last row. He was one of the fourteen passengers contacted by Human Factors Group Chairman Haden Leroy. Quill described the sensation in his testimony in the Holly Wicker civil trial. "Well, I think the most vivid memory was that—just an awareness that the plane was veering off to the right, sort of a continuous pattern."[10]

Figure 45 A yaw damper-induced rudder hardover of the lower rudder fits all of the available evidence.

It would be unfair to say that the NTSB investigators never considered the yaw damper as a possible initiator of the event. They did conduct limited testing both in the simulator as well as during the flight test. Kampschror was quoted in a few aviation periodicals as saying that investigators had ruled out the yaw damper and autopilot as possible contributing factors. But the evidence also indicates that any examination of the yaw damper system or rudder hardover scenario was perfunctory at best.

So if all of the evidence points to a discrepant rudder as having caused the upset, and since there have been no major changes to the Boeing 727 rudder/yaw damper system since the first planes rolled off the assembly line, what evidence is there of this problem occurring before or after TWA 841? As it turns out, there have been numerous instances of un-commanded roll due to rudder/yaw damper system malfunction on the 727. In fact, ALPA had a report of one such incident that had occurred several months prior to TWA 841.

The earlier incident involved a 727 on a flight from LaGuardia airport in New York to Atlanta, Georgia, on January 21, 1979. The pilot reported rudder control problems. Here the pilot describes what happened shortly after taking off from LaGuardia with thunderstorms in the vicinity.

. . . At 400' I felt a skid to the left which I attributed to expected wind shear. We turned to 170 degrees. Around 800' another skid was felt. We were in heavy rain and considerable turbulence at the time. This time the skid seemed to increase and hold. I thought we had lost an engine and made the comment to my crew. The reply was everything was normal. My thoughts were this was the most unusual wind shear I have ever experienced as it was apparently overcoming the 727 yaw system.

We were instructed to turn right to 240 degrees. It was then apparent that there was a problem with the aircraft, as I had full aileron input in to the right and the aircraft was in a left skid and not turning. ATC made the request again to turn. I told my crew that I would fly the airplane and for them to check the systems. Someone announced to look at the rudder indices as they were split in opposite directions between the yaw damper and full travel pointers. The aircraft then went into a 35 degree right bank as apparently the rudders went to the right. I was controlling the aircraft with aileron, as I did not want to aggravate the rudder problem.

At this time the aircraft was in a right bank with considerable left aileron input. It stopped and I had positive control of the aircraft again. I then made a turn to the west, experiencing several rudder inputs in the turn.[11]

The pilot goes on to explain how they eventually determined that the problem was related to the upper rudder system. Once they turned off the upper rudder yaw damper, the problem went away. The pilot was describing a rudder hardover of the upper rudder. This important clue somehow was overlooked, most likely because all of the focus was on the number seven slat.

Since TWA 841 there have been a number of similar cases of un-commanded roll due to yaw damper system malfunction. Below is an aircraft service report involving Eastern Airlines Flight 56 on January 3, 1982.[12]

EAL Flight 56 reported aircraft "Dutch Rolling" @ 32,000 feet altitude over Memphis, Tennessee, autopilot on or off.

Reduced altitude to 26,000 feet, no change. Returned to IAH landing without incident @0207Z.

Maintenance investigation disclosed upper yaw damper coupler inop and lower coupler intermittent. EAL maintenance replaced both couplers, test flew aircraft. No further control problems.

Here is an aircraft incident report filed on December 17, 1989.[13]

TWA Flight 70, N5430, a Boeing 727-231, departed St. Louis (STL) on 12/16/89 2326 CST en route to Newark (EWR). At approximately 40 nautical miles NW of Dayton (DAY) at FL 370, mach .825, the crew suddenly experienced un-commanded aileron and rudder input with the autopilot engaged. The crew reported they needed full right input of the autopilot to maintain level flight. They then disconnected the autopilot. The crew then reported that the aircraft required major forceful control inputs to maintain control of the aircraft. Captain Martinez declared an emergency to (IND) center and then diverted to Dayton Int'l (DAY) . . . The aircraft was ferried to Kansas City for maintenance. TWA maintenance accomplished the following: (1) Replaced both upper & lower rudder power control units. (2) Re-rigged rudder control system. (3) Replaced both autopilot yaw damper couplers. (4) Checked flap position indicators. (5) Re-rigged flap control system. (6) Test flew aircraft. The aircraft was released to resume service on December 29, 1989. There have been no further maintenance discrepancies reported.

Here is a report of a rudder induced un-commanded roll that occurred on March 12, 1991.[14]

At cruise FL 280 aircraft yawed to the right and the autopilot corrected with left aileron. At that time we noticed the upper rudder indices showed approximately 25 percent deflection to the left and the lower rudder indices showed approximately 50 per cent deflection to the right with the autopilot still engaged, the upper and lower rudder returned to center and everything appeared normal with [the] autopilot disconnected. The aircraft felt normal also.

Here is a flight debrief filed on May 27, 1991.[15]

90 DME east [of] ZUN, 28,000, 265 kts, autopilot coupled, VMC conditions (visual meteorological conditions), aircraft yawed to right (indices approximately 20 percent right). I disconnected the autopilot and maintained wings level with 30 to 40 degrees left aileron. After 6 seconds rudder returned to normal condition. Fifteen minutes later both rudder indices went to left (lower rudder leading upper). Autopilot again disconnected.

None of the incidents above resulted in loss of control. But none of them occurred under the same flight conditions as TWA 841, which was at cruise at 39,000 feet, mach .80, with an outboard right aileron suspected of up-floating, restricting the amount of lateral control available for recovery.

A look through the accident record of the Boeing 727 reveals that there have not been any unexplained accidents that might have been attributed to a malfunctioning rudder/yaw damper system. But the evidence clearly shows that the 727 was and is susceptible to discrepant rudder input.

So, what really happened on that fateful night April 4, 1979? Without the ability to do functional testing on the original yaw dampening system of N840TW, there is no way to conclusively state the exact chain of events that led to the rollover and dive. It is possible, however, by a thorough analysis of the available evidence in the form of the damaged aircraft report, the debris field, the FDR data, and passenger and crew testimony, to come up with a scenario that fits all of the evidence.

The scenario begins with an old airplane that had exhibited signs of fatigue, from the misaligned number seven slat and broken T-bolt to the fractured bolt that was supposed to lock out the right outboard aileron. The aircraft had been flying at altitude in very cold temperatures for more than an hour. A short time before the upset a bolt that was supposed to lock out the right outboard aileron fractured and allowed the aileron to free-float up. The aileron likely fluttered in the airstream. This created the slight buzz described by Hoot and several passengers.

As the right aileron floated up, the plane began to bank to the right. The autopilot, which was on heading hold, attempted to maintain heading by turning the control wheel to the left. Once the control wheel reached more than 10 degrees of left bank the spoiler panels on the left wing raised to aid in roll control.[16] This caused the slight buffet described by crew and some passengers.[17]

The yaw dampening system for the lower rudder, and possibly the upper rudder, sensed the plane yawing and made several corrective rudder inputs. The combination of the aircraft's tendency to bank to the right due to the right outboard aileron, and the autopilot's inputs to turn to the left in order to maintain heading, led to a cross-controlled condition. The yaw damper rate gyro and/or coupler sensed a worsening condition, which resulted in a rudder hardover of the lower rudder.

As the plane yawed nose right, airflow to the right engine was interrupted, which resulted in a compressor stall. Ram air was introduced into the static ports on the left side of the aircraft, which resulted in an indicated speed decay. The decrease in speed was misinterpreted by investigators as an indication of drag. As the yawing increased, the left wing was brought forward, creating more lift on the left wing and less lift on the right wing. This resulted in a roll to the right. Lateral control needed to counter the roll was reduced due to the free-play in the right outboard aileron.

When the plane rolled over, and while it was inverted, Hoot applied back pressure on the control wheel in order to maintain positive G's in an effort to keep people in their seats. This would have had the undesired effect of pulling the nose down into the dive. It's possible that the nose would have fallen through the horizon regardless of any action on Hoot's part. Hoot testified that he felt the nose dropping and that's why he pulled back. Also, the rate of the roll would have lessened the impact of elevator inputs. During the simulator tests, one pilot pushed on the control wheel while inverted rather than pull and was able to recover with an altitude loss of about 6,000 feet. But the simulator tests were programmed for an extended slat condition and not a rudder hardover.

The plane next entered an uncontrollable spiraling dive, making a complete rotation every three to four seconds. At around fifteen thousand feet, Scott Kennedy lowered the landing gear. The gear overextended on the right side due to a combination of the high speeds and a right sideslip condition. The over-extension of the right landing gear ruptured a system A hydraulics cooling line. The loss of system A hydraulics caused the number seven slat to extend due to a combination of the loss of hydraulic pressure and a failed locking mechanism. The number seven slat was immediately ripped from the plane. This caused the loud boom that the crew described as sounding like an explosion.

Other pilots who have experienced a slat separation have described the sound in a similar fashion. The slat was torn in half. Both halves of the slat were found in close proximity to other parts ripped from the plane when the gear was extended, indicating that the failures likely occurred at the same time. The loss of system A hydraulics, which also powered the lower rudder, resulted in the lower rudder centering, thus stopping the rotation of the aircraft. This occurred at around 5,000 feet. At that point Hoot had control of the aircraft, and he started to pull back on the yoke, eventually bottoming out of the dive less than a hundred feet from the ground.

———•◦•———

A review of this incident would not be complete without also addressing a number of other unanswered questions and controversial subjects. We'll look at each of these controversies, starting with the question of whether or not Gary Banks left and returned to the cockpit moments before the upset.

The idea that the upset occurred within close proximity to the flight engineer leaving and then returning to the cockpit came about as a result of Holly Wicker's written statement taken the night of the accident. She repeated the claim several times in depositions and in her testimony at her civil trial. At her civil trial she added that she was certain that it was Gary Banks because she had met all four flight attendants prior to the incident. Holly's coworker Sheryl Fisher, who was sitting in the aisle seat opposite Holly Wicker, testified at trial that she, too, saw Gary Banks hand the meal trays to the flight attendant just prior to the event. No one, and that includes Holly and Sheryl Fisher, saw Gary return to the cockpit. It's also important to note that neither Holly nor Sheryl Fisher testified to actually seeing Gary Banks leave the cockpit, only that he "came" from the cockpit.

The theory that Gary's movements just prior to the upset were somehow connected was bolstered by Hoot's statement to FAA inspector Ronald Montgomery the night of the accident. Hoot had erroneously said that Gary had taken his seat prior to the upset after returning the meal trays. Hoot claims that his statement to Montgomery was in error. The action of Gary taking his seat had occurred prior to the beginning of the climb from 35,000 feet to 39,000 feet. That timing coincides with the testimony of flight attendant Mark Moscicki, who said that he took the meal trays from Gary Banks midway in the first class section at least thirty minutes before the disruption began. So who are we to believe? Two passengers sitting in coach and preoccupied with an infant and three small children? Or four professional flight attendants?

None of the first class passengers saw Gary Banks leave the cockpit. But none of the first class passengers saw the meal tray exchange either. It's known from the testimony that all four flight attendants were in the first class section just prior to the upset. Flight attendant Carol Reams had taken seat 2F to eat her crew meal. Flight attendants Mark Moscicki and Carlos Machado-Olverdo were sitting in the aft-facing jump seats next to the cockpit door with their crew meals resting on their laps. And flight attendant Francine Schaulleur was in the galley warming a bottle of milk.

Mark Moscicki testified that he took the meal trays from Gary. None of the other three flight attendants witnessed the meal tray exchange. It could be argued that Mark Moscicki simply was confused about whether or not Gary handed him the trays. Maybe he was remembering a previous flight or leg. The problem with that assumption is that TWA 841 was Mark's first flight back after his vacation. He had not flown with any of the three cockpit crew members before. It's highly unlikely that he would get this particular flight confused with another in light of those important facts. It's improbable that Gary could have exited the cockpit, handed the meal trays to Mark, returned to the cockpit, and then Mark, Carol, and Carlos all had time to get their meals and take their places in the minute that Holly Wicker claims transpired between when she saw Gary Banks and the upset. Additionally, Holly claims that she saw the flight engineer hand the meal trays to a female flight attendant. Carol Reams and Francine Schaulleur both testified that they did not witness the meal tray exchange.

So what does the evidence suggest happened? The most likely chain of events goes like this: Gary Banks and Hoot both finished their crew meals while at cruise at flight level 350. Scott Kennedy did not eat his crew meal. Gary placed it on the floor in the cockpit. Just prior to making the climb to 390, Gary opened the cockpit door to hand his and Hoot's meal tray to one of the flight attendants. He saw lead flight attendant Mark Moscicki working in the galley, so Gary stepped out and handed the meal tray to Mark, with Mark meeting him halfway in first class for the exchange. None of the first class passengers witnessed this exchange. Mark testified that after taking the meal trays from Gary, he had time to pick up the meal trays in first class and prepare meals for his crew.

Flight Attendant Francine Schaulleur testified that at one point during the flight she had entered the cockpit to eat her apple pie. Since Francine wasn't eating her meal with the other three flight attendants, she most likely did not eat her meal. Instead, she grabbed the apple pie from the tray and took it with her to the cockpit. None of the three cockpit crew members remembered Francine in the cockpit. Francine said that the flight crew looked busy, so she ate her apple pie and left without saying anything, which would have been the case while Hoot was hand flying up to flight level 390.

As the plane leveled off at 390, Mark made another pass through first class and picked up additional meal trays, which he then handed to Francine who was in the galley. That is most likely what Holly Wicker saw. Holly also testified that the two crew members she saw had chatted for a while after the meal tray exchange. Mark testified that the meal tray exchange was brief and that there was no conversation between him and Gary Banks. Francine took the first class meal trays from Mark. The two chatted, perhaps in reference to getting the flight attendant crew meals ready. That sequence of events most closely fits the evidence and testimony. So the answer to this important question is that yes, Gary Banks did leave the cockpit, but he did so at least thirty minutes prior to the upset, and there is no correlation between his movements and what took place.

Another important fact supporting the scenario above is Gary Banks' seated position at the initiation of the event. In the NTSB scenario, Gary would have been standing as he pushed in the circuit breaker. Hoot testified that Gary had passed out during the high-G portion of the dive and had fallen face-forward onto the center console. Both Hoot and Gary testified that after leveling off, and just prior to the incident, Gary was making minor power adjustments. The flight engineer seat can swivel from the FE panel position to a forward-facing position. To get the seat facing forward toward the instrument panel, the flight engineer has to first sit down in the seat and face the FE panel and then slide the seat to his left. It would have been extremely difficult for Gary to take his seat and slide it forward while the plane was rolling and diving.

There are many cases on record where criminal investigations have resulted in wrongful convictions due to inaccurate eyewitness testimony. In this instance, Holly Wicker's written statement, and to a lesser extent Hoot's inaccurate statement to FAA inspector Ronald Montgomery the night of the upset, resulted in an investigation that was focused on crew involvement to the exclusion of all other possibilities.

⎯⎯•◦•⎯⎯

The next mystery involves the yaw damper fail flag for the lower rudder noticed by the crew after the recovery. There's no way to know whether the fail flag occurred prior to, or occurred as a result of the accident. The aircraft manual states that the fail flag indicates a loss of electrical power to the yaw damper system or that the engage switch is turned off. Loss of system A hydraulics is unrelated to the fail flag. Material provided by ALPA in their findings and recommendations to the NTSB indicated that the fail flag could also indicate a yaw damper rate gyro malfunction. At the very least the fail flag indicated a problem or malfunction with the lower rudder yaw dampening system and warranted more attention from the investigators.

⎯⎯•◦•⎯⎯

In the same category as the yaw damper fail flag was the discovery of the up-float in the right outboard aileron. The NTSB investigators first claimed the bolt that locked out the aileron most likely fractured as a result of the high-G dive. Later, when the logic of the delay scenario was called into question, they changed their minds and said that the free float in the outboard aileron would have reduced lateral control. Instead of losing control after a delay of 16.5 seconds, the pilots would have lost control after a delay of only 12.5 seconds, according to the NTSB's revised theory.

The topic of the up-float in the outboard aileron came up in the first Sunshine meeting on January 17, 1980. Board Member Patricia Goldman asked about it when referring to the ALPA report on the accident. "And did you take care, in talking about various possible mechanical functions and disfunctioning of the plane, that the ALPA submission with regard to the aileron misfunction or—I'm not sure if that was covered."

"The report submitted by the aircraft manufacturer did, in depth, treat the effects of the aileron problem free-float," replied William Laynor, the chief of the Vehicle Factors Division. "The simulation also included some examination of the effect of aileron float on the controllability of the aircraft."

"And we have included that?"

"Did not," Kampschror replied. "No. Not at the time."

"How have we resolved the contention made by the Airline Pilots Association about the aileron?"

"Well," Kampschror began, "the question arises even assuming that the aileron did float because of the result of a—"

"We don't—you're saying we have no evidence that it necessarily was floating?"

"That is correct," Kampshror said. "There was a broken bolt in the aileron actuator attachment. But we don't know when the bolt broke, in the first place. We feel that it is quite likely that it broke as a result of the heavy—very heavy loads imposed on the aircraft during its descent. However, assuming that the bolt broke while the aircraft was at 39,000 feet in a cruise condition, it would have allowed the aileron, the right outboard aileron, to float upward about one inch. And the question becomes, what are the aerodynamic effects of the upward float of the aileron? And how might those aerodynamic effects impinge on the loading of the number seven leading edge slat, which is on the fore part of the wing, where the aileron is on the trailing edge of the wing?

"We looked at this. The upward float of the aileron we feel – or, we believe, would have had virtually no effect on the leading edge of the wing. There would be some slight reduction in the angle of attack, localized reduction, but this would not alter the pressure pattern sufficiently to unload the slat, so to speak, to aerodynamically unload the slat.

"So, even if the bolt was broken before the problem began, it should have no effect on the leading edge slat. It would have some effect in the cockpit by causing a slight roll. It would require 13 degrees deflection of the wheel to the left to counteract that rolling action. But that would be the sole effect."[18]

The above explanation by lead investigator Leslie Kampschror demonstrates the tunnel vision investigators had with the number seven slat. He in effect describes the exact condition of the plane before the rollover, but no one on the Board, and not one investigator considered the up-floating aileron as a possible initiator of the upset.

————◦•◦————

Why did the airplane demonstrate a tendency to roll left after the recovery, a condition that began when the crew selected flaps using the alternate flap checklist and remained from that point on until touchdown in Detroit? The initial roll had been to the right. When Scott and Gary performed the alternate flap checklist to lower the flaps, the plane rolled left when the flap selector was placed in the five-degree detente. Hoot immediately told Scott to put the flaps back up. Scott did as requested, but the slats could not be retracted because they had been extended using the alternate flap procedure. The number seven slat had departed the aircraft and left a gaping hole in the right leading edge of the wing. The loss of the slat and the additional drag created by its absence should have caused the aircraft to want to roll to the right.

During the pull-up from the dive, Hoot described the aircraft as swaying left to right. It's quite possible that the upper rudder was also receiving discrepant rudder inputs from the upper yaw damper system. In other cases of a yaw damper system malfunction on the Boeing 727, the rudders have indicated differing displacements. In some cases one rudder led the other. In other cases the upper and lower rudder displaced in opposite directions, creating a split rudder condition. There have also been reports of one or both rudders displacing in one direction and then moments later displacing in the opposite direction. Hoot described the aircraft yawing to the left as he struggled for control. One possible explanation for the left-rolling tendency is that the upper rudder yaw dampening system, which is powered by system B hydraulics, was also receiving discrepant rudder inputs.

———•◦•———

How low was the aircraft before recovery was made? The official report is that the plane recovered around 4,900 feet. Hoot, however, claims that the recovery was much closer to the ground. Hoot says that when he walked around the aircraft after the landing in Detroit he noticed a tree branch stuck in the right landing gear, which he removed. He also states that he saw mud in the right gear well. Could this mean the aircraft actually touched the ground? Hoot brought up this possibility to Jim McIntyre and Harold Marthinsen, both of whom believed the probability of that happening to be so remote they told Hoot to keep that thought to himself. There is, however, another possible explanation for the mud Hoot said he saw in the right gear well and on the underside of the plane—ground effect. Hoot has a clear memory of entering a ground fog and passing by a building and lot filled with cranes and heavy road working equipment. It's quite possible that as Hoot was pulling up from the dive he flew close enough to the ground for the ground effect from the speeding plane to force mud, branches, and water skyward.

What do the radar and FDR data indicate? The radar report shows a bottom altitude of 4,750 feet. But the radar used to provide that report had a line-of-sight limit in that part of Michigan that didn't allow the radar to provide reliable data below 5,000 feet. As for the FDR altitude trace, the trace had missing data points but still showed the plane descending rapidly until disappearing off the chart, which ended at 4,000 feet.

In the civil trial Hoot talked about his perception of the altitude during the recovery. He doesn't mention the tree branch or the mud, but he does indicate that the plane was much lower than what the official record shows.

"All right," Don Mark began. "What was the altitude loss from 390, 39,000 feet?"

"Well, I am not really sure because the flight recorder was 600 feet off, which is within tolerance, the altimeter in the flight recorder," Hoot replied. "But it—I think it went from 39,000 feet down to about 4,800 feet above sea level."

"Now, when you regained control of the aircraft at 4,800 feet, tell us then what happened to the attitude of the aircraft from that altitude."

"Well, I am not sure I really had regained control of the aircraft yet, but as it went through 4,800 feet it continued—all this time it had been spinning—I'd seen the lights that were—the lights that were far away when we started this maneuver, as the airplane spun down toward the ground and then we stopped it from spinning, and it was doing the oscillating part like this, we ended upright in one of the lights in one of the cities, and I thought we were much closer to the ground than we were. I thought that we were going to hit the ground. But I was so intent on [not] hitting the ground I could have pulled back harder, I could have given it more back pressure, but I didn't think the airplane could take it structurally.

"And so I was so intent on not hitting the ground and pulling back just as much as I could possibly—that I thought, you know, that I thought the airplane would take, that I hadn't thought past hitting the ground.

And it didn't hit the ground. It pitched up, and it came out somewhere between 30 to 50 degrees nose up out of the clouds."[19]

There was ground fog present in Michigan that evening. Ground fog typically extends from the ground to not much beyond three or four hundred feet above the ground.

———•◦•———

Did Hoot erase the CVR? The issue surrounding the alleged CVR erasure is one part of this story that isn't so easily dismissed. The action of a captain deliberately erasing a CVR after a serious incident such as this would be hard to ignore if it were true. Some would argue that whether or not it was his habit to erase the CVR after every flight, Hoot should have realized the significance of that action in this instance and been able to break that habit.

Some speculation arose indicating that perhaps some unflattering comment or scream was made by one or more crew members in the moments just before the recovery and the CVR was intentionally erased to save the crew from that potential embarrassment. Hoot, however, stated on more than one occasion that the CVR never crossed his mind. Additionally, it would be difficult to believe that not one of the three crew members would confess to this action after the controversy surrounding the CVR came to light.

A close review of the available evidence is enough to show that Hoot most likely did not press the erase button. Pressing the erase button was part of a flow Hoot followed at the completion of every flight. That flow was interrupted when Hoot noticed several switches weren't in their normal position. There were also too many other distractions going on at that time for Hoot to follow a typical shutdown routine.

While most media outlets reported that the tape was completely blank, the nine minutes of audio that were on the tape do not support a deliberate attempt by the crew to cover something up.

Lastly, there is a real possibility that even had Hoot, through force of habit, managed to overcome the interruption to his flow and the numerous distractions, and pushed the erase button, it probably wouldn't have worked. In order to erase the CVR, two conditions must be met: The aircraft has to be on the ground, and the brakes have to be parked. Late in the investigation someone came to the realization that perhaps those two conditions had not been met. The CVR had been removed the night of the accident. The electrical wiring that sent signals to the CVR that the plane was on the ground and that the brakes were parked was severely damaged. The electrical wiring was repaired within days of the incident. The Investigator-in-Charge, Leslie Kampschror, contacted TWA to ask them if there had been any problems with the electrical connections to the CVR. Someone from TWA replied that there were no problems found. Here is how the official report reads: "Tests of the CVR in the aircraft revealed no discrepancies in the CVR's electrical and recording systems."

That is a false statement. For one, there had not been any tests done on the CVR before or after it was removed. Here is what mechanic Mel Brown, who removed the CVR within hours of the incident, had to say about the CVR electrical system when questioned eighteen months after the incident:[20]

A. One other thing I was thinking about, you know all the wiring around the gear switches were ripped right out. I don't know if this had any effect on that voice recorder.

Q. Was the right gear safety switch completely gone?

A. The right and left gear switches, yes. All the warning switches. I'm sure you could find that through the inspection department in Kansas City. They had a detailed write-up on all this.

Q. So, in other words, the wiring to the boxes was actually loose.

A. Yes, some of it was just ripped right off and the boxes pulled away and the linkage was just hanging there . . .

The fact that the two main gear indicators were red, indicating that the gear was not down and locked, led some to speculate that the squat switch that would have indicated that the plane was on the ground might also have precluded the CVR erase button from working. This theory was discounted, however, because of evidence that the crew had started the APU. The APU can be started only with the aircraft on the ground. So the squat switch had to have been working properly.[21]

So what else could have caused the CVR erasure? The actual CVR has long since been lost, and no functional testing is possible. The CVR could have been experiencing issues long before this incident, with the problem never detected. Checking the functionality of the CVR is not part of regular maintenance. Leigh Johnson, who authored the ALPA petition for reconsideration, speculated that the CVR may have experienced a fault during the power change-over that caused the CVR to activate the bulk erase field instead of the power change-over tone.[22] This possibility was described to Leigh by Fairchild's own CVR expert. This theory, however, has its own problems. Mechanic Mel Brown stated that when he first got to the airplane, the APU was running and the engines were shut off, indicating that the power switchover had already taken place. Mel next states that after trying to place gear pins into the main gear, he plugged into the intercom to advise the captain of the leaking fuel and the need to evacuate the passengers. That conversation is not on the tape. What is on the tape is Mel Brown contacting the captain to ask if he had notified operations to arrange transportation to the terminal for the passengers. So the CVR erasure had to have occurred sometime between Mel's first contact with the crew and his second contact.

———•◦•———

Lastly, while there will always be those unwilling to accept any theory contrary to what they have long believed, the evidence does raise serious concerns about the findings in the original investigation. Even though the crew was charged with endangering the lives of passengers, they were never charged criminally. They were not charged for perjury for lying under oath. There were no certificate actions taken against any of the crew members. TWA did not take any actions against Hoot and promoted him on schedule. All three cockpit crew members received awards from the TWA Master Executive Council (MEC) of ALPA for their handling of the TWA 841 emergency. Additionally, at no time over the ensuing decades did any one of the three crew members come forward to say that they had done anything in the cockpit that could have led to the rollover and dive.

Does it matter that the NTSB might have gotten this one wrong? The answer is yes, it matters. Just as there are lessons to be learned from accidents where mistakes are made, the same is true in an investigation where investigator biases and preconceived beliefs taint their work. Investigators working on future accidents must let the evidence guide the investigation and not the other way around. There were numerous instances in the TWA 841 investigation where investigators tried to fit or manipulate evidence to better fit their theory of the upset. When the logic of Hoot waiting 17 seconds was questioned, Boeing and the NTSB revised their estimate to 12.5 seconds. When investigators could not explain the rapid heading changes at the beginning of the upset without a corresponding increase in g-loads, they explained away the discrepancy as its being the result of a tumbled gyro. When the comparison of the acceleration traces from the October 1980 test flight did not match the acceleration traces of TWA 841, investigators claimed that the differences were attributed to a different autopilot and a test switch left in the wrong position.

Had the NTSB investigators not let the supposed CVR erasure implant a bias on the investigation, they might have considered possibilities other than crew involvement. They might have talked to the crew in greater detail and would have learned that the plane had yawed prior to the upset.

Epilogue

A*fter leaving TWA, Hoot grew restless in Costa Rica.* He was still five years away from mandatory retirement. Hoot learned about opportunities flying overseas as a captain for foreign carriers who were in desperate need of experienced pilots like Hoot. The foreign carriers were offering lucrative contracts to expat pilots. Hoot took a job flying an L-1011 for Iran Air. Hoot was single and making more money than he had ever made in his career, but the experience wasn't as glamorous as he envisioned. In an interview in November of 2012, Hoot talked about his time as an expatriate pilot. "When I retired, I found work around the world, the first being for the Shah of Iran; actually, Iran Air. I spent time in Korea as a Marine, but I was not close to being prepared to even walk the streets in that country and left very quickly and quietly. I then went to Sri Lanka and hired on with Air Lanka. They were having a civil war and walking or driving home from the airport I would see at least fifteen bodies. I moved to Bombay and then to Goa, Singapore, and finally back to the USA."

Hoot continued flying well into his sixties. He stopped when he could no longer pass his FAA physical. When Hoot retired as a pilot after thirty-plus years, he had accumulated more than 30,000 hours of accident- and violation-free flight time. That is quite a feat considering that Hoot was also a stunt pilot, balloon pilot, helicopter pilot, crop duster, and flew a wide range of aircraft from the Ford Tri-Motor to the Boeing 747. Additionally, Hoot was a flight instructor, gave check rides, and taught air safety.

Despite his best efforts to put the debacle of TWA 841 behind him, he could never escape it completely. He couldn't go for more than a few months before the subject was brought up in one way or another. He would get calls from former TWA pilots wanting to know how he was doing. Jim McIntyre and Harold Marthinsen would each call at least once a year to reminisce. He received Christmas cards for many years from the Rakowskys, the passengers who came to his defense on more than one occasion. Hoot was always gracious and genuinely glad to hear from the many people who stayed in touch.

The story surrounding TWA 841 had grabbed the attention of the media from the start. A commercial airliner comes within seconds of killing everyone on board. What happened? Was the crew involved? It was a story filled with drama, intrigue, and mystery.

The petitions for reconsideration by ALPA in October of 1990 and Hoot's in May of 1991 reignited interest in the story. Several local and national publications ran stories with the theme that the NTSB may have wrongfully accused the crew for causing the upset. "11 years after plane took a dive, pilot tries to clear his reputation," was the title of an article by Buzz Bissinger. "Conclusions by NTSB were 'made for TV,' but were they hasty?" was the title of an article by writer John Galipault. The *Wall Street Journal* ran an article titled, "Fighting Blame for Near Crash of a Boeing 727, Pilot Raises Questions about Safety of the Plane." Television news shows *Inside Edition* and *Hard Copy* ran segments about the possible new findings. ABC *Prime Time Live* aired a segment about TWA 841 with host Chris Whipple.

Then there were the book and film offers. Hoot's personal attorney Landon Dowdey proposed writing a book about Hoot's story using three different writers: Landon, a freelance writer Landon hired to write legal briefs, and an aviation expert they had used in their research for the libel suit. Other prospective authors came forward, but nothing went beyond the initial talks.

In January of 1991, after news broke about his petition for reconsideration, Hoot received an offer from a film studio in Los Angeles. A producer wanted to tell Hoot's story with a book and film. The offer seemed almost too good to be true, especially for someone who had been retired for two years and was already regretting that decision. Highlights of the offer included $15,000 as a script consultant on a TV deal, $25,000 as a script consultant on a movie deal, $50,000 for rights to his story upon receipt of a firm offer from a movie studio, another $40,000 and screen credit as "technical adviser" if a film were to be made. There were additional bonuses for appearances on *60 Minutes*, another $25,000 bonus if a book was published in conjunction with a movie deal, and Hoot was also to receive a percentage of the profits for all projects based on his story.

The book and film deals fell through. Hoot's hopes of having his story told and his reputation restored were dashed. One problem with Hoot's story was that it was a story without an ending. There were still open petitions for reconsideration.

Hoot's story of saving the plane moments before impact could just as easily have played out the same way a similar story had surrounding the ditching of USAir Flight 1549 on January 15, 2009. USAir pilot Chesley (Sully) Sullenberger became a national hero when he landed his powerless plane in the Hudson River after running into a flock of geese. Sully and First Officer Jeffrey Skiles were lauded for their efforts. Both appeared in numerous documentaries and TV specials. Sully would eventually land a $3 million book deal to write his story. The resulting book, co-written by writer Jeffrey Zaslow, was published less than a year later.[1]

In the summer of 2001, Hoot was approached with yet another film offer, this time by HBO. Buzz Bissinger, who by this time had found success with his best seller *Friday Night Lights* about a high school football team in West Texas, was set to write the script. Despite several meetings with HBO executives, the project never got off the ground.

The truth was that Hoot was never looking to cash in on his story. His only goal was to restore his reputation and for the cause of the upset to be properly investigated. Fearing that his memory might fail him, Hoot hung on to the thousands of pages of documents he had collected over the years. He kept the documents in plastic containers piled high in a storage shed. A large percentage of those documents, however, were destroyed by a landlord who needed room in the shed for other items. To Hoot it was like losing his life savings. He was certain that any chance of someone being able to reconstruct his story was lost forever.

Over the years Hoot's health suffered as a direct result of the constant adverse attention he received. In late 1999, Hoot's health had deteriorated to the point where one physician told him that he wouldn't live to see the parking lot. He had congestive heart failure. He was put on a waiting list for a heart transplant.

While he waited for a new heart, he stayed with Kathleen Dowdey, the daughter of his personal attorney Landon Dowdey. Kathleen worked in the film industry. She interviewed Hoot while he stayed in her home over the course of several weeks. She used the material from her interviews to write a screenplay based on Hoot's life. She was well aware of Hoot's battles with Boeing and the NTSB. She was about ready to start shopping the screenplay when Hoot told her to hold off.

He had promised his story to someone else and didn't want to go back on his word.

Hoot's problems with his heart had begun long before his dealings with the NTSB. In his late thirties, Hoot learned that he had several blocked arteries. He underwent a coronary angiogram procedure to unblock the clogged arteries. Then there was the time in 1973 when he almost died from electrical shock. He and a friend were doing some electrical rewiring in his house in Vegas. It was summertime and he was working in the attic above his garage, where the temperature climbed to 145 degrees. Prior to commencing work, Hoot made sure that the main circuit breakers for the house were turned off. He was straddling a gas pipe, which he felt would serve as a good ground. He had a screwdriver in one hand and an exposed electrical wire in the other. His friend meanwhile wanted to use a saw but had no power, so he switched the circuit breakers back on. Hoot was hit with 220 volts of electricity in the hand that was holding the exposed wire. He tried but couldn't let go of the wire. He nearly lost consciousness before his friend realized his mistake and tripped the circuit breakers. Hoot believes his heart actually stopped for a brief time during the electrical shock. He went to the hospital and underwent a series of tests. Hoot was a heavy smoker prior to the accident, a chain smoker, going through four or five packs a day. The medical scare convinced him to give up smoking. He quit cold turkey and never smoked again.

Hoot's health worsened while he was staying with Kathleen Dowdey. Besides a weakened heart, Hoot had a number of other health issues that doctors refused to treat because of his poor condition. So while he waited for a new heart he also had to deal with a bad back, a torn rotary cuff in his right shoulder, two hernias, and a sinus condition. Hoot complained that he was falling apart and no one was willing to put him back together.

Kathleen had Hoot admitted to the hospital when his condition worsened. It was not looking good. His son Kevin drove to California in hopes of seeing his dad one last time. Hoot was in his hospital room when he was told that someone from CBS was on the phone. The television news show *60 Minutes* was researching a story on the crash of TWA 800. They wanted a comment from Hoot. Reporter Lesley Stahl was on the other end.

"Is this Captain Gibson?" Lesley asked.

"Yes," Hoot answered.

"How do you feel about getting a new heart?"

"What are you talking about?" Hoot replied.

"We just learned that you're getting a new heart."

Before he could even finish the conversation with Lesley Stahl, a team of doctors raced into the room and tore open his hospital gown, marking his chest with a big yellow X. It was December 1, 1999. Hoot would start the new decade with a new heart provided by a female donor. He moved back in with Kathleen Dowdey during his recovery.

The health scare with his heart was just one of a long list of near-death experiences for Hoot. Before his brush with death from electrical shock, and long before TWA 841, Hoot was involved in an automobile accident that nearly killed him. Hoot drove race cars as a hobby. He had been racing cars since he was a teenager. On one particular day, while recently employed with TWA, he was driving a Shelby AC Cobra race car on a local racetrack. A friend of his, Bob Angeline, rode along for a few laps. Hoot got the Cobra up to 160 mph but told his friend he thought he could do better. What he needed was a longer straightaway. So he took the car off the track and onto a long stretch of highway that ran along the Pacific coast. He was doing about 140 mph when he lost a front wheel. The car careened through a fence and slammed into a couple of utility poles before coming to a stop. The car disintegrated around him. Even the engine left the vehicle. Hoot's injuries included two broken legs, a fractured right ankle, several broken ribs, a broken right arm, and over fifty facial fractures that required reconstruction surgery. It took a full year for him to recover. Hoot's friend miraculously escaped without any serious injuries.

Then there was the time in Costa Rica when he was working on the fuel tank of an amphibious airplane. He was wearing a gas mask, but the gas mask failed and he ended up inhaling noxious fumes that damaged his lungs.

As a pilot, Hoot had experienced numerous emergencies that could have ended badly if not for his skill and a little luck. This includes numerous engine failures, precautionary engine shutdowns, and other in-flight emergencies. TWA 841 certainly falls into this category. One aviation-related incident that could have ended badly involved an attempted hijacking.

Hoot was the first officer on a Boeing 747 scheduled to fly from Athens, Greece, to Tel Aviv, Israel. While inside the aircraft parked alongside the passenger terminal, Hoot heard what sounded like an explosion. The captain was out of the cockpit at the time, so Hoot moved to the captain's seat to see what was going on. What he saw was shattered glass and smoke. Militants had set off an explosion inside the terminal. Hoot was in communication with ground personnel on the intercom system. He told the ground crew to clear away from the aircraft because he intended to start all four engines.

By this time the captain had stormed back into the cockpit and jumped into the first officer's seat. "Let's get the hell out of here!" the captain yelled.

As soon as all four engines started, they contacted the tower for taxi clearance but were told that the airport was closed. Hoot could see militants heading for the plane. He glanced at the captain, who was signaling for him to go. So Hoot advanced the throttles and the huge 747 lumbered forward.

The terminal building was a long distance from the runway. When Hoot turned the 747 onto the runway, he saw a fuel truck racing to block his path. The fuel truck pulled out onto the departure end of the runway. Hoot wasn't sure he could clear it, so he turned off the runway and pulled onto the parallel taxiway.

If there had been any doubt as to whether or not they were possible targets, the fuel truck and a swarm of armed militants running toward the plane convinced them that they had to get out of there by any means possible. Hoot gunned the throttles and the plane sped down the taxiway, with gun-toting men in close pursuit. The plane lifted off before the fuel truck had a chance to turn around. They would later learn that more than thirty people had been killed or injured in the attack inside the terminal. They also learned that the plane and its passengers were the intended target.[2]

After receiving his new heart in 1999, Hoot was required to take organ-rejection medication. The prolonged use of that medication led to kidney failure. Hoot needed a new kidney. Once again he was placed on a waiting list. In the interim, while he was undergoing dialysis, the wife of a close friend was tested and found to be a compatible match. Once the match was confirmed, she didn't hesitate in offering to donate her kidney to Hoot. When it came time for the operation, an unexpected visitor showed up at the hospital—the daughter of the woman whose donated heart had kept Hoot alive. She had learned of the operation and wanted to be there. In her own way she had a vested interest in Hoot's outcome. The operation was a success and Hoot once again had a new lease on life.

In early 2013 Hoot learned that he had lung cancer. He was in the hospital for a circulation problem in his legs when the doctor informed him that they had found a large cancerous tumor in his lung, a condition that may have formed back when he was a heavy smoker. Hoot decided to try alternative medicine along with daily radiation therapy to fight the cancer. Hoot's positive outlook along with an aggressive treatment schedule sent the cancer into remission.

In the decades since TWA 841, Hoot's ability to recall the specific details of his experiences with the flawed TWA 841 investigation diminished. He claimed that his lack of recall was due to his attempts to "block out" negative memories, but his age and declining health were likely contributing factors.

Hoot's donated heart finally gave out in early 2015. He passed away in his sleep on January 31, 2015. The daughter of the woman whose donated heart kept Hoot going for another fourteen years, and who was present when Hoot received his kidney, attended his memorial service in Las Vegas. Though Hoot never remarried, he did find a companion who stayed by his side in his later years. Anyone who knew Hoot in the last fifteen years of his life also knows Lois Tribett.

Scott Kennedy and Gary Banks did not receive the amount of vitriol reserved for Hoot, but they both were affected by the events of April 4, 1979. Gary Banks had trouble sleeping for a full year after the dive. He had recurring nightmares of the dive and the plane rolling onto its back. The dreams were vivid and as time went on they evolved along with the circumstances of the investigation. One of his recurring nightmares involved Hoot's head turning around and his face turning into that of lead investigator Leslie Kampschror. When Gary was furloughed from TWA, he never returned to the flight deck. He became a professor of marketing and organizational behavior at a small business college outside of Pittsburgh. Gary worked as a teacher for the remainder of his career. His relationship with his wife Autumn suffered as a result of his inability to get and pay for psychiatric counseling. He eventually divorced and did not remarry. To this day Gary is reluctant to talk about TWA 841 for fear of dredging up unpleasant memories. He declined numerous requests to be interviewed for this book.

Scott Kennedy left the hustle and bustle of Los Angeles and moved to the wide-open spaces of Durango, Colorado. Scott was a fan of everything western. It was not unusual to see him riding one of his horses, decked out in a cowboy hat, boots, and western attire. Scott was the least affected by the events surrounding TWA 841. While he was angered over being falsely accused, he was mostly grateful to TWA for supporting him and the rest of the crew. He remained a devoted employee even when he ran into difficulty during his upgrade training. Upgrading to captain is a multistep process. After the initial training, there is a simulator check ride. That is followed by several flights under the supervision of a check airman in what is known as initial operating experience (IOE). It was during this portion of his training that he ran into difficulty. Scott's IOE training occurred within close proximity of his mother's passing. Pilots who flew with Scott say he was a safe and conscientious pilot. After failing to upgrade, TWA offered Scott an opportunity to fly as a flight engineer on the Boeing 747. While some would consider such an offer an insult, Scott put a positive spin on the news. He looked forward to flying international flights for the first time in his career. Scott ended his career a few months shy of mandatory retirement due to health concerns. Scott and his wife Sandra live in Arizona.

The Holly Wicker civil trial ended in June of 1983. The verdict in that trial determined liability and damages for Holly and Tim Wicker. There were, however, a number of other passengers who had also brought suit and were awaiting their turn to go to court to ask for damages. The liability issue had been resolved in the Wicker trial with TWA responsible for seventy percent of future damage claims and Boeing responsible for thirty percent.

To expedite the proceedings, individual suits were combined. In November of 1983, four passenger suits were tried simultaneously. Boeing elected to settle. The lawyers for the individual plaintiffs argued what they believed the damages should be and Boeing agreed to pay their thirty percent share. Boeing had nothing to gain by going to trial. They were more than happy to distance themselves from trials involving passengers who were injured on one of their planes.

TWA on the other hand had incentive to lessen the damages as much as possible. For one, they were responsible for a much larger chunk of the total damages. But there was also a belief by many that the investigators had got it wrong and that a defect with the plane was what had caused the upset.

Don Mark again represented TWA in the damages cases. The first trial ended after only five days with all of the plaintiffs agreeing to settle rather than risk having a jury side with TWA's valuation of what the damages, if any, should be.

In January of 1984, three more damage claims were combined and tried at the same time. The three cases were Barbara and William Merrill and their daughter Susan. Barbara and Susan Merrill were traveling together on TWA 841. Barbara Merrill was the passenger who had left her seat to freshen up her makeup just prior to the upset. She had injured her hip and elbow as she was forced to the floor of the lavatory during the high-G dive and recovery. Barbara and her husband settled just two days into the trial. Susan, however, who had no physical injuries but was claiming emotional distress and a fear of flying, decided to gamble and let a jury decide. It was a gamble that didn't pay off as the jury came back with a verdict in favor of TWA and no damages were awarded.

Many of the passengers who had brought suit did not have physical symptoms. They were claiming emotional distress, anxiety, and a fear of flying. They were hard cases to prove. The law required some physical manifestation that could be measured, treated, or otherwise documented. The intent of the law was to prevent baseless claims that were impossible to prove. Don Mark appealed a few of the damage claims where the plaintiffs did not seek medical or psychiatric care. The court ruled in favor of the plaintiffs who claimed that sweaty palms and elevated blood pressure were physical symptoms of their anxiety.[3]

Of all of the damage cases brought against TWA, the suit brought by passenger Alan Mahler was the only one with the potential to equal or surpass the damages awarded to Holly Wicker. Alan was an Obstetrician-Gynecologist. Alan claimed to suffer from vertigo and hand tremors that left him unable to work. Prior to his flight on TWA 841, he had accepted a high-paying position in California that he subsequently had to relinquish. He had more education than Holly and a much higher earning potential. But when he saw the effort Don Mark was willing to put forward to discredit some of his claims, he decided to settle.

As of this writing, Donald Chance Mark still practices as an attorney in Minneapolis, Minnesota. He is currently working on a book about his experiences as a trial lawyer. He plans to include his experience working on TWA 841 and the Holly and Timothy Wicker civil trial.

Charles Hvass took on the job of the plaintiff's attorney strictly on a contingency basis. He and his firm knew that they probably wouldn't recoup their costs in preparing for trial. After all, none of the cases being tried involved a death. So the potential for a large damage award was minimal. The thinking by Hvass and his firm was that the trial had the potential for the firm to gain recognition as a law firm with experience trying commercial airline accidents. There certainly was the potential to gain a high level of publicity for the firm both locally and nationally. The trial might open up the doors for much larger cases down the road. The strategy paid off just one year later when Hvass represented the sole survivor of a Galaxy Airline crash in Reno, Nevada. The Galaxy accident, however, would be Hvass's only other trial involving a commercial airline accident. Hvass and his firm continued to be involved in general aviation cases, but there hadn't been any major airline accidents in Minnesota in which their expertise would be required.

During the course of the preparatory work leading up to the trial, Charles Hvass and his wife adopted a baby girl from Korea. The knowledge that Hvass was going through the adoption process may have helped Holly Wicker decide to select him and his firm to represent her. And while Holly didn't assist Hvass with his adoption, she did offer some advice about the process. Once Holly was onboard she paved the way for Sheryl Fisher, who had worked with Holly, to hire Charles Hvass to represent her, as well.

At the time of the writing of this book, Charles Hvass is still practicing law. He continues to work on aviation-related cases, but time devoted to his legal work has made it impossible for him to maintain currency for his private pilot license. He hopes to resume flying in the near future.

———◆———

Leslie Dean Kampschror, who served as the Investigator-in-Charge on TWA 841, was promoted to higher administrative positions within the

NTSB. He did not serve again as an accident investigator. Kampschror also rose to the rank of Brigadier General in the D.C. Air National Guard. Kampschror's career with the NTSB, however, ended with a demotion. He appealed the decision and lost on the grounds that his performance did not demonstrate the excellence required to meet the goals of the SES (special executive service of civilian government).

Acknowledgements

This book is the culmination of three years of research, interviews, and a thorough review of thousands of pages of depositions, transcripts, and petitions for reconsideration. The individuals interviewed for this book are mentioned elsewhere, but I would like to single out Hoot Gibson and Scott Kennedy. Not only did Hoot give graciously of his time, but he also provided the vast majority of the source material that was used to reconstruct his story. Scott was interviewed late in the process but provided valuable details and insight which helped with the finished manuscript.

I would like to thank the following individuals: Cynthia Corsetti, Bob Pastore, Andrew Baffi, William Price, Dale Bebee, Neil Hoppe, Internet researcher Vicki Pate, proofreader Frank W. Kresen, and Leigh Johnson. My thanks also go to my editor Kathleen Marusak whose attention to detail helped shape the finished manuscript. Finally, I would like to thank my wife Lynn who was not only an early reader and a first-rate editor but a sounding board from the project's conception through to its completion.

About the Author

Emilio Corsetti III is a professional pilot and author. Emilio has written for both regional and national publications including the *Chicago Tribune, Multimedia Producer*, and *Professional Pilot magazine*. Emilio's first book, *35 Miles From Shore: The Ditching and Rescue of ALM Flight 980*, tells the true story of an airline ditching in the Caribbean Sea

Emilio Corsetti III

and the efforts to rescue those who survived. Emilio is a graduate of St. Louis University. He and his wife Lynn reside in Dallas, TX. To learn more, please visit the author's website at www.EmilioCorsetti.com.

Appendix

NTSB Response to Hoot's Petition for Reconsideration

As of this writing, the NTSB has yet to respond to the petition for reconsideration submitted by ALPA and authored by Leigh Johnson. The same is true for the petition submitted by TWA. The NTSB did, however, respond to Hoot's petition. In their response to Hoot's petition, the NTSB had this to say regarding the other two petitions:

> On October 9, 1990, ALPA submitted another Petition for Reconsideration of probable cause. This petition consists of 116 pages and claims that the Safety Board and all parties to the investigation erroneously assumed that the No. 7 leading-edge slat, which separated from the airplane in flight, was the initiating cause of the accident. ALPA stated that it now believes that the previous premise is erroneous. In a cover letter to its petition, ALPA stated that a malfunction in the rudder control system most likely contributed to the initial upset. The response to the ALPA petition is being handled separately in a manner independent of the subject petition from Captain Gibson.
>
> On December 2, 1991, Trans World Airlines, Inc. filed a petition to reopen the investigation, hold a public hearing, and reconsider the

probable cause in the subject accident. TWA's stated purpose of the petition was to "finally put to rest the questions raised in the petition of Captain Gibson . . ." The TWA petition is also being handled independent of the subject petition from Captain Gibson.

Leigh Johnson's petition was much more detailed and specific than Hoot's standalone petition. By excluding the TWA and ALPA petitions, the NTSB avoided the need to counter the numerous investigative errors and technical issues raised by Leigh Johnson. A review of the NTSB's response to Hoot's petition for reconsideration is revealing in its total disregard of a number of pertinent facts. A summary of some of the more important issues raised and how the NTSB responded follows: (The complete NTSB response to Hoot's petition is available at http://www.iprr.org/comps/pet727/PFR2.html)

CVR system checkouts—If there is one thing that any non-partial observer could single out as the point at which the TWA 841 investigation went awry, it was the discovery that 21 minutes of the 30-minute cockpit voice recorder tape were blank. That fact implanted a bias in the minds of the NTSB investigators that permeated every aspect of the investigation. The supposed CVR erasure was alluded to twice in the final report, and both made unsubstantiated claims. The first unsubstantiated claim appeared on page six of the final report: "Tests of the CVR in the aircraft revealed no discrepancies in the CVR's electrical and recording systems."[1] Hoot's petition argued that this was a false statement. The truth is that the CVR and FDR were removed from the aircraft the night of the incident and placed in the trunk of the station manager's car, where they remained until they were shipped first to TWA's maintenance base in Kansas City and then to the NTSB. There is no evidence that any testing of any kind at any time was conducted on the CVR before or after it was removed from the aircraft.

The second unsubstantiated claim concerns the alleged intentional erasure of the CVR by the captain. "We believe the captain's erasure of the CVR is a factor we cannot ignore and cannot sanction."[2] Here the report insinuates that the NTSB has evidence that conclusively shows that the captain erased the CVR. No such evidence exists. The evidence that does exist lends credence to the possibility that no one pushed the erase button intentionally or otherwise.

So how would the NTSB handle these important discrepancies? Here is the NTSB response to the issues surrounding the CVR.

> The Safety Board recognizes that the CVR on board the accident airplane, with its 30-minute recording duration, did not contain contemporaneous information about the accident scenario. The only audio evidence from the CVR that was available to the investigation was a brief crew conversation that was determined to have taken place after the airplane had landed in Detroit. As a result, the Safety Board concludes that the CVR information is largely irrelevant to the investigation and should not be a subject for reconsideration.[3]

Crew participation frustrated—During the course of the two-year investigation into TWA 841, NTSB investigators questioned the crew about the upset only two times. The first time was the day after the incident during the impromptu mini-hearing held in a hotel conference room in Detroit. The second time was at the televised depositional proceedings held in Los Angeles, California, eight days after the incident. When Hoot told his union advisers that he wanted to speak directly with the investigators, he was advised instead to provide an affidavit. No one from the NTSB took the time to follow up directly with the crew or made any attempt to clarify contradictory evidence. Requests for a public hearing were denied. Hoot volunteered to take a polygraph test. That request was ignored. When Board member McAdams requested that the crew be allowed to answer questions related to evidence brought against them, lead investigator Leslie Kampschror insisted that the crew not be given that opportunity. At the final Sunshine meeting held in June of 1981, the crew was told to not attend. When they ignored that unwarranted request, they were physically barred from entering the meeting room. The response by the NTSB to this issue shows complete ignorance of the facts.

During the investigation, crew members were formally deposed on two occasions. They were represented by their employer and their labor organization at all times. Investigative activity was undertaken in the traditional group manner, with the participation of representatives of the flight crew's employer and labor organization as parties to the investigation. In addition, 49 CFR 831.14 provides those concerned persons with an avenue through which to communicate directly with the Safety Board. The flight crew did not avail themselves of this opportunity during the progress of the investigation. However, it should also be noted that it is not the practice of the Safety Board to invite or permit the involved crew members to participate actively as a member of an investigative group during the investigation process. With regard to issue No. 8, the Safety Board believes that there was ample opportunity for the flight crew to have made its views known during the investigative process either directly or through their union or company representatives; however, they chose not to do so. As a result, the Safety Board concludes that the petitioner has not presented material on which to base a reconsideration.[4]

No 7 slat extension was the result of the dive rather than cause—Extended No. 7 slat could not have caused the upset—All references to the slat were combined into one response.

Petitioner states No. 7 slat extension was the result of dive rather than its cause. Petitioner refers to a portion of the Boeing Company's report that states ". . . with no pre-existing damage, that slat would have departed the aircraft when its speed reached 363 KIAS when the aircraft descended to approximately 31,500 feet."

As part of the research directed toward this reconsideration, the Boeing Company on January 11, 1993, provided the Safety Board with a revised Figure B.2.1(7), Estimated Time of Slat Separation, which corresponds with the discussion in the Boeing Report, paragraph B.2.2.1.2. That discussion states that slat separation and departure could occur between 360 and 400 knots equivalent airspeed.[5]

The NTSB response to this issue is telling on a number of fronts. First, the response indicates that the NTSB found this particular claim to be problematic. The revised rate of speed, however, is not backed up by any new evidence or test data. The new slat separation speed provided by Boeing also ignores direct evidence of several actual slat separation incidents where the slats separated at much slower speeds. The revised data also does not consider the existing misalignment of the number seven slat, which would have resulted in the slat departing even sooner.

Petitioner theorizes that the No. 7 slat did not fail until the end of the dive maneuver. Offered as evidence are the ground trail of debris and the ability of the flight crew to extend the landing gear with 'A' system hydraulic pressure.

Petitioner advances the theory that, "Had the No. 7 slat departed the aircraft early in the dive, at 31,500 feet as calculated by the Boeing Company, then 'A' system hydraulic pressure could not have been available to extend the landing gear."

Petitioner's theory appears to be based on the premise that a complete failure of hydraulic system "A" is coincident with the separation of the No. 7 slat. This is not the case. Due to the small diameter of the hydraulic lines in the leading edge slat system, the hydraulic system operating pressure of 3,000 pounds per square inch (psi) will remain available after the system has been breached until the reservoir is drained, a period of several minutes.

Investigators on scene in Detroit found the area aft of No. 7 slat bathed with hydraulic fluid. However, no such bathing or evidence of escape of a considerable quantity of hydraulic fluid was observed in the wheel well.

Petitioner's statement regarding the extension of the landing gear also indicates a general assumption that the "A" hydraulic system is necessary to "extend" the landing gear. While this statement is true regarding an overall systems description, the statement requires operational clarification. When the landing gear handle is moved to the down position while positive "G's" are applied to the airframe, the main landing gear will extend by themselves provided there is sufficient hydraulic pressure available to (1) open the internal gear door actuator locks and (2) open the landing gear uplocks. It should also be noted that opening the gear doors causes fluid to be displaced into the return lines, thereby temporarily "increasing" system quantity.

The Safety Board believes that the time interval between the loss of No. 7 slat (with concurrent hydraulic fluid escape) and the movement of the gear handle to the down position was short enough that sufficient system "A" hydraulic pressure remained to open the gear door actuator locks and the landing gear uplocks. Thereafter, positive "G's" provided sufficient force to extend (and to overextend and damage) the main landing gear. However, insufficient hydraulic fluid remained in the system to bathe the landing gear area from the hydraulic line when it ruptured.

With regard to issue No. 9, Safety Board review indicates that the analysis contained in Aircraft Accident Report AAR-81-8 was based on an appropriate speed range and appropriate reference to the degree of damage noted on the slat actuator and landing gear components as they relate to the hydraulic system "A" of the accident airplane. As a result, the Safety Board concludes that the petitioner has not presented material on which to base a reconsideration."[6]

Here the NTSB concedes that even if the slat somehow managed to stay attached until reaching a speed of between 360 and 400 knots-equivalent airspeed, the slat would have separated prior to the gear extending. The response then claims that there would have been enough residual hydraulic pressure to extend the gear. There are, however, a number of important facts missing from the response that are not so easily explained. First, had the slat departed the aircraft prior to the gear being extended, why didn't the crew recover earlier? Had the slat separated earlier in the dive, how is it that broken slat pieces were found in close proximity to other recovered parts? There is no explanation for the over-extension of the right landing gear. Additionally, no evidence or test data was provided to back up the NTSB's response concerning residual hydraulic pressure or how long it would take to lose hydraulic pressure from a separated slat.

Additionally, the NTSB response contradicts the Systems Group Chairman report, which stated the following: "It was noted that the 'A' system reservoir was depleted to two quarts of hydraulic fluid (Skydrol 500). The loss of fluid was attributed to the fractured actuator body and the crushing of the fluid cooling line at the right wheel area."[7] In other words, the hydraulics loss came as a result of the right gear "crushing the fluid cooling line," not from a separated slat.

Petitioner quotes the following, "The Boeing Company further stated that an extension of the No. 7 leading edge slat at .80 mach and 39,000 feet would have been easily controllable requiring only approximately half lateral control authority to counter the right rolling movement."

The Safety Board concurs with the above statement. However, the petitioner goes on to present a statement of conclusion, "Therefore, an extended No. 7 leading edge slat could not have caused the upset." However, the petitioner does not offer any basis in fact for this conclusion.

With regard to issue No. 10, the Safety Board analysis of the accident indicated that the asymmetrical slat condition resulting from the extended No. 7 slat was part of a series of events that led to the flight crew's loss of aircraft control. The Safety Board's probable cause statement recognizes a series of events, including slat asymmetry and, in addition, 'the captain's untimely flight control inputs to counter the roll resulting from the slat asymmetry.' Thus, in these circumstances, the Safety Board concludes that the petitioner has not presented material on which to base a reconsideration.[8]

This response also ignores a number of important facts: 118 simulator tests were conducted and not one pilot lost control except for two cases where pilot input was contrary to crew testimony and later ruled as improbable.

"Buzz" as a result of outboard aileron bolt failure with the possible yaw damper and rudder actuating system malfunctions.

Petitioner suggests that the 'buzz and turning' at the beginning of the accident flight upset was the result of outboard aileron bolt failure in flight and aileron "float" upwards. Petitioner further suggests that resultant yawing movement may have resulted in a malfunction of the yaw damper and rudder actuating system.

The Safety Board recognizes that a malfunction of either of these systems would produce recognizable yawing moments and roll response. However, the Petitioner has not provided any evidence that yawing moments associated with these systems were observed by the flight crew or the passengers. Also, such yawing moments were not identifiable on the FDR. However, flight tests conducted after the accident did produce FDR vertical acceleration traces as a result of flap movement that were consistent with the evidence from the accident airplane's FDR. Likewise, drag coefficients resulting in speed changes on the flight test airplane following flap configuration changes were consistent with the speed changes observed on the FDR indicated airspeed traces from the accident airplane. With regard to issue No. 13, the Petitioner has not provided any new evidence to substantiate the premise that a malfunction of the yaw damper or the rudder actuating system was present on the accident airplane. As a result, the Safety Board concludes that the Petitioner has not presented material on which to base a reconsideration.[9]

The NTSB response to this issue contains the most egregious statements expressed in the entire document. The author states that there was no evidence found on the FDR of a yawing aircraft. The author also claims that there was no evidence that any flight crew member or passenger observed a yawing aircraft.

The rapid heading changes at the beginning of the upset recorded on the FDR clearly show the aircraft yawing. While Hoot didn't use the word "yaw" during the two times he actually spoke to NTSB investigators, he mentioned it numerous times during the course of the investigation and subsequent to the investigation. He also made the following statement during his deposition on May 12, 1979: "Okay. Well, as it rolled over, when it became inverted, I had just a slight back pressure on it, and it did go off to the right. I'm not sure how many degrees, but it went maybe 10 degrees off to the right on this heading before it rolled."[10] Hoot's affidavit contains the following reference: ". . . Thereinafter something seemed to let go and the airplane yawed and rolled slowly to the right . . ."

The Human Factors report also contained references to a yawing aircraft. "Five passengers mentioned movement to the right as the initial indication, ranging from: "an ordinary change of course"; through—"veered to the right, like a sharp turn"; to—"pitching-off/shorting-off to the right."[11]

Holly Wicker's Written Statement

On the night of the incident, TWA 841 passenger Holly Wicker provided a written statement to TWA station manager Frank Cook. That statement was given to the NTSB, which promptly lost it. As the investigation proceeded, NTSB lead investigator Leslie Kampschror realized that he needed another statement from Holly to support his contention that the upset occurred within close proximity to the time of Gary Banks' leaving and then returning to the cockpit.

Holly repeated her claim of seeing Gary Banks hand meal trays over to a flight attendant, moments before the event, during her deposition for her civil trial. Kampschror read the deposition and then asked Holly if she would provide another written statement. This is the statement she provided.

> Before the incident, a member of the crew came back toward the galley with three trays. He came from the cockpit and he had insignias on his shoulder, which indicated he was one of the flight crew. I had met the stewards and stewardesses when I got on because I was transporting three children back from India for adoption. I was watching the galley because one of the stewardesses was heating up a bottle for one of the children I was with. It was within a minute or two, or maybe less, later that the incident began. The bottle that I had been given still did not have its cap on properly.[12]

Passenger List

(This is the most complete list from the available records. Numbers in parentheses represent the passengers' age at the time of the incident. Ages and seat position are shown if known.)

- Robert Reber seat 22F (pronounced Rayber)
- Dr. Peter Fehr seat 12D
- Holly Wicker (29) seat 14C
- Sheryl Fisher (34) seat 14D
- Atul Bhatt (27) seat 16F
- Barbara Merrill (41) and Susan Merrill (14)
- Alan Mahler and Donna Marie Boulet
- Joe Williams seat 4A
- Keith Kyle (42) seat 4C
- Dr. Dean Abrahamson (45)
- Chell Roberts (22) and Louise Roberts (21)
- Arthur Gaultier (70) and Geraldine Gaultier
- Frederick Rascher (64) and wife
- Roger Peterson (20's) seat 21A
- Comillo and Luisa Andretta
- Silvia Buhler
- Robert Rakowsky (41) and Jeannine Rakowsky (38) seats 3D and 3F
- Floyd and Patricia Carlson seats 1A and 1C
- Mary and Charles Butera
- Leonard Adler
- Shelly Backstrom
- Bob Carter
- Jaminie Dorner
- David Hoddeson

- Hobart Jarrett
- Mary Knudsen
- George Logan
- Patricia Morgan
- Bill Nelson
- Dr. Twila Papay
- Debra Price
- Gene Selenski
- Una, Mark, and Cherisse Valanski
- Asha (2 1/2 months)
- Jasmine (8)
- Teppy Smith (6)
- Debi (22 months)
- Douglas Page seat 22D
- Lou Dougherty
- Thomas H. Quill Jr. seat 15C

Illustrations and Photo Credits

Illustration 1 Seating diagram provided by author

Illustration 2 FDR Readout from actual TWA 841 trace recordings

Illustration 3 FDR Readout Close from actual TWA 841 trace recordings

Illustration 4 B727 Flight controls—illustration by Mike James, mike-jamesmedia.com

Illustration 5 B727 Flight controls deployed—illustration by Mike James, mikejamesmedia.com

Figure 1 Photo courtesy of Roger Peterson

Figure 2 Photo courtesy of John Proctor

Figure 3 AP Photo

Figure 4 Image courtesy of Roger Peterson

Figure 5 Image by Mike James, mikejamesmedia.com

Figure 6 Photo courtesy of Roger Peterson

Figure 7 Photo courtesy of *Air Line Pilot* Magazine

Figure 8 AP Photo

Figure 9 Image by Mike James, mikejamesmedia.com

Figure 10 Photo courtesy of *Air Line Pilot* Magazine

Figure 11 Photo courtesy of *Air Line Pilot* Magazine

Figure 12 AP Article

Figure 13 AP Article

Figure 14 Photo courtesy of Peter Fehr

Figure 15 Photo courtesy of Doug Page

Figure 16 Photo courtesy of Hoot Gibson

Figure 17 Photo courtesy of Hoot Gibson

Figure 18 Photo courtesy of Hoot Gibson

Figure 19 Photo courtesy of Hoot Gibson

Figure 20 Photo by author

Figure 21 Image by Mike James, mikejamesmedia.com

Figure 22 Image by Mike James, mikejamesmedia.com

Figure 23 Image by Mike James, mikejamesmedia.com

Figure 24 Image by Mike James, mikejamesmedia.com

Figure 25 Defendant's exhibit

Figure 26 Photo by author

Figure 27 Image by Mike James, mikejamesmedia.com

Figure 28 NTSB Publication

Figure 29 NTSB publication

Figure 30 Image courtesy of David Haase

Figure 31 Image by Mike James, mikejamesmedia.com

Figure 32 Image courtesy of Leigh Johnson

Figure 33 Photo courtesy of Jeannine Rakowski

Figure 34 Photo courtesy of *Air Line Pilot* Magazine

Figure 35 Photo courtesy of Scott Kennedy

Figure 36 Photo courtesy of Roger Peterson

Figure 37 Photo courtesy of Roger Peterson

Figure 38 Photo courtesy of Hoot Gibson

Figure 39 Image courtesy of Don Mark

Figure 40 Image courtesy of Don Mark

Figure 41 Image courtesy of Leigh Johnson

Figure 42 Image by Mike James, mikejamesmedia.com

Figure 43 Photo courtesy of Hoot Gibson

Figure 44 Photo courtesy of Hoot Gibson

Figure 45 Image by Mike James, mikejamesmedia.com

Author photo provided by author

SELECT SOURCES AND BIBLIOGRAPHY
(A complete list of sources is available on request)

Newspapers

"87 on Airliner Survive a Nose Dive In Michigan Near Speed of Sound." *Associated Press* April 6, 1979.

"Ex-Pilot Likens 1979 Spiral to '94 Fatal Crash." *Associated Press* January 15, 1995.

"Four Passengers Are Injured, Jetliner Damaged in Mishap." *The Kansas City Star* April 5, 1979.

"Jetliner's Crew Blamed for Dangerous Dive" *United Press International* June 10, 1981.

"Nosedive jet tape is erased." *United Press International* April 10, 1979.

"NTSB report blames six-mile dive on crew." *United Press International* June 9, 1981.

"Pilot Presses Safety Board to Reconsider 1979 Incident." *Associated Press* January 13, 1995.

"Pilot Saves Jetliner Diving Faster Than Speed of Sound." *Associated Press* April 1979.

"Pilot says Boeing, safety unit covering up crash." *Reuters, Limited* January 13, 1995.

"Pilots Wait, Wonder after Baffling Incident." *The Kansas City Star* May 20, 1979.

"Safety Board to Interview TWA 727 Pilots Under Oath Today." *Aviation Daily* April 12, 1979.

"Says TWA Tape Was Erased On Purpose." *Associated Press* April 11, 1979.

"TWA jetliner survives 'miraculous' ordeal." *Associated Press* April 1979.

"Want Help in Finding Pieces of Jetliner." *Associated Press* April 16, 1979.

Acohido, Byron. "Former Pilot Seeks to Reopen Case." *The Seattle Times* January 13, 1995.

Anderson, Dave. "Pilot testifies how TWA jet went out of control, into dive." *Minneapolis Star and Tribune* May 18, 1983.

Anderson, Dave. "Test pilot testifies crew performed well during 6 ½-mile dive." *Minneapolis Star Tribune* May 20, 1983.

Anderson, Dave. "Woman awarded $350,000 for injury received when jetliner fell six miles." *Minneapolis Star and Tribune* Jun 1983.

Andrews, Robert M. "Breaking of Jet's Slat May Have Averted Crash." *The Washington Post* July 5, 1979.

Berton, Justin. "Flight Diversions: Rumors won't fly with those who lost their loved ones in Colorado Springs crash." April 1, 1999.

Bissinger, H. G. "The plane that fell from the sky." *St. Paul Pioneer Press* May 24, 1981.

Cannon, Lou. "TWA's 727 Might Not Have Rolled before Dive, Cockpit Data Indicate." *The Washington Post* April 13, 1979.

Bissinger, H. G. "11 years after plane took a dive, pilot tries to clear his reputation." *St. Paul Pioneer Press* Oct 1990.

Bissinger, H. G. "Nose Dive." *The Chicago Tribune* June 2, 1991.

Cassano, Dennis. "Reasons for jetliner's 6.5-mile plunge argued." *Minneapolis Star Tribune* May 12, 1983.

Clarke, Norm. "Vegas pilot relives miracle flight." *Associated Press* April 7, 1979.

Crank, B. Arnold. "Flight Engineer Testifies as . . ." *The Kansas City Star* April 1979.

Feaver, B. Douglas. "Did 'coffin' corner catch 727, send it into near-fatal plunge?" *Washington Post* May 1979.

Feaver, Douglas B. "TWA Jet's Accidental Aerobatics under Exhaustive Study." *The Washington Post* May 13, 1979.

Gardner, Bill. "Area trial to decide liability." *St. Paul Pioneer Press* May 9, 1983.

Gardner, Bill. "Passengers relive trauma." *St. Paul Pioneer Press* May 9, 1983.

Karr, Albert R. "Tighter FAA Control over Maintenance of Planes is Likely to Follow DC10 Probe." *The Wall Street Journal* July 5, 1979.

Kilian, Michael. "Unwinding the (expletive) cockpit tape mystery." *The Chicago Tribune* (Note: date not known)

Lamberto, Nick. "'Hoot' Gibson of plunging jet fame is still in the saddle." *Des Moines Register* August 19, 1979.

Lindsey, Robert. "Pilot Says Extending Landing Gear Was Near Last Resort to Stop Dive." *The New York Times* April 13, 1979.

Love, Thomas. "Crew Gets Blame for Jet's Dive." *The Washington Star* June 10, 1981.

McGinley, Laurie. "Fighting Blame for Near Crash of a Boeing 727, Pilot Raises Questions About Safety of the Plane." *The Wall Street Journal* May 3, 1991.

Morrison, Jane Ann. "Pilot, crew file lawsuit over plane's nosedive." *Las Vegas Review Journal* April 4, 1981.

Morrison, Jane Ann. "Lawsuit by flight crew dismissed." *Las Vegas Review Journal* May 14, 1983.

Pipp, Edwin G. "'Reflex action?' may have erased tape—TWA pilot." *Detroit News* April 13, 1979.

Pipp, Edwin G. "Tape of jet's dive erased by crewman." *Detroit News* April 10, 1979.

Regan, Judith. "Passengers Tell of Terror on Jetliner That Plunged 6 Miles At the Speed of Sound." *National Enquirer* April 1979.

Serrano, Richard A. "FAA Arrives To Begin TWA Study." *The Kansas City Times* April 24, 1979.

Stoffer, Harry. "Former TWA pilot pushes for NTSB study." *Pittsburgh Post Gazette* January 14, 1995.

"TWA Pilot Denies He Erased Tape" (details other than title unknown. Most likely dated April 5-7, 1979)

Walek, Gordon. "Terror of plane's fall from the sky is retold on CBS." *The Daily Herald* Jul 14, 1983.

Watson, Susan. "'Hoot' Still High After Saving 727." April 7, 1979 .

Witkin, Richard. "Crew Will Testify Today on near-Fatal Jet Plunge." *New York Times* April 12, 1979.

Zack, Margaret. "Passengers tell of ordeal in plane that rolled over." *Minneapolis Star Tribune* April 6, 1979.

Books and Periodicals

"727 Damage Slight after Dive Incident." *Aviation Week & Space Technology* April 23, 1979.

"Safety Board Studies Transport Incident." *Aviation Week & Space Technology* Oct 5, 1981.

Adair, Bill. *The Mystery of Flight 427: Inside a Crash Investigation.* Washington, D.C.: The Smithsonian Institution Press, 2002.

C. V. Glines. "Flight 841: The Nightmare Continues Parts I & II." *Air Line Pilot* Nov 1981.

Cotia, Rick. "The Case of the Extended Slat." *Aviation* June 14, 1979.

Dornheim, A. Michael. "NTSB Probes Rudder Anomaly as Factor in United 585 Crash." *Aviation Week & Space Technology* August 10, 1992.

Faith, Nicholas. *Black Box: Inside the World's Worst Air Crashes.* Monday Books, September 13, 2012.

Garrison, Peter. "In Quest of Extra Performance." *Flying Magazine* March 1982.

Mansfield, Harold. *Billion Dollar Battle: The Story Behind the "Impossible" 727 Project.* David McKay Company, Inc., 1965.

Noland, David. *Safeguard.* Aviation Consumer Oct 15, 1979.

North, M. David. "Focus Narrowing in TWA 727 Incident." *Aviation Week & Space Technology* April 16, 1979

Steenblik W, Jan. "A New Look at TWA Flight 841." *Air Line Pilot* January 1991

Stewart, Stanley. *Emergency! Crisis on the flight deck.* The Crowood Press, September 20, 2002.

Miscellaneous Reports, letters, websites, and Official Documents

Aircraft Accident Report. "Trans World Airlines, Inc., Boeing 727-31, N840TW Near Saginaw, Michigan April 4, 1979." NTSB-AAR-81-8. July 13, 1981.

ALPA Petition for Reconsideration of Probable Cause. TWA Flight 841 on April 4, 1979. Oct 9, 1990.

ALPA Petition for Reconsideration. North Central Airlines Convair 580 July 25, 1978, Kalamazoo, Michigan.

Appellant-Petitioner's Brief. H.G. Gibson Petitioner vs. National Transportation Safety Board (NTSB) Respondent. United States Court of Appeals for the Ninth Circuit No. 95-70525. June 30, 1995.

Banks, Autumn. Letter to Hoot in response to correspondence from Hoot. February 21, 1982.

Bates, Walt. Letter to ALPA National with dissenting opinion over ALPA's support of the crew. Nov 23, 1981.

Bezek, Stanley. Letter to Landon Dowdey concerning Hoot's visit to his medical clinic in Utah. Nov 1, 1980.

Boeing technical report on TWA 841. September, 1979.

Cleaver, E. Leon. Personal Statement. Cleveland Air Route Traffic Control Center. May 4, 1979.

Deposition of Carlos Machado-Olverdo. "National Transportation Safety Board. An Accident Involving a Trans World Airlines, Inc. B727, Flint, Michigan, April 4, 1979." Accident number CHI-79-AA-040 Jan 29, 1980.

Deposition of David Noland April 21, 1983.

Deposition of Francine Schauller. "National Transportation Safety Board. An Accident Involving a Trans World Airlines, Inc. B727, Flint, Michigan, April 4, 1979." Accident number CHI-79-AA-040 Jan 29, 1980.

Deposition of Gary N. Banks. "National Transportation Safety Board. An Accident Involving a Trans World Airlines, Inc. B727, Flint, Michigan, April 4, 1979." Accident number CHI-79-AA-040 April 12, 1979.

Deposition of Gary N. Banks. "National Transportation Safety Board. An Accident Involving a Trans World Airlines, Inc. B727, Flint, Michigan, April 4, 1979." Accident number CHI-79-AA-040 January 29, 1980.

Deposition of Harold Francis Marthinsen March 30, 31, 1983.

Deposition of Harvey G. Gibson August 11, 1981, April 20, 21, 23, 1982.

Deposition of Harvey G. Gibson. "National Transportation Safety Board. An Accident Involving a Trans World Airlines, Inc. B727, Flint, Michigan, April 4, 1979." Accident number CHI-79-AA-040 April 12, 1979.

Deposition of Harvey G. Gibson. "National Transportation Safety Board. An Accident Involving a Trans World Airlines, Inc. B727, Flint, Michigan, April 4, 1979." Accident number CHI-79-AA-040 January 29, 1980.

Deposition of Holly Wicker June 27, 1980.

Deposition of James William Kerrigan January 10, 11, 1983.

Deposition of Jess Scott Kennedy November 18, 1981.

Deposition of Jess Scott Kennedy. "National Transportation Safety Board. An Accident Involving a Trans World Airlines, Inc. B727, Flint, Michigan, April 4, 1979." Accident number CHI-79-AA-040 April 12, 1979.

Deposition of Jess Scott Kennedy. "National Transportation Safety Board. An Accident Involving a Trans World Airlines, Inc. B727, Flint, Michigan, April 4, 1979." Accident number CHI-79-AA-040 January 29, 1980.

Deposition of Leslie D. Kampschror. "Timothy and Holly Wicker vs Trans World Airlines, Inc. and the Boeing Company." January 12, 13, 1982, April 26, 27, 28, 1982.

Deposition of Mark Moscicki. "National Transportation Safety Board. An Accident Involving a Trans World Airlines, Inc. B727, Flint, Michigan, April 4, 1979." Accident number CHI-79-AA-040 Jan 29, 1980.

Deposition of Robert Von Husen April 28, 1982, June 22, 23, 1982.

Deposition of Roger Gordon. "National Transportation Safety Board. An Accident Involving a Trans World Airlines, Inc. B727, Flint, Michigan, April 4, 1979." Accident number CHI-79-AA-040 Jan 29, 1980.

Deposition of Ronald Montgomery. "National Transportation Safety Board. An Accident Involving a Trans World Airlines, Inc. B727, Flint, Michigan, April 4, 1979." Accident number CHI-79-AA-040 Jan 29, 1980.

Deposition of Samuel Lewis Wallick Jan 12, 1983.

Deposition of Timothy Wicker June 27, 1980.

Dowdey, Kathleen recorded interview with Hoot November, December 1999.

Dowdey, Martin telephone conversation June, 2013.

Gibson, H. G. Affidavit November 19, 1979.

Gibson, H. G. Petition for Reconsideration TWA Flight 841 on April 4, 1979. May 2, 1991.

Gibson, H. G. Petition in the Nature of Mandamus. United States Court of Appeals for the District of Columbia Circuit. November 1, 1991.

Human Factors Specialist's Report of Investigation National Transportation Safety Board June 22, 1979.

Husen, Von Robert. Addendum to Performance Chairman's Report of Investigation. May 27, 1981.

Hvass, Charles Closing Arguments June 8, 1983.

Hvass, Charles Opening Statements May 10, 1983.

Leppard, D. Letter to Captain Tom Buttion Vice President Flight Operations Eastern Airlines concerning TWA 841 rumors being taught as fact in recurrent training. Sep 12, 1980.

Mark, Chance Donald Closing Arguments June 8, 1983.

Mark, Chance Donald Opening Statements May 10, 1983.

Marthinsen, Harold. Letter to Leroy A. Keith FAA. June 5, 1991.

Marthinson, Harold. Letter to Leroy A. Keith, Manager Transport Airplane Directorate Federal Aviation Administration concerning rudder hardover incident. Jun 5, 1991.

McAdams, Francis. Written statement to Chairman James King regarding the scope of the January 29 depositions. Jan 29, 1980.

McIntyre, Jim. Letter to NTSB Chairman James King regarding new documents related to the investigation. Jun 8, 1981.

McIntyre, Jim. Letter to NTSB Chairman James King regarding the TWA 841 investigation. March 30, 1981.

McIntyre, Jim. Affidavit regarding statements made by Leslie Kampschror. January 3, 1991.

Mel Brown interview September 9, 1980.

National Transportation Safety Board Sunshine Meeting in the Matter of Aircraft Incident Report. TWA Inc., B-727, near Saginaw, Michigan. April 4, 1979. January 17, 1980.

O'Donnel, J.J. Letter to NTSB Chairman James King regarding the Board's findings. Jul 30, 1981.

O'Donnel, J.J. Letter to NTSB Chairman James King regarding the negative effects of the unsubstantiated rumors regarding crew wrong-doing. April 2, 1981.

P. J. Neufeld and N Colman, "When Science Takes the Witness Stand," *Scientific American*, 262:5 (May 1990), 46-53.

Planecrashinfo.com

Quill v. Trans World Airlines, Inc. Court of Appeals of Minnesota Jan 29, 1985.

Radio Transcripts. Cleveland Air Route Traffic Control Center. April 10, 1979.

Ratchye, Boyd H. Opening Statements May 10, 1983.

Ratchye, Boyd H. Closing Arguments June 8, 1983.

Recommendations to the National Safety Board with regard to the Accident Involving TWA 841, Near Flint, Michigan, April 4, 1979. Air Line Pilots Association March 27, 1981.

Recommendations to the National Transportation Safety Board with regard to the Accident involving TWA Flight 841, Near Flint, Michigan. Airline Pilots Association. April 4, 1979.

Response to Petition for Reconsideration. National Transportation Safety Board. May 4, 1995.

Statistical Summary of Commercial Jet Airplane Accidents, 1959–2008, Boeing

Sunshine Meeting. National Transportation Safety Board. June 9, 1981.

Systems Group Chairman Report National Transportation Safety Board May 7, 1979.

Testimony of Andy Davis Yates, Jr. May 19, 1983.

Testimony of Carlos Machado-Olverdo May 18, 1983.

Testimony of Carol Reams May 18, 1983.

Testimony of Charles O. Miller May 24, 1983.

Testimony of Charles R. Higgins Jun 1, 1983.

Testimony of Clifford Phibbs May 16, 1983.

Testimony of Deldon Rich May 25, 1983.

Testimony of Dr. Charles I. Barron May 19, 1983.

Testimony of Earl Robinson Jun 2, 1983.

Testimony of Eugene L. Morgan May 25, 26, June 6, 1983.

Testimony of Floyd Carlson May 26, 1983.

Testimony of George Maurice Andre May, 23, 24, 1983.

Testimony of Harold Buchstein May 20, 1983.

Testimony of Holly Wicker May 16, 1983.

Testimony of Hoot Gibson May 16, 17, 1983.

Testimony of Irene Carlson May 11, 1983.

Testimony of James Bailey May 12, 13, 1983.

Testimony of James William Kerrigan May 31, 1983.

Testimony of Jeannine Rakowsky May 20, 1983.

Testimony of Mark Moscicki May 18, 1983.

Testimony of Nancy Carlson May 11, 1983.

Testimony of Patricia Carlson May 26, 1983.

Testimony of Robert Davis May 26, 27, 1983.

Testimony of Robert Rakowsky May 20, 1983.

Testimony of Robert Rassmussen May 11, 1983.

Testimony of Robert Reber May 11, 1983.

Testimony of Salvatore Fallucco May 23, 1983.

Testimony of Samuel Louis Wallick May 27, 31, 1983.

Testimony of Scott Kennedy May 18, 1983.

Testimony of Sheryl Fisher May 10, 1983.

Testimony of Timothy Wicker May 12, 13, 1983.

Testimony of Walter J. Hansen Jun 2, 7, 1983.

Turner, C. Paul. Cockpit Voice Recorder Factual Report. April 16, 1979.

Yorke, Duane. "Discussion and Analysis of Incident Involving TWA Flight 841 on April 4, 1979." Monograph. Massapequa, NY, November 16, 1984.

Documentaries

"Chicago Air Crash: American Airlines Flight 191." Seconds from Disaster National Geographic Channel Feb 14, 2013.

"Hidden Dangers." Air Emergency National Geographic Channel May 13, 2007.

"Silkair 185: Pilot Suicide?" National Geographic Channel Asia 2006.
"The Plane That Fell From The Sky." CBS July 14, 1983.

Videotaped Interviews

Charles Hvass — September 23, 2013.
David Haase — September 6, 2013.
Donald Chance Mark — September 23, 2013.
Floyd and Patricia Carlson — September 22, 2013.
Gene York — April 25, 2013.
Hoot Gibson — November 2012.
Jerry Lawler — Feb 2013.
John Rohlfing — November 2, 2013.
Peter Fehr — April 3, 2013.
Roger Peterson — April 4, 2013.
Scott Kennedy — November 21, 2015.
Vern and Randall Deshano — July 1, 2013.

Telephone Interviews

Anthony Mealy — November 9, 2013.
Douglas Page — November 3, 2013.
Glen Smith — November 19, 2013.
James Berry — June 19, 2013.
Kevin Gibson — March 18, 2013.
Leon Cleaver — January 29, 2014.
Martin Ries — June 21, 2013.
Randal DeShano — June 5, 2013.
Robert and Jeannine Rakowsky — May 22, 2013.
Sandy Meyer — May 30, 2013.

Skype Interviews

John Cox — August 7, 2014

The following individuals were contacted but declined to be interviewed:

Gary Banks
Mark Moscicki
Leigh Johnson
Ron Schleede
Holly Wicker

Endnotes

HEADWINDS

1. The difference between ticketed passengers and souls on board would lead a number of newspapers to report erroneous passenger totals in the first news accounts of TWA 841.
2. Testimony of Mark Moscicki, May 18, 1983. P. 887
3. Deposition of Francine Schauller, "National Transportation Safety Board: An Accident Involving a Trans World Airlines, Inc. B727, Flint, Michigan, April 4, 1979." Accident number CHI-79-AA-040 Jan 29, 1980.
4. Aircraft Accident Report: "Trans World Airlines, Inc. Boeing 727-31, N840TW. Near Saginaw, Michigan, April 4, 1979." NTSB-AAR-81-8. Jul 13, 1981. P. 19
5. Leon Cleaver telephone interview with author. Jan 29, 2014.

WE'VE HAD A SLIGHT PROBLEM

1. There are three different accounts as to whose idea it was to extend the landing gear. Hoot claims it was his idea. Scott told Jerry Lawler, the first person from TWA to speak to the crew after the incident, the version told in the text. Gary Banks' wife says that Gary told her he was screaming for them to put the gear out.
2. Deposition of Gary N. Banks, "National Transportation Safety Board: An Accident Involving a Trans World Airlines, Inc. B727, Flint, Michigan, April 4, 1979." Accident number CHI-79-AA-040 April 12, 1979.
3. The Breech Academy was the name given to the TWA training facility in Kansas City, Missouri.
4. Anthony Mealy telephone interview with author, Nov 9, 2013.
5. Mel Brown interview, Sep 9, 1980.

6. Bissinger, H. G. "The plane that fell from the sky." *St. Paul Pioneer Press* May 24, 1981.

Roller Coaster

1. Testimony of Carol Reams, May 18, 1983. P. 917
2. Bissinger, H. G. "The plane that fell from the sky." *St. Paul Pioneer Press* May 24, 1981.
3. Douglas Page telephone interview with author, Nov 3, 2013.
4. Peter Fehr interview with author, Apr 3, 2013.
5. Randall Deshano interview with author, Jul 1, 2013.
6. Testimony of Sheryl Fisher, May 10, 1983, P. 8
7. Deposition of Holly Wicker, Jul 7, 1980, P. 38
8. *Ibid*. P. 43
9. Holly's actual written statement was handed over to the NTSB. The NTSB misplaced that statement. Holly would be asked to provide another statement nearly two years later by Leslie Kampschror.

Hero for a Day

1. C. V. Glines. "Flight 841: The Nightmare Continues Parts I & II." *Air Line Pilot*, Nov 1981.
2. Deposition of Ronald Montgomery. "National Transportation Safety Board. An Accident Involving a Trans World Airlines, Inc. B727, Flint, Michigan, April 4, 1979." Accident number CHI-79-AA-040 Jan 29, 1980.
3. Jerry Lawler interview with author Feb 2012.
4. "87 on Airliner Survive a Nose Dive In Michigan Near Speed of Sound." *Associated Press*, Apr 6, 1979.
5. Witkin, Richard. "Plane's Dive is Laid to Malfunctioning Wing Flap. *New York Times*, Apr 7, 1979.

An Inquisition

1. Pipp, Edwin G. "Tape of jet's dive erased by crewman." *Detroit News* Apr 10, 1979.
2. *Ibid.*
3. The term "Go Team" refers to the group of NTSB investigators who initially travel to the scene of an accident to begin an investigation. Each group member becomes the head of one or more investigative groups, such as those investigating human factors, weather, maintenance, etc. The "Go Team" is usually assembled in advance so they can get to the scene of the accident as quickly as possible.

4. Deposition of Harvey G. Gibson. "National Transportation Safety Board. An Accident Involving a Trans World Airlines, Inc. B727, Flint, Michigan, April 4, 1979." Accident number CHI-79-AA-040 Apr 12, 1979.

5. Deposition of Harvey G. Gibson. "National Transportation Safety Board. An Accident Involving a Trans World Airlines, Inc. B727, Flint, Michigan, April 4, 1979." Accident number CHI-79-AA-040 Apr 12, 1979. P 7

6. *Ibid.* P 9-10

7. *Ibid.* P 45-46

8. *Ibid.* P 46

9. *Ibid.* P 62-97

10. Deposition of Jess Scott Kennedy. "National Transportation Safety Board. An Accident Involving a Trans World Airlines, Inc. B727, Flint, Michigan, April 4, 1979." Accident number CHI-79-AA-040 Apr 12, 1979.

11. *Ibid.* P 12-13

12. *Ibid.* P 19

13. *Ibid.* P 20

14. *Ibid.* P 39

15. Deposition of Gary N. Banks. "National Transportation Safety Board. An Accident Involving a Trans World Airlines, Inc. B727, Flint, Michigan, Apr 4, 1979." Accident number CHI-79-AA-040 Apr 12, 1979. P 12

16. *Ibid.* P 21

17. *Ibid.* P 26-27

18. *Ibid.* P 30-31

Shifting Winds

1. Serrano, Richard A. "FAA Arrives to Begin TWA Study." *The Kansas City Times* Apr 24, 1979.

2. Feaver, Douglas B. "TWA Jet's Accidental Aerobatics under Exhaustive Study." *The Washington Post* May 13, 1979.

3. Kilian, Michael. "Unwinding the (expletive) cockpit tape mystery." *The Chicago Tribune.*

4. C. V. Glines. "Flight 841: The Nightmare Continues Parts I & II." *Air Line Pilot* Nov 1981.

5. Crank, B. Arnold. "What Occurs at 39,000 Feet?" *The Kansas City Star* April 1979.

6. Hoot had been awarded the L-1011 captain's slot before TWA 841. Since there were no L-1011 classes scheduled when Hoot returned from his medical leave, he was required to fly the 727 until the next L-1011 class was scheduled.

Fear of Flying

1. A factor in Holly's decision to not seek medical treatment immediately after the incident was her concern and responsibility for the children she was escorting.
2. Deposition of Holly Wicker Jul 7, 1980. P 46-47
3. Bissinger, H. G. "The plane that fell from the sky." *St. Paul Pioneer Press* May 24, 1981.
4. *Ibid.*
5. *Ibid.*
6. *Ibid.*
7. Charles Hvass interview with author.
8. Noland, David. "Safeguard." *Aviation Consumer* Oct 15, 1979.
9. Bissinger, H. G. "The plane that fell from the sky." *St. Paul Pioneer Press* May 24, 1981.

Born to Fly

1. Hoot wasn't old enough to hold a commercial pilot's license. He was paid as an employee of the grain company and not directly for crop dusting.
2. Sandy Meyer interview with author.
3. Dowdey, Kathleen recorded interview with Hoot Nov, Dec 1999

A Fly on the Wall

1. CVRs today can record up to two hours.
2. Adair, Bill. "The Mystery of Flight 427: Inside a Crash Investigation." Washington, D.C.: *The Smithsonian Institution Press*, 2002, P 38-39
3. Deposition of Harvey G. Gibson Aug 11, 1981. P 113-114
4. Hoot also testified during the civil trial that he had learned it was Mel Brown who first spoke to the crew.

Miss Piggy

1. The visibility and ceiling requirements at that time for two engines was a three hundred-foot ceiling and a mile visibility, except when there was a takeoff alternate within fifteen minutes flying time, in which case the requirements were reduced to a ceiling of two hundred feet and visibility of a half mile.
2. Gilchrist, Peter. "Modern Civil Aircraft: 13 Boeing 727." *Ian Allan Publishing*, 1996. P 81

Putting the Pieces Back Together

1. Vern DeShano interview with author Jul 1, 2013.
2. The coordinates where the parts were found are 43 39n 84 05w
3. Statistical Summary of Commercial Jet Airplane Accidents, 1959-2008, Boeing.
4. "Safety Board Studies Transport Incident." *Aviation Week & Space Technology* Oct 5, 1981.
5. *Ibid.*
6. It was later determined that the backward-in-time movement of the heading trace was the result of the gimbal for the heading trace hitting its maximum limit.
7. Deposition of Lou Wallick, Jan 12, 1983. P 30
8. One interesting development that arose from the test flight flown on May 12, 1979 concerned the flight data recorder. Unknown to either George Andre or Lou Wallick was the fact that TWA had removed the FDR after the test flight in order to have it analyzed. That analysis showed that the acceleration trace was not recorded.
9. Testimony of Charles Higgins, Jun 1, 1983. P 53

The Boeing Scenario

1. "Safety Board Studies Transport Incident." *Aviation Week & Space Technology* Oct 5, 1981.
2. The reported failures were all Decoto slat actuators. TWA 841 had a Ronson slat actuator. There was no evidence of a similar failure on the Ronson actuator; however, there is also no evidence to indicate that a similar failure could not occur to a Ronson slat actuator.
3. "Safety Board Studies Transport Incident." *Aviation Week & Space Technology* Oct 5, 1981.
4. Deposition of James William Kerrigan Jan 11, 1983. P 64
5. Boeing also released a training bulletin to pilots that described a procedure for dealing with asymmetrical flaps and or slats. That procedure was the Boeing scenario in reverse.
6. Testimony of Robert Davis May 26, 27, 1983.
7. Noland, David. "Safeguard." *Aviation Consumer* Oct 15, 1979.
8. Deposition of Leslie D. Kampschror Apr 26, 1982. P 85.
9. Deposition of Harold Francis Marthinsen Mar 31, 1983. P 88

LIBEL

1. Lamberto, Nick. "'Hoot' Gibson of plunging jet fame is still in the saddle." *Des Moines Register*, Aug 19, 1979.
2. Leppard, D. Letter to Captain Tom Buttion, Vice President of Flight Operations, Eastern Airlines, concerning TWA 841 rumors being taught as fact in recurrent training. Sep 12, 1980.
3. Deposition of Timothy Wicker Jun 27, 1980. P 4-6
4. Sandy Meyer interview with author.
5. Leppard, D. Letter to Captain Tom Buttion, Vice President of Flight Operations, Eastern Airlines, concerning TWA 841 rumors being taught as fact in recurrent training. Sep 12, 1980.

PRELIMINARY FINDINGS

1. A law passed in 1976 intended to provide transparency in government.
2. National Transportation Safety Board Sunshine Meeting in the Matter of Aircraft Incident Report. TWA Inc. B-727, near Saginaw, Michigan. April 4, 1979. Jan 17, 1980. P 5-6
3. *Ibid.* P 8-9
4. *Ibid.* P 10-11
5. *Ibid.* P 12-14
6. *Ibid.* P 17
7. *Ibid.* P 22-24
8. *Ibid.* P 42
9. *Ibid.* P 48
10. *Ibid.* P 64
11. *Ibid.* P 65
12. *Ibid.* P 67
13. *Ibid.* P 68
14. *Ibid.* P 156-157
15. *Ibid.* P 158
16. *Ibid.* P 168-170
17. *Ibid.* P 175
18. Each of the five crew members submitted a written report to TWA describing the upset from their perspective.
19. *Ibid.* P 176
20. *Ibid.* P 177

21. *Ibid.* P 177-178

22. *Ibid.* P 178

23. *Ibid.* P 179-180

Where Was the Flight Engineer?

1. McAdams, Francis. Written statement to Chairman James King regarding the scope of the January 29 depositions. Jan 29, 1980.

2. C. V. Glines. "Flight 841: The Nightmare Continues Parts I & II." *Air Line Pilot* Nov 1981.

3. Speiser, Martin. Opening statements for the January 29, 1980 depositions. Jan 29, 1980. P 9

4. Deposition of Ronald Montgomery. "National Transportation Safety Board. An Accident Involving a Trans World Airlines, Inc. B727, Flint, Michigan, April 4, 1979." Accident number CHI-79-AA-040 Jan 29, 1980. P 18

5. Deposition of Roger Gordon. "National Transportation Safety Board. An Accident Involving a Trans World Airlines, Inc. B727, Flint, Michigan, April 4, 1979." Accident number CHI-79-AA-040 Jan 29, 1980. P 45

6. Deposition of Mark Moscicki. "National Transportation Safety Board. An Accident Involving a Trans World Airlines, Inc. B727, Flint, Michigan, April 4, 1979." Accident number CHI-79-AA-040 Jan 29, 1980. P 64

7. *Ibid.* P 66-67

8. Deposition of Gary N. Banks. "National Transportation Safety Board. An Accident Involving a Trans World Airlines, Inc. B727, Flint, Michigan, April 4, 1979." Accident number CHI-79-AA-040 Jan 29, 1980. P 97-109

9. Sandra Kennedy interview with author.

10. Deposition of Jess Scott Kennedy. "National Transportation Safety Board. An Accident Involving a Trans World Airlines, Inc. B727, Flint, Michigan, April 4, 1979." Accident number CHI-79-AA-040 Jan 29, 1980. P 110-121

11. Deposition of Harvey G. Gibson. "National Transportation Safety Board. An Accident Involving a Trans World Airlines, Inc. B727, Flint, Michigan, April 4, 1979." Accident number CHI-79-AA-040 Jan 29, 1980. P 122-123

12. *Ibid.* P 124-125

Fabricating Evidence

1. Dave Haase interview with author.

2. When the author interviewed Randal Deshano, the brother of the farmer who had found a piece of the number 7 slat, Randal had in his possession a metal part later identified as a section of anti-icing ducting from TWA 841.

3. The flight engineer station was manned by Boeing engineer Ken Storms.

4. Deposition of Robert Von Husen Apr 28, 1982. P 25

5. Aircraft Accident Report. "Trans World Airlines, Inc., Boeing 727-31, N840TW Near Saginaw, Michigan April 4, 1979." NTSB-AAR-81-8. Jul 13, 1981. P 22

6. Deposition of Robert Von Husen Apr 28, 1982. P 21

7. "Safety Board Studies Transport Incident." *Aviation Week & Space Technology* Oct 5, 1981.

8. McIntyre, Jim. Letter to NTSB Chairman James King regarding new documents related to the investigation. Jun 8, 1981.

9. Deposition of Harold Francis Marthinsen Mar 31, 1983. P 314-315

10. *Ibid.* P 321-323

11. *Ibid.* P 325

12. Deposition of James William Kerrigan Jan 10, 1983. P 65-66

13. P. J. Neufeld and N Colman, "When Science Takes the Witness Stand," *Scientific American*, 262:5 (May 1990), P 46-53

14. ALPA Petition for Reconsideration of Probable Cause Oct 9, 1990. P 18-20

15. Testimony of Andy Davis Yates, Jr. May 19, 1983. P 1125-1126

16. Deposition of Harold Francis Marthinsen Mar 31, 1983. P 338-340

17. Testimony of George Maurice Andre May 23, 1983. P 23

Eye of the Storm

1. Minutes from TWA MEC regular meeting Nov 1-13, 1980.

2. Telephone interview with Kevin Gibson. Mar 18, 2013.

3. Bezek, Stanley. Letter to Landon Dowdey concerning Hoot's visit to his medical clinic in Utah. Nov 1, 1981.

4. Deposition of Harvey G. Gibson, Aug 11, 1981. P 131-132

5. The documents that Hoot so meticulously saved would later prove to be an invaluable resource in reconstructing his story.

Circumnavigation

1. Recommendations to the National Transportation Safety Board with regard to the Accident involving TWA Flight 841, Near Flint, Michigan. Airline Pilots Association. Apr 4, 1979. P 18

2. *Ibid.* P 36-37

3. McIntyre, Jim. Letter to NTSB Chairman James King regarding the TWA 841 investigation. Mar 30, 1981.

4. O'Donnel, J.J. Letter to NTSB Chairman James King regarding the negative effects of the unsubstantiated rumors regarding crew wrong-doing. Apr 2, 1981.

An Improbable Probable Cause

1. Sunshine Meeting. National Transportation Safety Board. Jun 9, 1981. P 85

2. *Ibid.* P 38-40

3. *Ibid.* P 40

4. There is evidence to suggest that this new theory of the incident came from one or more TWA accident investigators and subsequently was adopted by the NTSB.

5. *Ibid.* P 72-73

6. *Ibid.* P 78

7. *Ibid.* P 86

8. *Ibid.* P 98

9. *Ibid.* P 5

10. *Ibid.* P 116–117

11. *Ibid.* P 125–127

12. *Ibid.* P 126–127

13. McIntyre, Jim. Affidavit regarding statements made by Leslie Kampschror. Jan 3, 1991.

14. Laurie McGinley. "Fighting Blame for Near Crash of a Boeing 727, Pilot Raises Questions about Safety of the Plane." *The Wall Street Journal* May 3, 1981.

Turbulence

1. "Jetliner's Crew Blamed for Dangerous Dive" *United Press International* Jun 10, 1981.

2. There is some confusion over whether the correct name is Haden Leroy or Leroy Haden.

3. Deposition of Leslie D. Kampschror Apr 26, 1982. P 20-25

4. O'Donnel, J.J. Letter to NTSB Chairman James King regarding the Board's findings. Jul 30, 1981.

5. Bates, Walt. Letter to ALPA National with dissenting opinion over ALPA's support of the crew. Nov 23, 1981.

6. Deposition of Harold Francis Marthinsen Mar 30, 1983. P 82-89

7. Other passengers also complained about having spells of dizziness after the incident.

8. It was never established during the deposition which leg Hoot had broken.

9. Deposition of Harvey G. Gibson Aug 11, 1981. P 157-158

10. *Ibid.*

11. Bissenger's article won the 1981 Livingston Award for National Reporting and was also a runner up for a Pulitzer. H.G. "Buzz" Bissenger would later go on to write the best-selling book *Friday Night Lights*. The documentary based on Bissenger's article also won a Peabody award for best television documentary.

12. Phone interview with Glen Smith.

13. Some flight attendants wore the "I flew with Hoot" button as a show of support and did not consider it derogatory.

14. Gardner, Bill. "Passengers relive trauma." *St. Paul Pioneer Press* May 9, 1983.

Questioning The Investigators

1. Deposition of Leslie D. Kampschror Jan 12, 1982.

2. Deposition of Leslie D. Kampschror Jan 13, 1982.

3. Excerpts of Kampschror's deposition were played at trial; however, the video played to the jury was an edited version of depositions taken over three days. Because the depositions were taken on different days and Kampschror was dressed differently each time, the edited video had no continuity. The jarring effect of the different backgrounds and the obvious changes in clothing had the effect of lessening the impact of the damning testimony Mark was trying to present to the jury.

4. Ironically, the cockpit voice recorder would play a crucial role in the investigation that followed, placing the blame for the accident on the crew.

5. Deposition of Robert Von Husen Apr 28, 1982.

6. Deposition of Robert Von Husen Jun 22, 1982. P 51-58

Lawsuits, Lawyers, and Liability

1. Gardner, Bill. "Area trial to decide liability." *St. Paul Pioneer Press* May 9, 1983.

2. An infant's lungs are not developed enough to withstand such high G forces.

3. Hvass, Charles Opening Statements May 8, 1983. P 11

4. Mark, Donald Chance Opening Statements May 8, 1983. P 29

5. *Ibid.* P 29

6. *Ibid.* P 40-41

7. *Ibid.* P 41-42

8. Ratchye, Boyd H. Opening Statements May 8, 1983. P 46-47

9. *Ibid.* P 47

10. *Ibid.* P 61

11. Testimony of Robert Reber May 11, 1983 P 154

12. Testimony of James Bailey May 12, 13, 1983. P 298

13. *Ibid.* P 298-306

14. *Ibid.* P 349

15. *Ibid.* P 351

16. Testimony of Thomas Quill May 12, 1983 P 359

17. Don Mark in chambers May 12, 1983 P 373
18. Holly's friend was Judith Haavig. The two went on to author several books related to adoptions.
19. Testimony of Holly Wicker May 16, 1983. P 534
20. *Ibid.* P 494-497

CHALLENGE AND RESPONSE

1. Testimony of Hoot Gibson May 16-17, 1983. P 744
2. *Ibid.* P 752
3. *Ibid.* P 58
4. *Ibid.* P 762-763
5. *Ibid.* P 810
6. *Ibid.* P 843
7. *Ibid.* P 851
8. Testimony of Mark Mosciki May 18, 1983. P 900
9. *Ibid.* P 902
10. Testimony of Carol Reams May 18, 1983. P 920
11. *Ibid.* P 922
12. Testimony of Carlos Machado-Olverdo May 18, 1983. P 932
13. Testimony of Harold Buchstein May 20, 1983. P 1138
14. Testimony of Charles O. Miller May 24, 1983. P 1458
15. During the investigation of TWA 841, Miller had reached out to Hoot and had invited him down to his ranch in New Mexico. He told Hoot then that he didn't know what had happened to cause the plane to roll out of control, but he was confident that it didn't have anything to do with the theories being touted by Boeing and the NTSB. When Paul and Holly Fine, the documentary filmmakers working on the TWA 841 documentary, learned that a former NTSB employee had voiced some criticisms about the TWA 841 investigation, they interviewed him and included some of his comments in the documentary.

WEIGHT & BALANCE

1. Testimony of Robert Davis May 26, 27, 1983. P 1959-1960
2. Testimony of James William Kerrigan May 31, 1983. P 2163
3. *Ibid.* P 2165
4. Ratchye, Boyd H. Closing Arguments Jun 8, 1983. P 2561
5. *Ibid.* P 2563
6. *Ibid.* P 2574

7. *Ibid.* P 2574-2575

8. *Ibid.* P 2578

9. Mark, Donald Chance Closing Arguments Jun 8, 1983. P 2596-2597

10. *Ibid.* P 2603

11. *Ibid.* P 2626

12. Hvass, Charles Closing Arguments Jun 8, 1983. P 2628-2629

13. *Ibid.* P 2631

14. *Ibid.* P 2635-2636

15. *Ibid.* P 2637-2638

16. *Ibid.* P 2639

17. *Ibid.* P 2647-2648

18. The Wickers eventually settled for a lesser amount rather than go to trial again on a promised appeal by TWA.

Breaking Point

1. Landon did file an appeal, but it was dismissed on Jul 7, 1997 without review due to a lack of jurisdiction.

2. Phone interview with Glen Smith.

A Cold Case Gets a Second Look

1. Yorke, Duane. Independent analysis of the TWA 841 incident. Nov 16, 1984.

2. *Ibid.*

3. ALPA Petition for Reconsideration of Probable Cause. TWA Flight 841 on Apr 4, 1979. Oct 9, 1990. P 1

Rudder Hardover

1. Mandatory retirement at that time occurred when a pilot reached the age of 60.

2. Testimony of Hoot Gibson May 17, 1983. P 695

3. Berton, Justin. "Flight Diversions: Rumors won't fly with those who lost their loved ones in Colorado Springs crash." Apr 1, 1999.

4. Bissinger, H. G. "Nose dive." *Chicago Tribune* Jun 2, 1991.

5. The TWA 841 investigation, like all investigations where a finding of probable cause is issued, was never officially closed. The NTSB is obligated, however, to reconsider a probable cause finding when presented with new evidence.

6. Adair, Bill. "The Mystery of Flight 427: Inside a Crash Investigation." Washington, D.C.: *The Smithsonian Institution Press*, 2002. P 14-15

7. *Ibid.* P 54-55

8. *Ibid.* P 151-152

9. Jon Cox interview with author.

10. Adair, Bill. "The Mystery of Flight 427: Inside a Crash Investigation." Washington, D.C.: *The Smithsonian Institution Press*, 2002. P 14-15. P 175

11. There was a standby rudder PCU that did have the valve within a valve design.

12. The author has been unable to verify some facts such as the exact amount of the captain's trading losses as well as the amount of his life insurance policy, due to conflicting reports.

13. Adair, Bill. "The Mystery of Flight 427: Inside a Crash Investigation." Washington, D.C.: *The Smithsonian Institution Press*, 2002. P 197

14. *Ibid.* P 198

15. "Silkair 185: Pilot Suicide?" National Geographic Channel Asia 2006.

WHAT REALLY HAPPENED?

1. Deposition of Harvey G. Gibson. "National Transportation Safety Board. An Accident Involving a Trans World Airlines, Inc. B727, Flint, Michigan, April 4, 1979." Accident number CHI-79-AA-040 Apr 12, 1979. P 25–29

2. Witkin, Richard. "Crew Will Testify Today on Near-fatal Jet Plunge." *New York Times* Apr 12, 1979.

3. Gibson, H. G. Affidavit Nov 19, 1979.

4. Deposition of Harvey G. Gibson Aug 11, 1981. P 81

5. *Ibid.* P 97-98

6. Kathleen Dowdey Interview of Hoot Gibson November and December 1999. Side 2.dat.

7. Recommendations to the National Safety Board with regard to the Accident Involving TWA 841, Near Flint, Michigan, Apr 4, 1979. Air Line Pilots Association Mar 27, 1981.

8. Recommendations to the National Transportation Safety Board with regard to the Accident involving TWA Flight 841, Near Flint, Michigan. Airline Pilots Association. Apr 4, 1979. P 5

9. Pipp, Edwin G. "Tape of jet's dive erased by crewman." *Detroit News* Apr 10, 1979.

10. Testimony of Thomas H. Quill May 12, 1983. P 359

11. Morrill, C. William. Flight 201, January 21, 1979 flight summary. Jan 22, 1979.

12. Aircraft Incident Report. Eastern Airlines Flight 56. Jan 3, 1982.

13. Aircraft Incident Report. TWA Flight 70. Dec 17, 1989.

14. Marthinsen, Harold. Letter to Leroy A. Keith FAA. Jun 5, 1991.

15. Parisc, E. Flight 169 debrief. Sep 9, 1991.

16. Boeing's analysis indicated that it would require 13 degrees of bank to counter the upfloat in the aileron.
17. Hoot has always maintained that the buzz he first felt increased to a gentle buffet when the plane was in about a 30-degree right bank. That is consistent with the control yoke turning to the left enough to activate the left spoilers, which would account for the buffeting. In testimony Hoot gave during the civil trial, he stated that the only time he had ever felt a similar buffet was when making a steep turn in the Boeing 707 when the spoilers deployed.
18. National Transportation Safety Board Sunshine Meeting in the Matter of Aircraft Incident Report. TWA Inc., B-727, near Saginaw, Michigan. April 4, 1979. Jan 17, 1980. P 86-88
19. Testimony of Hoot Gibson May 16-17, 1983. P 711-712
20. Mel Brown interview Sep 9, 1980.
21. The APU on the 727 was located in the center fuselage. The exhaust for the APU was over the right inboard wing. Because of this unique arrangement, the APU had a limitation that it could not be used or started in flight.
22. ALPA Petition for Reconsideration of Probable Cause. TWA Flight 841 on April 4, 1979. Oct 9, 1990. P 4

Epilogue

1. A film based on the book, starring Tom Hanks as Sullenberger, is scheduled for release in September of 2016.
2. While Hoot and his crew managed to escape the hijackers, the crew of a Boeing 727 was not as lucky. TWA 847, scheduled to fly from Athens to Rome, was hijacked on June 14, 1985. The crew and passengers were held hostage over a prolonged period, involving stops at several different airports. Two passengers were killed by the hijackers, who released the final hostages weeks later after negotiating the release of 700 Shia prisoners.
3. Quill v. Trans World Airlines, Inc. Court of Appeals of Minnesota Jan 29, 1985.

Appendix

1. Aircraft Accident Report. "Trans World Airlines, Inc. Boeing 727-31, N840TW Near Saginaw, Michigan April 4, 1979." NTSB-AAR-81-8. Jul 13, 1981. P 6
2. *Ibid.* P 33
3. Response to Petition for Reconsideration. National Transportation Safety Board. May 4, 1995. P 5
4. *Ibid.* P 9

5. *Ibid.* P 9-10

6. *Ibid.* P 10-11

7. Systems Group Chairman Report National Transportation Safety Board May 7, 1979. P 2

8. *Ibid.*

9. *Ibid.* P 14-15

10. Deposition of Harvey G. Gibson. "National Transportation Safety Board. An Accident Involving a Trans World Airlines, Inc. B727, Flint, Michigan, April 4, 1979." Accident number CHI-79-AA-040 Apr 12, 1979. P 25–29

11. Human Factors Specialist's Report of Investigation National Transportation Safety Board Jun 22, 1979. P 3

12. Passenger Sheryl Fisher, who was traveling with Holly, later testified to the same sequence of events in her testimony at trial. Sheryl Fisher Testimony P 144-145

Index